ROOTS OF MODERN GERONTOLOGY AND GERIATRICS

This is a volume in the
Arno Press collection

AGING AND OLD AGE

Advisory Editor

Robert Kastenbaum

Editorial Board

Joseph T. Freeman
Gerald J. Gruman
Michel Philibert

See last page of this volume
for a complete list of titles.

ROOTS OF MODERN GERONTOLOGY AND GERIATRICS

Frederic D. Zeman's
"Medical History of Old Age"
and Selected Studies
by Other Writers

Edited by
Gerald J. Gruman

ARNO PRESS
A New York Times Company
New York • 1979

Editorial Supervision: Joseph Cellini

Reprint Edition 1979 by Arno Press Inc.

Arrangement copyright © by Arno Press Inc.

AGING AND OLD AGE
ISBN for complete set: 0-405-11800-7
See last pages of this volume for titles.

Manufactured in the United States of America

Library of Congress Cataloging in Publication Data

Main entry under title:

Roots of modern gerontology and geriatrics.

   (Aging and old age)
   Includes bibliographical references.
   1. Geriatrics--History--Addresses, essays, lectures.
2. Gerontology--History--Addresses, essays, lectures.
I. Gruman, Gerald J. II. Series.
RC952.5.R665   618.9'7'009   78-22184
ISBN 0-405-11801-5
   2. Aged--Addresses, essays, lectures. 3. Aged--
Care and hygiene--Addresses, essays, lectures.
I. Beard, George Miller, 1839-1883. Legal responsi-
bility in old age. 1979. II. Osler, William, Sir,
bart., 1849-1919. Aequanimitas. The fixed period.
1979. III. Crichton-Browne, James, Sir, 1840-1938.
The prevention of senility and a sanitary outlook. The
prevention of senility. 1979. IV. Gruman, Gerald J.
V. Series.
HD6279.F58   301.43'5   78-22186
ISBN 0-405-11804-X

A Note About This Book

"Old age is a topic that has been almost totally ignored by historians," states David Hackett Fisher in his fascinating survey history *Growing Old in America* (New York, Oxford University Press, 1977). In another recent work, Peter N. Stearns' *Old Age in European Society: The Case of France* (New York, Holms and Meier, 1976), we read that "the historical literature is sparse." Fisher and Stearns, both of whom seem generally unaware of the studies in this volume, predict that a rapidly growing number of historians will be entering this area of research and writing. Clearly it is imperative to collect some of the pioneer historical efforts in this field and make them available. Gruman, who is both physician and historian, has performed the function of selecting significant historical work now scattered in journals unlikely to come to the attention of general historians. As editor, Gruman also pays tribute to the late Frederic D. Zeman, a physician and administrator, who truly loved the history of his profession, and who planned to publish in book form a series of articles called "Life's Later Years: Studies in the Medical History of Old Age." It was a source of regret to Zeman's admirers that he was not able to carry the story beyond the early years of this century. Those who read the series come away with a deep respect for the author and a feeling of inspiration for the subject matter. Gruman's "Introduction to the History of Literature on Gerontology" (1957) is reprinted here as a guide to the situation in the field at that time, and because it includes evaluations of three of the writings in this volume and mentions many lesser works. A review of Grmek's 1958 monograph follows. Like Zeman, Joseph T. Freeman is another amateur historian whose love of the subject shines through in his classic 1938 article on the history of geriatrics. Freeman too, is one of the inspired personalities who have led American efforts on behalf of the elderly. Steudel's 1942 article published in German is the polished production of a professional medical historian only minimally marred by wartime nationalism. "A Brief History of the Psychology of Aging" (1961) by James E. Birren is more comprehensive than its title suggests and includes invaluable information on the formative years of American gerontology as an organized specialty. Like Zeman and Freeman, Birren has had a career span and personal influence that illuminate the heroic years of American geriatrics and gerontology. Next there is reprinted the 1965 project of the History Committee of the Gerontological Society: this consisted of articles covering the four major branches of the Society — medicine, biology, psychology and social welfare. A fine theoretically oriented article on "Concepts of Aging" by R. L. Grant is included. The volume ends with Freeman's lively 1961 memoir of Nascher, founder of geriatrics, whose great work *Geriatrics* (1914) is reproduced as a separate volume in this series.

CONTENTS

Introduction

Zeman, Frederic D., LIFE'S LATER YEARS: Studies in the Medical History of Old Age, Parts 1-12 (Reprinted from *Journal of the Mount Sinai Hospital Hospital, Vols. VIII-XVII*) New York, 1942-1950

Gruman, Gerald J., AN INTRODUCTION TO LITERATURE ON THE HISTORY OF GERONTOLOGY (Reprinted from *Bulletin of the History of Medicine, Vol. 31, No. 1*) Baltimore, Md., 1957

Gruman, Gerald J., REVIEW OF M. D. GRMEK'S ON AGEING AND OLD AGE: Basic Proglems of Gerontology and Geriatrics (Reprinted from *Bulletin of the History of Medicine*, Vol. 34, No. 3) Baltimore, Md., 1960

Freeman, Joseph T., THE HISTORY OF GERIATRICS (Reprinted from *Annals of Medical History, Vol. 10*) 1938

Steudel, Johannes, ZUR GESCHICHTE DER LEHRE VON DEN GREISENKRANKHEITEN (Reprinted from *Sudhoffs Archiv fuer Geschichte der Medizin und der Naturwissenschaften*, Vol. 35) Wiesbaden, West Germany, 1942

Birren, James E., A BRIEF HISTORY OF THE PSYCHOLOGY OF AGING (Reprinted from *The Gerontologist, Vol. 1, Nos. 2-3*) St. Louis, Mo., June and September, 1961

Freeman, Joseph T. and Irving L. Webber, editors, PERSPECTIVES IN AGING (Reprinted from *The Gerontologist,* Vol. 5, No. 1, Part 2) St. Louis, Mo., March 1965

Grant, Richard L., CONCEPTS OF AGING: An Historical Review (Reprinted from *Perspectives in Biology and Medicine,* Vol. 6) Chicago, Summer, 1963

Freeman, Joseph T., NASCHER: Excerpts from His Life, Letters and Works (Reprinted from *The Gerontologist,* Vol. 1, No. 1) St. Louis, Mo., March, 1961

ACKNOWLEDGMENTS

"Life's Later Years" by Frederic D. Zeman has been reprinted by permission of The Mount Sinai Medical Center.

"An Introduction to Literature on the History of Gerontology" by Gerald J. Gruman, *Bulletin of the History of Medicine,* Vol. 31, No. 1, pp. 78-83 and "Review of M. D. Grmek's *On Aging and Old Age" Bulletin of the History of Medicine,* Vol. 34, No. 3, pp. 283-85 have been reprinted by permission of The Johns Hopkins University Press.

"A Brief History of the Psychology of Aging" by James E. Birren, "Perspectives in Aging" by Joseph T. Freeman and Irving L. Webber, editors, and "Nascher" by Joseph T. Freeman have been reprinted by permission of The Gerontological Society.

"Concepts of Aging" by Richard L. Grant from *Perspectives in Biology and Medicine,* Vol. 6, Summer, 1963 has been reprinted by permission of The University of Chicago Press. All rights in *The Gerontologist* and its Supplement are reserved under the copyright held by The Gerontological Society.

INTRODUCTION

My original initiative in this project was to see at last into print in a one-volume format the fascinating series of articles written between 1942 and 1950 by Dr. Frederic D. Zeman on the history of gerontology and geriatrics. That had been Dr. Zeman's own goal: his articles typically begin with a footnote stating his intention "upon completion" of the set to have them published as a monograph. However, when he reached the early decades of the twentieth century, as his subject subtly changed from "past" to "present" in terms of his own lifetime and as the lines of development in care of the aged became increasingly manifold and complex, Zeman hesitated. His method of singling out individual persons and books no longer seemed adequate. To the keen disappointment of his friends and admirers, the final sections never appeared. Nor could he be persuaded to publish the series as it was—a most valuable, although incomplete, introduction to the medical and philosophical heritage of gerontologists and geriatricians.

There is something very personal about Frederic Zeman's essays; he writes with the unconcealed enthusiasm of a collector. The reader feels that he has met the author and come to know him. In a charming mélange of scholarly and antiquarian effort, Zeman describes and gives due homage to a line of key personages (with portraits from his own collection and characteristic selections from their writings) who prepared the way for the medical science of Zeman's time and our own. It is appropriate here to observe that many of the books reprinted in this Arno project, *Aging and Old Age,* are discussed in his articles. Those who, like myself, wrote to him or met him, and were given generous encouragement and help, felt all the more gratitude and affection. Therefore, I had no doubt that this volume, greatly extended as it is by the writings of others, should be dedicated to the memory of Dr. Zeman.

Frederic David Zeman was born on March 25, 1894 in Brooklyn, New York. It is said his parents were of German-Jewish origin, educated and sufficiently wealthy to send young Frederic to college at Columbia University, where he majored in Chemistry and German. Always a fine student, he was elected to Phi Beta Kappa and graduated summa cum laude in 1913. He then entered Columbia University's famed College of Physicians and Surgeons, again was elected to the honor fraternity (Alpha Omega Alpha), and in 1917 he earned his medical degree. As it happened, the remainder of Dr. Zeman's long career was to pass in the area of Manhattan just south of the Columbia campus—Mt. Sinai Hospital, the Jewish Home and Hospital for the Aged, the New York Academy of Medicine, his private office and his residence—all between 86th and 106th streets. The one notable exception occurred during World War I. After an internship in pathology at City Hospital, Zeman became an army medical officer and received special training at the Rockefeller Institute concerning bacterial infections then causing many deaths in the 1918-1919 pandemic of viral influenza. After this, he served in Virginia and Indiana. Upon concluding his wartime duties, Zeman held a two-year medical internship at Mt. Sinai, and this was followed by five years as a fellow in pathology; his relationship to this hospital was to be a close one until the mid-1950s.

The turning point in Dr. Zeman's life took place in 1925, but probably was not much noted at the time: this was his agreement to be the medical director of the Home for Aged and Infirm Hebrews, an institution limited to custodial care. During his forty-five long years as medical director, Zeman guided the transformation of this retirement residence into the Jewish Home and Hospital for the Aged, with clinical, research and teaching facilities recognized as models both nationally and internationally. At first, the home for the elderly was a subsidiary interest, because Zeman, as a specialist in internal medicine, had important duties at Mt. Sinai Hospital and its School of Nursing. Moreover, he could have devoted all his attention to his growing private practice. But the problems involved in applying his medical skills to the elderly more and more attracted his intellectual curiosity and his time. His inquiries in the 1940s and 1950s into history enabled him to see himself in the succession of scientists, philosophers and physicians who, over the centuries, had contributed to gerontology and geriatrics. He came to realize that this area of medicine was destined to increase greatly in scope and significance in the coming years.

It is striking how Zeman's seeming retreat from the "practical" world into the realm of scholarly literature actually came to augment his ability to face, in an inspired way, the needs of the real world. The wide range of his innovations is indicated by the diverse activities he added to the Home and Hospital—e.g., physical and occupational therapy, and rehabilitation as well as psychiatric services. In 1960, he conceived his most remarkable creation: a Center for Instruction in the Care of the Aged, which gained funds from the federal government and expedited the training of professionals in the new and expanding field.

Frederic Zeman did not retire, although he was slowed by age and afflicted with severe arthritis. Indeed, his patients at the Home and Hospital continued to be much older than he—their average age was well above eighty. While following a busy schedule, Zeman died suddenly on March 26, 1970, one day after his seventy-sixth birthday. There were numerous tributes, and they recalled the various facets of his character. A prominent article in the *New York Times* spoke of him as "a man of forceful personality." In a memorial article, medical colleagues praised him for his "warm compassion," "great good cheer" and "unfailing humor." And, in a memorial notice, other physicians recalled his "sweet and gentle nature." The differing emphases all were justifiably applicable to him, but perhaps the last-quoted phrase is the most perceptive and willbe the lasting remembrance of those who knew Dr. Frederic ("Fred") D. Zeman.

My "Introduction to Literature on the History of Gerontology" (1957) is reprinted here mainly because it offers an opportunity to recall the situation two decades ago and to cite a number of events in the historiography of the field that have taken place since that time. Also, three of the writings in this volume are described in it—the Zeman series, Freeman's article of 1938 and the Steudel article of 1942; they would be given approximately the same high evaluations today. A survey now would have to include the strong papers by Birren (1961) and Grant (1963) and the valuable essays edited by Freeman and Webber (1965) which appear in this volume. The only selection here that is not general in compass is

Freeman's study of Nascher, which not only is an especially fine example of the memoir genre but also recalls the Father of American Geriatrics whose precedent-setting book *Geriatrics* (1914) is reprinted in this Arno collection. Sona Rosa Burstein's historical writings should be rated more highly than they were: see Freeman's article on Burstein in the bibliography below. The recent "Historical Perspectives on Care" (1975) by Robert Kastenbaum and Barbara Ross also should be consulted. The one major addition to these studies is the medical history of old age by Grmek.

The very real merits of Grmek's monograph of 1958 are detailed in the review which I have appended to my "Introduction" survey. Unfortunately, the book still is relatively little known; it should be reprinted and made generally available as soon as possible. At the time of the review, Mirko Drazen Grmek already was, at the age of thirty-four, a distinguished physician and historian in Yugoslavia. He became a French citizen in 1967 and has pursued an illustrious career, first at the French government's National Center for Scientific Research and then as Professor of Biomedical History at the Ecole pratique des hautes études. He has been very active as an author and editor and has been a Laureate of the Académie française.

My "Introduction" article of 1957 was written as I prepared for my doctoral thesis in History of Science under the direction of Professors I. Bernard Cohen and Crane Brinton at Harvard University. The thesis (1960), *A History of Ideas About the Prolongation of Life: The Evolution of Prolongevity Hypotheses to 1800,* was published in 1966 by by the American Philosophical Society and republished by Arno Press in 1977.

Several developments since 1957 in the organizational aspects of the history of aging may now be mentioned. In the 1950s, I carried out studies of an early American gerontologist, C. A. Stephens, who already in 1871 was exploring theoretical and empirical dimensions of senescence. The difficulty in locating material about Stephens and other pioneer scientists led to my editorial in *Science* (1958) on the need for action by scientific organizations to preserve primary source materials. At the same time, I initiated a resolution that the Gerontological Society establish a committee on history. It was this Committee on History that brought about the symposium reprinted in this volume, *Perspectives in Aging,* edited by J. T. Freeman and I. L. Webber. The Society's Committee on History continues to be active and to wrestle with the problems of archival preservation of source materials.

Another area of interest to historians was opened by Prof. David D. Van Tassel of Case Western Reserve University, who organized a symposium on "The Aged in History" for the 1973 annual meeting of the American Historical Association: in addition to Van Tassel, Thomas F. Glick (Boston U.), Barbara G. Rosenkrantz (Harvard U.) and myself took part. It was the first time that dilemmas of an aging society were discussed before the American Historical Association. Since then, several general historians, including David Hackett Fischer, Peter N. Stearns and W. Andrew Achenbaum, have published books on the elderly (see bib. below). That these writers have predicted a rapid increase in the number of students and historians doing research and writing in this field provided an imperative reason for the publication of the present volume.

The A. H. A. symposium had an additional sequel in a project on "Aging and Human Values," sponsored by the National Endowment for the Humanities and directed by Prof. Van Tassel. Thirty scholars from a spectrum of the humanities were selected as Research Associates; ten of them were historians. A first conference was held in Cleveland in 1975, and papers were read by senior scholars in the social sciences, medicine and the humanities. At a second conference, in New York in 1976, at the time of the annual meeting of the Gerontological Society, the papers of the Research Associates were presented and discussed; many of them have since been published in *Aging and the Elderly: Humanistic Perspectives in Gerontology,* edited by Spicker, Woodward and Van Tassel (see bibliography), and more than half of them are historical. These efforts were brought to the attention of the Gerontological Society by Dr. Joseph T. Freeman and others, and a Committee on Humanism and the Humanities was established under the chairmanship of Prof. Van Tassel.

Returning to the selections in the present volume, Dr. Joseph T. Freeman, one of the editors of this Arno series *Aging and Old Age,* has, I believe, done more to encourage the organized study of the history of gerontology and geriatrics than any other person in this country. Diplomatic and self-assured, Dr. Freeman has served as vice-president of the American Geriatrics Society (1948-1952) and as president of the Gerontological Society (1961). As an "elder statesman" and as a distinguished scholar, Freeman has been able to reach a wide professional audience; he had a key role in the formation of theGerontological Society's Committee on History and, recently, its Committee on Humanism and the Humanities.

Joseph T. Freeman was born on May 25, 1908 in McKeesport, an industrial city near Pittsburgh. An outstanding student, Freeman was able to attend college at Harvard University, where he was elected to Phi Beta Kappa and graduated magna cum laude in 1930. He then enrolled at the Jefferson Medical School in Philadelphia and received his medical degree in 1934. After serving as intern and resident at the Philadelphia General Hospital, he did special work in pulmonary diseases. It was during these years in internal medicine that Freeman produced the remarkable "History of Geriatrics" (1938) described in my "Introduction" and reprinted in this volume. It should be noted that such a polished performance reflected the fact that Freeman had decided, in his third year in medical school (1933), to devote himself to geriatrics and since then had pursued a self-directed course of reading on the subject. Also one must recall his deep interest and excellent training in history and the other humanities at Harvard. It was the first considerable article on the medical history of aging: the term "geriatrics" still was general enough to cover much of gerontology. Another factor of help to the young author was the fact that both Nascher, whose text had appeared in 1914, and Thewlis, his early disciple, paid some attention to the historical origins of the subject. For example, in Thewlis' text of 1919, the preface briefly sketches the contributions of Floyer, Canstatt and Charcot, and, in the bibliography, there are listed quite a number of the works later analyzed by Freeman, Steudel and Zeman.

Freeman's 1938 article was the first of more than a hundred papers and several books he has written on geriatrics and gerontology. In 1942, he began the clinical and educational work in geriatrics he has carried out during the past thirty-seven years at Philadelphia's medical institutions. Along with this, there has been his private practice and his long years of dedicated collecting, scholarship and personal and organizational relationships to further the growth of historical knowledge about the care of the elderly and the amelioration of senescence.

In reviewing the biographies of our writers, we must not neglect the events of general history that were arousing concern about aging. 1938, for example, was a propitious year for an article like the one by Freeman. The Great Depression after

1929 had made the elderly a major issue in 1930s American politics: e.g., the Townsend Plan; Social Security legislation; the proposal to "rejuvenate" the Supreme Court. The intellectual climate was favorable to the opening of "new frontiers" of medical research: witness the 1937 conference at Woods Hole that prepared the way for the publication, with preface by philosopher John Dewey, of Cowdry's *Problems of Aging* in 1939. In 1938, the Soviet Union convened in Kiev the first large-scale biomedical convention on problems of aging, an occurrence that stirred both friends and foes of that nation. The outbreak of World War II in 1939 brought urgent needs to re-employ older workers, and medical officialdom took a new look at the more practical aspects of geriatrics. Moreover, statements of "war aims" were promising, with victory, greater welfare for the population, the elderly included—as in America's "Economic Bill of Rights" and Britain's "Beveridge Plan."

However, in 1942, the year of Zeman's and Steudel's first publications on the medical history of aging, we confront a horrendous phenomenon that seems to make a mockery of our analysis. It happens that Zeman, Freeman and Steudel all were of German descent. And their scholarship, humanism and philanthropy indicate the common motives of their studies. Yet if the forebears of the first two had remained in Germany, Frederic Zeman and Joseph Freeman probably would have been killed in the "Final Solution" unleased by the Nazi regime in 1942. That fate might have been mine also, if my grandparents had not left the Ukraine and Moldavia, territories overrun after June 1942 by the Nazi invasion.

I should agree with the statement by the novelist Heinrich Böll, that in this sort of question, the tactic of irony is not enough:

. . . irony wasn't enough, and never would be . . . it was only an opiate for a few privileged ones . . .

It is necessary for the historian to face the problem and take a stand. At a minimum, the humanist efforts of geriatricians and gerontologists, in healing, research or scholarship, constitute constructive steps that tend to diminish the destructive forces of *"Thanatos"* (Freud). And, as I have reasoned in a paper on the aging population and "cultural decline," the elderly today are in a real danger from lethal measures—geriatric genocide. The defense (and self-defense) of the older population, in my view, brings into cohesion the striving of Frederic Zeman, Joseph Freeman and Johannes Steudel.

Johannes Steudel was born on March 9, 1901 in a small town in Thuringia in the eastern-central part of Germany (now in the German Democratic Republic): the great, historic cultural center, Weimar, is the major city of the region. Steudel always was fascinated by Graeco-Roman archeology and art history; in 1923 he earned a degree from the University of Königsberg (in former East Prussia) for a study of Hadrian's Villa. During the remainder of the 1920s and 1930s, he worked in the scholarly area between philosophy and medicine, e.g., the history of medical terminology; and he especially investigated the medical aspects and implications of the thought of Leibniz and Goethe. It was not until 1941 that Steudel took his degree at the medical school of the University of Leipzig, a center of medical history made famous by the genius of Karl Sudhoff and two of his outstanding students, Henry E. Sigerist and Owsei Temkin who emigrated to the United States in 1932.

At the University of Bonn, Steudel established an Institute of Medical History modeled on the one at Leipzig. Bonn, best known for its university and as the birthplace of Beethoven, also was an industrial center strategically located on the Rhine (south of Cologne). The city was heavily bombed during the last two years of World War II, and the university was devastated. However, in 1949, Bonn became the capital of the Federal Republic of Germany, and the city and university prospered. Steudel attracted many students and exerted a congenial kind of direction on several "generations." When he was honored on his sixty-fifth birthday, the title for the *Festschrift* was *Medical History in Spectrum*, for he was a specialist whose humanism attracted him to diverse subjects. His relative permissiveness to students in that regard fit well with the post-war attitude of the young and strengthened his reputation among them. Nonetheless, Steudel was a diligent and conscientious worker and administrator. Twice he served as rector of the entire university. His most notable studies were centered on three areas of the intellectual and cultural history of medicine: first, the question of medical terminology; second, the evolution of European spas and physical therapy; and third, gerontology and geriatrics. In continuance of the inquiries into care of the aged, he added to his 1942 article new summaries in 1956 and 1965 (see bibliography).

A deep feeling of loss was expressed by his students and colleagues when Johannes Steudel died on May 31, 1973; they spoke of him as a wise adviser and as a friend. Of particular interest is the fact that his studies in the medical history of aging seemed to enable him to cope with his own aging in a creative way. Despite the painful illness of his last years, the ongoing integrity of Steudel's life and thought won him renewed admiration and respect.

As one reads James E. Birren's brief history of geronto-psychology, it seems that not only is the subject matter new, but also that the basic approach is very different from that of the previous selections in this volume. To Birren, the history of the study of aging really begins only with the victory of science, which he defines in terms of systematic research of an empirical, quantitative kind with intensifyingly sophisticated, organized and specialized methods of interpretation. The author's particular interests in research methodology and psychometrics seem to outweigh the humanism that pervasively informs the writings of Zeman, Steudel and Freeman.

In one respect, however, the historical approach is similar in the first four writers: all are attracted to the heroic theory of history. To the busy practitioner, whether in the clinic or the laboratory, there is something irresistibly absorbing in the life and work of an individual predecessor, especially if one considers the earlier person a creator of processes followed in one's own professional employ, or if the forerunner opened the path to the subject in which one's own specialty is located. Thus, Birren allotted more attention to Quetelet and his successor Galton than to any other individuals. Such an attitude to history is not necessarily anti-humanist; indeed, classical humanism tended to focus on the biographical mode. Much of the charm of Zeman's series is due to his skill in this genre. And even in the studies of Steudel, an expert, full-time historian, the biographical bias, so strong in the medical tradition, makes its appearance.

But in Birren's article, heroic biographical humanism came into conflict with objective methodology based on probabilities, the concept of the "average man" and ever-increasing specialization. Perhaps these are contradictions inherent in twentieth-century American science. On one hand, Birren centered on scientists who broke through the limits of traditional specialties: e.g., Quetelet, Galton, Pavlov, Miles, Pressey, Cowdry and Welford. On the other, he foresaw a future in which the creative psychologist will choose to be a small part of an organized research unit; and if he wishes to glimpse the larger implications of his work, he will have to submit humbly to the systematization of electronic data-collecting devices. This struggle between the specific and the general also reflects Birren's own lifework, divided between precise studies and comprehensive administration and editing. Among the most valuable features of his article are his memories of persons met and events experienced in the course of his duties as a major organizer of the expansion of gerontology after 1945.

James Emmett Birren was born in Chicago on April 4, 1918; he graduated from Chicago Teachers College in 1941 and in 1947 received his Ph.D. in psychology at Northwestern University. His years at Northwestern coincided with federal government and U.S. Navy research work in psychology and statistics during World War II. The key step in Birren's career came in 1947, when he joined the Gerontology Unit at the rapidly developing National Institutes of Health. In the twenty years between 1947 and 1965, he took part, often as chief administrator, in exciting meetings and decisions (described in his article), as the aging program underwent its spectacular period of growth. From 1953 to 1964, he was chief of the Section on Aging, and in 1962 he served as president of the Gerontological Society. It was from the Section on Aging that, in time, the present National Institute on Aging was to evolve. In 1965, however, Birren left for Los Angeles to lead the new gerontology center at the University of Southern California. At present, he is executive director of the Andrus Gerontology Center and dean of the Leonard Davis School of Gerontology.

It should be noted that despite an apparent diffidence about history and philosophy, Birren, as an administrator and editor, has followed a most benevolent policy regarding these two subjects. Thus, the landmark work *Handbook of Aging and the Individual,* edited by Birren in 1959, included chapters on the philosophy of time and on comparative cultural and historical patterns of aging. In 1961 as president-elect of the Gerontological Society, he was an active member of the Committee on History and wrote the article reprinted in this volume. The second edition of the *Handbook*, co-edited with K. Warner Schaie in 1977, features chapters on the history of psychological gerontology and on the cross-cultural, comparative psychology of aging. And in the textbook *Aging,* co-edited by Diana S. Woodruff and James E. Birren in 1975, there is a good chapter on the history of gerontology.

We turn now to *Perspectives in Aging,* consisting of four survey articles, edited in 1965 by Joseph T. Freeman and Irving L. Webber. The career of Dr. Freeman, who also wrote the perspective article on the medical history of aging, already has been discussed. Prof. Webber worked devotedly as the first chairman of the Gerontological Society's Committee on History (1960-1964). Irving Leonard Webber was born in 1915 in Minnesota. He attended college at the University of Florida (Gainesville) and in 1956 earned a Ph.D. in sociology at the Louisiana State University. He taught sociology at the University of Florida and the University of South Florida (Tampa) from 1953 to 1971. He carried out sociological research with the Health Department of Pinellas County: i.e., the Clearwater-St. Petersburg area. he also was a visiting professor, for three years, in South America at the University of Valle in Colombia. Since 1971, he has been professor of sociology at the University of Alabama.

The historical article on the biology of aging was written by Alfred Henry Lawton. Born in 1916 in a small town in western Iowa, Lawton graduated from Simpson College near Des Moines and then moved to Chicago, where he attained an M.D. in 1941 and a Ph.D. in 1943 at Northwestern University. During World War II, he was an officer in the U.S. Public Health Service; and in the post-war decades, he distinguished himself in a series of high positions, mostly governmental, administering biomedical research, education and the public health. At the time he wrote the article, he was director of the Department of H. E. W. study center in human development (St. Petersburg). After 1966, he held leading posts at the University of South Florida and the V. A. hospital at Tampa, and in 1973, he served as president of the Gerontological Society. Since 1974, Dr. Lawton has directed geriatric research at the V. A. Center at Bay Pines, Florida.

Walter Miles was the author of the perspective on the history of psychology; his research efforts in aging are described and honored in Birren's paper. Born in North Dakota in 1885, Walter Richard Miles gained his Ph.D. in psychology at Iowa State University in 1913. Miles' approach to psychology was experimental and physiological; from 1914 to 1922, he did studies in nutrition for the Carnegie Institution. Next was his creative period at Stanford University (1922-1932), where his work on senescence was done after 1928. In 1932, Miles' presidential address to the American Psychological Association dealt with aging, and in 1939, his fine chapter appeared in the classic *Problems of Aging,* edited by E. V. Cowdry. From 1932 to 1953, he taught at Yale. During World War II, Miles dropped his work on the psychology of senescence in order to help the Air Corps. After becoming emeritus at Yale, he again turned to applied science as an expert on submarine habitation and the new domain of Space Age psychology. The latter research, done in his own advanced age, indicates his pioneering energy Walter R. Miles died in 1978 at the age of ninety-three.

The paper on the history of social-welfare gerontology was prepared by Olli A. Randall, who was born in Kansas in 1890 and graduated from Brown University in 1912. A social worker, Ms. Randall took the initiative in organizing in 1925 a division on the welfare of the elderly as part of the New York City Welfare Council—this was the first such organization for older people in this country. Randall worked with the Community Service Society of New York from 1925 to 1945. During the Great Depression, she served on the Emergency Unemployment Relief Commission. She was awarded a special citation at the first White House Conference on the Aged in 1950. In 1955, Ms. Randall was president of the Gerontological Society, and after 1955, she was consultant to the Ford Foundation's program in aging. Now at an advanced age herself, Ollie A. Randall continues to be active and is the only one in the Gerontological Society designated "Honorary Member."

Finally, to introduce the writer of the paper on "Concepts of Aging," Richard Locke Grant was born in Oklahoma in 1933, graduated from De Pauw University in 1956 and received his M.D. from the University of Chicago in 1959. Dr. Grant's article on the history of gerontology reflected his interest in internal medicine while he was a resident at the University of Oregon Medical School; he turned to psychiatry, however, teaching that subject at Oregon until 1971. After 1971, he taught at the University of Vermont; and since 1975, Richard L. Grant has been an associate professor of psychiatry at the University of Colorado Medical Center in Denver.

—Gerald J. Gruman

BIBLIOGRAPHY

I. What is Ageism?

Butler, Robert N. "The Effect of Medical and Health Progress on the Social and Economic Aspects of the Life Cycle." *Industrial Gerontology*, 1, no. 2 (June 1969), pp. 1-9.

_____. "Age-Ism: Another Form of Bigotry." *The Gerontologist*, 9 (1969), pp. 243-246.

Freedman, Richard. "Sufficiently Decayed: Gerontophobia in English Literature." *Aging and the Elderly: Humanistic Perspectives in Gerontology*. Eds. Stuart F. Spicker, Kathleen M. Woodward and David D. Van Tassel. Atlantic Highlands, NJ: Humanities Press, 1978, pp. 49-61.

Gruman, Gerald J. "Cultural Origins of Present-day 'Age-ism': The Modernization of the Life Cycle." *Aging and the Elderly: Humanistic Perspectives in Gerontology*. Eds. Stuart F. Spicker, Kathleen M. Woodward and David D. Van Tassel. Atlantic Highlands, NJ: Humanities Press, 1978, pp. 359-387.

Kastenbaum, Robert. "Should We Have Mixed Feelings About Our Ambivalence Toward the Aged?" *Journal of Geriatric Psychiatry*, 7 (1974), pp. 94-107.

Neugarten, Bernice L. "The Old and the Young in Advanced Industrial Societies." Lecture presented 29 August 1969 to 8th International Congress of Gerontology, Washington, DC.

II. Cultural Origins of Ageism

Achenbaum, W. Andrew. *Old Age in the New Land: The American Experience since 1790*. Baltimore: The Johns Hopkins Univ. Press, 1978.

Allen, Walter. *The English Novel: A Short Critical History*. New York: Dutton Everyman, 1954.

Beauvoir, Simone de. *The Coming of Age*. Tr. Patrick O'Brian, New York: G.P. Putnam's Sons, 1972.

Boorstin, Daniel J. *The Lost World of Thomas Jefferson*. 1948; rpt. Boston: Beacon, 1960.

Butler, Robert N. "The Destiny of Creativity in Later Life." *Psychodynamic Studies on Aging*. Eds. Sidney Levin and Ralph J. Kahana. New York: International Universities Press, 1967, pp. 20-63.

Cowgill, Donald O. and Holmes, Lowell D., Eds. *Aging and Modernization*. New York: Appleton-Century-Crofts, 1972.

Cumming, Elaine and Henry, William E. *Growing Old: The Process of Disengagement.* 1961; rpt. New York: Arno Press, 1979.

Erikson, Erik H. *Childhood and Society.* 2nd ed. New York: W. W. Norton, 1963, pp. 247-274.

Fischer, David Hackett. *Growing Old in America.* New York: Oxford Univ. Press, 1977.

Foucault, Michel, *The Birth of the Clinic: An Archaeology of Medical Perception.* Tr. A. M. Sheridan Smith. New York: Vintage, 1975, pp. 124-148, 195-199.

Fyodorov, Nicholas F. "The Question of Brotherhood, or Relatedness." Trs. Arleigh E. Moorhouse and George L. Kline. Reprinted in *Death as a Speculative Theme in Religious, Scientific, and Social Thought.* New York: Arno Press, 1977.

Graubard, Mark. "The Frankenstein Syndrome: Man's Ambivalent Attitude to Knowledge and Power." *Perspectives in Biology and Medicine,* 10 (1967), 419-443.

Grmek, Mirko D. *On Ageing and Old Age: Basic Problems and Historic Aspects of Gerontology and Geriatrics.* The Hague, Netherlands: W. Junk, 1958.

Gruman, Gerald J. *A History of Ideas About the Prolongation of Life: The Evolution of Prolongevity Hypotheses to 1800.* 1966; rpt. New York: Arno Press, 1977.

_____. "Longevity." *Dictionary of the History of Ideas.* Ed. Philip P. Wiener. New York: Charles Scribner's Sons, 1973-1974, III, 89-93.

_____. "The Modern Intellectual Crisis About an Aging Population and Cultural Decline." Presented to Colloquium on "Aging: Myths, Rituals, and Values," Univ. of Southern California, 2 May 1975.

Kett, Joseph F. "History of Age Grouping in America." *Youth: Transition to Adulthood.* Report of the Panel on Youth. Washington: Government Printing Office, 1973, pp. 9-29.

Parsons, Talcott. "Old Age as Consummatory Phase." *The Gerontologist,* 3 (1963), pp. 53-54.

Richardson, Bessie ellen. *Old Age Among the Ancient Greeks.* 1933; rpt. New York: 1969.

Rose, Arnold M. "A Current Theoretical Issue." [Disengagement]. *The Gerontologist,* 4 (1964), pp. 46-50.

Smalley, Donald. *Trollope: The Critical Heritage.* New York: Barnes and Noble, 1969.

Temkin, Owsei. "German Concepts of Ontogeny and History around 1800." [German Romantic origins of the idea of stages of life]. *The Double Face of Janus, and Other Essays in the History of Medicine.* Baltimore: The Johns Hopkins Univ. Press, 1977, pp. 373-389.

Toynbee, Arnold *et al.,* Eds. *Man's Concern with Death.* New York: McGraw-Hill, 1969.

III. The Controversy: The Three Chief Actors

A. George Miller Beard

"George Miller Beard." *Dictionary of American Biography.* Ed. Allen Johnson. New York: Scribner's, 1955, I, pp. 92-93.

"George Miller Beard." *Dictionary of American Medical Biography.* Howard A. Kelly and W. L. Burrage, Eds. New York: D. Appleton, 1928, pp. 80-81.

Ellenberger, Henri F. *The Discovery of the Unconscious: The History and Evolution of Dynamic Psychiatry.* New York: Basic Books, 1970, pp. 242-245.

Rosenberg, Charles E. "The Place of George M. Beard in Nineteenth-Century Psychiatry." *Bulletin of the History of Medicine,* 36 (1962), pp. 245-259.

B. Sir James Crichton-Browne

Crichton-Brown, Sir James. *The Doctor Remembers.* London: Duckworth, 1938.

"Sir James Crichton-Browne." *Dictionary of National Biography: 1931-1940.*

"Crichton-Browne, Scottish Surgeon." Obituary. *New York Times.* 1 February 1938, p. 21, cols. 2,[a]; photo.

C. Sir William Osler

Cushing, Harvey. *The Life of Sir William Osler* (1925). One volume ed. New York: Oxford Univ. Press, 1940.

Graebner, William. "The Osler Valedictory." Chapter mss. *Between Work and Death: The Meaning and Function of Retirement in America, 1885-1979.* New Haven: Yale Univ. Press, in press.

Sigerist, Henry E. *The Great Doctors.* Tr. Eden and Cedar Paul. 1933; rpt. Garden City, NY: Doubleday Anchor, 1958, pp. 379-386.

Sullivan, Mark. *Our Times: The United States: 1900-1925.* New York: Scribner's, 1927, II, pp. 632-633.

Dr. Frederic D. Zeman, 1894-1970

DEDICATION

This work is dedicated to the memory of Frederic D. Zeman, M.D. (1894–1970), a pioneer in the medical care of the aged and in the writing of its history.

LIFE'S LATER YEARS

Studies in the Medical History of Old Age

Frederic D. Zeman

LIFE'S LATER YEARS

Studies in the Medical History of Old Age

FREDERIC D. ZEMAN, M.D.

[*New York City*]

Part 1*

"*From history we have to learn not only what our ancestors conceived, and made, but also why they thought and acted so. For if the world-drama is, in part, of man's conflicts with nature, it is far more a drama of his conflicts with his kind and with himself.*"

Sir Clifford Allbutt—*Greek Medicine in Rome*

INTRODUCTION

The story of man's struggle against old age and its maladies is a significant but rarely differentiated part of medical history. Since the tremendous advances of the last century in increasing the expectancy of human life have forcibly brought the problems of the advancing years to the attention of the practising physician, he must seek a sound foundation for present day thinking in a clear realization of the historical perspective. He must look back over several thousand years, follow carefully the devious paths of superstition, folk-belief, magic and religion to trace the uneven progress of medicine until the relatively recent development of a scientific viewpoint is finally attained. Contact with the great minds of the past, whose thoughts and observations are so often remarkably fresh and unimpaired by time, will bring the humility that history alone can teach.

Old age in its relation to medicine is a part of that larger field of inquiry, old age and society, consideration of which must be deferred until the time when the social implications of old age may be taken up as a whole. For the present our concern is limited to the theories and practices of priests, magicians, philosophers and physicians, as related to aging man and his diseases. We shall find that some of the most notable contributions in the past have been made by individuals entirely untrained in the healing art. Of the three most famous descriptions of advanced age, one is attributed to an unnamed preacher, and two have emanated from great poets. During the Renaissance many great thinkers turned their attention to the problem, but the widest influence was exercised by a reformed rake, whose theory of longevity through undernutrition was dramatically demonstrated by his actually living past the century mark. In our own time real leadership has often been found in the teachings of the biologists; unusual insight and objectivity were combined in the last work of a great psychologist. On the other hand, the bulk of the investigative endeavor, to say nothing of the diag-

---

* This is the first in a series of articles dealing with Studies in the Medical History of Old Age. Upon completion of their publication, the installments will be collected and reprinted in a single volume, constituting the third in the Series of Monographs of The Mount Sinai Hospital Press.—Ed.

nostic and therapeutic responsibility, has been in the hands of the medical profession. These instances of lay participation serve notably to illustrate the intense preoccupation of all mankind with our problem which, in the words of Dawson (1), forms "the history of human effort to prolong life and avert extinction—an effort out of which the magician, priest and doctor had their origin."

PRIMITIVE MAN

The skeletal anatomy of the early races of man has been carefully studied in the scanty material made available by the archeologists. On the basis of field and laboratory studies, definite time and cultural correlations have been set up. Professor Krogman's chart of the Pleistocene Period (fig. 1), shows vividly many essential features of the life and the culture of primitive man.

The recent work of Vallois (2) and Weidenreich (3) now furnishes interesting, although meager data as to the longevity and pathology of early and late Paleolithic man. The age determinations are largely based on the times of closure of various skull sutures (4). The first mentioned investigator studied the remains of Neanderthal man, and concluded that his life duration was very brief, inasmuch as out of 20 individuals only 5 per cent reached an age of more than 40 years, while 40 per cent died as children of 11 years or less. Late Paleolithic man, in contrast, shows a distinct lengthening of his life, 10.8 per cent of the individuals reaching an age of 40 and 1 per cent even more than 50 years, whereas the percentage of children dying before 11 years decreases to 24.5 per cent.

In the series of Sinanthropus bones reported by Weidenreich, numbering 38 persons, 15 or 39.5 per cent were children 14 years or less, judging by dentition; 3 skulls may have belonged to individuals less than 30 years old, 3 may have ranged between 40 and 50 years, and only 1, apparently that of a woman, of whom unfortunately only small fragments remain, may have been 50 or even 60 years of age. The location of the remains in the famous cave at Choukoutien, near Peiping, indicate that the existence of these people must be dated back at least 25,000 years, probably even more. Late Paleolithic man, as compared with Sinanthropus, is represented by only 7 individuals, 3 definitely juvenile, 4 adults, of whom 2 were probably women slightly over 20, the age of the third being indefinite, but not old. The fourth adult was certainly an old man of at least 60 years. These figures for the East are to be compared with Vallois' for the Western parts of the old world. In both the Sinanthropus and the later Paleolithic series from the East, all died violent deaths from skull injuries.

These contributions are quoted in detail to bring out that there *seems* to be evidence for a difference between early and late Stone Age life duration based on the examination of actual remains, and that anatomical findings point to few individuals reaching an advanced age. Such scanty data can at best be hardly more than suggestive. Vallois believes that the more refined civilization of later Paleolithic time permitted survival of individuals who under the coarser conditions of more primitive living would surely have been exterminated. Weidenreich is of the opinion that primitive man, like undomesticated animals, had

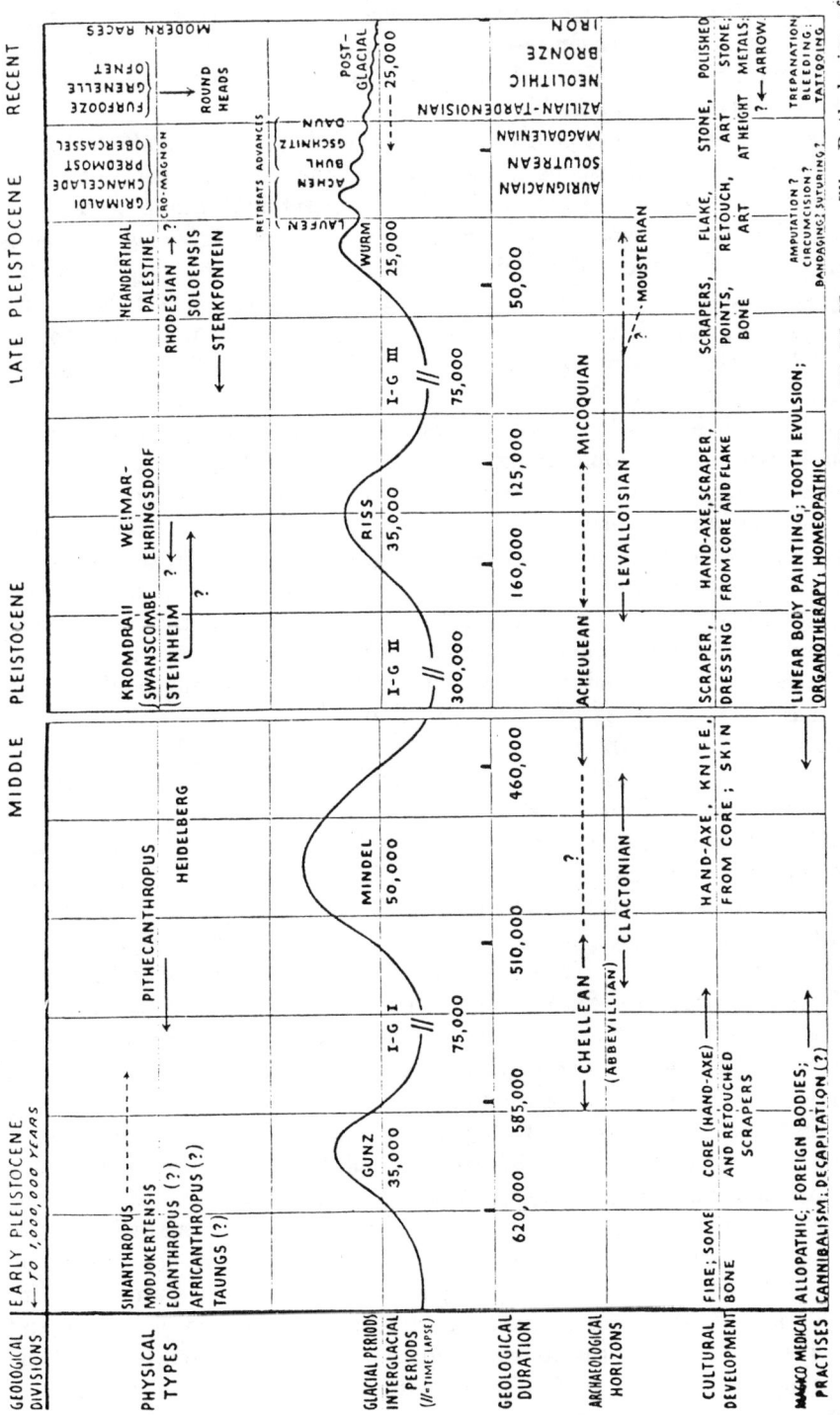

FIG. 1. The Pleistocene History of Man and His Culture (after Daly, Nelson, Zeuner). (From W. M. Krogman, The Pathologies of Pre- and Protohistoric Man, Ciba Symposia, Vol. 2, No. 2, May 1940. Reproduced by permission of Ciba Symposia and Prof. Krogman).

greater resistance to infectious disease in general. He calls attention to the attrition of teeth due to the coarse diet, to the total absence of signs of dental caries or pyorrhea alveolaris, and finally to the osteoarthritic changes in the vertebrae of the old man in his late series (5).

The bare bones of ancient peoples (6), while yielding much valuable information as to the size and the shape of the brain and the relative proportions of its component parts, give us but little insight into their actual mental processes and customs. For this information we turn to comparative anthropology, which is concerned with the study of so-called savage peoples living today, or in the recent past, whose cultural development is thought to approximate that of our Stone Age ancestors. The study of folk-lore throughout the world, in civilizations of all degrees of complexity, has likewise thrown much light on primitive patterns of thinking.

In his monumental work "Folkways," Sumner (7) devotes a whole chapter to the consideration of abortion, infanticide and killing the old, pointing out that the rearing of children and the caring for the weak were, under rigorous conditions of living, burdens that required summary action from the standpoint of group welfare. He describes "two sets of mores as to the aged: (a) in one set of mores the teaching and usages inculcate conventional respect for the aged, who are therefore arbitrarily preserved for their wisdom and counsel, perhaps also sometimes out of affection and sympathy; (b) in the other set of mores the aged are regarded as societal burdens, which waste the strength of society, already inadequate for its tasks. Therefore they are forced to die either by their own hands, or those of their relatives." Abundant ethnographic illustrations are given of both viewpoints. Civilized men face to face with primitive conditions may find their sentiments temporarily overcome by grim necessity. Sumner emphasizes that with the improvement of living conditions there was less and less necessity for doing away with the weak, and in borderline cases men would be apt to be swayed by repugnance of the act rather than by the dislike of hardship. He points out that a kindly sentimental attachment to the old is a product of civilization, possible only to men for whom the struggle and competition of life had become definitely moderated. One need hardly be reminded that even today these primitive attitudes keep coming to the fore, and have formed an intrinsic part of the political program of the most bestial scoundrels who have ever sought to enslave the world.

Dawson (8) has emphasized that "primitive man was not an abstract thinker and long ages had elapsed before he had accumulated the knowledge necessary to convince him that death is the inevitable fate of all living creatures." To the mitigation of this fate primitive religion devoted itself, for in many lands and among many peoples we find the concept that death is the result of avenging spirits or gods, and that in the beginning of the world man was immortal. Innumerable legends and myths have arisen to explain the origin of old age and death, all of which embody the same basic ideas with varying amounts of elaboration. Many are based on the forbidden fruit theme exemplified by the Biblical story (9), and on the punishment resulting from disobeying the instructions of the deity. Others have to do with the casting off of the skin. Savages had naturally observed the periodic renewal of the surface coverings of snakes, lizards, crabs and beetles, with their apparent rejuvenation following this process. The far-reaching meaning of this natural process for the primitive mind is attested by the illuminating observation of Richardson (10) that "in both Greek and Latin the words for old age, γῆρος and *senectus*, are used to designate the casting off of the skin of an animal." Philology thus confirms the intimate association of the ideas of old age and rejuvenation by prehistoric man.

It will be recalled that in Greek mythology the snake is the symbol of rejuvenation and was intimately associated with Asklepios, the god of healing. While this property of the snake plays no rôle in the Biblical story of the Fall of Man, the choice of this animal as the villain of that piece is not accidental, and in Frazer's opinion indicates the essential unity of the two fundamental themes.

"*The Arawaks of British Guinea say that man was created by a good being whom they call Kurunumany. Once on a time this kindly creator came to earth to see how his creature man was getting on. But men were so ungrateful that they tried to kill their Maker. Hence he took from them the gift of immortality and bestowed it on animals that change their skins, such as snakes, lizards and beetles. Again, the Tamanachiers, an Indian tribe of the Orinoco, tell how their creator kindly intended to make man immortal by telling them that they should change their skins. He meant to say that by so doing they should renew their youth like serpents and beetles. But the glad tidings were received with such incredulity by an old woman that the creator in a huff changed his tune and said, 'Ye shall die!'* " (*11*)

Having once lost the gift of immortality, the efforts of mankind in the form of religion were designed to propitiate the gods, in order to prolong life and to avert bodily sufferings whether due to injury or disease. This last mentioned distinction, when finally achieved, represents one of the greatest of advances in the medical thinking of all time. That external violence could cause pain, raise a swelling, break a bone or even kill was an actual commonplace of primitive experience, but for long ages all other forms of bodily suffering were ascribed to supernatural causes. "What we call natural death is nearly always attributed to witchcraft, sorcery or divine interference in human affairs. Such are the prevailing ideas among primitive peoples today, and by analogy, such was probably the belief of primitive man before the advent of civilization." (Dawson).

An additional fact of primitive experience was the association of advancing years with the diminution of bodily powers, the loss of sexual attractiveness, and increased likelihood of death. Here, too, the myths attempt to explain away reality, and primitive religion holds forth the hope of a better life to come. Malinowski's studies among the Trobriand Islanders, inhabiting a part of British New Guinea in Northwestern Melanesia, furnish enlightening detail and explanation on these points. These quotations from his work bear also on the preceding discussions.

"*To enjoy life and love it is necessary to be young. Even in Tuma (paradise), old-age, that is, wrinkles, grey hair and feebleness, creeps from the spirits. But in Tuma there exists a remedy, once accessible to all mankind, but now lost to the world. For old age to the Trobrianders is not a natural state— it is an accident, a misadventure. Long ago, shortly after mankind had come upon the earth from underground, human beings could rejuvenate at will by casting off the old withered skin; just as crabs, snakes and lizards and those creatures that burrow underground will every now and then throw off the old covering and start life with a new and perfect one. Humanity, unfortunately, lost this art—through the folly of an ancestress, according to legend—but in Tuma, the happy spirits retained it. When they find themselves old, they slough off the loose, wrinkled skin, and emerge with a smooth body, dark locks, sound teeth and full vigor. Thus life with them is an eternal recapitulation of youth with its accompaniment of love and pleasure." (12)*

"Old age is felt to be a serious handicap in affairs of gallantry. The contrast between repulsive old age and attractive youth is brought out clearly in the myth. A hero, who is unsuccessful because of his elderly appearance, becomes rejuvenated and gets everything he wants. First, the marks scored upon him by the hand of time are ruthlessly enumerated: a wrinkled skin, white hair and toothless jaws. Then the magical change is described: his rounded face, the smooth full lines of the body, his sleek glossy skin, the thick black hair covering his head, the beautiful black teeth showing between vermilion lips. Now he can win the favors of desirable women and impose his wishes on men and Fate. Such pictures are drawn in two of the chief myths of the Kula (the ceremonial interchange) which plays such a great part in tribal life and shows so many psychological affinities to their erotic interests. Similar pictures are also to be found in the ideas of the natives concerning a future life and in one or two fairy tales." (12)

In drawing the picture of primitive man's attitude toward his environment, his fellows and to himself, we have spoken chiefly of religion, which may be defined here as the belief in the control of man's destiny by higher powers whose favor and good-will must be cultivated. Closely linked with it and perhaps preceding it historically, are the rites which today we call magic; rites in which incantations appropriate to the occasion and the purpose are recited, and certain definite manual activities performed, in order to bring about a desired result, usually without appeal to higher beings. Frazer has differentiated two varieties of magic, the *contagious*—according to which special properties are ascribed to objects once in contact with an object or thing, or which once formed part of it; the *sympathetic*—according to which magical effects may be projected at a distance, and also may be produced for good or evil by working upon objects of similar appearance. In the earliest times the treatment of diseases and injuries was in the hands of the priest-magician, who thus became in effect priest-magician-physician. The history of medicine, of human culture in fact, is concerned with the gradual differentiation of these three functions.

Today, according to Rivers (13), "medicine, magic and religion are abstract terms each of which connotes a large group of social processes, processes by means of which mankind has come to regulate his behavior towards the world around him. Among ourselves these three groups of processes are more or less sharply marked off from one another. One has gone altogether into the background of our social life, while the other two form distinct social categories widely different from one another and having few elements in common. If we survey mankind widely this distinction and separation does not exist. There are many peoples among whom the three sets of social process are so closely interrelated that the disentanglement of each from the rest is difficult or impossible; while there are yet other peoples among whom the social processes to which

FIG. 2 Pottery Portrait of an Old Woman. This wrinkled, round face, with button nose and toothless mouth adorns a pottery vase which was found on the coast of Northern Peru by the sons of the Vice-President of Peru, Senor don Rafael Larco Herrera. This remarkable art work is a product of Cupisnique Indian culture, probably the earliest settlers in Peru, long antedating the Incas. (Reproduced by permission of Science News Service, from Science News Letter, November 15, 1941).

we give the name of medicine can hardly be said to exist, so closely is man's attitude toward disease identical with that which he adopts towards other classes of natural phenomena."

We shall find, as we proceed in our depiction of old age, that of all the stages of human life to which the physician devotes his attention, it has longest remained an equally anxious concern of the priest and to some degree also of the magician. That such is even today evident is to be explained by the biological limitations of the healing art. Throughout the centuries there has, therefore, been a struggle between the three forces, with the physician attaining the ascendancy during the classic period of Greek medicine, the priest again dominant during the Middle Ages, and in our own time a brief resurgence of the magician in the form of "spiritualism" and in pseudo-scienific efforts at rejuvenation.

REFERENCES

(1) DAWSON, W. R.: Magician and Leech. London, Methuen & Co., p. 1, 1929.
(2) VALLOIS, H. V.: Life Duration of Primitive Man. Compt. rend. Acad. d. Sci. 204: 60, 1937.
(3) WEIDENREICH, F.: Longevity of Fossil Man in China and Pathologie Lesions Found in His Skeleton. Chinese M. J., 55: 34, 1939.
(4) TODD, T. W. AND LYON, D. W.: Cranial Suture Closure, its Progress and Age Relationships. Am. J. Phys. Anthropology, 7: 325, 1924.
(5) Studies of mortality in prehistoric peoples have also been made by the following:
   SMITH, G. E. AND JONES, F. W.: The Archeological Survey of Nubia; Report for 1907-08; Vol. 2; Report on Human Remains, Cairo, 1910.
   FRANZ, L. AND WINKLER, W.: Mortality in Early Bronze Age of Lower Austria, Ztschr. d. Rassenk., 4: 157, 1936.
   KROGMAN, W. M.: The Skeletal and Dental Pathology of an Early Iranian Site. Bull. Hist. Med., 8 (1): 28, 1940.
(6) See among others: SIR ARTHUR KEITH: New Discoveries Relating to the Antiquity of Man, The Interpretation of Brain Casts. New York, W. W. Norton, Chap. 31, 1932.
(7) SUMNER, W. G.: Folkways, New York, Ginn & Co., 1906.
(8) DAWSON, op. cit.
(9) Genesis 3: 1-24. For an illuminating study of this passage see Sir J. G. FRAZER: Folk-Lore in the Old Testament, London, Macmillan & Co., 1: 70, 1919.
(10) RICHARDSON, B. E.: Old Age among the Ancient Greeks. Baltimore, Johns Hopkins Press, p. 69, 1933.
(11) FRAZER, SIR J. G.: The Golden Bough, Part 6, The Scapegoat, 3rd Ed., p. 302, London, Macmillan, 1913.
(12) MALINOWSKI, B.: The Sexual Life of Savages, London, Halcyon House, 1929.
(13) RIVERS, W. H. R.: Medicine, Magic and Religion, New York, Harcourt Brace, 1924.

OLD AGE IN ANCIENT EGYPT

A Contribution to the History of Geriatrics

FREDERIC D. ZEMAN, M.D.

[New York City]

"Blessed is the man of science who enjoys the great companionship of the ancients; they are flesh of his flesh, sharers of his successes and errors, of his joys and his deceptions."

Sudhoff—Essays.

Primitive man is believed to have first appeared in the Pleistocene or Glacial Period, generally considered to have covered about one million years. Since many geologists now place the origin of *Homo Sapiens* in the period preceding the Pleistocene, the Miocene, the age of prehistoric man is further increased. These figures, although only approximate, contrast strikingly with the very brief time which has elapsed since the dawn of "antiquity," inaugurated by the Egyptians with the discovery of the use of metals and the development of the art of writing. According to Breasted (1), the transition from prehistory to the historic period in Egypt occupied the thousand years from 4000 B.C. to 3000 B.C. Relatively speaking, the Egyptian civilization is modern, and the progress of the past 5000 years absolutely breath-taking, however little the mind of man may have been altered in its essential nature. Hooton (2) writes that "the period of human civilization is as inconsiderable in man's cultural history as is post-glacial time in the age of the earth".

At the opening of the Age of the Pyramids in the year 3000 B.C. we find already a highly developed Egyptian civilization, characterized by intricate social organization, extensive industrial and agricultural activity, and a religious system notable for its beliefs not only in life after death but also in "right living, in kindness to others, and that a good life here was the only thing that could bring happiness in the next world" (1). This period is outstanding in giving us Imhotep, the first physician known by name, whose activities covered with distinction the fields of medicine, priestly wisdom, magic and architecture. His reputation increased steadily after his death until he became deified and later was identified by the Greeks with their own Asklepios.

The development of Egyptian medicine from the rites of the priest-magicians has been traced by Dawson (3). He has pointed out in detail how these practices were copied by Greek and Roman writers, were transcribed in the leech books of the sixteenth century (4), and reappear from time to time in the folk medicine of our own day. The art of the magician consisted in the utterance of spells and incantations, accompanied by manipulation of figures, amulets or a variety of natural substances. These procedures have been differentiated by Gardiner (5) into the "oral rite" and the "manual rite." In the medical papyri preserved to us from these remote times we find abundant illustrations of these two rites.

"The prescriptions in the medical papyri are but elaborations of the manual rite of the magician, and it is for this reason that the papyri are interspersed with magical spells that constitute the oral rites belonging to each group of prescriptions that follows and that are recited by the magician in order to make the doses effective. Some of these remedies contain drugs that are really beneficial and appropriate, and such prescriptions, actually accomplishing their purpose, would tend to survive their more fantastic fellows. By such means more and more reliance came to be placed on the drugs themselves and less upon the magicians' spells, and the persons who would be most in request in cases of sickness would be those who were skilled in knowledge and preparation of drugs. Such men were no longer magicians, but physicians." (3)

In the famous medical document known as the Edwin Smith Surgical Papyrus (1600 B.C.), and recently published by Breasted (6) in a brilliant translation, with a beautiful reproduction of the original text, we find a remarkable description of surgical conditions of the head. These clinical records of actual cases are comparable for detail and accurate description to those of Hippocrates. Our present interest centers on the incantations and recipes which are found on the back of the papyrus in the hand of the same scribe. Among these is one entitled, "The Book for Transforming an Old Man into a Youth of Twenty". This may be divided into two parts, the first containing directions for compounding the ointment, the second, the directions for its use. These read as follows:

"*Anoint a man therewith. It is a remover of wrinkles from the head. When the flesh is smeared therewith it becomes a beautifier of the skin, a remover of blemishes, of all disfigurements, of all signs of age, of all weaknesses which are in the flesh. Found effective myriads of times.*"

In this recipe of an Egyptian priest for rejuvenation we find the earliest written history of medicine in the aged.

The medical papyri are written in the Egyptian script known as hieratic, which must be transcribed into hieroglyphic before an English translation is possible. Study of Breasted's hieroglyphic text of the Smith Papyrus brought to this writer's attention an interesting feature of the hieroglyph meaning "old" or "to grow old". It is a clear representation of a bent human figure resting on a staff (figs. 1 and 2). This ideograph delineates old age as typified by muscular and bony weakness, and may be considered the earliest artistic representation of senile debility. The symbol is first found in inscriptions of the period 2700 to 2800 B.C. It is to be compared with the hieroglyph for youth which consists of a sitting child with its finger in its mouth.

The Papyrus Ebers (c.1550 B.C.) (7, 8) is made up of a great collection of prescriptions for various ailments, some observations on symptomatology and diagnosis, and an unusually perspicacious description of the function of the heart and great vessels. Among the diseases and symptoms, which are

Fig. 1. Hieroglyphic sentence from the Papyrus Prisse (c. 1580 B.C.) containing the Precepts of Ptah-hotep: "To be an old man is evil for people in every respect". (Quoted by Breasted, The Edwin Smith Surgical Papyrus, p. 493). Note the seventh symbol from the left, which is enlarged in Fig. 2.

Fig. 2. This bent human figure resting on a staff is the hieroglyphic ideograph indicating "old age" or "to grow old", and used as a determinative in phrases involving the concept of old age. First noted in inscriptions of 2700 to 2800 B.C.

associated with old age, treatment is prescribed for the following: polyuria, accumulation and obstruction of urine, cystitis, cardiac pain, weakness, and palpitation, tumors, both innocent and malignant, deafness, and eye diseases. The identification of many Egyptian medical terms is often beyond the ability of the translator, who is forced to reproduce in his text the consonants representing the original word. The drugs and medicaments are of infinite variety, being derived from the animal, vegetable and mineral worlds. Many remedies are offered for constipation, grey hair, baldness, wrinkles, as well as the more serious diseases of old age.

In the section of definitions of medical terms we find an explanation of the manifestations of age. "As to debility through senile decay, it is (due to the fact) that purulency is on his heart" (8). Although the importance of the heart for life seems to have been sensed, the Egyptians can in no way be said to have foreshadowed Harvey's great discovery (9). In the section devoted to ocular diseases we find a recipe for cataract which serves to exemplify many of the features characteristic of Egyptian medicine.

> *Another to expel water suffusion in the eyes:*
> "Come, malachite! Come, malachite!
> Come, thou green one, come discharge from Horus' eye,
> Come secretion from Atum's eye, Come fluid that has come out of Osiris!
> Come to him and expel for him water, matter, blood, dim sight, BJDJ, blindness, blear-eyedness, afflictions caused by a god, by a dead man or woman, all kinds of purulency, all evil things that are in these eyes."
> *Is recited over malachite, pounded with honey NTHPRJI, with them is pounded rush nut, applied to the eye. Really excellent* (8).

This typical incantation embodies the oral and manual rites, the reference to the healing power of the gods and to the possible etiology in the disfavor of the gods or of a dead person, and the use of a copper compound in the eye, a practice prevailing at the present time.

All studies of Egyptian thought indicate that not only was old age held in highest respect but that the attainment of 110 years was the ultimate in achievement for an Egyptian. The inscription on a statue of Amenophis, the son of Hapu, who rivalled Imhotep as a healer, bears the inscription: "I have attained the age of 80 years, may I live to be 110." In the Papyrus Prisse (c. 1580 B.C.) we find the precepts of Ptah-hotep, a vizier in the reign of Pharaoh Assa of the Fifth Dynasty, who endeavored in his book to pass on to his children the knowledge he had accumulated during a long life. Dawson (10) calls it the oldest Wisdom Book in the world. The final words of the papyrus are: "I have gathered 110 years of life, for the King granted more favors than my ancestors, because I acted with truth and justice for the King until my old age."

Egyptian medicine flourished among a people in whom family life was highly developed. The children showed the greatest respect for their parents, and every son was required to maintain the tomb of his father. High value was placed upon the affection of one's parents and family. The inscription is found commonly in tombs: "I was one beloved of his father, praised by his mother, whom his sisters and brothers loved" (11). Thus we find here in the ancient land of Kemi not only the beginning of the medical study and treatment of the old, but also the earliest indication of the mores that were to characterize the religion of the ancient Hebrews and find lasting preservation in the Old Testament.

The writer is indebted to Mr. Ambrose Lansing, Curator of Egyptian Art, Metropolitan Museum of Art, New York, for the kindly encouragement and helpful advice of a true scholar.

REFERENCES

(1) BREASTED, J. H.: The Conquest of Civilization. New York, Harper & Bros., 1926.
(2) HOOTON, E. A.: Apes, Men and Morons. New York, G. P. Putnam's Sons, 1937.
(3) DAWSON, W. R.: Magician and Leech. London, Methuen & Co., 1929.
(4) DAWSON, W. R.: The Leech-Book. London, MacMillan & Co., 1934.
(5) GARDINER: Quoted by DAWSON (4).
(6) BREASTED, J. H.: Edwin Smith Surgical Papyrus. Chicago, University of Chicago Press, 1930.
(7) The Papyrus Ebers, translated from the German version of H. Joachim by Cyril Bryan, New York, D. Appleton & Co., 1931. This work is valuable for the introduction by G. Eliot Smith and the comments of Dr. Bryan. The Joachim translation is now discredited.
(8) The Papyrus Ebers, The Greatest Egyptian Medical Document, translated by B. Ebbell, London, Oxford University Press, 1937. This volume represents the latest and best translation, although itself incomplete in many particulars. Dates ascribed to the medical papyri in the text are from Ebbell, as are the quotations.
(9) RANKE, H.: Medicine and Surgery in Ancient Egypt, University of Pennsylvania Bicentennial Conference, 1940.
(10) DAWSON, W. R.: The Bridle of Pegasus,— Studies in Magic, Mythology and Folk-Lore. London, Methuen & Co., 1930.
(11) BREASTED, J. H.: A History of Egypt, New York, C. Scribner's Sons, 1912, p. 85.

LIFE'S LATER YEARS

STUDIES IN THE MEDICAL HISTORY OF OLD AGE

FREDERIC D. ZEMAN, M.D.

[*New York City*]

PART 3*

THE ANCIENT HEBREWS

Give glory to thy father with thy whole heart; and forget not the pangs of thy mother. Remember that of them thou wast born; and what wilt thou recompense them for the things that they have done for thee?

Ecclesiasticus, Chap. VII.

A new translation of the Bible has been made available in recent years by James Moffatt (1) in an effort "to offer the unlearned a transcript of Biblical literature in the light thrown upon it by modern research. The Bible is not always what it seems to those who read it in the great prose of the English version or, indeed, in any of the conventional versions." The present writer has been attracted to the Moffatt translation by its clarification of hitherto obscure passages, such as Ecclesiastes XII: 1–8. All quotations are therefore from Moffatt's rendering, and bring not only new wording but often new meaning to the familiar verses.

In the enlightening introduction to his work, Moffatt speaks aptly of the "little library, which we call the Old Testament." As revelation and inspiration to untold millions, as ethical guide, as lawgiver, as history and literature, it has long lived up to its title as *The Book*. It has been studied by scholars for centuries for its contributions to the most varied fields of interest. There is a large body of literature devoted only to its medical aspects (2). For our present study the Bible has abundant meaning. In its pages we read descriptions of old age and learn the precepts laid down for the guidance of the Jews in their attitude to the old. The meaning of old age to the individual himself is discussed from many viewpoints.

Historically it must be emphasized that the books of the Old Testament are not older than the eighth century B.C., and some are as recent as the second century, B.C. The older ones are thought to represent the literary preservation of more ancient traditions. All show evidence of the fusion of parallel stories, of editorial changes and of elements taken over from other civilizations.

In Genesis (XLVII, 8–9) we find in the audience accorded by Pharaoh to Jacob as Joseph's father, a striking contact of the Egyptian and Hebrew viewpoints on longevity, and are able, as Miles (3) has pointed out, to read more significance in the brief lines than is at first apparent.

---

* Part two of this study was published in Journal of The Mount Sinai Hospital, Vol. 8, Nov. 6, January–February, 1942, as "Old Age in Ancient Egypt." This is the third in a series of articles dealing with studies in the Medical History of Old Age. Upon completion of their publication, the installments will be collected and reprinted in a single volume, constituting the third in the Series of Monographs of The Mount Sinai Hospital Press.—Ed.

> *Then Joseph brought his father Jacob in, and placed him before the Pharaoh. Jacob saluted the Pharaoh. The Pharaoh asked Jacob, "How many years have you lived?" Jacob answered, "For a hundred and thirty years I have had a wandering life of it; few and hard have been the years I have lived; fewer than the years my father lived and wandered." Then, saluting the Pharaoh, Jacob withdrew from his presence.*

In view of the respect of every Egyptian for advanced age and his desire to attain the maximum of 110 years, Jacob must surely have impressed the Pharaoh. Certainly his humility of expression avoids the suspicion of boasting. Miles emphasizes that "both Jacob and the Pharaoh received renewed sense of the breadth and the continuity of life from the social experience," and that "in fact, interracial friendship was here balancing itself on longevity as a pivot-point of common interest."

From a medical viewpoint certain observations are essential. The knowledge of hygiene shown in the Bible is far ahead of that of medicine proper. The Mosaic Code, establishing a day of rest, regulating labor, promulgating the dietary laws, and attempting to prevent and treat pestilence and venereal disease, was a unique achievement in its own time, and stands on its merits even today. The cause of disease was sought in the anger of the Lord, and its cure to be found in sacrifice, repentance, fasting and prayer for Divine forgiveness. According to Neuburger, "the Old Testament, true to its strict monotheism, frowns on all belief in the demonic origin of disease, a belief universally prevalent among all peoples who attained to a certain cultural stage." By 22 B.C. the belief in God as the cause of disease and at the same time its healer had been reconciled with the actual practice of medicine, as we learn from the words of Ecclesiasticus (4) who points out in the greatest of all tributes to the physician, that there is place for medicine and prayer, since both have been created by the Lord.

In the early chapters of the Book of Genesis, the vital statistics, if taken literally, indicate an amazing length of life for Adam and his descendants. Noah is said to have died at the age of 950 years and the far-famed Methuselah prolonged his existence to 969 years. It is clear that the figures either imply the exaggeration often associated with mythical personages, or are based on some long forgotten calendar. When individuals of somewhat greater historical solidity appear, such as Abraham, Isaac and Jacob, the figures more nearly approach the plausible, being 175, 180 and 140 respectively, while Joseph lived to 110 years, Aaron to 123 and Moses to 120. The celebrated words of the Psalmist indicate a life span which approximates present-day experience.

> *Our life is seventy years at most, or eighty at best; a span of toil and trouble, soon over, and we flit away.*
>
> Psalm XC: 10.

The Book of Proberbs (16: 31) indicates the manner of attaining old age: "*Grey hairs are a crown of honour, gained by a good life.*"

In the Bible one finds objective reference to old age based usually on sound observation. Commonly mentioned are weakness of vision, loss of sexual power and mental deterioration.

> "Well," said the Eternal, "I will come back to you next Spring, when your wife Sarah shall have a son." Sarah was listening behind the door. She and Abraham were old, well on in years and the custom of women had ceased with Sarah. So Sarah laughed to herself, "Imagine marriage bliss for a worn old creature like me with an old husband."
>
> *Genesis 18: 20.*
>
> Now when Isaac was an old man, his eyes so dim that he could not see, he called his son Esau and said to him, "My son." Esau answered. "Here I am." He went on: "I am an old man now. I do not know how soon I may die."
>
> *Genesis 27: 1–3.*
>
> Moses was 120 yeard old when he died, but his eyes were undimmed and his vigor unabated.
>
> *Deuteronomy 34: 7.*

Brim (2) in commenting on this passage points out that the Hebrew words *lo nuss lecho*, rendered as "his vigor unabated," means literally "his secretions did not escape"; and reminds us how very characteristic of old people are such weaknesses as lachrymation, salivation, rhinorrhea, urinary frequency and incontinence.

> King David was an old man, well advanced in years, and although they covered him with bedclothes he could not keep himself warm. So his attendants said to the King, "Let some young girl be sought for my lord, the King, let her wait upon the King and take care of him: let her lie in your bosom, that my lord, the King may get warmth." All over Israel they sought for a beautiful maiden, and found Abisag of Shunem, whom they brought to the King; she was most beautiful, and she took care of the King and attended to him. But the King had no intercourse with her.
>
> *1 Kings: 1.*

We are indebted to McKenzie (5), whose History of Health, 1758, is a valuable source book, for an interesting collection of commentaries on this famous passage. Referring to David and Abishag, McKenzie considers this method "a very proper means to warm and cherish him, and which when kept within the bounds of innocence and decency is justified by the opinions of Galen, Paul of Aegina, Francis Bacon, and Boerhave." "Nothing contributes so much to a good digestion as a sound healthy human body touching the stomach." (*Galen, Meth. med., lib. 7, cap. 7* and *De Simpl. med. facult. lib. 5, cap. 6.*) "It is very difficult to relieve a person who is cold and dry at the same time; and a plump healthy boy to lie in his bosom is one of the best remedies he can use." (Paul of Aegina, *Lib. 1. cap. 72.*) Lord Verulam recommends fomentations of living animals for the coldness of age (*Hist. vit. et mort. p. 300*). Boerhave frequently told his pupils that an old German prince in a very infirm state of health, being advised to lie between two virtuous young women, grew so healthy and strong that his physicians found it necessary to remove his companions. In Hufeland's version (6) of the Boerhave story it was an old burgomaster of Amsterdam who enjoyed such a remarkable recovery as a result of this treatment. Cohansen (1749) in *Hermippus Redivivus or the Sage's Triumph over Old Age and the Grave, wherein a Method is laid down for prolonging the Life and Vigour of Man*, devotes a volume to the efficacy of the breath of young girls in furthering longevity.

> *Eli was ninety-eight years old, and his eyes were so dim that he could not see.*
> *1 Samuel 4: 15*

He is told of the disastrous outcome of the battle, the death of his two sons and the capture of the Ark of God by the Philistines.

> *When he mentioned the Ark of God, Eli fell back from his seat by the gate; his neck was broken, and he died—for he was old and heavy.*
> *1 Samuel 4: 18*

Barzillai the Gileadite ranks among the truly great old men of history because he wisely knew his own limitations, and declined King David's invitation to spend his remaining years in Jerusalem:

> *How many years have I to live, that I should go up with the King to Jerusalem? I am now eighty years old. Have I a taste for pleasure? Can your servant taste what he eats and drinks? Can I still hear the voice of singing men and women? Why, then, should your servant be a burden to my lord, the King? Pray let your servant return, that I may die in my own town, near the grave of my father and mother.*
> *2 Samuel 19: 34-37.*

We are also told of the last illness of Asa, Solomon's great-grandson, who long ruled wisely and devoutly as King of Judah:

> *In the thirty-ninth year of his reign Asa's feet became diseased; the disease was very painful, and Asa had recourse to his physicians, not to the Eternal. Asa slept with his fathers, dying in the forty-first year of his reign.*
> *3 Chronicles 16: 12-13.*

This illustrates the conflict between divine or priestly healing and the practical physician,—a conflict not settled until much later by Ecclesiasticus.

Two familiar tales from the Apocrypha must have brief mention here since they round out the picture of the character of old men, since one celebrates their perfidy and the other their nobility. The story of Susanna's false accusation by the lecherous elders and her acquittal by Daniel's intervention have inspired painters from Rembrandt van Rijn to Thomas Benton; and even today the narrative moves one to sympathy for the wronged woman and to disgust at the vile old men.

In contrast stands Eleazar the scribe (Maccabees, ii, chap. vi), who chose death rather than renounce his religion by eating swine's flesh, even though his jailers out of pity, begged him only to go through the motions. "For it becometh not our years to dissemble," said he, "that through this many of the young should suppose that Eleazar, the man of fourscore years and ten, had gone over into an alien religion; and so they, by reason of my dissimulation, and for the sake of this brief and momentary life, should be led astray because of me, and thus I get to myself a pollution and stain of mine old age."

The attitude towards parents and older people in general is clearly set forth in the Old Testament. It is made part of man's duty to God and appropriate rewards are promised. The Fifth Commandment (Exodus 20: 12) states emphatically, "Honour your father and your mother that you may have a long life in the land which the Eternal, your God is giving you." On this sentence has depended for over 2,000 years our mores regarding the old. In Leviticus (20: 9) it is more drastically phrased, "For any one who curses his father or his mother, his blood be on his own head"; and again more softly, (19: 32), "You shall rise up before a man with white hair and honour the person of an old man."

A gentle plea is voiced by the Psalmist (70: 9–10), "Cast me not off in my old age, forsake me not when my powers fail." In Ecclesiasticus many admonitions are given relating to the duties of children to their parents, of which these are typical:

Dishonor not a man in his old age; for some of us are also waxing old.

Miss not the discourse of the aged; for they also learned of their fathers; because from them thou shalt learn understanding and to give answer in time of need.

In thy youth thou hast not gathered, and how couldest thou find in thine old age? How beautiful a thing is judgement for gray hairs, and for elders to know counsel? How beautiful is the wisdom of old men, and thought and counsel to men that are in honour! Much experience is the crown of old men; and their glorying is the fear of the Lord.

For the other side of the picture, youth resenting age, we turn to the Book of Job, where Elihu the son of Barakel the Buzite "blazed out in anger against Job for making himself to be better than God," but also against the three friends for compromising God by failing to refute Job.

I am young and you are aged men;
So I held back; afraid to tell you my opinion.
I felt the word lay with a long life, and years
entitled men to instruct wisely,
Yet God inspires a man, 'tis the Almighty who
breathes knowledge into him;
It is not always seniors who are sage, or aged
men who understand.

Job 32: 8–16

It is clear from the vehemence and stringency of the admonitions and the violence of the penalties, that there was an active tendency on the part of the young people in the opposite direction, and that the early Hebrews were not far removed from the days when the summary disposal of the old and weak was a necessary condition of existence. That this was particularly common among nomadic tribes has been emphasized by Sumner (6).

Among the many precepts laid down in the Mosaic Code, only one bears on the relation of age to working capacity. In Numbers 8: 24–30, we find that the Levites who enter upon their duties in the Tabernacle at the age of twenty-five, are relieved of active service after fifty. They may assist, but are not required to perform any duties.

The general attitude throughout the Bible toward old age is one of great pessimism; it is inevitable, it is distressing, and after life is done, there is nothing more.

> *Poor man! his days are like grass,*
> *He blooms like a flower in the meadow;*
> *At the breath of a breeze it is gone,*
> *And its place never sees it again.*
> *Psalms 103: 15–16.*

> *My days are few! let me alone awhile,*
> *that I may have life bright with a brief smile,*
> *Before I leave it to return no more.*
> *Job 10: 20.*

The great poetry from the mouth of the unknown preacher of Ecclesiastes sums up the futility of life, and describes the infirmities of age in one of the most noted utterances of all time.

> *But remember the Creator in the flower of your age,*
>   *ere evil days come on,*
> *and years approach when you shall say,*
>   *"I have no joys in them;"*
> *ere the sun grows dark,*
>   *and the light goes from moon and stars,*
>   *and the clouds gather after rain;*
> *when the Guards tremble in the home of Life,*
>   *when its upholders bow,*
> *when the maids that grind are few and frail,*
>   *and ladies at the lattice lose their lustre,*
> *when the doors to the street are shut,*
>   *and the sound of the mill runs low,*
> *when the twitter of birds is faint,*
>   *and dull the daughters of song,*
> *when old age fears a height,*
>   *and even a walk has its terrors,*

> *when his hair is almost white,*
>   *and he drags his limbs along,*
>   *as the spirit flags and fades.*
> *So man goes to his long, long home,*
>   *and mourners pass along the street,*
> *on the day when the silver cord is snapped,*
>   *and the golden lamp drops broken,*
> *when the pitcher breaks at the fountain,*
>   *the wheel breaks at the cistern,*
> *when the dust returns to earth once more,*
>   *and the spirit of God who gave it,*
> *Utterly vain—such is the speaker's verdict,*
>   *everything is vain.*
>   *Ecclesiastes XII: 1–8 (8).*

These lines, so long considered as the epitome of pessimism, seem to have found an answer in the words of one who probably lived only some hundred years later than the Unknown Preacher. In the wisdom book called Ecclesiasticus, from which so many opinions about the old have been quoted, we read a courageous, robust admonition to all men, a message of understanding and compassion, founded in a truly religious spirit.

> *O death, how bitter is the remembrance of thee to a man that is at peace in his possessions, unto the man that hath nothing to distract him, and hath prosperity in all things, and that still hath strength to receive meat! O death, acceptable is thy sentence unto a man that is needy, and that faileth in strength, that is in extreme old age, and is distracted about all things, and is perverse, and hath lost patience! Fear not the sentence of death; remember them that have been before thee, and that come after; this is the sentence from the Lord over all flesh. And why dost thou refuse, when it is the good pleasure of the Most High? Whether it be ten, or a hundred, or a thousand years, there is no inquisition of life in the grave.*
>   *XLI: 24.*

These quotations *in extenso* are revealing as an insight into a traditional attitude which reflects the spirit of the times, but they have a far greater significance in that, with the rise and spread of Christianity, they became the foundation for all priestly and lay thinking for nearly twenty centuries, and today constitute a vital part of our intellectual heritage. The contribution of the Old Testament writers to our present historical narrative has therefore less strictly medical significance, and more of a religious, ethical and philosophical bearing. As a matter of fact, the emphasis of the Old Testament on the frailty of the human body and the futility of life acted during the Middle Ages to impede and hinder medical progress. Taken in the broader aspects, however, this review refreshes our memory of the wisdom of our forebears and strengthens our feeling of kinship and continuity with men whose essential problems and conflicts differed but little from our own.

The writer is indebted to his life-long friend and teacher, Rabbi Nathan Krass, for helpful advice and encouragement in the preparation of this chapter.

REFERENCES

1. Moffatt, J.: A New Translation of the Bible Containing the Old and New Testaments, New York, Harper & Bros., 1935.
2. Spivak, C. D.: Jewish Encyclopedia, New York, 8: 409, 1904.
    Preuss, J.: Biblisch-Talmudische Medizin, Berlin, Karger, 1911.
    Neuburger, M.: Essays in the History of Medicine, New York, Medical Life Press, 1930.
    Brim, C. J.: Medicine in the Bible, New York, Froben Press, 1936.
3. Miles, W. R.: Age and Human Society, in Handbook of Social Psychology, Worcester, Mass., Clarke University Press, 1935.
4. Ecclesiasticus, Chap. 38, The Apocrypha, trans. out of the Greek and Latin Tongues, London, Oxford Univ. Press, 1898.
5. McKenzie, J.: History of Health, Edinburgh, Gordon, 1758.
6. Hufeland, C. W.: Makrobiotik, Die Kunst das Menschliche Leben zu verlängern, Jena, 1798.
7. Sumner, W. G.: Folkways, New York, Ginn & Co., 1906.
8. Rolleston has summarized the best known medical interpretations of these lines. His remarks were published first in "Aspects of Age, Life and Disease," New York, Macmillan, 1929, p. 31, and later with minor changes, in "Medical Aspects of Old Age," London, Macmillan, 1932, p. 144. See also Jastrow, M.: A Gentle Cynic, Philadelphia, Lippincott, 1919.

LIFE'S LATER YEARS

STUDIES IN THE MEDICAL HISTORY OF OLD AGE

FREDERIC D. ZEMAN, M.D.

[*New York City*]

PART 4[1]

THE CONTRIBUTION OF GREEK THOUGHT

Let us then reaffirm the toast: 'Whatever is Greek must, in the end, prevail!' for Greek thought abides on the heights of freedom, on upward pathways which science once deserted, indeed, but at the risk of its very existence.

Sudhoff-Essays

In the year 1550 B.C., as the Papyrus Elbers was being written, nomad tribesmen from the North were engaged in the conquest of the Greek peninsula and the islands of the Aegean Sea. These rude folk learned from their predecessors, their neighbors, and also from far away peoples; "slowly they built up the greatest civilization that the world had seen" (1). In the poems of Homer (c. 1,000 B.C.) celebrating the battles for the domination of the shores of Asia Minor, we find the earliest records of the religion and customs of this remarkable people whose great contribution was to be the achievement of intellectual freedom. The Orient, exemplified by the Egyptians, Babylonians, Hittites, Assyrians and Hebrews had made great strides forward in the physical and mental development of mankind, but "suffered from a lack of freedom of the mind, a kind of intellectual bondage to religion and old ideas" (1).

In the last book of the Odyssey, line 258, Ulysses gives advice to his father Laertes which indicates a sound understanding of the care of the aged:

> *Warm baths, good food, soft sleep and generous wine,*
> *These are the rights of age, and should be thine.*
> (*Pope's translation*)

Mackenzie (2) records Galen's opinion of this passage. "The poet's rule was excellent, which directed an old man after bathing and refreshing himself with food, to take some rest; for old age being naturally cold and dry, those things which moisten and warm, as bathing, eating and sleeping, are the most proper for it."

The great distinction achieved by Greek medicine may be traced to two primary sources, first, to the temples of Aesculapius, where the priests acted as physicians and through a mixture of faith and practical methods brought healing to the sick; and second, to the philosophical schools of Athens and its

---

[1] This is the fourth in a series of articles dealing with Studies in the Medical History of Old Age. Upon completion of their publication, the installments will be collected and reprinted in a single volume, constituting one of the Series of Monographs of The Mount Sinai Hospital Press.—Ed.

island outposts. There taught men learned in the wisdom of Egypt and the East, such as Thales of Miletus (639–544 B.C.), Empedocles of Grigentum (504–443 B.C.) and Pythagoras (580–549 B.C.). These thinkers put aside the idea that the gods controlled the world, and attempted to explain the phenomena of life by ingenious hypotheses based in part on observation. From both sources came the knowledge of Hippocrates, the foremost physician of the age of Pericles, when philosophy was represented by Socrates and Plato, dramatic literature by Sophocles and Euripides, poetry by Pindar, satire by Aristophanes, art by Phidias and Polygnotus. A product of the temple school of Cos, a thinker in the best philosophic manner, the founder of modern medicine, he divorced medical thinking from both philosophy and religion, formulated its ethical code, and demonstrated for all time the value of sound observation and clear-headed reasoning. Among his many and varied contributions to the art of medicine is his emphasis on the patient himself, his habits, his food and his environment. In differentiating the peculiarities of man according to age, Hippocrates has recorded many sharp observations about the advanced years.

"And if at the rising of the Dogstar rain and wintry storms supervene and if the etesian winds blow, there is reason to hope that these diseases (dysentery) will cease, and that the autumn will be healthy; but if not, it is likely to be a fatal season of children and women, but least of all to old men."

Airs, Waters and Places, par. 10. (3)

"Of persons having empyema after peripneumonic affections, those that are advanced in life run the greatest risk of dying; but in the other kinds of empyema younger persons die."

On the Prognostics, par. 18.

"Acute pain of the ear, with continual and strong fever, is to be dreaded. Younger persons die of this disease on the seventh day, or still earlier, but old persons much later; for the fevers and delirium less frequently supervene upon them, and on that account. The ears previously come to a suppuration, but at these periods of life, relapses of the disease coming on generally prove fatal."

On the Prognostics, par. 22.

"Old persons are subject to cancers, both deepseated and superficial, which never leave them. They are particularly intractable when seated in the armpits, the loins and the thighs."

Ibid, p. 227.

"With regard to persons affected by the gout, those who are aged, have tophi in their joints, who have led a hard life, and whose bowels are constipated, are beyond the power of medicine to cure. But, the best natural remedy for them is an attack of dysentery, or other determination to the bowels. Persons, under opposite conditions, may be cured by a skillful physician."

Ibid, p. 217.

"*With regard to the time when this (recovery from paralysis) may occur, it is to be prognosticated by attending to the severity of the disease, to its duration, to the age of the patient, and to the season, it being known that of all cases the inveterate, and such as are the consequence of repeated attacks, are the worst and the most difficult to remove, and those in aged persons.*"
Ibid, p. 222.

"*Ischiatic diseases are to be thus judged of:—In the case of old persons, when the torpor and coldness of the loins and legs are very strong, and when they lose the power of erections, and the bowels are not moved, or with difficulty, and the feces passed with much mucus, the disease will be very protracted, and it should be announced beforehand that the disease will not last shorter than one year from its commencement.*"
Ibid, p. 223.

"*When a person suddenly loses his speech, in connection with obstruction of the veins,—if this happens without warning or any other strong cause, one ought to open the internal vein of the right arm, and abstract blood more or less according the habit or age of the patient. Such cases are mostly attended with the following symptoms: redness of the face, eyes fixed, hands distended, grinding of the teeth, palpitations, jaws fixed, coldness of the extremities, retention of airs in the veins.*"
Appendix to the Regimen in Acute Diseases, par. 4.

"*. . . In elder persons, and those in whom the heat is already more subdued, these cases (fever associated with headache, delirium and ocular symptoms) end in paralysis, mania and loss of sight.*"
The Epidemics, Book One, par. 6.

"*In many cases erysipelas, from some obvious cause, such as an accident, and sometimes from even a very small wound, broke out all over the body, especially, in persons about sixty years of age, about the head, if such an accident was neglected in the slightest degree.*"
The Epidemics, Book Three, par. 4.

"*Growing bodies have the most innate heat, they therefore require the most food, for otherwise their bodies are wasted. In old persons, the heat is feeble, and therefore they require little fuel, as it were to the flame, for it would be extinguished by much. On this account, also, fevers in old persons, are not equally acute, because their bodies are cold.*"
Aphorisms, Section One, No. 14.

"*Largeness of person in youth is noble and not unbecoming; but in old age it is inconvenient, and worse than a smaller structure.*"
Aphorisms, Section Two, No. 54.

"*Diseases about the kidney and bladder are cured with difficulty in old men.*"
Aphorisms, Section Six, No. 6.

"Persons are most subject to apoplexy between the ages of forty and sixty."

Aphorisms, Section Six, No. 57.

"People over forty years who are affected with frenzy do not readily recover; the danger is less when the disease is cognate to constitution and age."

Aphorisms, Section Seven, No. 82.

These quotations need no explanation and but little comment. They illustrate the amazing ability of Hippocrates both in observation and description. He realized the changing picture of disease with advancing age and continually drives home its special importance in prognosis. It is impossible here to quote all the relevant material, but the reader is strongly urged to turn again to the works of the master, where he will find familiar clinical pictures depicted vividly by one whose only instruments of precision were his five senses.

Edelstein (4) in a recent study of the relation of Greek medicine to religion and magic, points out it was essentially rational and empirical, but nevertheless influenced by religious ideas. God and his actions are powers reckoned with by physicians in their theory and practice. They refused to treat certain serious diseases where the result was foreordained, not from heartlessness, but on the assumption that the patient will seek treatment at the temple. The temple-cures boast of the god's success where the physician failed. A frequently quoted opinion of antiquity was that when the art of the physician fails, everybody resorts to incantations and prayers. Plutarch says, "Those who are ill with chronic disease and do not succeed by the usual remedies and the customary diet turn to purifications and amulets and dreams." Although Greek physicians acknowledged the power of religion, they rejected every form of magic as wrong, and never wavered in denunciation of superstition. These observations are to be correlated with similar discussions of the relation of medicine and religion in the preceding sections devoted to Primitive Man, Egypt, and the Old Testament.

In acclaiming the discernment of the Greek physician for his recognition of age generally as a factor in disease and for his emphasis on old age as a special stage of life, we must not fail to look into the general cultural attitudes and viewpoints of that period. For this purpose we have in Richardson's work (5) a contribution of the greatest value and relevancy. In a rare combination of erudition, insight and understanding, she has drawn a broad, detailed picture of the role of the aged in Greek life, based on a painstaking study of all possible original sources. We learn of the emphasis placed upon the respect for one's parents, and the high value placed upon the wisdom of the old. Certain duties and responsibilities belonged to the aged as well. On the other hand, the peculiarities, foibles and eccentricities of the hoary-headed were not only recognized but formed a frequent source of humor and satire. The Greeks did not delude themselves about old age, for all references to it are highly realistic, and stress its unfavorable and unpleasant nature, at times regarding it as a punishment sent for that purpose by Zeus. Dr. Richardson's study of the artistic representations is no less comprehensive than the survey of the literary sources.

The excellent reproductions of the paintings on pottery and of sculptures indicate clearly that the Greek artist had a keen eye for the physical characteristics of the aged (fig. 1). The treatment of the old man as a clown in the Greek drama

Fig. 1. Old Woman on the Boston Counterpart of the Ludovisi Altar (Boston Museum of Fine Arts). Reproduced by permission from Old Age Among the Ancient Greeks, by Bessie Ellen Richardson, Baltimore, Johns Hopkins Press, 1933.

Dr. Richardson points out that "this is a remarkable picture of old age for the period (480–470 B.C.). . . . The profile of the old woman reveals a hooked nose; the lips suggest toothless gums; the cheeks are slightly sunken; the chin sags; and the bones of the shoulder almost show through the wasted flesh; the hair is bobbed and treated in rather severe straight waves. It is a picture of respectable old age, not the courtesan type, and the bobbed hair may be taken as a sign of mourning."

was imitated centuries later in the Italian *commedia dell 'arte*, where he became the character Pantaloon, a word used as a synonym for old man by Shakespeare.

The opinions of Plato and Aristotle on old age have served for over two thousand years as either model or inspiration for untold numbers of writers, many of whom, like Cicero, neglected to quote their authorities. In the opening pages of the first book of the dialogue known as *The Republic*, Plato tells of Socrates' conversation with Cephalus, the aged father of Polemarchus, in which the philosopher urges the old man to tell him his opinion and experience of the advancing years.

"*I will certainly tell you, Socrates, what my experience of it is. I and a few other people of my age are in the habit of frequently meeting together, true to the old proverb. On these occasions, most of us give way to lamentations, and regret the pleasures of youth, and call up the memory of amours and drinking parties and banquets and similar proceedings. They are grievously discontented at the loss of what they consider great privileges, and describe themselves as living well in those days, whereas now, by their own account, they cannot be said to live at all. Some also complain of the manner in which their relations insult their infirmities, and make this a ground for reproaching old age with the many miseries it occasions them. But, in my opinion, Socrates, these persons miss the true cause of their unhappiness. For if old age were the cause, the same discomforts would have been felt also by me, as an old man, and by every other person that has reached that period of life. But, as it is, I have before now met with several old men who expressed themselves quite in a different manner; and in particular I may mention Sophocles the poet, who was once asked in my presence, 'How do you feel about love, Sophocles? are you still capable of it?' to which he replied, 'Hush! if you please: to my great delight I have escaped from it, and feel as if I had escaped from a frantic and savage master.' I thought then, as I do now, that he spoke wisely. For unquestionably old age brings us profound repose and freedom from this and other passions. When the appetites have abated, and their force is diminished, the description of Sophocles is perfectly realized. It is like being delivered from a multitude of furious masters. But the complaints on this score, as well as the troubles with relatives, may all be referred to one cause, and that is, not the age, Socrates, but the character of the men. If they possess well-regulated minds and easy tempers, old age itself is no intolerable burden: if they are differently constituted,: why in that case, Socrates, they find even youth is irksome to them as old age.*"

"*. . . . And to those, who, not being rich, are impatient under old age, it may be said with equal justice that while on the one hand, a good man cannot be altogether cheerful under old age and poverty combined, so on the other hand, no wealth can ever make a bad man at peace with himself.*"

"*. . . . But if his conscience reproaches him with no injustice, he enjoys the abiding presence of sweet hope, that 'kind nurse of old age,' as Pindar calls it. For indeed, Socrates, these are beautiful words of his, in which he says of the man who has lived a just and holy life, 'Sweet Hope' is his companion, cheering his heart, the nurse of age,—Hope, which more than aught else steers the capricious will of mortal men*" (6).

This pleasant kindly attitude of the philosophers contrasts sharply with the views of Aristotle (384–322 B.C.), who, in Garrison's words, "gave to medicine the beginnings of botany, zoology, comparative anatomy, embryology, teratology and physiology, and the use of formal logic as an instrument of precision." Aristotle's theory of old age is that heat is lost by gradual dissipation, very little remaining in old age — a flickering flame that a slight disturbance could put out. The lung hardens by gradual evaporation of the fluid and so is unable to perform its office of heat regulation. He assumes that heat is gradually developed in the heart. The amount produced is always somewhat less than that which is given off and the deficiency has to be made good out of the stock which with the organism started originally, that is, from the innate heat in which the soul was incorporate. This eventually is so reduced by constant draughts made upon it that it is insufficient to support the soul. The natural span of life, he says, differs greatly in length in different species, due to material constitution and the degree of harmony with the environment. But still, as a general rule, big plants and animals live longer than small ones; sanguineous or vertebrates longer than the invertebrates; the more perfect longer than the less perfect; and long gestation generally goes with long duration. Thus bulk, degree of organization, period of gestation, are correlated. Great size goes with high organization.

In his Rhetoric, as is well known, Aristotle gives old age an unfavorable aspect. He says in substance that the old have lived many years and been often the victims of deception, and since vice is the rule rather than the exception in human affairs, they are never positive about anything. They "suppose" and add "perhaps" or "possibly," always expressing themselves in doubt and never positively. They are uncharitable and ever ready to put the worst construction upon anything. They are suspicious of evil, not trusting, because of their experience of human weakness. Hence they have no strong loves or hates but go according to the precept of bias. Their love is such as may one day become hate and their hatred such as may one day become love. The temper of mind is neither grand nor generous—not the former because they have been too much humiliated and have no desire to go according to anything but mere appearances, and not the latter because property is a necessity of life and they have learned the difficulty of acquiring it and the facility with which it may be lost. They are cowards and perpetual alarmists, exactly contrary to the young; not fervent, but cold. They are never so fond of life as on their last day. Again, it is the absent which is the object of all desire, and what they most lack they most want. They are selfish and inclined to expediency rather than honor; the former having to do with the individual and the latter being absolute. They are apt to be shameless rather than the contrary and are prone to disregard appearances. They are dependent for most things. They live in memory rather than by hope, for the remainder of their life is short while the past is long, and this explains their garrulity. Their fits of passion though violent are feeble. Their sensual desires have either died or become feeble but they are regulated chiefly by self-interest. Hence they are capable of self-control, because desires have abated and self-interest is their leading passion. Calculation has a character that regulated their lives, for while calculation is directed to expediency, morality is directed to virtue as its end. Their offenses are those of petty meanness rather than of insolence. They are compassionate like the young, but the latter are so from humanity while the old suppose all manner of sufferings at their door. When the orator addresses them he should bear these traits in mind. Elsewhere he says a happy old age is one that approaches gradually and without pain, and is dependent upon physical excellence and on fortune. although there is such a thing as a long life even without health and strength (7).

The great naturalist believed that gray hair resulted from weakness and deficiency of heat, and that baldness arose from overdeveloped sexual feeling. Grayness, he held, results from decay of the liquid nutrient of the hair, but does not necessarily indicate physical deterioration.

The important contributions of the Alexandrian School are well known but do not bear directly on our theme. As the power of Rome grew in the ancient world, the influence of the Greek physician broadened, and for our further investigations we shall turn to the Imperial City. Many centuries will pass before mankind learns to build on the broad strong foundations laid out by Greek scientists and philosophers.

REFERENCES

(1) BREASTED, J. H.: The Conquest of Civilization, New York, Harper & Bros., p. 234, 1926.
(2) MACKENZIE, J.: History of Health, Edinburgh, W. Gordon, 1758.
(3) HIPPOCRATES, Genuine Works of; trans. by F. Adams, New York, Wm. Wood and Co. All translations following are from this work. A more modern translation of the Hippocratic Corpus, by Jones and Worthington, is to be found in the Loeb Classical Library, London, 4 Vols., 1923-27.
(4) EDELSTEIN, L.: Greek Medicine in its Relation to Religion and Magic. Bull. Inst. Hist. Med., 5: 201, 1937.
(5) RICHARDSON, B. E.: Old Age Among the Ancient Greeks,—the Greek Portrayal of Old Age in Literature, Art and Inscriptions, with a Study of the Duration of Life Among the Ancient Greeks on the Basis of Inscriptional Evidence. Baltimore, Johns Hopkins Press, 1933.
(6) PLATO, The Republic, English trans. by Davies, J. L. and Vaughan, D. J., London, Macmillan & Co., 1921, paragraphs 329, 330, 331.
(7) Adapted from HALL, G. STANLEY, Senescence, The Last Half of Life. New York, D. Appleton & Co., p. 64, 1923.

LIFE'S LATER YEARS

Studies in the Medical History of Old Age

FREDERIC D. ZEMAN, M.D.

[New York City]

Part 5[1]

ROMAN ATTITUDES AND OPINIONS

"When Greece was at its height Rome was the land of the soldier, the peasant, and the small trader; a people without art, without literature, and without philosophy" (1). The force of this statement is enhanced by the realization that southern Italy was an important part of Magna Graecia and shared actively in all the manifestations of Greek culture. The resistance of the Roman to the infiltration and the absorption of new ideas was one of his outstanding qualities. Pliny the Elder points out that for 600 years Rome existed without doctors. In 146 B.C. after the fall of Corinth, Greek physicians established themselves in Rome and later achieved recognition through the professional success of Asclepiades of Bythynia (124 B.C.). He is notable to us as a pioneer in the humane treatment of mental diseases, allowing the patients to enjoy daylight, employing occupational therapy, and using wine and music as sedatives.

Of the numerous individual practitioners whose names have come down to us, only a few stand out above all the rest. Celsus, who flourished in the first century A.D., is one of the great medical amateurs. He wrote the famous *De Re Medicina*, entirely neglected in his own day, but greatly celebrated during the Renaissance, not only for its medical content but also for its linguistic and rhetorical excellence. The comments on old age and its diseases are almost altogether repetitions of Hippocratic observations. Dioscerides, living in the second half of the first century was, according to Garrison, the originator of materia medica, the first to write on medical botany as an applied science. Aretaeus the Cappadocian, in the second century A.D., is notable for his exact descriptions of disease in the Hippocratic style, and particularly for his full differentiation of the types of mental disease, contrasting the variability of manic-depressive mental states with the fixed unchanging picture of senile melancholia.

The greatest physician of this period was Galen (131–201 A.D.) whose versatility and varied talents combined with untiring energy produced a whole library of publications on all phases of medicine. He made real contributions to anatomy, physiology and pathology; he was actually the first to introduce the experimental method in medicine. Galen nevertheless was essentially a philosophical theorist with an explanation for everything in a highly dogmatic manner. The resulting effect on medical progress is incalculable. "After his death

---

[1] This is the fifth in a series of articles dealing with Studies in the Medical History of Old Age. Upon completion of their publication, the installments will be collected and reprinted in a single volume, constituting the third in the Series of Monographs of The Mount Sinai Hospital Press.—Ed.

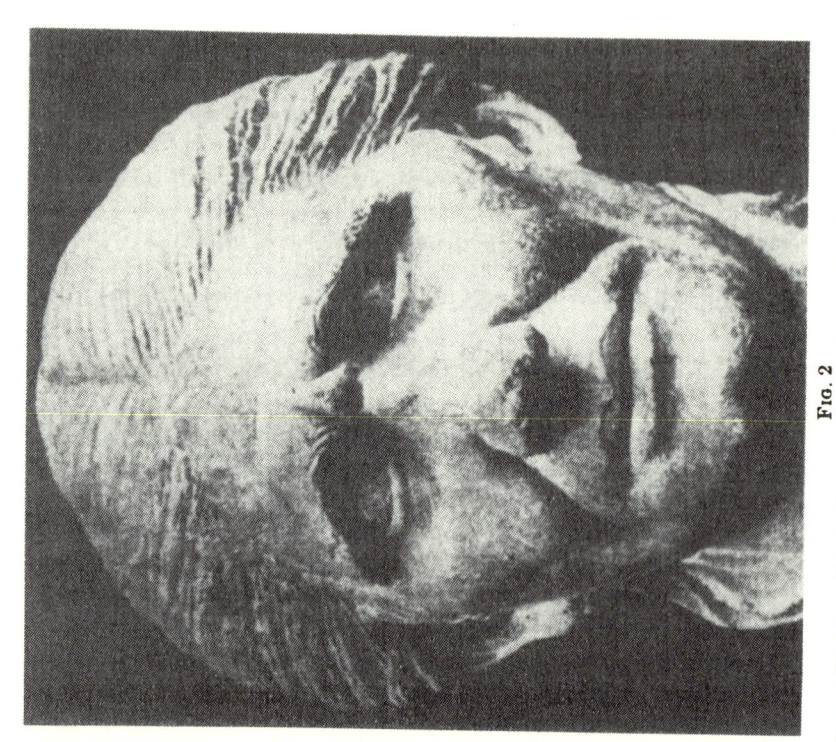

Figs. 1 and 2. Marble portraits of elderly women from the period of the Roman Empire. No attempt has been made to flatter the subject. (Reproduced by permission from "Art Without Epoch," by L. Goldscheider, New York, Oxford University Press, 1937).

European medicine remained at a dead level for nearly 14 centuries" (Garrison). He was regarded as the court of last resort in all medical disputes and his assumption of infallibility was particularly acceptable to those who cherished every regard for his authority. Galen's complicated explanation of physiology was based on the qualities (hot, cold, moist, dry) and the humors (blood, phlegm, yellow bile, black bile). He describes four ages, youth (hot and moist), manhood (hot and dry), age (cold and dry), senility (cold and moist) (2). This interpretation of human physiology will recur again and again, as we trace our theme through succeeding centuries.

In *"De sanitatem tuendam"* Galen discusses the hygiene of old age in great detail, emphasizing exercise, diet, the care of the bowels, sleep, and the use of wine. Although it is the style to belittle this great physician because his teachings became medical dogma for so many centuries, it must be admitted that the problems of caring for the aged are analysed with rare good sense. In emphasizing that an old man's experience must determine whether a milk diet be proper for him or not, Galen says, "I knew a husbandman above an hundred years old, whose principal food was goat's milk, with which he mixed sometimes bread and sometimes honey; and now and then he ate it boiled with tops of thyme. A neighbor of his imagining that milk was the cause of the old man's long life, would try it in imitation of him, but could never bear it in any form, for it lay heavy on his stomach, and soon raised a swelling in his left side. Another making the same experiment, found milk agreed with him perfectly well, till after the seventh day of trial, when he felt a hard tumor in his right side which occasioned a tension with spasms quite up to his throat. I have also known some, who, from long use of milk, had contracted a stone in the kidneys, and some who lost their teeth; while others have lived upon it many years in health" (3).

Garrison (4) points out how rich as medical sources are the Roman secular writers, the poets, dramatists and essayists. Here we also find important observations bearing on the political and social status of the aged, pictures of their peculiarities and moralising on their sad fate. In Terence's *Phormio* (Act 4, Scene 1) we find the famous line, *"Senectus ipsa est morbus,"* "Old age is itself a disease," which epitomizes the attitude of the physician from ancient times down almost to our own day Even now we have difficulty in differentiating between the diseases that occur in the aged, and the involutionary changes that occur with age in all living matter. Cicero, Horace and Seneca made contributions of this kind that in the succeeding centuries were repeated over and over again, often in modified forms which, passed off as original, are still recognizable.

In his "Cato the Elder on Old Age," (5) Cicero (106–43 B.C.) places in the mouth of the aged Cato the exposition of a point of view of an old age which may be considered as representative of the opinion of aging Romans. While it leans heavily on Plato's "Republic," Chapters 2 and 3, as well as on Xenophon's *Oeconomicus* and *Cyropaedia*, it is distinctive as an attempt to define the values of old age and is unique in its optimistic tone. These qualities have insured its immortality. As recently as 1867, Charcot (6), the eminent French clinician, could say without exaggeration, "Most of the medical works of the past century which touch, in a special manner, upon the senile period of life, have a literary or philosophical bearing; they are more or less ingenious paraphrases of the famous treatise *De Senectute* of the Roman Orator." In the introduction dedicating the work to his friend, Titus Pomponius Atticus (then 65 years old), Cicero (then 62) explains that his purpose has been to "lighten both for you and for me our common burden of old age; which, if not already pressing hard upon us, is surely coming on apace." The writer's views are brought out in the following excerpts from the essay.

> "*It is their own vices and their own faults that fools charge to old age.*"
>
> "*It is not by miracles, speed, or physical dexterity that great things are achieved, but by reflection, force of character, and judgement; in these qualities old age is usually not only not poorer, but is even richer.*"
>
> "*Rashness is the product of the budding-time of youth, prudence of the harvest-time of age.*"
>
> "*The aged remember everything that interests them.*"
>
> "*...Solon, whom we see boasting in his verses that he grows old learning something every day. And I have done the same, for in my old age, I have learned Greek, which I seized upon as eagerly as I had been desirous of satisfying a long continued thirst, with the result that I have acquired firsthand the infomation which you see me using in this discussion by way of illustration.*"
>
> "*An intemperate youth delivers to old age a body all worn out.*"
>
> "*But it is our duty, my young friends, to resist old age; to compensate for its defects by a watchful care; to fight against it as we would fight against disease; to adopt a regimen of health; to practice moderate exercise and to take just enough food and drink to restore our strength and not to overburden it. Nor, indeed, are we to give our attention solely to the body; much greater care is due to the mind and soul; for they, too, like lamps, grow dim with time, unless we keep them supplied with oil. Moreover exercise causes the body to become heavy with fatigue, but intellectual activity gives buoyancy to the mind.*"
>
> "*... if reason and wisdom did not enable us to reject pleasure, we should be very grateful to old age for taking away the desire to do what we ought not to do. For casual pleasure hinders deliberation, is at war with reason, blindfolds the eyes of the mind, so to speak, and has no fellowship with virtue.*"
>
> "*Bear well in mind that in this entire discussion I am praising that old age which has its foundation well laid in youth. Hence it follows—as I once said with the approval of all who heard it that old age is wretched which needs to defend itself with words. Nor can wrinkles and gray hair suddenly seize upon influence; but when the preceding part of life has been notably spent, old age gathers the fruits of influence at the last.*"

> "But, the critics say, old men are morose, troubled, fretful and hard to please; and, if we inquire we shall find that some of them are misers, too. However, these are faults of character, not of age."

Cicero closes with a philosophic duscussion of death, expressing his belief in the immortality of the soul. "And, if I err in my belief that the souls of men are immortal, I gladly err, nor do I wish this ever, which gives me pleasure, to be wrested from me while I live." In this essay we have old age defended, it is true, by a man of means, position and intellectual resource, and yet portrayed with great insight and real understanding in such a way as to convey a message that after many centuries brings real cheer to many an old man (7). Among the writers of antiquity, in fact of all time, no one has more effectively and earnestly endeavored to bring forward the positive side of the picture of old age.

In his *Ars Poetica*, Horace (65–8 B.C.), (well known to high school and college students of the last generation, and far more highly regarded by them than the author of *In Catilinam*), attempts to instruct an aspirant in the technique of writing. In the course of this poetic discourse he describes the various kinds of characters which one must put into a play or a story. His description of old age, complete in a few lines, is so vivid, so realistic, so searching, that it ranks as one of the great classical treatments of the subject and has had the most widespread and varied influence throughout succeeding generations.

> "Grey hairs have many evils; without end
> The old man gathers what he dare not spend,
> While, as for action, do what he will,
> 'Tis all half-hearted, spiritless, and chill;
> Inert, irresolute, his neck he cranes
> Into the future, grumbles and complains,
> Extols his own young years with peevish praise,
> But rates and censures these degenerate days" (8).

These lines of Horace have been traced by G. R. Coffman in a charming and scholarly essay (9), from their appearance in the time of Augustus to their reappearance in Chaucer's "Canterbury Tales" where they form part of the Prologue to the Reeve's Tale. In following the adventures of these verses over a period of 13 centuries one encounters many little known social and religious associations. Some of these throw light on the medical history of old age and will be quoted in due course and with grateful acknowledgement of Professor Coffman's erudition. The sources of Horace's inspiration are to be found in Aristotle rather than Plato, as the passages quoted in the previous sections will amply testify. The reader of Horace's poetry will find many other allusions to old age and its woes. The realism is bitter, almost savagely brutal, especially as regards women. One recalls particularly such poems as "The Shortness of Life" (*Eheu fugaces*), "Vanity of Riches" (*non ebur neque aureum*), "Be your age, Chloris" (*uxor pauperis Ibyci*) and "Too Old for Love" (*intermissia, Venus, diu*).

Seneca (c. 3 B.C.–A.D. 65) was famed as a philosopher, dramatist and statesman. Of his many works, the best (so thought Montaigne) is his "Letters to Lucullus," which are not really letters but collections of maxims and moral remarks, representative of the Stoic philosophy of which he was a leading exponent.

"Of what use to such a man are 80 years spent in doing nothing? It is not in having lived; he has merely passed through life. It is not in dying late; he has been dead very long. It is by actions and not by its duration that life must be measured. He has lived for 80 years; say rather that he has existed for 80 years so long as you understand by that he has lived as we say the tree lives."

"...It is in mankind to preserve old age with care—that age whose fruit is more abundant, and the guardianship less irksome—that age which makes a more vigorous use of life when it knows that it is agreeable, useful and desirable to someone in the household. Besides this care is accompanied by joy in the house which is its reward. What is sweeter than to be sufficiently dear to a wife as to become dearer to yourself thereby?"

"We make the mistake in common of only believing in the approach of death in old age and in our declining years, while childhood, youth and other periods of life are leading up to the same end. Infancy is swallowed up by childhood, childhood by the age of puberty, the age of puberty by youth, youth by old age. Consider well, and you will find that our growing powers are but a series of losses."

"Let us try to make our life like to precious metals which have much weight in little compass; it is by our actons and not by length of life that we measure it. It is possible and even common to have lived little although long."

This discussion of the Roman lay contributors to our narrative serves to reinforce that feeling of nearness to ancient Rome, to which Sir Clifford Allbutt has called attention, pointing out that it seems no further off than the time of Queen Anne, and indicating how much more alien to us is the Middle Age with its many strange customs and viewpoints.

The centuries that followed the Golden Age of Augustus were marked throughout the Roman world by the steady deterioration of science in general and medicine in particular The fine free spirit of the classical Greek tradition was hopelessly corrupted by the mingling of the old Roman superstitions with cults from Phrygia, Egypt, Persia and Syria, all glorifying the supernatural and the mystical and led to an increasing respect for Oriental magic and occultism. The physician, according to Garrison, became more and more a mercenary parasite and vendor of quack medicines. Oribasius (325–403 A.D.), Aetus (sixth century A.D.), Alexander of Tralles (525–605 A.D.), Paul of Aegina (625–690 A.D.) comprise the notables of these latter days, whose chief interest lies in their having based much of their writings on the works of other men which would otherwise have been lost forever. In originality of thought or observation their efforts are largely lacking An outstanding effect of Christian teaching with its emphasis on aid to the poor, the helpless and the sick, was the establishment of hospitals. This movement had its start following closure of the Asclepieia and other pagan temples by Constantine in A.D. 335. Gradually (10) these institutions became specialized and were differentiated according to their purposes: "Nosocomia or claustral hospitals, for the reception and care of the sick alone; Brephotrophia, for foundlings; Orphanotrophia, for orphans; Ptochia, for the helpless poor; Gerontochia, for the aged; and Xenodochia, for the poor and infirm pilgrims." At this early date between the fourth and sixth centuries were laid the patterns of public and private philanthropy which are familiar in our own communities.

To regain the tenuous thread of our theme we must turn again to a poet, Maximianus, who lived in the middle of the sixth century A.D., and who is known only from six elegies on old age (11). Coffman describes them as "lamentations on the ills of old age, inspired in the mind of the hero by memories of his youth and early manhood and by the realization of his failing powers in general and of his physical (sexual) impotence in particular. The first voices a prayer for death The second is the pleading of an old man to his mistress to whom he no longer appeals, not to leave him, and a lament over his present impotency. The third and fourth are memories of the amorous thwarted experiences of his youth. The fifth is a sensual account of the highly erotic experiences of the old man with a young mistress and the lament of both over its ineffectual issue because of his old age. The last—only 12 lines in length, gives the final conclusion of the old man: Be reconciled to old age; be content that you are coming to the inevitable—death and the grave! In essence these elegies are a blending of lascivious eroticism, in degenerate Ovidian or Ausonian vein, and of universal cynicism and pessimism with a final touch of stoicism." The effect of old age upon the senses through loss of hearing, taste, sight, touch and smell, along with the colorless face, the dried-up skin and the rheumatic tears, is vividly described in Elegy I, pp. 119–150.

Coffman believes that this poem may have had a part in initiating certain cliches as a literary fashion, which were later improved upon by Pope Innocent III, in his *De contemptu mundi*, and afterwards popularized as a part of the stock in trade of Middle English descriptions of old age.

In retrospect we see clearly that to the problem of old age Rome contributed the medical influence of Galen, that in this field lasted far beyond Vesalius, and the contrasting views of Cicero the optimist, and Horace, who with Juvenal, spared no detail of the unpleasant side of the senium. The continuance of this narrative will reveal just how much farther we have advanced in our present thinking.

REFERENCES

(1) ALLBUTT, SIR CLIFFORD: Greek Medicine in Rome, London. Macmillan & Co., 1921.
(2) GARRISON, F. H.: History of Medicine, 4th ed., Philadelphia, Saunders, p. 117, 1929.
(3) SINCLAIR, SIR JOHN: The Code of Health and Longevity, Edinburgh, Vol. 2, 1807.

(4) GARRISON, F. H.: op. cit. p. 113.
(5) CICERO: *De Senectute*, etc., with English trans. by W. A. Falconer, Loeb Classical Library, Cambridge, Mass., Harvard Univ. Press, 1938.
(6) CHARCOT, J. M.: Lecons Cliniques sur les Maladies des Vieillards, Paris, Delahaye, 1867. English trans. by L. H. Hunt, New York, Wm. Wood & Co., p. 18, 1881.
(7) See W. A. Falconer's preface to his translation of *De Senectute* in the Loeb Classical Library describing how he first rendered the essay into English for the pleasure of his 81 year old uncle.
(8) HORACE: Ars Poetica, Conington's translation, London, G. Bell & Sons, 1905. For the benefit of the minority who still enjoy the classics in the original, we append the much quoted Latin verses:

> "Multa senem circumveniunt incommoda, vel quod
> Quaerit et inventis miser abstinet ac timet uti,
> Vel quod res omnis timide gelideque ministrat
> Dilator spe longus, iners avidusque futuri
> Difficilis, querulus, laudator temporis acti
> Se puero, castigator censorque minorum."

(9) COFFMAN, G. R.: Old Age from Horace to Chaucer: Some Literary Affinities and Adventures of an Idea: Speculum, 9: 249, 1934.
(10) GARRISON, F. H.: op. cit. pp. 176–177.
(11) The elegies were wrongly attributed to one Ca. Cornelius Gallus, as appears in the English translation by Sir Hovenden Walker, London, 1688, entitled "Elegies of Old Age made English from the Latin of Ca. Cornelius Gallus. (Coffman.)

LIFE'S LATER YEARS

Studies in the Medical History of Old Age

FREDERIC D. ZEMAN, M.D.

[New York City]

Part 6[1]

THE MEDICINE OF ISLAM
(732–1096 A.D.)

"Looking back from the vantage point of A.D. 1925 we are tempted to look upon the Middle Ages as one of ignorance, superstition, bigotry and lawlessness, while fighting and religion occupied the whole attention of the great men of these ages; and standing amid the great leaders of the misty past, we see the great figures looking down upon us from the visor of the knight and the cowl of the monk; but the Arabist tradition of Mediaeval Europe brings to our minds yet another great figure, that of the Arab physician-philosopher and his gold and silver brocaded turban and his halo of intellectual curiosity and broad tolerance, and who are they amongst us who would place him among the least of these?"

D. Campbell—*Arabian Medicine.*

The manifold contributions of the Moslem world to our culture are well known. The fascinating tale of the preservation of Greek philosophy and science in the shape of Arabic translations is familiar to all students of history. At a time when western Europe found itself in intellectual darkness, the Caliphs of Bagdad and Cordova were actively encouraging the study of the Greek texts and the application of their lessons to the practice of medicine in hospitals founded by them. The success of these efforts is to be seen in many Arabic manuscripts that have come down to us, making known the thoughts of the great medical men, whose opinions, of much weight in their own day, were later to be enshrined as the authoritative word in medicine for many centuries.

The Arab physicians have been accused of many sins, and often with justice. Under their influence surgery languished; they encouraged unquestioning respect for authority; they indulged in over-elaborate classifications and delighted in hairsplitting discussions. They frequently misinterpreted their idol Galen, and thereby caused worse confusion. On the other hand they did preserve the Greek texts, even if at times in garbled form; they contributed excellent descriptions of disease, as seen at the bedside; they devoted great study to therapeutics in general and especially to dietetics; they contributed many new drugs and endeavored to study their action, and finally, raised the position of the healer to

---

[1] This is the sixth in a series of articles dealing with Studies in the Medical History of Old Age. Upon completion of their publication, the installments will be collected and reprinted in a single volume, constituting the third in the Series of Monographs of The Mount Sinai Hospital Press.—Ed.

the dignity of a learned profession. Their contributions to the medical study of old age are particularly noteworthy. They include discussion of the nature of aging, the differences between old age and youth, the proper regimen for the old, and the peculiarities of disease in the aged. One Ibn al Haitham or Alhazan (996–1038) of Bassora, according to Garrison, published a Thesaurus of Optics (Basel 1572) which contains the first note of ocular refraction and of the fact that a segment of a glass ball will magnify objects. The interest of the great Arab writers in the problems of advanced age is directly reflected in the works of later writers, such as the eminent Roger Bacon (1210–1292) and Arnold of Villanova (1235–1312), whose consulting practice covered France, Italy and Spain.

The Eastern Caliphate, with its center at Bagdad, produced three renowned figures, Rhazes (860–932), Haly Abbas (d. 994) and Avicenna (980–1037). The latter was truly a universal genius, for he not only wrote many volumes on medical subjects, but also contributed to geology an epoch-making description of the origin of mountains. He is said to have been a convivial spirit, enjoying life to the full, and meeting an early end as the result of excesses. One group of scholars attributes to him the authorship of the celebrated poem ascribed to Omar Khayam, and known to us in Fitzgerald's magnificent rendition. But Avicenna's greatest work was the *Canon*, described by Garrison, as "a huge unwieldy storehouse of learning, in which the author attempts to codify the whole medical knowledge of his time and to square its facts with the systems of Galen and Aristotle." Gruner (2) has provided a translation of the first book of the *Canon*, and here we find abundant references to old age.

> "*There are four periods of life:*—
> 1—*The period of growth,—adolescence—up to 30 years.*
> 2—*The prime of life,—period of beauty—up to 35 or 40.*
> 3—*Elderly life,—period of decline—senescence—up to about 60.*
> 4—*Decrepit age,—senility—to the end of life.*
> *In the fourth period, the best vigor has passed, and the intellectual vigor begins to decline.*"

> "*To sum up, the equable temperament of the period of juvenility and youth is hot, whereas that of the last two periods is cold. The body in juvenility is additionally of a moist (equable) temperament, in that growth is proceeding; the moistness is shown by the softness of their bones, nerves and other members, and by the fact that at this age it is not going to be long before the semen and ether will come to manifestation. Old persons and those in the decrepit age are not only colder but drier in temperament. This is evidenced by the hardness of the bones, the roughness of their skin, and the long time which has elapsed since they produced semen, blood and the vaporal (ether) breath.*"

> "*In summertime the humors are dispersed; the faculties and natural functions are impaired due to the excessive dispersion. The blood and*

serous humor are diminished in amount; the bilious atrabilious humor increases in amount as a result of the dispersion of attenuated matters, whereby the heavier particles stay behind in increasing amount. This is why old persons and those of similar nature feel stronger in summer.

The first part of autumn is to some extent beneficial to old people, but the last part is very injurious to them. (In the first place there is the cold, in the second place there is the residue of the oxidation of humors of summertime.)

Winter is inimical to old persons and to those akin to them in nature. Middle aged persons are likely to be in health."

The effect of age and sex on the pulse:—

"Elderly persons,—The pulse is here smaller because of the weakness of the vital power; the swiftness is lessened both because of this and because of the lessened resistance. Such a pulse is therefore more sluggish.

Old age,—In the advanced years of life, the pulse becomes small, sluggish, slow. If it be also soft this is because of extraneous, and not natural humors."

Variations of the urine according to age:—

"Infancy,—The urine tends to the character of milk, considering the food and their moist temperament. Hence it is nearly colorless.

Childhood,—The urine thicker and coarser than in adolescents, and more turbid. This has already been mentioned.

Adolescence,—The urine tends to igneity, and to homogeneity.

Later life,—The urine tends to be white and tenuous but it may be coarse ("thick") because of the effete matters which are now being evacuated to a greater extent by way of the urine.

Decrepit age,—The urine whiter and still more tenuous. A similar coarseness to the proceeding may develop but this is rare. If the urine becomes very thick it intimates liability to develop calculus."

Following the detailed description of the manifestations at different times of life, we find an entire chapter devoted to "General Remarks on the Regimen of Old Age." The opening paragraph indicates how the treatment of the old proceeds logically from the observations on the "coldness" and "dryness" of the body at that time of life.

"In brief, the regimen appropriate for old people consists in giving those offerings of aliment, drink and baths which render the body warm and moist (i.e. moistening, calefacient food; warm or hot soft water baths). There should be plenty of sleep; and the time spent on the couch should be liberal; more than is legitimate for adults. The flow of urine should be continually assisted by diluents; the mucus should be helped out of the stomach by way of the bowels and urine. The nature is too soft and this needs correcting."

Then follows a detailed discussion of the food for the elderly. Judging by the frequency with which they are quoted these rules had wide influence on all later writers for several hundred years,—and is on the whole so rich in commonsense as to have validity even to-day, however antiquated the underlying reasons have become. The following paragraphs are typical:—

"Food should be given in small amounts at a time. There may be two or three meals a day; divided up according to the digestive power, and according to the general condition, whether robust or weakly. In the latter case, at the second or third hour they may partake of well-baked bread and honey. At the seventh hour after the bath they may partake of some one or another of the foods we shall name later, which are laxative in action. At bedtime some laudable nutriment may be allowed.

When they are robust, old persons may have a rather more liberal supper as long as they avoid any gross aliment which is likely to give rise to atrabilious or serous humour, and avoid all hot, sharp, or desiccative foods, such as dishes made with vinegar, salt or hot aromatics, seasoning, pickles, etc. These may, however, be allowed as medicaments."

Following Galen, stress is laid on its value for those "who like and can digest milk." Asses' milk is recommended. The effect of food on the bowels is stressed and the importance of easy evacuations for the decrepit is emphasized. The kinds of wine best suited to the old are discussed. Exercise receives very detailed attention. The whole chapter is a carefully considered contribution to the physical hygiene of old age.

The Western Caliphate, with its capital at Cordova, is noted medically for Albucasis (1013–1106), Avenzoar (d. 1162), Averroes (1126–1198) and Maimonides (1136–1204). The latter, most famous of all the Jewish physicians who played such influential rôles in Moslem and medieval medicine, is known both for his religious and medical works. His "Guide to the Perplexed" attempted to reconcile the duties of the Jew to his faith and to the world in which he lived. While rejecting much orthodox tradition, he contributed biblical commentaries and legal elucidations to the Talmud. He is to be thought of as one who endeavored to bring about a fusion of Greek and Hebrew viewpoints, a task to which he brought an unusually independent mind.

In his "Aphorisms," a book which attained great popularity, he dares to call attention to more than forty inconsistencies in Galen. This questioning of authority is unique in the medical literature of the time. Oddly enough one of the examples has to do with Galen's saying in one place that body temperature is unaltered by age and in another saying that it decreases as a person grows older. Maimonides was much concerned with the significance of old age, especially in regard to treatment. In his "Treatise on Hemorrhoids" (3) he recommends incision in cases of thrombosed veins, but if the patient is too old, the application of dry cups to the lumbar region.

His "Book of Poisons" was written in 1199 at the request of his patron the Kadi al-Fadil, to avert the great danger of snake bites so prevalent in Egypt at

FIG. 1. Avicenna or Ibn Sina (980–1037), known as the "Prince of Physicians." (Reproduced from print in the collection of the Home for Aged and Infirm Hebrews, New York).

FIG. 2. Moses ben Maimon or Maimonides (1135–1204). A traditional portrait. (Reproduced from "Spanish Influence on Medical Science," Wellcome Foundation, Ltd., London, 1935.

the time. For internal poisoning as opposed to snake bite, he recommends the use of mandrake, bezoar, theriac and the like. With regard to the size of the dose, Maimonides tells us that this depends upon the intensity of the poison, the age of the patient, and the season of the year. He relates an interesting story in connection with this point. When he was a young man at Fez, there lived in that city a Vizier by the name of Ali ibn Yussuf. This man had reached the age of 120 years when he took seriously sick. Two doctors were called to his bedside, and they prescribed half a dram of theriac to be taken in the middle of the night. Just before dawn they came into his room and found him dead. The doctors looked solemnly at the body and gave two different opinions as to the cause of the Vizier's death. The first doctor said that the dose of theriac was too small, and the other that it was too large. A third doctor was called in and wisely decided that the Vizier had died not because of the medicine, but because of his old age (4).

Maimonides' writings are often popular in character, emphasizing rules of hygiene for his highly placed patrons at the court. He advised that convalescents and elderly people especially should consult their physicians frequently. He warned against over-indulgence in coition (5), particularly stressing the dangers to the aged and sufferers from heart disease. He believed in the moderate use of wine, as more conducive to health in older people than in younger ones and of special tonic value to the aged and enfeebled (6). He was an untiring foe of superstition and astrology.

The doubts expressed by Maimonides as to the credibility of Galen were slow in influencing medical thinking. The Arabization of Western Europe was due to the efforts at Salerno of Constantinus Africanus (c. 1020-1087), the translator into Latin of many of the Arab classics. This mode of thought achieved wide and unquestioned acceptance until the seventeenth century. We must remind ourselves that the great revival of learning, the Renaissance, was anticipated in the original thinking and the expression of honest doubts by many courageous men whose activities covered the centuries preceding.

REFERENCES

(1) CAMPBELL, D.: Arabian Medicine and Its Influence on the Middle Ages. London, Kegan Paul, Trench, Trubner & Co., Ltd., 1926.
(2) GRUNER, O. C.: A Treatise of the Canon of Medicine of Avicenna, incorporating a translation of the first book, London, Luzac & Co., 1930.
(3) German translation by H. Kroner, Janus, 16: 441 and 645, 1911.
(4) MUNZ, M.: Maimonides—The Story of His Life and Genius, trans. by Schnittkind, Boston, Winchell-Thomas Co., 1935.
(5) MEYERHOF, M.: The Medical Work of Maimonides, in Essays on Maimonides, N. Y., Columbia Univ. Press, 1941. Meyerhof points out that works such as the book on poisons and on sexual intercourse, belong to a well known type, popular with the princes and other prominent personages of that day. An Arabic bibliography lists several hundred such books written between the 9th and 13th centuries.
(6) ZEITLIN, S.: Maimonides. A Biography, New York, Bloch Publishing Co., Chap. 13, 1935.

LIFE'S LATER YEARS

Studies in the Medical History of Old Age

FREDERIC D. ZEMAN, M.D.

[New York City]

Part 7[1]

THE MEDIEVAL PERIOD (1096–1438)

"But amonge all other thynges there is nothynge, the which so strongly doth cause a man to look oldely, as feare and desperacioun. For because in that passion and effectyon, all the naturall hete of the body doth resort inwarde and forsaketh the outward partes, and ye most chefely, when the manes complexyon is disposed to the same, and that is the cause that many beyng toste, turmoyled, and vexed with this worldly stormes so vaynly, theyr heer waxe hore, or whyte."

Arnold of Villanova—*The Conservation of Youth and Defense of Age.* (Drummond's translation—*1544 A. D.*)

The social and political chaos, which preceded and followed the fall of the Roman Empire, brought about spiritual confusion, disillusionment, and hopelessness in the minds of men. To the suffering multitudes, as well as to their rulers, the Christian Church brought a message of comfort, and the hope of a better life in the hereafter for the faithful. Its preachment of sympathy for the sufferer and of care for the poor, the sick, and the old, led to the establishment of ecclesiastical hospitals and nursing orders. Medicine during the Dark Ages in Western Europe found its only home in the monasteries where the works of the great Greeks and Romans were copied and preserved; but rigid adherence to accepted rules and blind respect for authority suppressed all striving for new knowledge.

The supercilious attitude of the church toward the human body was officially expressed in the book of Pope Innocent III, "*De Contemptu Mundi sive de Miseria Humanae Conditionis.*" Chapter X of the treatise treats of the brevity of life. Chapters XI and XII take title from Horace's opening line, "*De incommodis senectutis*" (1). The description of old age enlarges that of Horace in stating that the aged are "easily provoked, stingy, avaricious, sullen and quarrelsome, quick to talk, slow to hear, but not slow in wrath, praising former times, despising moderns, censuring the present, commending the past." The moral of this discourse is, "Young man, be not proud in the presence of a decaying old man; he once was that which you are, he now is that which you in turn will be." Coffman points out how this epitomizes the change from Augustan paganism

---

[1] This is the seventh in a series of articles dealing with the Medical History of Old Age. Upon completion of their publication, the installments will be collected and reprinted in a single volume, constituting one of the Monographs of The Mount Sinai Hospital Press.—Ed.

to medieval asceticism and the supplanting of the *carpe diem* of Roman stoicism by the *memento mori* theme of medieval Christianity (2). Another feature of Church policy inimical to medicine was a series of edicts listed by Garrison (3), whose object was primarily aimed at malpractice by monks, but had the general effect of not only discouraging clerical medicine, but also of placing their odium on the whole medical profession.

The Medical School of Salerno, first of its kind in Western Europe flourished in the eleventh and twelfth centuries. If not founded by the clergy it was at

ARNALDVS — VILLANOVANVS —

FIG. 1. Arnold of Villanova (1238–1311). (Reproduced from print in the collection of the Home for Aged and Infirm Hebrews, N. Y.)

least under church auspices. This institution of learning gradually came to form the focal point of Monastic, Greek, Jewish and Arabic medical learning, and exerted a wide influence in Italy and other parts of Western Europe. The Salernitan masters covered many fields of medicine in their writing, of which the most famous is the *Regimen (Sanitatis) Salernitanum or Flos Medicinae* (1260–1300), a popular work in poetic form, written for the King of England, the purpose of which was, in the words of the subtitle of the English translation of Sir John Harington (4), "the perfect preserving of the body of Man in continual health."

This famous medical work, known to have had a wide currency in manuscript form and to have gone through some 200 editions after the invention of printing, follows the precepts of healthful living as laid down by Avicenna, Maimonides and other Arab writers, quoted in the previous sections. In discussing the various herbs and their properties, the unknown author exclaims:—

> "*But who can write thy worth (O soveraigne Sage!)*
> *Some aske how man can die, where thou dost grow;*
> *Oh that there was a medicine curing age,*
> *Death comes at last, though death comes ne're so slow.*"

The importance of age in the indications for phlebotomy is twice stressed.

> "*Of seventy from seventeene, if bloud abound,*
> *The opening of a veine is healthfull found.*"

> "*Too old, too young, both letting bloud displeases,*
> *By years and sicknesse make your computation.*"

A famous commentary on this poem was written by Arnold of Villanova (1238–1311), the distinguished Spaniard, whose fame spread far and wide as the result of his sound medical ability, his books on medical subjects and his chemical investigations. In his famous "Parables of the Healing Art", he discusses the value of drug therapy and inveighs against the indiscriminate use of drugs in a manner more modern than medieval.

> "*A conscientious and thoughtful physician will never hurry with drug therapy, when necessity does not force him since even weakly acting remedies may be harmful, if the body has no need of them.*
> *With children and older people one must hesitate before administering drug remedies, even in youth the frequent taking of drugs is of doubtful value.*
> *People who frequently take drugs in youth, will complain early of the troubles of old age.*" (5)

At the request of King James of Spain, Arnold published in 1290 a treatise entitled, "*De Conservatio Juventutis et Retardatione Senectutis*" (6). The English translation by Dr. Drummond did not appear until 1544, over 250 years later and was called "The Conservation of Youth and the Defense of Age" (7). Arnold's theory of old age was based on the old Galenical pathology, as set forth by the Arabian school. Health depends on the equilibrium between the four temperaments, hot, cold, wet and dry, and the four humors, blood, phlegm, yellow bile, black bile. In old age cold and dry humors predominate and deplete the body. To overcome this the warm and moist humors must be stimulated. Arnold presents a regimen for each humor and temperament, and attention to these prevents old age. In general, his advice is eminently rational. Moderation in all things is advised. Life is to be regularly divided between moderate excercise, physical repose, waking and sleeping, mental work and some kind of amusement. Intellectual diversions are stressed, such as music, story-telling, theaters, travelling. He advocates well ventilated homes, proper clothing and frequent bathing. His drug therapy, largely vegetable remedies and medicinal wines, is secondary to hygienic measures of a general nature.

Of old folys that is to say the longer they lyue the more they ar gyuen to foly.

Howe beit I stoup, and fast declyne
Dayly to my graue, and sepulture
And though my lyfe fast do enclyne
To pay the trybute of nature
Yet styll remayne I and endure
In my olde synnes, and them not hate
Nought yonge, wors olde, suche is my state.

Fig. 2. This wood-cut showing an old man with one foot actually in the grave is taken from a contemporary English translation of Sebastian Brant's famous satirical and didactic poem "Das Narrenschiff" (The Ship of Fools) published in 1494.

In Arnold of Villanova we see an inquiring mind, a keen observer, and a practical physician, who, while still imbued with Arabian theory, was not afraid to set forth his own views and to defend them. Something of this same spirit of independence stirred Maimonides when he ventured to criticize Galen, and is indeed, an outstanding characteristic of Roger Bacon (c. 1214-c. 1294), largely unappreciated in his own day, but described by Garrison as "comparative philologist, mathematician, astronomer, physicist, physical geographer, chemist and physician." His chief contribution to science was as a practical experimenter whereby he anticipated many modern inventions. He is important in this narrative of the development of our knowledge of geriatrics for his book on old age, and his contribution to the development of eye-glasses.

"Very rarely does it happen that anyone pays sufficient heed to the rule of health. No one does in his youth, but sometimes one in 3,000 thinks of these matters, when he is old and approaching death, but he cannot apply a remedy because of his weakened powers and lack of experience. Therefore fathers are weakened and beget weak sons, then by neglect of rules of health, the sons weaken themselves and thus the son's son has a doubly weak constitution, the shortening of life of this kind is accidental and therefore a subject to remedy, if from birth a man followed a proper rule of life he would reach the limit set by God and nature." (Opus Majus) (8)

"If a man looks at letters or other small objects through the medium of a crystal or a glass or of some other transparent body placed above the letters, and it is the smaller part of a sphere whose convexity is towards the eye and the eye is in the air, he will see the letters much better and they will appear larger to him. For in accordance with the truth—all conditions are favourable for magnification—Therefore this instrument is useful to the aged and to those with weak eyes. For they can see the letter, no matter how small, sufficiently enlarged."
  (*Opus Majus, Burke's translation, p. 574.*) (9)

Roger Bacon is celebrated *inter alia* for the invention of gunpowder, the result of his great interest in alchemy. This primitive chemistry, had, as the name implies, its origin in ancient Egypt, (Land of Kemi, Black Land, hence also the term Black Art, meaning alchemy or magic), and has its theoretical foundation, according to Davis, (11) the great historian of chemisty, in the doctrine of the two contraries. This concept also appeared in China (12) in the third and fourth century, B.C., in a state of maturity that leads Davis to conclude that it was probably an importation into that country.

"The positive and active principle was identified with the sun, the male, dry, light and fiery; the negative and passive principle with the moon, female, moist, heavy and cold. When men became interested in the chemical properties of metals, they of course supposed them to be the result of the confluence of the two groups of opposite forces and qualities, or in other words, of the combination of the two contrary prinicples. Zozimos and the Alexandrians of about the third century A.D. called the fiery principle Sulphur and the negative principle Mercury, and supposed all metals to be combinations of the Sulphur and Mercury principles. Jahir taught the doctrine in the eighth century. Albertus Magnus and Roger Bacon continued it. Becker in the seventeenth century gave the name of *terra pinquis* (fat earth) to the sulphur principle. Stahl shortly afterwards renamed it phlogiston (the fiery entity) and the doctrine dominated chemistry until the time of Lavoisier. Alchemy, understood as the pursuit of transmutation and the elixir, does not seem to have been practised by the Alexandrians but first appeared among the Arabs of about the eighth century" (13). The alchemists of that time believed that if the two contraries could be made to unite or combine, that the Real Gold, the Philosopher's Stone, the Pill of Immortality and the Grand Elixir could be produced. This brief outline helps us to comprehend how the research activities of a group of medieval thinkers in their efforts to solve the riddle of life and death, laid the foundations for a modern science, full of rich promise today for an eventual clarification of the same problem.

In his book "The Care of Old Age and Preservation of Youth," Bacon attempts to convey to the lay reader the knowledge necessary to attain the ideal mentioned in the quotation from his *Opus Majus*. This geriatric work, known only in Latin manuscript for centuries, finally was translated by Dr. Richard Browne of London in 1683 (10). Bacon depended largely on the Arabs for his opinions and quoted constantly from Isaac Bemiramis, Haly Abbas, Avicenna, Averroes, Rhazes, and Johannes Damascenus, as well as Aristotle, Pliny and Galen. The outline of the book as well as its substance depends largely on the Moslem prototypes. The infirmities of old age, their nature and prevention, proper regimen to be followed by the old, all these topics are covered, together with chapters on diet and wines. The final paragraph of the final chapter furnishes an excellent summary of the spirit as well as the content of the entire work.

> "*Whence in conclusion it is made manifest, that Mirth, Singing, Looking on Humane Beauty and Comeliness, Spices, Electuaries, warm Water, Bathings, some things lying in the Bowels of the Sea, some living in the Air, others taken from the noble Animal, well tempered and prepared, and many more such things are Remedies whereby the Accidents of Age in Young Men, the Infirmities of Old Age in Old Men, the Weakness and Diseases of Decrepit Age in very Old Age, may be restrained, retarded and driven away.*"

While the scientist of the Middle Ages worked with crucible and alembic, the people, both rich and poor, found solace not only in the religion that played so large and dominating a role in their lives, but also in romantic tales of high adventure, in part stimulated by the Crusades. While many stories had to do with love and battle, some told of the quest for the fountain of Juventa, celebrated in Greek folklore as the spring formed in the metamorphosis of the nymph Juventa by Jupiter, and capable of rejuvenating those who bathed in it (14). Many of these medieval tales are based on the life of Alexander the Great, whose adventures formed part of the literature of all countries. Poems of the Middle Ages, French, German and Italian, are consecrated to the hero and in each of these is found the discovery of the fountain. The oldest Roman d'Alexandre is the work of Lambert-li-Cora de Chatendun and Alexandre de Bernay in 1184 A.D.

The famous Sir John Mandeville discovered the place in 1372 and located it in a narrow valley between a bare rock and a verdant hill near the city of Polonibes (?) and described it as follows:—"It has the odor and taste of spices, and at each hour of the day exhales new perfumes, and whoever drinks this fountain is cured of every malady he has, and seems always to be young; all call it the Fountain of Juventa." The vain quest of Ponce de Leon in Florida is well known, and in many of the early tales of discoveries in the New World, the fountain was definitely located. De Soto is said to have had it as an object of his wide travels.

In a strange parallel the mystic religion of the epoch took up the same idea in attributing to the blood of the Saviour the merits of the marvelous water. This is explained in the Legend of the Holy Grail of Robert de Baron written toward the end of the twelfth century. The Grail is the cup used at the Last Supper by Jesus and his disciples. In it Joseph of Arimathea collected the blood flowing from the wounds of the Saviour. Put into prison, Christ appeared to him and said, "I shall not take you with me; stay here until they think you are dead, but have no fear; you shall suffer no pain, and thou shalt not die." The divine blood thus became the fount of immortality and inspired many of the artists of the Middle Ages. Frescoes, engravings, tapestries and paintings are based on the theme of the pagan fount and its religious counterpart. Of them all, the most famous is the painting of Lucas Cranach, the Elder, now in the Berlin Museum, executed in 1546, and showing in lively fashion the magical transformation of weak old ladies into gay and flirtatious young women. Curiously enough, the only men shown are those waiting to receive the rejuvenated females (Fig. 3).

In sharp contrast with Arabist medical lore, the efforts of alchemists, and the romantic strivings of the medieval poets and painters, stands the marvelous insight and objectivity of Geoffrey Chaucer (1340–1400) whose Canterbury Tales give an intimate and revealing picture of the life of his time. Coffman has traced Horace's lines on old age through fourteen centuries to their enriched reappearance in the Reeve's Prologue. Chaucer's use of a classic inspiration for his own original purpose is a characteristic fore-runner of the spirit of the Renaissance, when, starting afresh with the originals of the classics, men once more began to think as Hippocrates had done, 1800 years earlier.

"*But ik am old, me list not pley for age;*
Gras-time is doon, my fodder is now forage,
This whyte top wryteth myne olde yeres,
Myn herte is al-so mowled (a) as myne heres,
 But—if I fare as dooth an open-ers; (b)
That ilke fruit is ever long the wers,
Til it be roten in mullok (c) or in stree (d).
We olde men, I drede, so fare we;
Til we be roten, can we nat be rype;
We hoppen ay, whyl that the world wol pype.
For in oure wil ther stiketh ever a nayl,
To have an hoor heed and a grene tayl,
As hath a leek; for thogh our might be goon,

Our wil desireth folie ever in oon.
For whan we may nat doon, than wol we speke;
Yet in oure asshen olde is fyr y-reke (e).
Foure gledes (f) han we, whiche I shal devyse,
Avaunting, lying, anger, coveityse;
Thise foure sparkles longen un-to elde.
Oure olde lemes mowe wel been unwelde (g).
But wil ne shal nat faillen, that is sooth.
And yet ik have alwey a coltes tooth,
As many a yeer as it is passed henne,
Sin that my tappe of lyf bigan to renne.
For sikerly, whan I was bore, anon
Deeth drogh the tappe of lyf and leet it gon;
And ever sith hath so the tappe y-ronne,
Til that almost al empty is the tonne.
The streem of lyf now droppeth on the chimbe; (h)
The sely (i) tonge may wel ringe and chime
Of wrecchednesse that passed is ful yore;
With olde folk, seve dotage, is namore." (*15*)

(a) grown mouldy
(b) medlars
(c) rubbish
(d) straw
(e) spread about
(f) burning coal
(g) unwieldy
(h) rim of the barrel
(i) innocent

REFERENCES

(1) COFFMAN, G. R. Old Age from Horace to Chaucer: Some Literary Affinities and Adventure of an Idea. Speculum, 9: 249, 1934. This account of Pope Innocent III is based on Coffman's essay.
(2) For a scholarly treatment of the *memento mori* theme in medieval life, see F. Parkes Weber, Aspects of Death and Correlated Aspects of Life in Art, Epigram and Poetry, 3rd ed., New York, P. B. Hoeber, 1920.
(3) GARRISON, F. H.: History of Medicine, ed. 4, Philadelphia, Saunders, p. 168, 1929.
(4) The School of Salernum, Regimen Sanitatis Salernitanum, The English Version, by Sir John Harington, New York, P. B. Hoeber, 1920. All quotations in the text are from this translation.
(5) The Second Doctrine-Aphorisms 11, 12, 13; translated from "Des Meisters Arnold von Villanova, Parabel der Heilkunst, aus dem lateinischen uebersetzt, erklaert und eingeleitet", Paul Diepgen, Klassiker der Medizin, Leipzig, 1922.
(6) Contained in Arnoldus de Villa Nova, Opera omnia, Basiliae, Conrad Waldkirch, 1585, (Streeter Collection, New York Academy of Medicine).
(7) The Conservation of Youth and the Defense of Old Age (1290); Arnoldus Villanova (d. 1311), trans. by Dr. Jonas Drummond, A. D. 1544, with additions from the Breviarium of Arnoldus, edited by C. L. Dana, The Elm Tree Press, Woodstock, Vt. 1922. The writer is indebted to Dr. Dana's excellent introduction.
(8) WOODRUFF, E. WINTHROP: Roger Bacon, A Biography, London, James Clarke & Co., 1938, p. 111.
(9) Ibid, p. 142. For the early history of eye-glasses, the development of which has meant so much for the comfort and happiness of the old, see Garrison's full account, op. cit. p. 184 et seq.

(10) BACON, ROGER, The Cure of Old Age and Preservation of Youth, translated out of the Latin, with annotations and an account of life and writings, by Richard Browne; London, T. Flesher, 1683. (With this is bound, Madeira Arraiz, De Arbor Vitae, or a physical account of the Tree of Life.).
(11) Davis, T. L.: Pictorial Representations of Alchemical Theory, Isis, 28: 75, 1938; see also Problems of the Origin of Alchemy, Scientific Monthly, 43: 551, 1936.
(12) WILSON, W. J.: Alchemy in China, Ciba Symposia, 217, 1940, with an extensive bibliography.
(13) DAVIS, T. L.: Loc. cit.
(14) MASSON, L.: La Fontaine de Jouvence, Aesculape, 27: 244, 1937, and 28: 16, 1938. An excellent account of the legend in many countries with splendid illustrations.
(15) From the Reeve's Prologue, Canterbury Tales, Geoffrey Chaucer, with introduction by T. R. Lounsbury, New York, T. Y. Crowell & Co., 1903. Decidedly worthy of re-reading at this point is Chaucer's keen picture of the "Doctour of Physik", whose education and personal peculiarities are particularly well described.

LIFE'S LATER YEARS

Studies in the Medical History of Old Age

FREDERIC D. ZEMAN, M.D.

[New York City]

Part 8[1]

THE REVIVAL OF LEARNING

(1483–1600 A.D.)

> "*But if phisitions be angry, that I have wryten phislike in englyshe, let theym remember, that the Greeks wrote in greek, the Romanes in latyne, Avicenna, and the other in Arabike, which were theyr owne propre and maternal tonges. And if they had bene as moche attached with envy and covaytise, as some nowe seeme to be, they wolde have devysed somme particular language, with a strange syphre or forme of lettres wherein they wolde have writen their science, which language or lettres no man shoulde have knowen that had not possessed and practised phisycke; but those, altho they were painimes and Jewes, in this parte of charity they farre surmountid us Christianes, that they wolde not have soo necessary a knowledge as phisicke is to be hyd from them, whych wolde be studiouse aboute it.*"
>
> Sir Thomas Elyot-Castel of Helth (*1541*).

As we slowly pick our way through medical history, pausing here and there to dwell upon the work and opinions of men who have left behind evidence of their interest in our problem, let us not neglect the main stream of medical progress, upon which, in every epoch the advancement of the knowledge of old age has necessarily depended. The contributions of each period to a special field are made strictly in accordance with its general medical understanding. At no time has the topic of old age been actually neglected, as many professional and lay writers seem to think, but the quality of the thought and the amount of attention given to it, have varied widely.

We have observed at times during the preceding centuries individual efforts toward original thinking. These availed but little to loosen the bondage in which the Arabs and their medieval followers were held by the anatomy and physiology of Galen, verbosely reinterpreted through 10 or 12 centuries. With the fall of Constantinople in 1453, the first scholars came to Italy who could read and interpret the medical classics in the original Greek. As late as 1499, when Erasmus went to Oxford, he could find there no teacher of Greek, and the following year in Paris received only imperfect instruction.

---

[1] This is the eighth in a series of articles dealing with Studies in the Medical History of Old Age. Upon completion of their publication, the installments will be collected and reprinted in a single volume, constituting one of the Series of Monographs of The Mount Sinai Hospital Press.—Ed.

The forces of independent inquiry released by the revival of learning had profound effects on medicine. On every side, in Italy, later in France, Germany and England, men rose up to protest against scholasticism and superstition, to substitute direct observation for hair-splitting dialectic. The anatomical studies of the renowned artist Leonardo da Vinci (1452–1519) paved the way for the revolutionary anatomical teaching of Andreas Vesalius (1514–1564), whose *De Fabrica Humanis Corporis* (published at the age of 28) with the vivid and accurate illustrations of Jan Kalkar, was concerned with function as well as structure, with pathological as well as normal anatomy. This work is properly regarded as the foundation of modern medical thought. Fabricius of Aquapendente, a student of Vesalius, was the teacher of William Harvey and the inspiration of his immortal discovery.

The vernacular version of *De Fabrica* prepared by Ambrose Pare (1510–1590) had a wide influence on the surgery of the Renaissance and illustrates the growing tendency to substitute the mother tongue for the Latin of the university scholars. The controversy over this question is bluntly terminated by Sir Thomas Elyot in the passage which stands as epigraph to this chapter. During this period several famous old books on old age appeared for the first time in English. Arnold of Villanova's work *De Conservatio juventutis et retardationis senectutis* first appeared in English in Drummond's translation in 1544; Paynel's *Regimen Sanitatis Salerni* in 1528; Baker's version of Gesner's *The New Jewel of Health* in 1576; and Ward's translation of the French edition of Alexis of Piedmont's *Secrets* in 1560.

The last two works indicate clearly the persistence of superstition and folk medicine in spite of the enlightenment of the times. Although sometimes listed in bibliographies of the medical history of old age, neither of the works constitutes anything more than background for the development of our theme, as is apparent from the title-pages.

"The Secretes of the Reverende Master Alexis of Piedmont containing many excellent Remedies agaynst dyvers diseases, woundes, and other accidents, with the manner to make distillations, parfumes, confitures, dyings, colours fusions and meltynges. A work wel approved verye profitable and necessary for everyman. Translated out of Frenche into Englishe by William Warde, 1559."

"The newe Jewel of Health wherein is contained the most excellent of Secretes of Phisicke and Philosophie, divided into fower bookes. In the which are the best approved remedies for the disease as well as inwarde as outwarde, of all the partes of the mans bodie: treating very amply of all distillations of Waters, of Oyles, Balmes, Quintessences, with the extraction of artificial salts, the use and preparation of Antimony and Potable Gold. Gathered out of the best and most approved authors by that excellent Doctor Gesnesrus. Also the pictures, and manner to make the Vessels, Farmaces, and other instruments thereunto belonging. Faithfully corrected and published in Englysh by George Baker, Chirurgien."

Conrad Gesner (1515-1565) to whom this book is ascribed, was a master of botany, zoology and medicine. He wrote copiously on all branches of human knowledge, including Alpine scenery and mountain climbing. One cannot but wonder his thoughts on reading his translator's dedication of his work to the Count and Countess of Oxford in which he says that "this newe Jewell wyll make the blynde to see, and the lame to walk. This newe Jewell will make weake to become strong, and the olde crooked age to become lustye. This newe Jewell will make the soule seeme beautifull, and the withered face seeme smoothe and fayre, yea, it will heal infirmities and all paynes in the bodie of man." Among the remedies offered to work these wonders is one strangely reminiscent of the Smith Papyrus. "An Oyle of Myrre, that mayntaineth the person long youthful even as the naturall balme doth; for this oyle by his naturall virtue defendeth and preserveth all things from putrefying, which are layd into it; and this also anointed on the face, mayntaineth a freshe and comely face; and that youthful appearing."

Ranked by Garrison with Vesalius and Pare, as one of the three great medical leaders of the sixteenth century, is Aureolus Theophrastus Bombastus von Hohenheim (1493-1541), the self-styled Paracelsus, whose turbulent life and truculent teachings generated controversies in his own time which have prevented until recently his proper evaluation. While schooled in the classics, Hippocrates and Aristotle, he publicly burned the works of Galen and Avicenna. Lecturing in German he declared himself greater than the highly respected Celsus. His writings are everywhere permeated by alchemical therapeutics, but established in practical use such drugs as opium, mercury, lead, sulphate, iron, arsenic, copper sulphate and potassium sulphate. The mixture of mysticism and ranting with sound observation and studied experience in his writings render their interpretation most difficult.

The subject of long life was an important feature of all discussions of the Hermetic Mysteries. The following passage from Paracelsus represents the master "in his most arcane manner", to quote Waite, the translator and editor of the authoritative works (1).

> "There have been other men, indeed, not unworthy of mention, who surpassed the ordinary length of life. As Moses, who completed 120 years, yet not according to the method of magic, but rather of physical life, to whom was joined so strong a nature that it attained a great age without difficulty. Like instances occur in our days, and will be found occasionally to the end of the world. Some, again, by the help of magic, have lived to a century and a half, and yet some have attained to a life of several centuries, and that by the adjoined force of Nature, which exists fully in metals and in other things which they call minerals. This force lifts up and preserves the body above its complexion and inborn quality. Of this kind are the Tincture and the Stone of the Philosophers because they are elicited from antimony, and, similarly, the quintessence. These and other numerous arcana of the Spagyric Art are met with, which in all manners restore the body exhausted by age, returns it to its former youth, and free it from all sickness, a fact which is well known to all acquainted with this monarchia."

A similar confusion of thought, a mixture of what to us seems sense and nonsense is found in other eminent writers of this period. Erasmus (1467–1536), the famous Dutch scholar and humanist, combined learning, stylistic brilliance, humor and tolerance. In his *Praise of Medicine* (2) there occurs a striking

Fig. 1. Marsilius Ficinus (1433–1499). (From print in the collection of The Home for Aged and Infirm Hebrews, N. Y.).

passage quoted by Schwalbe in the Introduction to his *Lehrbuch der Greisenkrankheiten* (1907). "A heavy burden is old age, which can no more be eluded than death itself. But medical aid is often able to postpone its onset and to palliate its maladies in a striking fashion." By itself this is an impressive statement, but taken in its context, the words assume an entirely different significance, as Erasmus continues: "For it is no fable, but vouched for by several witnesses, that man by means of the so-called Fifth Essence can strip off senile weakness like a snake skin, and be rejuvenated." This Fifth Essence was the creation of Raymond Lully (1234–1315), the alchemist, and discussed in his *Libellus de secretis naturae*, Augsburg, 1518, where it is ascribed every imaginable power over disease, old age and death, as well as over minerals and plants.

Knowledge mixed with credulity and superstition are manifest in the work of Marsilius Ficinus the Florentine (1433–1499), noted as the translator of Plato into Latin and as a protege of Cosimo da Medici. His *De triplici vita*, privately printed at Basle not later than 1498, contains three books, *De Vita Sana, De Vita Longa* and *De Vita Coelitus Comparandi*. A German translation of the first two books, *Das Buch der Gesundheit*, was printed in Strassburg in 1505. That Ficinus followed the Arab pattern in his work is clear from the following chapter headings. "The first chapter says that for a perfection of art and the learning of widsom a long life is necessary which is to be desired and guarded." "The second chapter shows that the bodily heat and warmth is diminished by dampness." "The third chapter teaches how to preserve the warmth and heat of the body against moisture, as Minerva the goddess of wisdom advises." "The sixth chapter tells the common rules for eating and drinking, and the nature of foods and clothing." "The fourteenth and last chapter teaches how to avoid and prevent the serious accidents and injuries." He advised consultation with an astrologer every seventh year to find out what dangers threatened and resort to a physician to learn how to prevent the impending trouble. He recommended to old people the internal use of gold, frankincense and myrrh, since the wise men offered these three to the Creator of the stars in order to obtain from him the favorable influence of the three lords of the planets, Sol, Jupiter and Saturn.

Contrasting with Ficinus, is his contemporary, Gabriele Zerbi (1468–1505), celebrated as professor of anatomy at Padua, whose anatomic treatise published in 1502, was the first to separate organs into systems. Zerbi's book on old age (3), dedicated to Pope Innocent VIII, has never received the attention from medical historians that its rich content deserves. Thanks to the erudition of a friendly scholar, an abstract of this little known work has been made available (4). In it we find a wealth of practical information on the hygiene of old age, with a general similarity in form and content to Arab works of the preceding centuries. The preoccupation with astrology as shown in Ficinus is here also evident. In dividing old age into two periods, Zerbi describes first, "latent old age" ranging from thirty to sixty years, which is under the influence of the planet Jupiter, and second, "manifest old age," which is under the influence of Saturn. It is emphasized that there is no life extension beyond the natural limit of life and that gerontocomia should aim at retardation only. It is a special art consisting of conservative and preservative measures, and the use of the six "res naturales." The master of this art is a specialist in old age, and is called "gerontocomus" by the author. His qualifications and duties, as well as those of his assistants are described in detail. The best locations and climates for residences for the aged are discussed. The greater part of the book, Chapters 16 to 56, contain rules for exercise, bathing, rest, eating and drinking, sleeping, evacuations, and mental health. Among the therapeutic agents are viper meat, and broth, distillate of human blood, gold solutions, as well as rare stones and syrups for the retardation of old age. Sex hygiene and conservation of sight and smell are among other topics thoroughly discussed. In general this is a highly worthwhile, conscientious effort to elucidate the subject, and should be placed high among the works of Renaissance physicians on old age.

Antonius Fumariellus Veronensis wrote *De seniam regimine, anno 1540*, in which, according to MacKenzie, he declares that he "follows the sentiments of Hippocrates and Galen." Another Italian of this period was Tommaso Rangoni, known by his pen name of Thomas Philologus Ravenna. His *De Vita Hominis ultra CXX annos protrahenda* was addressed in 1553 to Pope Julius III. He is said to be the first physician to criticize the custom of having public burying places in populous cities because they contaminate the atmosphere and frequently spread fatal diseases.

In 1534 in England, Sir Thomas Elyot published *The Castel of Helth*. The first edition, of which no copy is known, is said to have been dedicated to Thomas Cromwell (see Bull. New York Acad. Med., 5:1, January, 1929). This fascinating nobleman had many interests, including political philosophy and the theory of education as well as medicine, in which by his own account he was extremely well read. Limited in actual medical experience he brought to the old established authorities a strong admixture of good sense and a forceful style. His book is devoted almost entirely to dietetics as then understood and as had been practiced for many centuries.

> *"Always remember, that aged man shuld eate often; and but litel at every time, for it fareth by them as it doth by a lampe, the lyght whereof is almost extincte, which by pouring oyle and litel is long kept bourninge: and with moch oyle poured in at once, it is clene put out."*

His list of "syckenesses of age" is reminiscent of Hippocrates' famous Aphorism.

> *"Difficultie of breth, reumes with coughes, strangulyon, and difficultie in pyssynge, ache in the ioyntes, diseases of the raynes, swymmynges in the head, palseyes, ytchynge of all the bodye, lacke of slepe, moysture in the eyes and eares, dulnesse of syght, hardnesse of hearynge,—or shortnesse of breth. Although many of the said sycknesses do happem in every tyme and age: yet because they be most frequent in the sayde tymes and ages I have written them, to the intent, that in the ages and tymes moste inclyned unto them, such thinges mought be than eschewed, which are as appte to ingendre sayde dyseases."*

Not the least of Sir Thomas' charm is his spelling. His work ran into at least three editions, and had a wide influence among the people, if not among the profession.

The old mans dietarie (5) of Thomas Newton, published in 1586, is noteworthy chiefly as a medical work that was current in Shakespeare's day. In it we find Elyot quoted very freely, sometimes with credit, but as often not.

An eighteenth century work, the *History of Health*, by MacKenzie contains references to works of old authors, which are not to be found in present day bibliographies. Among these writers is Ferdinandas Eustachius, son of the famous anatomist Bartholomaeus Eustachius, who in 1589 wrote *De vitae humanae a facultate medica prorogatione*, and dedicated it to Pope Sixtus V. In it

FIG. 2. Jerome Cardan (1501-1576). (From print in the collection of The Home for Aged and Infirm Hebrews, N. Y.).

he refutes many arguments alleged to prove that the medical art is of no use in prolonging life, but, as MacKenzie points out, is silent as to the means by which that end may be attained.

We come now to the fascinating figure of Jerome Cardan (1501-1576) who practiced in Milan and served as professor of medicine at Pavia and Bologna. His fame today rests on his mathematical work and on his contributions to physics, especially his efforts to measure the density of air. In his own time he was so highly regarded as a practitioner that he travelled to Edinburgh from Italy for consultation on the illness of the Archbishop Hamilton. Two medical works on old age are known (6), but among his many literary productions, his autobiography, *The Book of My Life*, stands out in the opinions of scholars as the first of the great introspective studies of a man's inner being. In it as well as in his essay *De Utilitate* are many bitter references to old age. According to Waters (7), Cardan declares old age to be the most cruel and irreparable evil with which man is cursed, and to talk of old age is to talk of the crowning misfortune of humanity. Old men are made wretched by avarice, by dejection and by terror. He bids men not to be deceived by the flowery words of Cicero when he describes Cato as an old man, like to a fair statue by Polycleitus, with faculties unimpaired and memory fresh and green. He next goes on to catalogue the numerous vices and deformities of old age, and instances from Aristotle what he considers to be the worst of all misfortunes, to wit, that an old man is well-nigh cut off from hope; and by way of comment, grimly adds, "If any man be plagued by the ills of old age he should blame no one but himself, for it is by his own choice that his life has run on so long." Cardan, as Waters points out, offers a few words of counsel as to how this hateful season may be robbed of some of its horror. Our bodies grow old first, then our senses, and last our minds. Therefore let us store our treasures in that part of us that will hold out the longest, as men in a beleaguered city are wont to collect their resources in the citadel, which albeit it must in the end be taken, will nevertheless be the last to fall into the foeman's hands. Old men should avoid society, seeing that they bring nothing thereto worth having; whether they speak or keep silent, they are in the way, and they are as irksome to themselves when they are silent as they are to others when they speak. The old man should take a lesson from the lower animals, which are wont to defend themselves with the best arms given them by nature; bulls with their horns, horses with their hoofs, and cats with their claws; wherefore an old man should at least show himself to be as wise as the brutes, and maintain his position by his wisdom and knowledge, seeing that all the grace and power of his manhood must needs have fled.

Cardan's pessimism was founded on his own life experience, and for sheer intensity, has probably never been rivalled. In spite of worldly success Cardan was essentially an unhappy person, due in part to the obstacles he had to overcome because of his illegitimate birth, and in part to the execution of his only son for murder. His personal sufferings did not prevent his mind from ranging, in true Renaissance fashion, over broad fields of activity. In addition to medicine, physics, mathematics and philosophy, he made practical suggestions of value for the education of the blind and deaf. His attitude toward the advanced years is summed up in this terse sentence: "Old age, when it comes, must make every man regret that he did not die in infancy."

At this time we leave the medical authorities and turn to two distinguished lay writers, Cornaro, the Italian (1467 or 1475–1566) and Montaigne, the Frenchman (1533–1592). Both had wide influence in their own and succeeding centuries. Both are well worth reading today, since in each we find originality of thought, action and expression, and unusual freedom from outworn scholasticism.

Although all the classical and medieval writers on old age had highly recommended sobriety and temperance, Cornaro developed an extreme regimen which he followed faithfully from about the age of forty until his death. He tells us how overindulgence in food and drink, as well as a strong propensity to anger and emotional outbursts had so upset his health that he was continually racked by pain and other bodily distresses. Wherefore he resolved to limit himself to twelve ounces of solid food, and fourteen ounces of liquids. In addition he determined to avoid heat, cold, fatigue, grief and other emotional strain. In order to carry out these resolves a highly secluded life would seem obligatory,

FIG. 3. Cornaro and His Family. An engraving after a painting by Titian

but such does not appear to have been the case. The ascetic way of life first planned at forty years, found Cornaro at an advanced age so robust and sturdy that he felt impelled to tell his contemporaries about his successful methods. This first essay, written at 83, was entitled, *A Treatise on a Sober Life*, and was followed, according to the customary dating, by three others, at the ages of 86, 91 and 95 years.

Readers of Thoms' work on *Human Longevity, Its Facts and Fictions* (8) will not be surprised to learn that the customary dates ascribed to Cornaro's life and writings require revision in the light of modern research. Professor Sarton (9) quotes Giordano to the effect that the usual ages given for Cornaro's discourses, 83, 86, 91 and 95 years, are based on the assumption that he was born in 1467, but that Rossi now considers most probable that Cornaro was born in 1475 and died on May 8, 1566. On that basis Cornaro's discourses were composed at the ages of 75, 78, 83 and 87. This new viewpoint revises Cornaro's age downward by eight years, and somewhat dims his absolute achievement in attaining long life through following his own prescriptions. On the other hand, it in no way detracts from the charm or value of Cornaro's work nor from its widespread influence. It was early translated into French and English, was recommended at length by Addison in the Spectator, October 13, 1711, and was reprinted as recently as 1912 by Butler, (Milwaukee) in an illustrated and annotated edition (10). Two paintings of Cornaro are extant, a portrait by Tintoretto in the Uffizzi Gallery in Florence, and an engraving after Titian showing the patriach surrounded by grandsons and their children (fig. 3).

Today Cornaro's methods have fresh significance for us in view of modern work in nutrition and becomes even more attractive in the light of McCay's work in promoting the longevity of his laboratory rats through systematic undernutrition. Cornaro's attitudes and ideas may best be understood from careful perusal of his little book, but a few quotations will serve to give some savor of this determined old Venetian.

"Now, Nature does not deny us the power of living many years. Indeed, old age, as a matter of fact, is the time of life to be most coveted, as it is then that prudence is best exercised, and the fruits of all the other virtues are enjoyed with the least opposition; because, by that time, the passions are subdued, and man gives himself up wholly to reason."
The First Discourse.

"In this manner, I accustomed myself to the habit of never fully satisfying my appetite, either with eating or drinking—always leaving the table well able to take more. In this I acted according to the proverb: 'Not to satiate one's self with food is the science of health'."
Ibid.

"And now, since some sensual and unreasonable men pretend that long life is not a blessing or a thing to be desired, but that the existence of a man after he had passed the age of sixty-five cannot any longer be called a living life, but rather should be termed a dead one, I shall plainly show they are much mistaken; for I have an ardent desire that every man should strive to attain my age, in order that he may enjoy what I have found—and what others, too, will find—to be the most beautiful period of life."
Ibid.

"In conclusion, I wish to say that, since old age is—as, in truth, it is— filled and overflowing with so many graces and blessings, and since I am one of the number who enjoy them, I cannot fail—not wishing to be wanting in charity—to give testimony to the fact, and to fully certify to all men that my enjoyment is much greater than I can now express in writing. I declare that I have no other motive for writing but my hope that the knowledge of so

great a blessing as my old age has proved to be, will induce every human being to determine to adopt this praiseworthy orderly and temperate life, in favor of which I ceaselessly keep repeating, Live, live, that you may become better servants of God!

The Fourth Discourse.

A contemporary reaction to Cornaro's work is to be found in Leonardus Lessius, a learned Jesuit of Louvaine, who according to Mackenzie, lived about the end of the sixteenth century, and was so much pleased by Cornaro that purely to recommend his efforts wrote a book entitled, *Hygiasticon, or the true method of preserving life and health to extreme old age.*

Michel Eyquem, Seigneur de Montaigne (1533–92) brings to the subject of old age the keen insight, sharp observation, kindly humor and realism that have kept his essays a part of the living literature of all time. His tolerant spirit and easy style give no room to false optimism, and nowhere does the writer allow himself any illusions about the discomforts of growing old. His attitude is summed up thus: "... old age stands a little in need of a more gentle treatment. Let us recommend it to God, the protector of health and wisdom, but withal, let us be gay and sociable." Compared with Cardan, who found nothing worthwhile in advancing years, Montaigne is still able to poke fun at himself, at physicians, and at those who put too much faith in physicians.

In attempting to choose extracts from the Essays, that may give the reader insight into Montaigne's spirit, the wealth of material worthy of quotation makes decision difficult. This work (11) and that of Cornaro, are required reading for both doctor and patient interested in old age.

> *"But nature, leading us by the hand, an easie, and, as it were, an insensible pace, step by step conducts us to that miserable condition, and by that means makes it familiar to us, so that we perceive not, nor are sensible of the stroak then, when our youth dies in us, though it be really a harder death than the final dissolution of a languishing body, which is only the death of old age."*
>
> *"No old age can be so ruinous and offensive in a man who has past his life in honour, but it must be venerable, especially to his children; the soule of which he must have train'd up to their duty by reason, not by necessity, and the need they have of him, not by roughness and force."*
>
> *"Our wits grow costive and thick in growing old."*
>
> *"Let us a little permit nature to take her own way; she better understands her own affairs than we. But such a one died, and so shall you, if not of that disease, of another. And how many have not escap'd dying who have their physicians always at their tails?"*
>
> *"The gout, the stone, and indigestion are symptoms of long years, as heat, rains, and winds are of long voyages."*
>
> *"Sometimes the body first submits to age, sometimes the soul, and I have seen enow who have got a weakness in their brains before either in their hams, or stomach; and by how much the more, it is a disease of no great pain in the infected party, and of obscure symptoms, so much greater the danger is."*

This review of the leading opinions regarding old age in the sixteenth century may be concluded with the work of Montaigne's countryman, Andre du Laurens, or Laurentius (1558–1609). This eminent practitioner, a physician to Marie de Medici and Henry IV, was not a great originator, and while no important discoveries are attributed to him, his writings achieved importance in his own day. In his *Opera Anatomica*, Lyon, 1593, he defended Galen against his detractors, Vesalius and Columbus, and yet he was far from being blindly bound by outworn authorities. This is well shown in his work on old age, published

Fig. 4. André du Laurens (1558–1609). (From print in the collection of The Home for Aged and Infirm Hebrews, N. Y.).

in French at Paris in 1597. There were nine French editions, two Italian and several Latin translations. The English translation by Richard Surphlet appeared in 1599, and is entitled, *Discourse of the Preservation of the Sight; of Melancholike Diseases; of Rheumes, and of Old Age* (12).

Laurentius was a thorough Galenist in his interpretation of aging, considering it as a result of the moisture of the body being consumed by its heat, and producing the characteristic coldness and dryness seen in the old. Nevertheless he was wise enough to make first hand observations bearing on certain questions which continued in dispute for centuries. "The Men of Egypt and Alexandria did believe that the naturall cause of olde age did come of the diminishing of the heart; they said that the heart did grow till fiftie yeares the weight of two drames every yeer, and that after fifty yeeres it waxed lesser and lesser, till in the end it was grown to nothing; but these are nothing but vaine imaginations and fooleness. We have caused many old men to be opened, whose hearts have been found as great, and heavie as them of younger sort." This question continued to perplex physicians until relatively recently, and the wide discrepancies in weight of the heart were not clarified until the rôle of hypertension in causing cardiac hypertrophy was appreciated.

In general all ancient writers on old age are concerned with it as an entity, as expressed in the epigram attributed to Terence, *Senectus ipsa est morbus*. Laurentius differentiates a natural old age, corresponding to what we call aging in the biological sense, and a pathological old age, *Senium ex morbo*. He defines external as well as internal causes of aging, the inevitability of which he emphasizes again and again, pointing out the worthlessness of the time honored quack remedies. "All the precious licours that are, Aurum potabile, conserves of Rubies and Emeralds, Elixir vitae, or the faimed and fabulous fountain of restored youth cannot withstand, but that our heate must at length grow weake and feeble."

"... I leave to speake of all other outward causes, (as over violent exercises, and idle and sitting life, long and continuall watching, the passions of the minde which of themselves can make us olde, as feare and sadness), because we may in some sort avoide and shun them. I leave also to say anything of chancing causes, or such as may befall us by haphazard as hurts: I am only purposed to shoew that it is of necessitie that every living creature must waxe olde, that he fostereth within himself the naturall causes of his death, and that he hath outward causes thereof hanging about him, which cannot be avoided."

Laurentius understands the significance of the mind, the importance of diet, of alcohol and of occupation for the aged. He points out too, that different men age at different rates of speed, some being old at forty and others young at sixty, attributing this to their bodily make-up. "They which are of a sanguine complexion, grow old very slowly, because they have a great store of heate and moysture; melancholike men which are cold and drie, become old in shorter time."

The views of this distinguished French physician may be taken to summarize the best thought of his day on old age and they represent the advance of learning to the point just antecedent to the great and sustained progress of medical science which followed upon Harvey's revolutionary discovery and the application of the microscope to anatomical study by Malpighi, which in turn led to the correlation of clinical and post-mortem findings by Morgagni. It is interesting to look ahead and see in the course of the years how many different causes have been assigned to aging, with the result that today we believe it to be a biological process, an inherent property of the germ plasm. *Senectus ipsa est morbus* may have re-established its right to serious consideration as a principle, but actually our modern interpretation is at the same time both broader and more restricted than the old time philosophers conceived it; broader in the sense that we think of aging as a fundamental property of living, and perhaps also of inanimate, matter; more restricted in that we are gradually becoming more and more precise in the differentiation of true aging from the superimposed disease processes.

REFERENCES

(1) WAITE, A. E.: The Hermetic and Alchemical Writings of Paracelsus the Great, London, Elliott, 1894. Quotations taken from, A Book Concerning Long Life, Vol. 2, p. 330.

(2) LOB DER HEILKUNST; aus dem lateinischen uebertragen und erlaeutert von Ludwig Enthoven, Strassburg, J. H. E. Heitz, 1907, vol. 7, p. 8.

The very rare English translation,—one copy in the Osler Library at McGill University, Montreal, Canada; the other in the Huntington Library, San Marino, Calif., —is entitled *Declamatio in laudem artis medicinae. A declamacion in the prayse of physyke, newly translated*, S. R. Redman. No author, date or place is given.

(3) ZERBI, G.: Ad Innocentam VIII, Pon. Max. Gerontocomia feliciter incipit. Prologus. Rome, 1489.

(4) ZEMAN, F. D.: The Gerontocomia of Gabriele Zerbi, A Fifteenth Century Manual of Hygiene for the Aged, J. Mt. Sinai Hosp., 8: 5, 1161, 1942.

(5) Only two copies of this odd little book are known, one in an English library, the other in the Huntington Library, San Marino, Calif., through whose courtesy the writer was privileged to read the book in microfilm. It is mentioned by S. V. Larkey in his excellent introduction to the Shakespeare Association's edition of Surphlet's translation of Laurentius' Discourse of Preservation of Sight.

(6) (1) De Senectute, J. Cardan, in his Opera, Lugdini 1663, VI, 242-298. (See Index Cat. S. G. L., vol. i.) (2) Hieronymus Cardanus, Opuscala medica senilia in quattier libros tributa, quorium i; De Dentitus, ii; De Rationali Curandiratione, iii; De facultatibus medicamentoram, praecipue purgatium, iv; De morto regio. Bunia nunc primium ex Ms. Bibliotheca romanam lucem data. Lugdini: Sumpt. L. Durand, 1638, p. 531.

(7) WATERS, W. G., CARDAN, J.: A Bibliographical Study. London, Lawrence and Bullen, Ltd., 1898.

(8) THOMS, W. J.: Human Longevity: Its Facts and Fictions, London, J. Murray, 1873.

(9) SARTON, G., HOEFER AND CHEVREUL, with an excursus on creative centenarians. Bull. Hist. Med., 8: 441.

(10) CORNARO, L.: The Art of Living Long. A New and Improved English Version, Milwaukee, Wm. F. Butler, 1915.

(11) The Essays of Michael, Seigneur de Montaigne, ed. 3, London, 1700, made English by Charles Cotton, London, Alex. Murray & Son, 1870. Reader is referred also to the Life of Montaigne, compiled from the Essays by Marvin Lowenthal, New York, Houghton Mifflin Co., 1935.

(12) See Shakespeare Association Facsimiles No. 15, published for the Shakespeare Association by H. Milford, London, Oxford Univ. Press, 1938, for reprint of Surphlet's Translation of Laurentius, with an excellent introduction by Sanford V. Larkey, to whom the present writer is indebted for his information on this author.

LIFE'S LATER YEARS

Studies in the Medical History of Old Age

FREDERIC D. ZEMAN, M.D.

[*New York City*]

Part 9[1]

THE SEVENTEENTH CENTURY

"For we have hope, and wish, that it may conduce to a common good, and that the nobler sort of physicians will advance their thoughts, and not employ their time wholly in the sordidness of cures, neither be honoured for necessity only; but that they will become co-adjutors and instruments of the Divine Omnipotence and Clemency, in prolonging and renewing the life of man; especially, seeing we prescribe it to be done by safe and convenient and civil ways, though hitherto unassayed."

Francis Bacon—Foreword to the
History of Life and Death.

Against a background of epoch-making achievements in art, literature, music, philosophy, mathematics and natural sciences, we find medicine striking an accelerated pace that has but rarely slackened in three hundred and fifty years. In the seventeenth century we behold the first fruits of the great intellectual emancipation that came with the overthrow of tradition and the application of what we now call the scientific method, the reasoned combining of observation, correlation and experimentation.

As a symbol of the transition between the old and new thinking, Shakespeare (1564-1616) stands preeminent as uniting with his great poetic gift a thorough grasp of the general knowledge of his time. It was given to him to cover the whole range of human experience with understanding such as no one had ever before possessed; but his imagery is all in terms of what had been learned and taught by the men who came before him (1). His physiological concepts of old age are apparent in these lines, based on the time-honored teachings of Galen that the quantity of blood in the body diminishes with advancing age, and that in characterizing old age as cold and dry, all its manifestations are explained.

"Yet who would have thought the old man
To have had so much blood in him?"

Macbeth—Act I, Scene V.

---

[1] This is the ninth in a series of articles dealing with Studies in the Medical History of Old Age. Upon completion of their publication, the installments will be collected and reprinted in a single volume, constituting the third in the Series of Monographs of The Mount Sinai Hospital Press.—Ed.

> "*Though now this grained face of mine be hid
> In sap-consuming winter's snow,
> And all the conduits of my life froze up,
> Yet hath my night of life some memory.*"
> Comedy of Errors—Act V, Scene I.

> "*These old fellows
> Have their ingratitude in them hereditary:
> Their blood is caked, 'tis cold, it seldom flows.
> 'Tis lack of kindly warmth they are not kind;
> And nature as it grows again toward earth,
> Is fashioned for the journey, dull and heavy.*"
> Timon of Athens—Act II, Scene II.

The roster of old men in the histories, the tragedies and comedies includes such well known figures as Lear, Prospero, Polonius and Falstaff, and several lesser ones, such as Aegeon, Nestor, Belarius, Capulet and Adam. The play *King Lear*, has been called by John Masefield the most affecting and grandest of Shakespeare's creations. For the present theme it not only furnishes the unequalled picture of senile deterioration aggravated by overwhelming misfortune, but also illustrates the conflict of parent and children in two separate examples, the old king and his three daughters, contrasted with Gloucester and his two sons, the legitimate but evil Edgar and the dutiful, unselfish bastard, Edmund.

His appraisal of life is to be found in the famous speech of Jacques, in which we recognize the familiar sad echoes of Ecclesiastes, Aristotle, Horace, Juvenal and Chaucer.

> "*All the world's a stage,
> And all the men and women merely players.
> They have their exits and their entrances;
> And one man in his time plays many parts;
> His acts being seven ages. At first the infant,
> Mewling and puking in the nurse's arms.
> And then the whining school-boy, with his satchel
> And shining morning face, creeping like a snail
> Unwillingly to school. And then the lover,
> Sighing like a furnace, with a woeful ballad
> Made to his mistress' eyebrow. Then a soldier,
> Full of strange oaths, and bearded like the pard;
> Jealous in honour, sudden and quick in quarrel,
> Seeking the bubble reputation
> Even in the cannon's mouth. And then the justice,
> In fair round belly with good capon lined,
> With eyes severe and beard of formal cut,
> Full of wise saws and modern instances;*

> *And so he plays his part. The sixth age shifts*
> *Into the lean and slipper'd pantaloon,*
> *With spectacles on nose and pouch on side;*
> *His youthful hose, well saved, a world too wide*
> *For his shrunk shank; and his big manly voice*
> *Turning again toward childish treble, pipes*
> *And whistles in his sound. Last scene of all,*
> *That ends this strange eventful history,*
> *Is second childishness, and mere oblivion,*
> *Sans teeth, sans eyes, sans taste, sans everything."*
> *As You Like It—Act II, Scene VII.*

From the greatest of English poets, we turn to one whose intellectual gifts are so impressive that some have even ascribed to his hand the whole of Shakespeare's endeavors. Francis Bacon, Baron St. Albans, Lord Verulam (1561-1621) presents from the standpoint of character one of the great enigmas of history, since in him we find both the philosopher's search for truth and a ruthless political opportunism. The poet, Alexander Pope, called him "the wisest, brightest, meanest of mankind." His influence on his contemporaries and on the following generations was due, not to his own original contributions which were negligible, but to his unremitting fight against authority, against uncontrolled flights of imagination and against wordy academic argument, all lucidly and forcibly expressed. His fundamental principles form the basis of modern scientific methods.

Among the many questions touched upon by Bacon in the wide range of his writings, the problem of old age, its nature and evaluation, is discussed at length. In the "Essays", reminiscent of Montaigne, and noted for their shrewd understanding and unusually vivid style, we find *Of Youth and Age*, a clearly drawn and well considered series of parallels, illustrating the salient mental characteristics of both periods of life.

> *"Young men are fitter to invent than to judge; fitter for execution than for counsel; and fitter for new projects than for settled business. For the experience of age, in things that fall within the compass of it, directeth them; but in new things, abuseth them. The errors of young men are the ruin of business; but the errors of aged men amount but to this, that more might have been done or sooner.... Men of age object too much, consult too long, adventure too little, repent too soon, and seldom drive business home to the full period, but content themselves with a mediocrity of success."* (2).

In the *History of Life and Death* (3) Bacon's aim is far more ambitious, seeking among other things, as the epigraph to this chapter indicates, to educate "the nobler set of physicians." He scoffs at "these things which the vulgar physicians talk of, radical moisture and natural heat, (which) are but mere fictions; and the immoderate praises of chemical medicines first puff up with vain hopes, and then fail their admirers." He differentiates death resulting from disease, and "death which comes by total decay of the body, and the inconcoction of old age." He ascribes old age to failure of the power of reparation of the tissues.

"There is, in the declining of age, an unequal reparation; some parts are repaired easily, others with difficulty, and to their loss; as, from that time, the bodies of men begin to endure the torment of Mezentius; that the

FIG. 1. Francis Bacon, Baron St. Albans, Lord Verulam (1561-1621), "The wisest, brightest, meanest of mankind." (Reproduced from print in the collection of The Home for Aged and Infirm Hebrews, New York.)

living die in the embrace of the dead; and the parts easily reparable, through their conjunction with the parts hardly reparable, do decay ... and that the cause of the termination of life is this; for that the spirits, like a gentle flame continually preying upon bodies, conspiring with the outward air, which is ever sucking and drying of them, do, in time, destroy the whole fabric of the body, as also the particular engines and organs thereof, and

make them unable for the work of reparation. These are the true ways of natural death, well and faithfully to be revolved in our minds; for he that knows not the ways of nature, how can he succour her, or turn her about?"
(3)

The author discusses longevity in relation to heredity, the physical attributes of the long-lived, rejecting astrology, and dwells at length on the subject of diet, endorsing Cornaro, but pointing out that some liberal eaters also live long. As in the Essays, he compares youth and age mentally, but also goes into great detail regarding the physical features. In general Bacon's observations are sound, as he seeks to disprove the time-honored explanations of the phenomena of youth and age.

At this point Sir Thomas Browne (1605-1682), the famed physician of Norwich, who endeavors in *Religio Medici* to reconcile faith and scepticism, must be included in our narrative, not so much as a significant example of contemporary thought, but for his own peculiar merits (4).

"But age doth not rectify, but incurvate our natures, turning bad dispositions into worser habits, and (like diseases) brings on incurable vices; for every day as we grow weaker in age, we grow stronger in sin, and the number of our days doth but make our sins innumerable. . . . I find my growing Judgment daily instruct me how to be better but my intamed affections and confirmed vitiosity make me daily do worse."

To make our record more complete and to remind readers that Galen still ruled medical thinking on old age, in spite of the efforts of original minds, we must here mention several unimportant works by physicians of this period. Rodericus a Fonseca, professor at Pisa and Padua, published in 1602 a treatise entitled *De tuenda valetodine et producenda vita, ad Ferdinandum Medicem magnum Hetruriae ducem,* based frankly on Galen. Aurelius Anselmus of Mantua, physician to the Duke of Mantua, in 1606, wrote *Gerocomice sive de senum regimine,* praising the old for excelling in prudence and understanding. Franciscus Ranchinus, professor at Montpellier, was the author of *Gerocomice de senum conservatione et senilium morborum curatione,* in the year 1625. Rodolphus Goelemius, a German physician, dedicated his efforts, entitled briefly *De vita proroganda,* to Frederic, Count of the Rhenish Palatinate, and to Otho, Landgrave of Hesse, in 1608. Claudius Diodatus, physician to the Bishop of Basle, is responsible for a bombastic effort, given to the world in 1628, and based on "the vain boasts of the chymists", *Pantheon Hygiasticon Hippocraticum Hermeticum de hominis vita ad centum et viginti annos salubriter producenda* (5). One conclusion seems clear: the good will of people in high places, then as always, was sought after by physicians through the medium of well aimed dedications. In addition, Stendel tells us, old age was a favorite theme for medical dissertations and speeches at academic celebrations. In 1664, Heinrich Meibom, the famous anatomist of Helmstedt, delivered his *Epistola de longaevis* as a birthday talk for the *Landherr* (6).

The significance, both immediate and remote, of the publication of William Harvey's (1578-1657) *De Motu Cordis* in 1628, needs no further enlargement here. The distinguished founder of modern physiology, whose discovery forms the cornerstone of all medical thinking, comes into our studies in an entirely different rôle, that of pathologist. On November 14, 1635, Harvey was called

FIG. 2. Thomas Parr (1483-1635), most famous of the supercentenarians. (Reproduced from print in the collection of The Home for Aged and Infirm Hebrews, New York.)

upon to perform an autopsy on Thomas Parr, "a poor countryman... having lived one hundred and fifty-two years and nine months and survived nine princes." Parr had been brough up to London by the Earl of Shropshire to be exhibited to the King as a prodigy of longevity. Harvey's own account (7) of his findings is a revealing picture of the medical reasoning of that day. Death is ascribed to change of climate and to the richness of the London diet.

> "*Whence the stomach at length failing, and the excretions long retained, the work of concoction proceeding languidly, the liver getting loaded, the blood stagnating in the veins, the spirit frozen, the heart, the source of life, oppressed, the lungs infarcted, and made impervious to the ambient air, the general habit rendered more compact, so that it could no longer exhale or perspire—no wonder that the soul, little content with such a prison, took its flight.*"

Death actually seems to have been caused by penumonia, but for all the details the whole protocol is worth reading. There is nothing in Harvey's words to indicate that he questioned the age of his subject (8). The centenarian has always fascinated both the layman and the physician, since he represents the attainment of the ultimate in longevity, and suggests that if his secret could be but fathomed, like success might be achieved by others. Since the time of Harvey a considerable literature has accumulated devoted to post-mortems of individuals 100 years and over (9).

Another famous medical experimenter and originator was Sanctorius (1561-1636) of Padua, who invented a clinical thermometer and a pulse-clock, as well as many surgical instruments. His *Ars de statica medicina* has been considered the earliest effort toward an experimental approach to the problems of metabolism, since his most celebrated accomplishment was the quantitative proof of the insensible perspiration. According to Stendel (10), old age to Sanctorius was an increasing difficulty in the insensible perspiration which finally led to suffocation and death. The frontispiece to the book shows the author seated in a chair suspended from a scale whereby he can weigh himself before and after eating. In this book occur several aphorisms on old age (11).

> "*There is a great deal more perspired in youth than in old age; and the quantity of perspiration differs according to different constitutions, ways of living, climates and seasons.*"
>
> "*If you know what quantity of food you ought to take daily, and can adjust your exercise to it, you know how to preserve your health to old age.*"
>
> "*Violent exercise of body and mind persisted in brings on an early old age, and a premature death.*"
>
> "*Old men are destroyed by indulgences (sexual) of this kind, which render them heavier, weaker and colder.*"

Revolutionary as were the techniques of Sanctorius in applying quantitative methods to medical problems, he had been anticipated a century and a half earlier by Nicholas Cusanus (1401-1464), Cardinal and Bishop of Brixen (12). This brilliant thinker in his *De staticis experimentis*, published in 1450, proposed to weigh the urine and blood and to evaluate the pulse rate by weighing the amount of water collected from a dropper-device while counting a standard number of beats. He believed that these methods would show marked differences in health and disease, in youth and in old age, and further, would have practical value.

On an entirely different level of medical endeavor, one that the eminent Lord Verulam would no doubt have found "less noble", we encounter Tobias Venner (1577-1660), "Doctor of Physicke at Bathe in the Spring and Fall, and at other times in the Borough of North-Petherton neere to the ancient Haven-Towne of Bridgewater in Somersetshire." Thus reads his address on the title

FIG. 3. Tobias Venner (1577-1660). This portrait at the age of 85 years indicates a state of well-being rivalling that of Cornaro whose regimen did not include whiskey. (Reproduced from print in the collection of The Home for Aged and Infirm Hebrews, New York.)

page of his curious work, *Via Recta ad Vitam Longam* (13), justly renowned for its ardent advocacy of whiskey for old age and other ills.

> "Now to the question I answer that for the most part there is not any water in use, which can better fortifie life and hinder the coming on of old age, than the aforesayd Aqua vitae; for it greatly comforteth a weak stomack, expelleth winde, putteth off all melancholike passions, preserveth the humours from corruption and excellently prevaileth against swounding; for by reason of a notable penetrable power that it hath, it quickly goeth to the heart and wonderfully raiseth up faint and feeble spirits. But the use thereof is not alike wholesome and good for all bodies, for unto them that are leane, and of a dry nature, and in the Summer it is very pernicious be-

cause it drieth up and (as it were) scorcheth their inward parts, especially the liver and destroyeth the naturall moysture, but to old men, to grosse and moyst bodies, it is very profitable, for it fortifieth their stomacks, concocteth excrement and all humours, discusseth winde, and defendeth them from the lethargie, apoplexie and other cold diseases unto which by reason of their moyst habit of body, they are very subject."

In an effort to limit the scope of this study we pass over the great achievements of the medical microscopists, Van Leevenhoeck (1632-1723), Malpighi (1628-1694) and De Graaf (1646-1673), to call to attention the beginning of vital statistics in England in the work of John Graunt (1620-1674), on the *Naturall and Political Observations upon the Bills of Mortality* (London, 1662), of Sir William Petty (1623-1689) who took the first census of Ireland and wrote *Essays on Political Arithmetic* (1687), and of the astronomer, Edmund Halley (1656-1742) who compiled the Breslau Table of births and funerals (1693). From these pioneer efforts gradually arose the great statistical studies furthered by governmental and private agencies that carry such weight in modern studies of life and death, as exemplified in the work of the late Raymond Pearl and in the publications of Dr. Louis Dublin.

In the field of clinical medicine we have such leaders as Thomas Sydenham (1624-1689), abnormally individualistic in his attitude to his medical predecessors and his colleagues but likewise abnormally gifted in the observation and differentiation of disease. In both his work on gout and on fevers he refers to the peculiar reactions of the old.

"But in aged persons, affected either with autumnal tertians or quartans, there is danger of these diseases becoming not only obstinate but mortal; for which reason, if the bark and every other method prove ineffectual to a cure, nature must at least be supplied with such helps, as may enable her to finish her work."

"In many persons the gout breeds the stone in the kidneys. It seldom attacks women, and only the aged of this sex, and those of a masculine habit of body. Children and young persons rarely have it." (*14*).

Thomas Willis (1621-1675) made significant contributions to the anatomy of the central nervous system, first describing the eleventh cranial nerve, to which his name is sometimes given, and pointing out the grouping of the arteries at the base of the brain which has ever since been known eponymically. Of all his notable achievements the most practical and important was the discovery that diabetic urine has a sweet taste, thus laying the foundation for the study of one of the most important diseases afflicting mankind and especially prevalent in the later years.

In this connection, it should be noted that Frederick Dekkers of Leyden in 1694 first detected albumin in urine in the presence of acetic acid. In pathology the work of Raymond Vieussens (1641-1716) of Montpellier in describing the course of the coronary arteries and the clinical picture as well as the pathology of mitral stenosis and aortic insufficiency, is outstanding. It is to be correlated with the work of Sylvius (1614-1672) on the nature of phthisis and of Lancisi (1654-1720) on the rôle of the heart in sudden death. Wepfer (1620-1695) of Schaffhausen in 1658 described the hemorrhagic brain lesion of apoplexy.

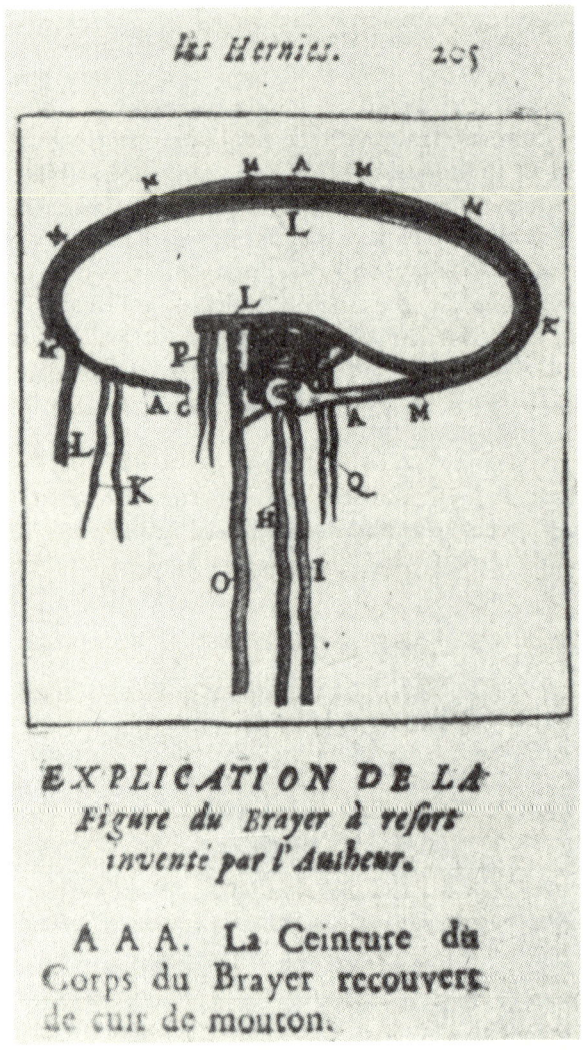

Fig. 4. The Elastic Truss of Nicolas de Blegny (reproduced from his *L'Art de Guerir les Hernies*, Paris, 1676, by courtesy of the Army Medical Library, Cleveland Branch.)

As for the medical specialties, mention must be made of the advancement of the physical theory of vision by Kepler the astronomer and Descartes the philosopher; by Marriotte (d. 1684) discoverer of the blind spot, and by the Jesuit astronomer Scheiner (d. 1650) who "illustrated accomodation and refraction by the pinhole test which bears his name" (15). The first book on dentistry in English was published by Charles Allen in 1686. Nicolas de Blegny (1652-

1722) invented the elastic truss, described in his treatise on hernia (1676). All of these advances have had particular meaning for those who have "so long marched hand in hand with time."

In reviewing the high lights of this highly productive period much has necessarily been omitted entirely and theoretical controversies have not been touched upon since they have not seemed germane to our theme. Many of the discoveries noted were of importance for the future of medicine and indicate the earliest observation of phenomena that only to-day are beginning to be understood. Garrison has drawn a vivid, fascinating picture of the cultural and social background of this period (16). As to the actual treatment of the old it seems likely that, in view of prevalent faith in magical remedies, such as the weapon-salve and Digby's "sympathetic powder", in astrology, in animal magnetism and in strange remedies of all descriptions, the aged fared badly whether they treated themselves or consulted physicians. The prevalence and frequency of blood-letting and the wide variety of conditions for which it was prescribed, make it evident that Dr. Sangrado of Le Sage's Gil Blas typified a large part of the profession in putting every possible obstacle in the way of the patient's recovery.

REFERENCES

1. For interesting comments on the medical aspects of Shakespeare, see:
    (a) Robin, P. A.: The Old Physiology in English Literature, London, 1911.
    (b) Sims, R. E.: The Green Old Age of Falstaff. Bull. Hist. Med., 13: 157, 1943.
2. Bacon, E.: Essays, and Colours of Good and Evil, W. A. Wright, London, Macmillan & Co., 1883.
3. Bacon, F.: History naturall and experimentall of Life and Death, or of the prolongation of life, London: for W. Lee and H. Mosely, 1650. This is an English translation of the Latin version, made under the direction of Dr. Rawley who wrote a life of Bacon.
4. Browne, Sir Thomas: Religio Medici, London, 1642.
5. MacKenzie, J.: History of Health, Edinburgh, Gordon, 1758.
6. Stendel, J.: Zur Geschichte der Lehre der Greisenkrankheiten, Sudhoff's Archiv. f. Geschichte d. Med. u. d. Naturwissen., 35: 12, 1942. As the result of difficulties in obtaining enemy publications, this excellent article did not come into the writer's hands until September, 1944.
7. Harvey, W.: Anatomical Examination of the Body of Thomas Parr. This account was first published in the work of Dr. Betts, entitled; "De Ortu et Natura Sanguinis", 8 vol., London, 1669, the MS. having been presented to Betts by Mr. Michael Harvey, nephew of the author.
8. For the first searching critique of the supercentenarian myths see: Thoms, W. J.: Human Longevity, Its Facts and Fictions, London, Murray, 1873.
9. Zeman, F. D.: The Pathological Anatomy of Old Age. An Historical Review, in preparation.
10. Stendel, J.: op. cit. p. 14.
11. Sanctorius, S.: Medicina Statica, or Rules of Health, London, 1676.
12. (a) Garrison, F. H.: History of Medicine, ed., 4, Philadelphia, W. B. Saunders Co., 1929, p. 259.
    (b) Mitchell, S. W.: The Early History of Instrumental Precision in Medicine, New Haven, 1892.

(c) GOTTFREDSEN, E.: Nicolaus Cusanus u. die Medizin, Muench. Med. Woch., 84: 1821, 1937.
13. VENNER, TOBIAS: Via Recta ad Vitam Longam, London, 1620.
14. SYDENHAM, T.: The Entire Works of.: ed. 2, revised by John Swan, M.D., London, 1749, p. 60 and p. 617.
15. GARRISON, F. H.: op. cit., p. 260.
16. Ibid. p. 304 et seq.

LIFE'S LATER YEARS

Studies in the Medical History of Old Age

FREDERIC D. ZEMAN, M.D.
[New York City]

PART 10[1]

THE EIGHTEENTH CENTURY

"But grant, the virtues of a temp'rate prime
Bless with an age exempt from scorn or crime;
An age that melts with unperceived decay,
And glides in modest Innocence away;
Whose peaceful day Benevolence endears,
Whose night congratulating Conscience cheers,
The gen'ral fav'rite as the gen'ral friend:
Such age there is, and who shall wish its end?"
Samuel Johnson—*The Vanity of Human Wishes.*

Although Garrison has characterized the Eighteenth Century as the "Age of Theories and Systems," and has described much of its thinking as "tedious and platitudinous philosophizing," we shall nevertheless find substantial achievements in the field of old age, such as the progress in pathological and clinical correlations, the increasing understanding of cardiac pathology, physiology and therapy, the rise of scientific surgery and dentistry, advances in ophthalmology and cerebral physiology, and finally an outstanding contribution to physical diagnosis (1). In addition we record the publication in 1724 of Sir John Floyer's *Medicina Gerocomica*, the first English work on old age (2), and in 1754 of Johann Bernhard von Fischer's pioneer book, *De senio eiusque gradibus et morbis* (3), in which the foundations were laid for the scientific approach to the problems of senescence and of disease in the aged.

Although the celebrated supercentenarian Thomas Parr died in 1635, Harvey's description of the post-mortem examination was not published until 1669, nine years after the death of the great physiologist (4). The influence of this classic necropsy was widespread and from time to time other post-mortem observations on the very old found their way into medical literature. In 1699 the French anatomist and surgeon, François Poupart (1616–1708) described the occurrence in a man aged 100 years, of marked spinal ankylosis, involving the nine lower vertebrae and characterized by extensive new bone formation (5). Dr. James Keill of Northampton, England, reported in 1706, "An Account of the Death and Dissection of John Bayles, of Northampton, Reputed to Have Been 130 Years Old" (6).

[1] This is the tenth in a series of articles dealing with Studies in the Medical History of Old Age. Upon completion of their publication, the installments will be collected and reprinted in a single volume, constituting one of the Series of Monographs of The Mount Sinai Hospital Press.—Ed.

In this paper Keill discussed his patient's habits, the evidence for his alleged age, and then described in detail his findings at the autopsy, comparing them frequently with those observed in Parr. He ascribed the fatal outcome to the weakness of Bayles' stomach, and to the hardness and dilatation of the aorta. In this connection, the keen physician, a worthy student of Harvey, made the following observation:

> "...and it was impossible that his blood could circulate duly while the great artery, having lost its elasticity, by being become cartilaginous, could give no motion to the blood: it is very probable that this was the cause of his irregular and intermittent pulse which I have felt some years before he died."

FIG. 1. Sir John Floyer (1649-1734). A line drawing, found in a volume in the Bodleian Library, said to be the only known portrait of Floyer.

This may well be the first description of the irregular pulse of auricular fibrillation in which the causative factor of arteriosclerosis was demonstrated postmortem. Keil believed that both Parr and Bayles owed their longevity to the strength of their hearts, the large size of their chests and the good quality of their lungs.

Scheuchzer, a Swiss physician and naturalist (1672-1733) published the clinical history and post-mortem findings in a man aged 109 years and 3 months. Here also the emphasis is laid on the marked arteriosclerosis, the aneurysmal dilatation of the aorta and the cartilaginous thickening of the aortic valve (7). Haller, the great physiologist, to whom we shall return later, recorded in 1747 the findings in a female centenarian (8). Cheselden (1688-1752) the renowned English surgeon, in his "Anatomy of the Human Body," first published in London in 1712, discussed the large size of the aorta in two men, each past the century mark and in one woman also of advanced age (9).

These isolated reports on the pathology of the aged indicate the widespread interest in the organic basis of disease that later found its highest expression in the work of Morgagni and Baillie. Before proceeding to these great figures we must break off to discuss other aspects of the medical interest in our theme, much of which, although of purely historical interest, serves nevertheless to round out the medical and social background of the period.

The unusual ability of Sir John Floyer (1649–1734) was first shown in his "Treatise on Asthma," published in 1698, which ascribes the disease to a "contraction of the bronchia" (10). In this work the post-mortem examination of a case of pulmonary emphysema was presented. He was an ardent advocate of the cold bath as a health promoting agent and advised its use in the treatment of disease. These views were set forth in "An Inquiry into the Right Use of the Hot, Cold and Temperature Baths in England" (11). Floyer was the first after Cusanus and Sanctorius to count the pulse (12) and is reputed to have been the earliest advocate of the use of mineral oil in constipation. Young Samuel Johnson's trip to London to be touched by Queene Anne for the "King's evil" was undertaken on Floyer's advice.

The *Medicina Gerocomica* or the "Galenic Art of Preserving Old Men's Healths," (1724) emphasized that old people are afflicted by characteristic forms of illness, which vary according to the individual constitution (13). For each type a different therapy is needed. Although his book is based on Galen, and all disease is ascribed to the *cacochymia*, or bad composition of the body fluids, Floyer's opinions are based on personal observations.

> "*Autumn and Winter are most injurious to old Men, whose Heat is weak, and the Circulation and the pulses are most stopt. In Spring and Summer they are the most healthful.... The florid and fat old men then are of a sanguine Constitution, and preserve that Temper, by avoiding all Excesses in the hot and cold Regimen. They are most healthful, and I reckon them in the middle of the acrid, chloeric, and salt tempers, which abound in the thin, hot old Men; and the pituitous and serous Humors and Slime, which appear in the cold, fat, pale, old Men.*" (12)

A contemporary of Floyer, George Cheyne (1671–1743) enjoyed the friendship of great physicians and of Samuel Richardson, the novelist. His popular reputation was large, in spite of the fact that he "preached temperance to an intemperate generation" (13). He was an extreme vegetarian; his own diet as well as that prescribed for his patients was chiefly vegetables and eggs. His views on diet and health were based on his personal experience, since his early excesses forced him to reform his way of life and to reduce his weight radically. His "Essay of Health and Long Life" achieved great popularity and ran to many editions, the 6th appearing in 1725 (14). The following paragraph is typical of Cheyne's viewpoint.

> "...*since 'tis certain aged Persons become Children, as to the weakness of their Digestions, they ought to diminish, as Children increase in their Food, from weaker to weaker, and from less to less. For as their Solids are unelastick, their concoctive Powders weak, their Perspiration little, and the Ex-*

penses of living scarce any, their Repairs (not to overlay the Spark of Life remaining) ought to lessen proportionally. And 'tis to the Neglect of this, in aged Persons that those Rheums, Catarrhs, Winds and Colicks, Loss of Memory and Senses, their Aches and Pains, and all that dismal and black Train of Miseries that wait on Long Life, is mostly owing. Which by a discreet and timeous lessening of their Diet, might, in a great measure be prevented."

Cheyne's book "The English Malady," was concerned with nervous diseases, spleen, vapors, and lowness of spirits, and contains much autobiographical material (15).

FIG. 2. George Cheyne (1671-1743)

Still another work on the hygiene of old age, *De Aetate Vergente Liber* (16), was published in 1724 by Dr. Robert Welsted (1671-1735). The author, holder of degrees from Oxford and Fellow of the Royal Society, was an industrious writer on medical and scholarly topics, but in this work is content to reiterate the admonitions against overeating and excessive drinking that Galen and the Arab physicians had impressed so deeply on medical thinking many hundreds of years before.

The celebrated Richard Meade (1673-1754), who inherited from Radcliffe the famous gold-headed cane, discussed old age in his *Monita et Precepta Medica* (1751) in the form of opinions whose source is likewise obvious.

> *"The frigidity of men advanced in years is a faithful monitor that points out to them the folly of forcing themselves to exert a vigor which they have lost, vainly expecting raptures, but finding only irksome labor which will shorten their days."*(17)

Meade's *Medica Sacra* or "A Commentary on the most remarkable Diseases mentioned in the Holy Scriptures," appeared in 1749 when he was in his 77th year, and in the preface he stated that the book resulted from his efforts "to pass his leisure pleasantly for himself and not useless for others." In Chapter VI, entitled the "Disease of Old Age," we find an ingenious interpretation of the famous twelfth chapter of Ecclesiastes. In an interesting essay, the late Sir Humphrey Rolleston compared Meade's version of these lines with that of many other commentators (18).

The earnest bibliographer in the field of old age will eventually encounter a reference to Dr. John Hill's "The Old Man's Guide to Health and Long Life" (19). Lest any time be wasted on this worthy, who also wrote "On the Virtues of Sage in Lengthening Human Life, with Rules to attain a Long Life" (20), we quote the summation of Hill's character to be found in the Dictionary of National Biography: "a versatile man of unscrupulous character, with considerable abilities, great perseverance and unlimited impudence" (21).

In the works of the great Dutch clinician and teacher, Hermann Boerhaave (1668–1738), there are only occasional references to old age as a medical problem. In the English translation of his famous aphorisms, we find in No. 1015 the following: "The greatness of an Apoplexy is therefore measured by the Age, Constitution and Make-up of the Patient" (22). In the commentary of the English translator on the aphorism devoted to urethral stone, we find a fascinating clinical recital, with a most unusual course and a happy ending.

> *"About ten years ago I was called to the late Sir William Langhorn, at Charleton in Kent, then aged Eighty-one, who had made no water for above thirty-six Hours. Whilst I sent an Express away to the late Dr. Cyprianus, I endeavored by all possible means to remove the stone out of the urethra; but finding it impossible, and that the old Knight was in a Lethargy, and all his lower Belly and Genitals burning hot, I sent in haste for the nearest Surgeon. We cut through the Penis longways into the Urethra, and let out the Stone; upon which the Urine flow'd abundantly, and he recovered well enough so as about three years afterward to be married to a young Girl of Fourteen; and, as they say, to consummate the Marriage. The Wound was cured in a few days with Unguentum Apostolorum."*(23)

Gerhard van Swieten (1700–1772), Boerhaave's most famous disciple, is noted as the founder of clinical instruction in Vienna, where he taught for many years. He introduced the use of mercuric chloride in the treatment of syphilis, and is remembered for his works on military medicine and for his commentaries on Boerhaave's aphorisms. In his *De senum Valetudine tuenda*, an address given at a university celebration, he recognized the age changes in the blood vessels and described shrinkage of the intervertebral discs, but at the same time repeated Galen's dicta on the dryness and coldness of the aging body. His hygienic and dietetic advice is entirely based on Galen, but he attacked such remedies for a long life as the heartbone of the deer and the flesh of mummies. He is pessimistic about the value of treatment in old people (24).

Among Boerhaave's students may also be reckoned Johann Heinrich Cohausen (1665-1750) who after extensive studies at the universities of Leyden, Amsterdam and probably Bordeaux, settled in Coesfeld, the summer residence of the Lord Bishop of Munster. Here, in 1699, he attracted the attention of the court by his book *Tentaminum physico-medicorum curiosa de vita humana theoretice et practice per Pharmaciam prolonganda Decas*, a learned review of all the efforts of mankind to lengthen life and to find means against death and disease (25). This early work is of significance only as it makes clear that the subject of longevity was a life-long interest of Cohausen, for in 1740, he wrote "*Hermippus Redivivus*" (26), which was based on a Roman tomb inscription, ascribing the advanced age, 114 years, of the deceased Hermippus to inhaling the breath of young girls. Cohausen with deliberate humor, conjures up a picture of the old Roman as a teacher in a young ladies seminary, and from there goes on to discuss David and Abishag as well as other instances in history and literature, both ancient and more recent, where odors and other sensations of many kinds seemed to refresh and comfort. Cohausen's concluding words made his purpose clear. "That I at my age should spend my time with the girls, no matter how properly god-like, neither my love of life nor my fear of death would bring me. At all events let no one take as serious medical advice that I have presented here about the exhalations and expirations of young women, but it is to be looked upon only as the last exercise of an old man to bring out that nothing is so improbable that it cannot be explained neatly and deceive the credulous with the appearance of truth, even stimulate them to imitation in hope of a long life." The book in spite of the author's avowal that it was "the recreation of an old man" was received with great seriousness and translated into several languages. The English version by the Scottish scholar, John Campbell, appeared in 1743 and was reprinted in 1749 with many additions by the translator. Of Campbell's version of Hermippus, Dr. Johnson pronounced the volume "very entertaining as an account of the hermetic philosophy and as furnishing a curious history of the extravagancies of the human mind; adding, "if it were merely imaginary it would be nothing at all" (27).

To Johann Bernhard von Fischer (1685-1772) goes the credit for the first medical work on old age to break away from medieval tradition and to attempt an approach to the problem in the modern spirit. His *De senio ciusque gradibus et morbis* (3), first published at Erfurt in 1754, vigorously attacked the prevailing medical pessimism about the aged, and emphasized in his introduction that he would prove the efficacy of therapy with actual cases. The author was persona physician to the Empress Anna Ivanovna and general director of Russian medi cal institutions. He was an active administrator, encouraging the foundation of new medical schools, and the preparation of texts to be used in the instruction of students. He served in Russia with great distinction from 1734 to 1742, and then returned to the practice of medicine in Riga, his birthplace.

The first part of the book Fischer devotes to the anatomy and physiology of old age, undertaking to differentiate normal and pathological aging and stressing the need for post-mortems to clarify these problems. His judgment is based on his own necropsies. As characteristic accompaniments of old age he lists the dilatation of the heart and aorta, the calcification of the smaller vessels, the firmness of the brain and the hardness of the glands, the absence of changes in

FIG. 3. Giovanni Battista Morgagni (1681-1771)

the lungs, the cartilaginous thickening of the splenic capsule, and the degeneration of the bones. He describes the characteristics of the respiration, pulse, sleep, nutrition and excretion. The second chapter is devoted to the diseases and their treatment. In the third he gives general rules of hygiene to be followed by the old. Steudel points out that to evaluate Fischer's work properly one must realize that it antedated Morgagni's *De sedibus et causis morborum* by seven years and that volume eight of Haller's *Elementa physiologiae corporis humani*, in which old age was discussed, did not appear until 1766. Von Fischer seems therefore to deserve consideration as the real pioneer of our present day attitudes, rather than Canstatt to whose book, first published in 1839, this honor has often been accorded in the past (28).

The famous Swiss physiologist, Albrecht von Haller (1708-1777), noted as a

German poet as well as for his medical contributions, gave evidence of his interest in old age on several occasions. In 1747 he published the post-mortem findings in a woman, aged 100 years (8) in whom were found aneurysmal dilatation of the aorta, stony hard excrescences and thickening of the aortic valves, arteriosclerotic changes in the aorta and its branches, and gall-stones. Haller's idea of the pathogenesis of arteriosclerosis is of great interest, since this publication antedated Scarpa.

> *"This...shows that the inner lining of the arteries as a result of continually repeated shocks of the heart finally becomes partially hardened, in part becomes torn between the ossified areas that the stem of the aorta is weakened and disposed to aneurysm formation. The autopsy shows that the blood carries with it everywhere true chalk particles, which may not only be deposited in the kidneys, but get caught and accumulate where the finest membranes are torn, and the attraction of chalk particles for rough uneven surfaces is greater than for smoother surfaces."*

This surprisingly well thought out description of both the chemical and mechanical factors in vascular sclerosis is further documented in Haller's "Pathological Observations" (1756) in which the gross changes in senile arteriosclerosis of the aorta are illustrated (29). Finally, in his famous *Elementa physiologiae corporis humani*, published in eight volumes in the years 1757 to 1763, one chapter is devoted to a discussion of the aging process, emphasizing both the physical and the mental changes (30).

> *"The rigidity of the whole body, the decrease of the muscular powers, and the diminution of the senses, constitute old age; which sooner, or later, oppresses mortals severely; sooner, if subjected to violent labor, or addicted to pleasure, or fed upon an unwholesome diet; but more slowly, if they have lived quietly and temperately, or if they have removed from a cold to a warm climate."*

Worthy of mention are Albertini (1762–1833), the teacher of Morgagni and a student of cardiac symptomatology and pathology, and de Senac (1693–1770), whose two volume work, *Traite de la structure du coeur, de son action, et de ses maladies* is a landmark in cardiology. In it the author stressed such physical signs of heart disease as dilatation and pulsation of the cervical veins, the pulsations of the cervical arteries, irregular heart action, the appearance of cardiac aneurysm and coronary artery sclerosis (31).

The active interest manifested by physicians both in Great Britain and on the continent in tracing the signs of disease through life and in seeking the explanation after death found its most authoritative and understanding expression in the *De sedibus et causis morborum* of Giovanni Battista Morgagni (1681–1771), published in 1761, when he was himself 79 years old, and embodied the accumulated experience of more than 50 years (32). According to Herrick, "The significance of Morgagni is seen when we realize that he was the efficient proponent of the method of diagnosing and explaining disease in terms of pathologic anatomy that gradually became more and more prevalent, especially after its adoption by Corvisart and Laennec, a method that for several decades was the one in general use and which to-day still bulks large in the practice of medicine" (33). For the student of old age Morgagni's work is full of examples of the various maladies that afflict the old, as the result of trauma as well as of disease. In the section devoted to apoplexy nearly all the patients are advanced in years. Here we find the celebrated case of the Cardinal Francesco Sanvitalis, aged 55, in whom Morgagni points out that the principal lesion was in the right side of the brain, while the paralysis resulting from it was on the opposite side. Many cases of aortic and cardiac aneurysms are described. Diaphragmatic hernia is divided into congenital and acquired types. Cholelithiasis and various new growths likewise are noted.

In Great Britain the vivid description of the clinical picture of angina pectoris published in 1768 by William Heberden the Elder (1710-1801) stimulated others to seek the cause of this striking symptom complex. John Fothergill (1712-1783) had post-mortems done on two of his patients with angina. In the necropsy on the second patient, a man aged 63 years, performed by John Hunter himself, the heart was "of ligamentous consistence and in many parts of the left ventricle almost white and hard.... The two coronary arteries from their origin to many of their ramifications upon the heart were become one piece of bone" (34). The association of angina pectoris and coronary disease was well known to Edward Jenner (1749-1823) of smallpox fame and Caleb Hillier Parry (1755-1822) of thyrotoxicosis renown, who predicted the vascular changes ante-mortem in the case of John Hunter himself, and proved the point at his death in 1793. This striking correlation of clinical manifestations and post-mortem findings was unappreciated and neglected for over 100 years, until, as Dock (35) has traced, the work of many clinicians including Herrick's conclusive contribution (36) finally made evident to physicians that coronary thrombosis occurred commonly and could be diagnosed accurately.

John Fothergill, who was an intelligent, highly successful and well beloved practitioner, re-enters the present narrative by reason of his work, published in 1762, entitled "Rules for the Preservation of Health, containing all that has been recommended by the most eminent Physicians, with the earliest Prescriptions for most Disorders incident to Mankind, through the Four different Periods of Human Life, being the Result of Many Years Practice" (37). This book is distinguished more by good sense than originality. Galen and Welsted are quoted approvingly, and emphasis is laid on the importance of diet, rest and mental calm and cheerfulness, the latter being helped by seeking the society of young people.

In stressing the advances of pathological anatomy, one must not overlook the progress in physiology. The chemical discoveries of Scheele, Priestly, Cavendish, Black and Lavoisier overthrew the old phlogiston theory and established the role of oxygen in respiration and fundamental bodily processes. Stephen Hales (1677-1761) in his *Hemodynamics* was the first to measure blood-pressure by inserting a glass tube into the carotid artery of a horse. The French school of neurologic surgeons, Du Petit (1664–1771), Lorry (1725–1783) and Saucerotte (1741–1814) made great advances in clarifying the functions of the brain and spinal cord. General surgery and dentistry were elevated to positions of standing in science by the work of John Hunter and his school. The introduction of digitalis by Withering, and his explanation of its proper mode of employment gave physicians a potent remedy in heart failure. Ophthalmology was advanced by the work of Daviel (1696–1762), originator of the modern surgical treatment of cataract, O'Halloran's (1728–1807) contribution to the study of glaucoma, and by Young's (1773–1829) description of astigmatism and the nature of accommodation. Increasing understanding of the structure and function of the ear by Valsalva and Scarpa led to improved methods of treating deafness and other ear disturbances.

In the field of internal medicine relating to the diseases common to old age, we call attention to Wollaston's discovery of urates in gouty joints, and Dobson's proof that the sweetness of the urine and blood serum in diabetes, first noted by Willis, was due to sugar. Rollo advocated and reported great success with a meat diet in diabetes. Of great significance for personal hygiene was the publication of Johann Zacharrias Platner's (1694–1747) *"Treatise on Cleanliness,"* in which he pointed out that the body reabsorbs the impurities from soiled clothing and that these provide a basis for disease by penetrating the fluids of the body. He also advised frequent change of underwear, and of the bed-linen of the sick (38).

In 1761 Leopold Auenbrugger published his classic *"Inventum novum,"* in which he described the method of percussion and its practical application to the diagnosis of chest diseases (39). This remarkable contribution to physical diagnosis was neglected by his contemporaries and might have been entirely forgotten had it not been for Corvisart, the forceful French clinician, who in 1808 took up Auenbrugger's method and gave to it his enthusiastic endorsement. Herrick has recently discussed the reasons for the long neglect of this great medical innovation, pointing out that not the least of the many factors operating was the unpleasant personality of the discoverer himself (40). Auenbrugger's clinical experience in the use of percussion is indicated by his direct reference to its interpretation of the diseases of old age. In discussing the absence of abnormal sounds in certain coughs and asthmas, which he ascribes to irritability of the nerves of the chest, he includes specifically "the nervous consumption and asthma of old persons." Elsewhere in discussing acute cardiac dilatation, where the enlargement of the area of precordial dullness can be demonstrated by percussion, he draws a vivid picture of the patient's appearance shortly before death, and points out that, "in contrast with the young, older persons, indeed, bear more tranquilly their sufferings." These passing references to the peculiarities of the aged serve to remind us once more that, in every period of medical development, contact with the pressing problems of sick old people has been an unavoidable part of every physician's experience.

The continuing stream of popular works on old age, devoted to much the same topics as were discussed by Galen and the Arab physicians, indicates a sound cumulative realization that old age is to some extent what the individual makes it, and that moderation in all things tends to prevent or at least postpone many of the unpleasant features commonly associated with senescence. Christian Wilhelm Hufeland (1762-1836) was at one time a member of the Weimar group that included Goethe and Schiller. A man of wide interests, of great human sympathy and an enthusiastic medical teacher, he left a deep imprint on German medicine, founding journals and, as professor at Berlin, making important improvements in methods of teaching. His book, entitled *Makrobiotik, oder die Kunst das menschliche Leben zu verlaengern*, appeared in 1796, and was translated into English and all the continental tongues (41). One American edition ap-

FIG. 4. Christian Wilhelm Hufeland (1762-1836)

peared as late as 1854. It is a well written work, sympathetic, optimistic and covers a wide field of topics. While in no sense original, its message is expressed in such a delightful way that its popularity is easily understood.

As a result of the persistence of the medieval university organization into the four faculties of theology, philosophy, law and medicine, the only pathway to the natural sciences lay through the study of medicine. The foundations of geology, mineralogy, physics, chemistry and botany were in many cases laid by gifted men trained as physicians. The converse, the contributions of non-medical individuals to medicine, is far less commonly encountered. Easily in the first rank of medical amateurs stands Benjamin Franklin (1706-1790). A study of his broad accomplishments is not in order here, but the reader will recall his substantial additions to the welfare of the elderly, such as the flexible catheter and the bifocal lens, as well as his studies on the ventilation and heating of houses (42).

Franklin's personal physician was the illustrious Benjamin Rush of Philadelphia (1745–1813), noted not only as a practitioner and teacher, but also for his active participation in politics and his leadership in matters of communal welfare. His writings cover a wide range of medical topics, including insanity and old age. In his work on the diseases of the mind, he does not seem to have recognized any specific type of mental disease in the aged, stating that "there is greater predisposition to madness between twenty and fifty than in any of the previous or subsequent years of human life." He gives several exceptions to

FIG. 5. Benjamin Rush (1745–1813)

this rule from his own experience, and attempts in the following quotation to explain the freedom of the aged from acute manic seizures.

> *"There are two reasons why this disease so rarely attacks old people. Their blood vessels lose their vibratility from age, and hence, they are less liable to fevers than in middle life; and from the diminution of sensibility in their nerves and brains, the causes of madness make but a feeble and transient impression upon their minds. In the latter condition of their bodies, they revert to that state which takes place in children and which I have said protects them from frequent occurrence of this disease."* (43)

His "Account of the State of the Body and Mind in Old Age, with observation on its diseases and their remedies" (1793) was the first American contribution to the subject, and was acclaimed both in this country, in England, and on the continent where it was widely circulated in translation. It is a simple direct little essay, based entirely on the author's own observations and a few authorities, to whom he gives full credit. A noteworthy feature is his reference to many of his distinguished patients by name. Dr. Franklin, we are told, "had two successive vomicas in his lungs before he was 40 years old." "Dr. Franklin informed me, that he recognized his friends after a long absence from them, first by their voices." "Dr. Franklin owed much of the cheerfulness and general vigor of body and mind, which characterized his old age, to his regular use of this remedy (the warm bath)." "An inflammation of the lungs, which terminated in an abscess, deprived the world of Dr. Franklin."

This is a practical work, well worth reading to-day, for its sharp comment and sound observations concerning the physical and mental characteristics of the aged, including such items as the broad gait, the failing memory, the eccentricities of appetite, the dysuria, the emotional disturbances and the lack of a fear of death. The clinical insight of Benjamin Rush into the problems of old age formed the foundation for the further pursuit of knowledge in this extensive field in the New World. In like manner it serves as a fitting conclusion to the accomplishments of one century and as an inspiring introduction to the greatest century of medical achievement yet recorded.

BIBLIOGRAPHY

(1) Garrison, F. F.: An Introduction to the History of Medicine, ed. 4, Philadelphia, Saunders, 1929, p. 310.
(2) Floyer, Sir J.: Medicina Gerocomica, or the galenic art of preserving old men's healths, explain'd in twenty chapters. To which is added an appendix concerning the use of oyls and unction in the prevention and cure of some diseases. As also a method from a Florentine physician of curing convulsions and epilepsies, by external operation. London, J. Isted, 1724.
(3) von Fischer, J. H.: De senio eiusque gradibus et morbis. Erfurt, 1754, ed. 2, 1760. German translation, Leipzig, 1777.
(4) The first publication of Harvey's autopsy on Thomas Parr, was in De Ortu et Natura Sanguinis, London, 1669, by Dr. Betts, to whom the manuscript had been presented by Harvey's nephew.
(5) Poupart, F.: Hist. de l'acad. royale des sciences. Annee 1699. Avec les memoires de Mathemat. et de Phys. pour la même annee, p. 50.
(6) Keill, J.: Phil. Trans. Royal Society, 25: 306, 2247, 1706. Abridged, vol. 5, (1703-1712), London, 1809.
(7) Scheuchzer, J. J.: Acta Vratislaviensa, p. 189, 1724. See also Phil. Trans Royal Society, 376: 313, March, 1723.
(8) Haller, A.: Observationes duae fabricae morbosae in cadaveribus repertae. Phil. Trans. Royal Society, 44: 483, 528, 1747.
(9) Cheselden, W.: The Anatomy of the Human Body, London, 1713. The 13th ed. appeared in 1792.
(10) Floyer, Sir J.: A Treatise of the Asthma, divided into four parts. In the first is given a history of the fits and symptoms preceding them; in the second, the cacochymia, which disposes to the fit, and the rarefaction of the spirits which produces it are described; in the third the accidental causes of the fit are observed; in the fourth the cure of the asthma fits and the method of preventing it is propos'd. ed. 2, London, R. Wilkins & W. & J. Innys, 1717.

(11) FLOYER, SIR J.: The ancient ΨΥΧΡΟΛΟΤΣΙΑ revived, or an essay to prove cold bathing both safe and useful. In four letters, London, S. Smith and B. Walford, 1702.
(12) FLOYER, SIR J.: The Physician's Pulse Watch, London, S. Smith and B. Walford, 1707.
(13) CHEYNE, G.: An Essay of Health and Long Life, London, G. Strahan, 1724.
(14) CHEYNE, G.: Article in Dictionary of National Biography, London, H. Milford, 1917, vol. 9.
(15) CHEYNE, G.: The English Malady, or a treatise of nervous diseases of all kinds, as spleen, vapours, lowness of spirits, hypochondriacal and hysterical distempers, etc., London, S. Powell, G. Risk, G. Ewing & W. Smith, 1733.
(16) WELSTED, R.: De Aetate Vergente Liber, London, 1724.
(17) MEADE, R.: Monita et precepta medica, London, J. Brindley, 1751.
(18) ROLLESTON, SIR, H. D.: Medical Aspects of Old Age, London, Macmillan, 1932. See Chap. 7—The description of old age in the twelfth chapter of Ecclesiastes.
(19) HILL, J.: The Old Man's Guide to Health and Long Life, London, 1761.
(20) HILL, J.: On the Virtues of Sage in Lengthening Human Life. With Rules to attain old Age, London, 1763.
(21) Dictionary of National Biography, London, H. Milford, 1917, vol. 9, p. 848.
(22) BOERHAAVE, H.: Aphorisms Concerning the Knowledge and Cure of Diseases. From the last edition printed in Latin at Leyden, 1728, with useful observations and explanations, London, 1742.
(23) BOERHAAVE, H.: op. cit., aphorism 1440.
(24) STEUDEL, J.: Zur Geschichte der Lehre von den Greisenkrankheiten. Sudhoff's Archiv. f. Geschichte d. Med. u. Naturwiss., 35: 1, 27, 1942.
(25) COHAUSEN, J. H.: Tentaminum physico-medicorum curiosa de vita humana theoretice et practice per Pharmaciam prolonganda decas. Coesfeld, 1699.
(26) COHAUSEN, J. H.: Hermippus Redivivus, or the sage's triumph over the grave, London, 1744.
(27) For additional material on this writer see following:
BEAUVOIS, A.: Un practicien allemand au xviiieme siecle. Jean-Henri Cohausen, 1665–1750, Paris, 1900.
PAAL, H.: Johan Heinrich Cohausen, 1665–1750, Leben u. Schriften eines bedeutenden Arztes aus der Bluetezeit des Hochstiftes Muenster, mit Kulturhistorischen Betrachtungen, Jena, Fischer, 1931.
(28) For further information on von Fischer, see the following:
RICHTER, W. M.: Geschichte der Medizin in Russland, Moscow, 1813–17, Vol. 3, p. 270–79.
Biographisches Lexicon, Berlin, Urban u. Schwarzenburg, 1932, vol. 2, p. 225.
(29) HALLER, A.: Pathological Observations, chiefly from the dissections of morbid bodies, London, D. Wilson and T. Darham, 1756.
(30) HALLER, A.: Elementa physiologiae corporis humani. 8 vols., Lausanne, vol. 1–5, 1757–1763. Vols. 6–8, Berne, 1764–66.
(31) DE SENAC, J. B.: Traité de la structure du coeur, de son action et de ses maladies. 2 vols., Paris, J. Vincent, 1749.
(32) MORGAGNI, G. B.: De sedibus et causis morborum, Venice, 1761.
(33) HERRICK, J. B.: A Short History of Cardiology, Springfield, Thomas, 1942.
(34) FOTHERGILL, J.: Works with Life and Notes by John Elliott, London, 1781. Angina cases, pp. 508 and 529.
(35) DOCK, G.: Historical Notes on Coronary Occlusion, from Heberden to Osler, J. A. M. A., 113: 563–568, 1939.
(36) HERRICK, J. B.: Clinical Features of Sudden Occlusion of the Coronary Artery, J. A. M. A., 59: 2015–2020, 1912.
(37) FOTHERGILL, J.: Rules for the Preservation of Health, London, M. Thrush, 1762.
(38) JENNY, J. J.: Problems of Clothing Hygiene, Ciba Symposia, 6: 1978–1984, 1944.

(39) On Percussion of the Chest, Being a Translation of Auenbrugger's Original Treatise, entitled "inventum novum ex percussione thoracis humani, ut signo interni pectoris morbos detegendi." (Vienna, 1761) Baltimore, the Johns Hopkins Press, 1936.
(40) HERRICK, J. B.: A Note Concerning the Long Neglect of Auenbrugger's "Inventum Novum." Arch. Int. Med., 71: 741–748, 1943.
(41) HUFELAND, C. W.: Die Kunst das Menschliche Leben zu Verlaengern, Jena, 1797.
(42) FRANKLIN, B.: The writings of, edited by Albert Henry Smythe, New York, Macmillan, 1907.
(43) RUSH, B.: Medical Inquiries and Observations upon the Diseases of the Mind, ed. 3, Philadelphia, Grigg, 1827.
(44) RUSH, B.: An Account of the State of Body and Mind in Old Age, with observations on its diseases and their remedies. In "Medical Inquiries and Observations," Philadelphia, 1793, vol. 2.

LIFE'S LATER YEARS

Studies in the Medical History of Old Age

FREDERIC D. ZEMAN, M.D.

[New York City]

Part XI*

THE NINETEENTH CENTURY

"When life has been well spent, age is a loss of what it can well spare,— muscular strength, organic instincts, gross bulk and work that belongs to these. But the central wisdom, which was old in infancy, is young at fourscore years, and dropping off obstructions, leaves in happy subjects, the mind purified and wise. I have heard that whoever loves is in no condition old...."
Emerson-Essay on Old Age.

The anatomists of the Renaissance taught physicians to study the structure of the human body. Harvey's great discovery revealed the fundamental truths of bodily function. The observation of structure and function both at the bedside and at the autopsy table led to the recognition of specific disease states, and by means of clinico-pathological correlations made possible the attempt at accurate ante-mortem diagnosis. The work of Morgagni was carried forward vigorously in the 19th century, and aided by stimulating biological concepts and methods of precision, furnished the groundwork for searching studies of the pathogenesis of all types of maladies. These efforts were crowned by the detection of the microscopic living agents of many diseases and finally by the development of methods of specific cure and prevention. These discoveries not only revolutionized medical thinking but altered the way of life of all civilized nations to such a degree that the death rate among children and young adults began to recede measurably. Longer and heathier life was assured to mankind.

In the understanding and the treatment of the aged sick the rapid advances of medicine had broad effects, leading to establishment of sound theoretical viewpoints, more careful observations and to the publishing of at least five major works and innumerable briefer contributions to the problem. The greatest activity is to be noted in the first sixty years of the century. Later the revelations of modern bacteriology and immunology seem to have absorbed the time and interest of all physicians who busied themselves in clinical research. The old profited in no small measure from the improvement in public hygiene, and were the particular beneficiaries of Listerian and aseptic surgery.

The pre-eminence of French medicine in the latter part of the 18th century and the first sixty or seventy years of the 19th is well known, and is to be explained

---

*This is the eleventh in a series of articles dealing with Studies in the Medical History of Old Age. Upon completion of their publication, the installments will be collected and reprinted in a single volume, constituting one of the Series of Monographs of The Mount Sinai Hospital Press.-Ed.

by the interest of Gallic investigators in fundamental chemical and physical studies as well as their practical applications. Lavoisier's discovery of the role of oxygen in combustion in 1775 and the application of this principle to respiration paved the way for the great physiological schools of Magendie and Claude-Bernard. Even the therapeutic excesses of Broussais and Bouillaud did not prevent these men from advancing medical thinking. The roster of famous French physicians in the early 1800's is in itself impressive, including Laennec (1781–1826), Bayle (1774–1816), Bretonneau (1771–1862), Louis (1787–1872).

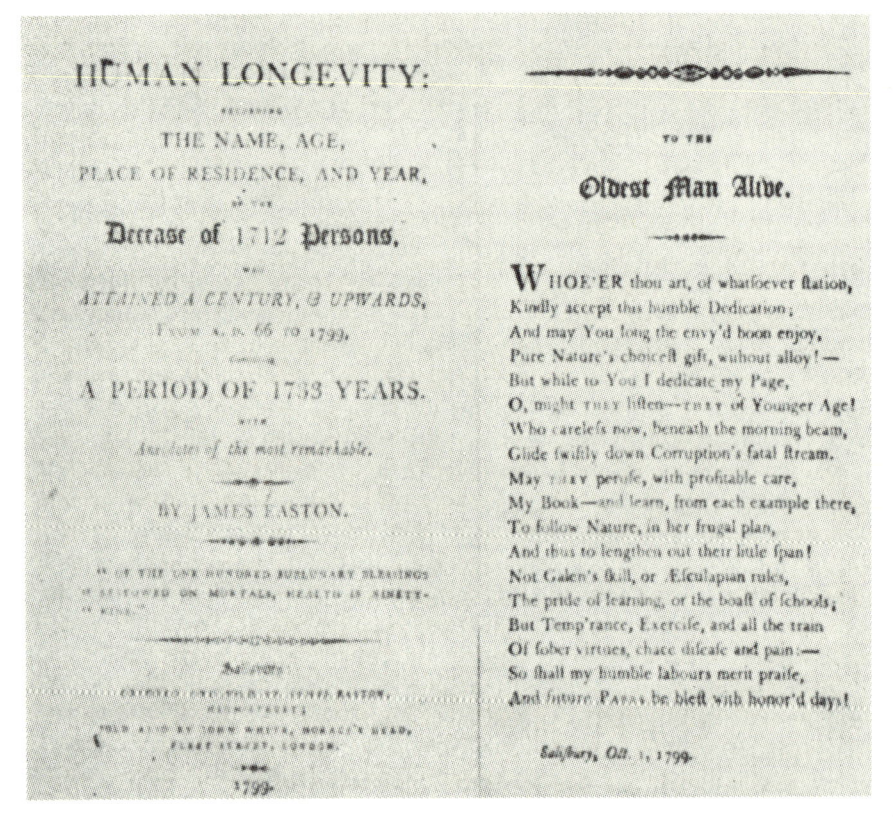

FIG. 1. Title page and Dedicatory Poem of Easton's curious work on Longevity, which reminds us of the fascination exerted by the centenarian on the popular mind.

Andral (1797–1876), Piorry (1794–1879), Pinel (1745–1826), Corvisart (1755–1821), Cruveilhier (1791–1873), Ricord (1799–1889) and Rayer (1793–1867)

That the Paris physicians devoted so much of their time to the study of the old is due to the fact that two of the city's most active centers of medical research were the Salpêtrière (1) and the Bicêtre (2), both hospices for the aged. They had been established by the decree of Louis XIV in 1656 as parts of the Hôpital-General which comprised, in addition, the institutions of the Pitié, the Réfuge and the Savonnerie. The Sâlpetrière, which derives its name from its previous use as a saltpeter factory, was used for women: prisoners, insane, aged and sick, all being housed under its broad roofs. The Bicêtre served the same mixed purposes for men. According to Guillain and Mathieu, "recalling the history of the Salpêtrière is to recall the history of three centuries of Paris." "Refuge of thousands of aged, great center of neurology, great center of psychiatry, the Salpêtrière has only become adapted to its actual role by stages. It has seen within its walls the men of the 17th, 18th, 19th and 20th centuries according to their successive conceptions, attempt to resolve the great problems of public and private charity, of aid to the poor and the aged, of the protection of society against the insane and the defective, of the protection of the insane and defective against society; it has seen...the creation of scientific psychiatry. The birth

FIG. 2. Interior Court of the Salpêtrière in Paris, with a view of the dome of the chapel in the distance.

and development of French neurology are inseparable from the name of the Salpêtrière" (3).

Since these institutions were built for the housing of three or four thousand inmates each, it can be easily understood that clinical material of great variety was never lacking. The Bicêtre is justly famous as the place where on May 24th, 1798 Philippe Pinel removed the chains from the insane and initiated the humane treatment of the mentally sick. Although his text book of insanity is to-day a medical classic, he also wrote about old age. His remarks on senile asthenia, written in 1812 and published posthumously by his son in 1823, emphasize that this condition is not a clinical entity but one found in a great variety of senile disorders, some of which he discusses briefly (4).

In addition to the easy access to the clinical material of these great institutions for the aged, another factor determining the attitude of French physicians must be pointed out. Marie-François-Xavier Bichat (1771-1802) has been described by Garrison as "the creator of descriptive anatomy" (5) because of his original contributions to this subject. His *"Recherches Physiologiques sur la Vie et la Mort"* (6) although based on the fallacious concept of vitalism, is noteworthy for its discussion of the changes preceding death in old age.

> *"Look at the man who comes to the end of long old age: he dies little by little; his external functions terminate one after another; all his senses close up successively; the ordinary stimuli of sensations strike them without response."*
>
> *"This is the great difference between death in old age from that which is the effect of a sudden blow. In the first, life begins to fade in all parts of the body, and ceases finally in the heart. Death extends its empire from the circumference to the center. In the second, life is extinguished in the heart, and later in all parts of the body. Death manifests itself from the center to the circumference."*

Bichat's works were translated into German and English and had a broad stimulating influence, often giving rise to violent controversy.

René-Théophile-Hyacinthe Laennec (1781-1826) touches on all aspects of medicine in his famous *"Traité de l'auscultation médiate"* published in 1819. Here too we find important comments on conditions seen in the aged, one referring to a lung abscess in a woman of 68 years, and another, often quoted, is described under the heading, "Occasional Causes of Tubercles."

> *"The ancients believed that phthisis attacks more particularly individuals between the ages of eighteen and thirty-five; it is true that at this period the disease is most frequently manifest and easiest of recognition...However no age is exempt from it...It is very common even in advanced old age. I once opened the body of a woman ninety-nine years and some months old, who had died of this disease. Women are more subject to it than men."* (7)

Among the contributions of French physicians of this period to the hygiene of old age, may be mentioned Tenon (8), Janin (9) and Terrier (10). Guyetant' popular work (11) was composed when the author had experienced 30 years in practice, and in general conforms to the old Arab formula for books designed for lay readers. It is a well written book, with a glossary of the few scientific terms used. He lays special emphasis on the problems of women, pointing out that they live longer than do men. Rostan, one of the celebrated teachers of the Salpêtrière, demonstrated that the so-called "asthma of old age" was due to an organic rather than to a nervous cause (12). He also contributed to the problem of cerebral softening, comparing it with the peripheral gangrene seen commonly in the aged (13). Magendie, the famous physiologist and pharmacologist demonstrated the changes in the tissues of the lung in the old (14), observations which were later well utilized by Hourmann and Dechambre in their celebrated study of pneumonia in the aged women of the Salpêtriére (15).

This famous clinical and pathological contribution contains many valuable observations. The authors point out the general dilatation of the bronchial tree in old age and that the mucous membranes of the bronchi are the habitual site of an abundant secretion, a true physiologic bronchorrhea. They describe the different types of chest in their patients, and the auscultatory findings in each. They record respiratory and pulse rates, mentioning pulse frequencies as low as 20 and 30 beats per minute. Pneumonia is discussed from the standpoint of the frequency in the aged, the pathological anatomy, together with the general and special symptomatology. They stress the frequent absence of any expectoration, especially of the blood tinged variety, the absence of dyspnea. The early physical signs are sonorous rales associated with diminished breath sounds. The picture they have drawn of latent pneumonia is famous through its quotation in part by Charcot in his "Lectures on Old Age" (1868). In 1916 this passage was read to the third year students at the College of Physicians and Surgeons of New York by the Professor of Medicine, Dr. Warfield T. Longcope. The present writer, a member of the class, has never forgotten the occasion and has always been aware of his debt to a great teacher.

"Finally in some even more obscure cases our old ladies complain neither of weakness nor of malaise. They do not seek admission to the infirmary; no one in their dormitory, neither the nurses nor the attendants nor their neighbors detect any change in their behavior. They arise, make their beds, walk about, eat as usual; then they feel somewhat fatigued, throw themselves on their beds and expire. This is called sudden death from old age at the Salpêtrière. One opens the bodies and finds a large part of the pulmonary parenchyma in suppuration. Remarkable feats of this class take place under our eyes at the infirmary among women admitted originally for diseases entirely remote from the lungs, of which they have been cured."

Hourmann and Dechambre also recorded observations on senile ankylosis of the spine (16).

Jean Cruveilhier (1791–1873) the great pathologist, was also a member of the staff of the Salpêtrière and there collected many of the cases which he used so well in his atlas of pathological anatomy where the clinical history of the patient was recorded with the post-mortem findings, beautifully illustrated by large colored plates (17). Prus, working at the Bicêtre, studied the pathological findings in 390 individuals in an effort that "the medicine of old age shall more and more cease to merit the reputation of inutility to which it is condemned by the ignorant and poorly informed". The causes of death classified anatomically were: respiratory, 149; nervous, 101; circulatory, 64; gastro-intestinal, 49; liver and biliary passages, 8; miscellaneous, 19. This study contains much valuable material (18).

Quetelet's (19) anatomical work on the developmental changes, in men and women contained many observations on age changes, especially with reference to weight. His findings were quoted with approval by later writers such as Geist and Charcot. The clinical studies of Beau at the Salpêtrière (20), especially his paper on spleno-hepatic relations (21) represent the best in straightforward bedside medicine. In the latter essay we find the following striking notation:

"*In the Salpêtrière infirmary few autopsies are made without there being found a greater or smaller number of calculi in the gall bladder, yet biliary colics are extremely rare at the Salpêtrière.*"

Another contribution from the same center of the clinical study of the old is that of Neucourt on the heart. Among his conclusions are the following:

"*Abnormal sounds arising in the cardiac orifices may exist without affecting its function.*"

"*Some cardiac abnormalities even with very profound alterations in the function of this organ may exist a large number of years without bringing about death.*" (22)

Gendrin's paper on the influence of age on sickness apparently impressed his contemporaries for it is often quoted with approbation. Like other similar efforts it contrasts infancy and childhood with old age. This writer uses the term "*senile cachexia*" to designate the sum of all the changes which we would to-day ascribe to the aging process itself. Following its introduction by Gendrin the term came into use in France and Germany as a diagnosis, even as a cause of death, corresponding to the use of "*old age*" in English speaking countries for the same purpose (23).

An interesting commentary on the medical thinking in France about the needs of the dependent aged is to be found in two notes published in the Annals of Hygiene. The one concerns a discussion by the eminent physicians Esquirol, Chevallier, Villermé and Parent-Duchatelet on the necessary features of hospitals designed to care for the sick aged (24). The emphasis is laid on low buildings because of the difficulty of the aged in climbing stairs. The second comprises the report of the committee on charitable establishments regarding the question of whether it is better to place aged persons in hospices or to board them out in the country. This discussion properly reaches no definite conclusion, since the same question is still being debated over 100 years later (25).

While the physicians of Paris worked faithfully at the problems presented by their aged patients, a gifted young German, practicing in the obscure village of Ansbach, published in 1839, what Charcot grudgingly admitted was "the first dogmatic treatise that has appeared upon the diseases of old age." Carl Friedrich Canstatt's "*Die Krankheiten des hocheren Alters und ihre Heilung*" (26) was the first attempt at a comprehensive treatment of the subject since Johann Bernhard Fischer's *De senio* in 1754. Before discussing this famous work it will be well to review some of its medical background.

According to Garrison, "up to the year 1850 and well beyond it, most of the advancements in medicine were made by the French" (27). He ascribes the backward position of German science to the prolonged depression resulting from the Napoleonic wars and to the prevalence of many fanciful medico-philosophical cults. In spite of a general tendency to unrestrained speculation on the part of some physicians, sound scientific achievement can be found in the work of such outstanding individuals as Johannes Mueller (1801-58), the distinguished physiologist and teacher, Matthias Schleiden (1804-81) and Theodor Schwann (1810-82), co-discoverers of the cellular structure of plant and animal tissues, Lucas

Schoenlein (1793-1864), founder of modern clinical teaching in Germany and teacher of Canstatt, Carl Rokitansky (1804-78) the noted Viennese pathologist and Jakob Henle (1809-85) the great histologist. It is thus apparent that the triumphs that German medicine achieved in the latter half of the century did not arise de novo, but were based on the work of men of the highest ability.

In tracing the work of German physicians on old age, we note the first monograph on the anatomy of the aged by Burkhard Wilhelm Seiler (1779-1843), *Anatomia corporis humani senilis specimen*, which appeared in Latin at Erlangen

Fig. 3. Carl Friedrich Canstatt (1807-1850). (from the Wolfe Collection, Syracuse University, through the courtesy of Dr. H. A. Weiskotten).

in 1800 (28), in a Dutch translation in 1804, and in German in the *Archiv für die Physiologie* in 1805 (29). It is a careful, critical but unoriginal compilation of the knowledge of his day, emphasizing, as Steudel (30) points out, that the anatomical features of the adult are greatly modified in old age and that man is so changed by prolonged functional activity as to become in old age a different being. He recognizes that most old people die of disease rather than old age, and that these disease changes must not be confused with results of the aging process itself. He advocates, in addition to dissection, the use of the microscope and chemical examination of the bodily fluids. He admonishes the physicians connected with homes for the aged to take advantage of the material at their disposal and stresses the necessity for repeated observations before any manifestation be ascribed to old age itself. Here Seiler indicates the progress that had been made since the days when old age was itself considered a disease. An often quoted observation of Seiler is that rigidity is the constant accompaniment of old age (*Rigiditas senectutis perpetua comes*).

The lengthy contribution of C. A. Philites in the year 1809 an old age and senile marasmus is typical of the German medicine of that day since the first half is taken up by a prolonged philosophical discussion (31). On the other hand he divides life into a period of increment and a period of decrement, a concept that is very close to Canstatt's concept of old age as involution. Philites uses the term senile marasmus to indicate the changes of senescence. Relatively little space is devoted to disease in the aged, but Philites states that in old age every effort must be made to conserve the vital energies.

In the year 1801 the Emperor Joseph Academy of Medicine and Surgery in Vienna offered a prize for the best essay on the diseases of the bladder and ureters in old men, with the exception of stones. For many years no award was made although in 1806 W. J. Schmitt published a work on this subject which apparently was not considered worthy (32). The contribution of Samuel Thomas Soemmering (1755–1830), famous anatomist (33), the first to describe achondroplasia and a prolific writer on a variety of topics, was finally awarded the palm. It is an excellent piece of work, richly annotated with many references to contemporary authors, covering each anatomical feature of the urinary tract except the kidneys. Part of the introduction is worth quoting.

"To every physician who busies himself with the thorough study of his science, it should be a personal obligation to learn to know exactly the variations from normal of the anticipated diseases, to trace their remotest causes, their smallest results, and to train himself in the easiest and safest removals of them with unconcern, when he realizes that these maladies become more threatening to himself with the advancing years, and that the highest rulers, the wisest statesmen, cannot escape them, but as sacrifices to them, arouse the compassion of their contemporaries."

Between the publication of Soemmering's work and the appearance of Canstatt's classic volumes, we find recorded in the Index-Catalogue of the Surgeon-General's office more than twenty Latin treatises devoted to some aspect of old age. With few exceptions none of these works appears to have created much impression on contemporary thinking and writing. During the same period about ten contributions to the subject written in German are to be found. These vary from Loo's paper on the use of drastic purgatives in the aged (34) and Mayer's on the changes in the female genitalia in old age (35), to Kruger's study of the natural healing power at various periods of life (36).

Carl Friedrich Canstatt (1807–1850), one of Schoenlein's most distinguished students, made a lasting impression on German medicine, crowding great accomplishments into a short life. While practicing in the Bavarian village of Anspach he published his work on old age. Two years later appeared his text book of medicine which was standard for many years, and was re-issued after Canstatt death under the editorship of E. H. Henoch. In 1844 he was called to Erlangen as professor of medicine. He is noted also for the journal which he founded in 1841, *Jahresbericht ueber die Fortschritte der gesamten Medizin in allen Laendern*, which was later carried on by Virchow.

The book on old age is divided into two volumes, the first or general part dealing with the anatomy and physiology of old age, and the second, or special part, devoted to the description and treatment of specific diseases. To Canstatt, old age is identical with involution, and he traces the various changes found in every part of the body, emphasizing that there is no rule about the order of their appearance. In his discussion of diseases he separates the essential involutional maladies from those conditions which are seen at all periods of life but are modified by the changes of old age.

Canstatt's book was sparingly admired by Durand-Fardel and Charcot, and at the same time subjected to the criticism that it is not based on careful personal observations, and that it indulges too much in the speculative philosophy so dear to the German mind. Actually these adverse comments are in part justified. Canstatt's clinical experience with old age must have been acquired chiefly during his practice in Anspach, the total population of which could not have equalled the number of old men and women in the Salpêtrière and the Bicêtre where Durand-Fardel and Charcot spent many years, as observed by Steudel. In spite of all shortcomings it is thoroughly modern in spirit, well written and worthy of reading even to-day. Felicitous expressions occur frequently, such as, "the old man dies off while living", which is reminiscent of Bichat, with whose works Canstatt was familiar. He has good understanding of the mental manifestations of old age, commenting that "psychic indifference may show itself in disgust with life and in suicide". His therapy is conservative, and his observations on the dosage of drugs very sound. All in all Canstatt's work set up a standard for all future workers in the field and laid the foundations for a scientific study of aging and disease, since the author does not hesitate to indicate the numerous unsolved problems and constantly urges his readers to fill up these gaps.

Although the merits of Canstatt's work were recognized by German and French physicians, it seems never to have been translated into English. The attention of the leaders in medical thinking in Great Britain was never attracted to disease in the aged as a special object of study. On the other hand the traditions of Sydenham, Heberden, the Hunters, Fothergill, Parry and Jenner had been carried on by a group of physicians whose contributions to general medicine frequently were concerned with diseases common in the old. We need mention only John Cheyne (1777-1836), Robert Adams (1791-1875), Robert Graves (1796-1853), William Stokes (1804-1878), Sir Dominic Corrigan (1802-1880), all of whom advanced the study of heart disease and described important clinical phenomena for the first time. Richard Bright (1789-1858) in his famous "Reports of Medical Cases" (1827) established nephritis as a definite clinical entity by the correlation of urinary findings with the pathology of the kidney, and differentiated between edema of renal and cardiac origin. In Garrison's opinion, "as an original delineator of disease, he ranks next to Laennec" (37). Thomas Addison (1793-1860) with his description of pernicious anemia, Thomas Hodgkin (1798-1866) with his contribution to glandular pathology, and Joseph Hodgson (1788-1869) with his studies of aortic aneurism, all increased the field of medical understanding. James Parkinson (1755-1824) contributed his "Essay on the Shaking Palsy" in 1817, describing the disease which has ever since borne his name.

Aside from Jameson's book (38), the first work of any importance on old age was published in London in 1818 by Sir Anthony Carlisle, the noted surgeon (39). This slender volume entitled "An Essay on the Disorders of Old Age", is written

FIG. 4. Sir Anthony Carlisle (1768-1840)

in epigrammatic style, without any references to other books on the subject. It contains good advice on hygiene, advocates the judicious use of blood-letting which can only be learned by experience, comes out against emetics for the aged and is strongly in favor of alkalis for a variety of purposes. He attributes urinary retention to cerebral and bowel diseases, describing the relief from catheterization as temporary and delusive. In general he is opposed to surgery in the aged: "even if the patients prefer the sacrifice of life to the endurance of protracted suffering, still the surgeon should refuse to comply with their improper wishes, and not become a party to homicide".

We recall at this point the publication in 1804 of Sir John Sinclair's four volume compilation, entitled "The Code of Health and Longevity, or a Concise View o the Principles Calculated for the Preservation of Health and the Attainment of Long Life, being an attempt to prove the practicability of condensing, within a narrow compass, the most material information hitherto accumulated, regarding the most useful arts and sciences, or any particular thereof" (40). In the first volume Sinclair, who also wrote extensively on finance and agriculture, summarizes the best opinions on diet and hygiene; in the subsequent three volumes he reprints extracts from the works of authorities such as Friar Bacon and Lord Bacon, bibliographies on old age and longevity from Ploucquet, as well as personal letters from friends in different parts of the world, including Dr. Benjamin Waterhouse of Cambridge, Massachusetts. This is on the whole a useful book of reference, and the author surely made a brave attempt to relieve others of the necessity of consulting as many books as he himself had to do.

Easton's volume on "Human Longevity" published only a few years before Sinclair's Code of Health, lists all the centenarians known since A.D. 66 (41). It is another illustration of the fascination of the very long-lived for the popular mind, which was pointed out in connection with Thomas Parr. The frontispiece and dedication of this odd work are reproduced in Figure I. Another popular work, "The Economy of Health", was published in 1837 by James Johnson (1777–1845), (42) naval surgeon and Physician Extraordinary to the King. The explanatory subtitle is almost an abstract of its contents.

Marshall Hall (1790–1857) who is noted for his work in neurology, was also the author of a work on the diseases of women (43). Part 3 is entitled, "Of the Disorders Incident to the Middle and Later Periods of Female Life." In Chapter VI he discusses the local diseases resulting from disorder of the general health in the later periods of life, commenting on the frequency of paralytic attacks, which he ascribes to a disordered state of the general health and loaded condition of the large intestines. In the final chapter, "Of the Decline of the Vital Powers in Old Age," three brief pages are devoted to quoting Sir Henry Halford's remarks on "the state of sinking in old age" (44).

A more ambitious effort in the interest of the hygiene of old age is to be found in Barnard Van Oven's "On the Decline of Life in Health and Disease: being an attempt to investigate the causes of longevity and the best means of attaining old age" (45). Written after thirty years in practice, the author points out that no similar volume has been attempted since Hufeland's *Macrobiotik*, 65 years earlier. The "Medical Notes and Reflections" of Henry Holland, published in 1840, has a chapter on the medical treatment of old age (46). J. A. Symonds contributed a carefully thought out article on "Age" to the Todd Cyclopedia of Anatomy and Physiology, 1835–6 (47). P. M. Roget was the author of the section on "Age" in the Cyclopedia of Practical Medicine, in which are described the changes of senescence and a few common diseases. He considered age as the state of transition between maturity and decay. "Spontaneous decay of the body and decline of its powers, invariably attending the lapse of years, arise altogether from causes that are internal and interwoven with the very condition and laws of its existence and are but little influenced by external circumstances" (48).

George Edward Day (1815–1872) was a graduate of Edinburgh and Cambridge, who later became professor of anatomy at St. Andrews. From his biographer we learn that he was a frequent contributor to medical journals and translated several German text books. It is therefore not surprising to find that in 1848 he published "A Practical Treatise on the Domestic Management and Most Important Diseases of Advanced Life" (49), with a foot-note acknowledging his debt to Canstatt, from whose work he states that he has drawn freely in several parts. Whatever his debt to his German colleague, Day has written the best text book on the subject in English in the whole 19th century, for while others later made single contributions, he remained without rival in his own country until Sir Humphrey Rolleston became interested in old age, more than a half century later. The volume is written in an interesting style, with many references to contemporary English and Continental clinicians, and with many personal case reports.

In the United States the valuable contribution to the study of old age made by Benjamin Rush in 1793 seems to have had but little influence in stimulating his colleagues to similar endeavors (50). The celebrated Dr. Benjamin Waterhouse of Cambridge, Massachusetts, one-time professor of medicine at Harvard University and first to practice vaccination in this country, expressed some views on old age in a letter to Sir John Sinclair.

"... During the natural change that takes place between 48 and 50, no particular organ suffers, but a gradual and uniform deterioration supervenes. At this time he first experiences a reluctancy to stoop; he prefers a carriage to riding on horseback, and he finds himself more affected by the weather ... regains his health, with a little diminution of muscular strength, until he turns sixty; then the gravity of age is more strongly marked, and he begins to boast of his age and its prerogatives. This is the result of my observations on others, compared with my own personal experience, which goes no farther than your own, being born in the same year, viz. 1754." (51)

In 1815 John Scudder presented as his inaugural dissertation at the College of Physicians and Surgeons in New York City, "On the diseases of old age, as connected with a plethoric state of the system." He stresses the value of bloodletting, quoting the authority of his preceptor, Hosack, as well as Lettsom, Boerhave and Van Swieten. He ascribes gout and palsy to plethora, and reports briefly four cases which he had observed, aged 74, 73, 48 and 34 years, all of whom were helped by phlebotomy (52).

Abel Lawrence Pierson (1794-1853) described in 1829 two cases of disease and dissection in old age (53). He states that the wearing out of organs varies in the individual due to his original formation, his occupation, habits and temperament. Imperfections in the vital organs are not incompatible with vigorous health. The first patient, a well known political figure who had served in the army at Yorktown, died at the age of 84 years after an eleven day illness. Necropsy showed a large left empyema, enlarged prostate, marked sclerosis of the abdominal aorta and iliac vessels. The pericardium was adherent and the heart showed areas of ossification in the myocardium and the semi-lunar valves

Pierson's second patient was the famous centenarian, Dr. Edward Holyoke of Salem, Massachusetts. The complete story of this aged physician is also to be found in a memoir prepared in book form by his medical colleagues and presented to his family as a mark of homage to his memory (54). This remarkable document contains not only the narrative of the doctor's life but also the clinical history of his last illness and the post-mortem findings. He had been honored at a public dinner on his 100th birthday when it is said, "he partook of the hilarity of the occasion with an ardent zest, and when called upon for a toast, offered in

FIG. 5. Edward A. Holyoke, M.D. of Salem, Massachusetts

his own handwriting, a sentiment perfectly appropriate and professional, accompanied with a paternal and touching benediction upon the medical brethren present". At his death less than a year later, the autopsy revealed the obvious cause of death as gangrene of the left leg to the knee, and in addition an asymptomatic and unsuspected carcinoma of the stomach. Pierson reported this case in his paper because of the small circulation of the memoir.

Another venerable physician of colonial days, John Redman (1722–1808) of Philadelphia has been recently discussed by McDaniel in a study of his speeches and letters (55). The old gentleman, who was the first president of the College of Physicians, constantly referred to his age and infirmity, always signing himself as, "your aged friend and fellow-servant."

No other contributions by Americans appear until 1837 when a report, signed only with the initials "J. M. W." is found in the Boston Medical and Surgical Journal, relating to post-mortem examination of a lady over 100 years old. Death had been accelerated by a fall resulting in a fracture of the hip. No obvious cause of death is apparent from the pathological findings. The author stresses the lack of ossification of the ribs, the absence of abnormal brittleness in the bones, the small size of the stomach and the presence of a large unsuspected fecal impaction (56).

In 1847 Caspar Wistar Pennock (1799-1867), Gerhard's colleague at Blockley, reported on the frequency of the pulse and respiration in the aged (57), pointing out that at one time the frequency of the heart's action was thought diminished with age until this was disproven by studies made at the Salpêtrière. His own observations on 170 men and 203 women led him to conclude that the frequency of the pulse of the aged is much greater than usually thought, while respiration is that generally admitted in reference to adults in middle life. This is the first quantitative clinical study of old age in American medical literature.

Jarrot (58) in 1849 described the amputation of the gangrenous leg of a Negro slave, aged 102 years. The patient stood the operation well but developed pleurisy on the fifteenth day and ceased. We are told that ether was ineffectual, that chloroform caused the patient to act as though intoxicated, and that brandy and laudanum were given to quiet him ante-operatively. Difficulty in management of the stump was experienced due to pressure of the adhesive plaster, and the use of sutures is advised.

In evaluating the knowledge of old age of the American physician in the first fifty years of the 19th century we must bear in mind that all of the outstanding men had studied in England and France. Pennock we know worked at the Salpêtrière, and Pierson learned the use of the stethoscope in Paris in 1832 (59). Likewise all the English medical texts were either imported or reprinted in the United States. The books of Carlisle and Day appeared in American editions, as did several of the encyclopedias of medicine. The paucity of contributions is perhaps best explained by the fact that medical literature in this country, in general, was very scanty until a much later date.

(To be Continued)

BIBLIOGRAPHY

(1) BOUCHER, L., La Salpêtrière, de 1656 à 1790, Paris, 1883.
GUILLAIN, G. AND MATHIEU, P., La Salpêtrière, Paris, Masson et Cie., 1925.
LARQUIER, L., La Salpêtrière (Les Vieux Hôpitaux Français), Les Laboratoires Ciba Lyon, 1939.
(2) FRANCK-FUNCK-BRENTANO, AND MARIADAZ, G., L'Hôpital General Bicêtre, Les Laboratoires Ciba, Lyon, 1938.
(3) GUILLAIN, G., AND MATHIEU, P., op. cit.
(4) PINEL, P., Considérations sur la constitution seniles et sur son influences dans les maladies aigües; Arch. gen. de med., Paris, 2: 5-15, 1823.

(5) GARRISON, F. H., An Introduction to the History of Medicine, ed. 4, Philadelphia, Saunders, 1929, pp. 444-5.
(6) BICHAT, M. F. X., Recherches physiologiques sur la Vie et la Mort, Paris, Brosson, Gabon et Cie., 1800.
(7) LAENNEC, R. T. H., Treatise on Mediate Auscultation and on Diseases of the Lungs and Heart, London, 1846, p. 312.
(8) TENON, J., Offrande aux vieillards, de quelques moyens pour prolonger leur vie, Paris, 1813.
(9) JANIN, H. F., Essai sur l'hygiene des vieillards, on de l'influence que les choses physiques et morales exercent sur les personnes agées, et des moyens de les conserver en santé, Paris, 1813.
(10) TERRIER, F., Essai sur l'hygiene des vieillards, Paris, 1817.
(11) GUYETANT, S., Le medecin de l'age de retour et de la vieillesse, ou conseils aux personnes des deux sexes, qui on passé l'age de quarante-cinq ans, Paris, 1836.
(12) ROSTAN, L., L'Asthme des vieillards, est-il une affection nerveuse, Paris, 1817.
(13) ROSTAN, L., Recherches sur une maladie encore peu connue, qui a reçule le nom de Ramollissement du Cerveau, Paris, 1820.
(14) MAGENDIE, F., Memoire sur la structure du poumon de l'homme. J. de physiol. exper. 1: 78, 1821.
(15) HOURMANN AND DECHAMBRE, Recherches cliniques pour servir á l'histoire des maladies des vieillards, Arch. gen de med., Paris, 2: s.8, 405-428, 1835; 2: s.9, 338-357, 1835; 2: 10, 269, 1836; 2: s.12, 27, 164, 1836.
(16) HOURMANN AND DECHAMBRE, Arch. gen. de med., Aug., 1835.
(17) CRUVEILHIER, J., Anatomie pathologique du corps humain, Paris, Bailliere, 1829-1842.
(18) PRUS, R., Recherches sur les maladies des vieillesse, Mem. acad. roy. de med., Paris, 8: 11-27, 1840.
(19) QUETELET, A., Sur l'Homme et le Developpement de ses Facultés, Paris, 1835.
(20) BEAU, J. H. S., Recherches cliniques sur les maladies des vieillards, J. de med. de Paris, 1: 289, 330, 353; 1843.
(21) BEAU, J. H. S., Études sur l'Appareil Splenohepatique, Arch. de Med., 1851.
(22) NEUCOURT, F., De l'état du coeur chez le vieillard, d'apres des observations au recueiller a la Salpêtrière, Arch. gen. de med., Paris, 45, 3: 1-24, 1843.
(23) GENDRIN, A. N., Influence des âges sur les maladies, Paris, Bailliere, 1840.
(24) Esquirol et al., Note relative à quelques conditions que doivent presenter les hôpitaux destinés à des individus agé plus de 60 ans, et infirmés, Ann. d'hyg., Paris, 9: 296-307, 1833.
(25) Lettre sur la question de savoir s'il est mieux de reunir les vieillards dans les hospices, oú de les placer en pension à la campagne, Ann. d'hyg., Paris, 7: 218-230, 1832.
(26) CANSTATT, C. F., Die Krankheiten des hoeheren Alters und ihre Heilung, Erlangen, 1939.
(27) GARRISON, F. H., op. cit., pp. 408 and 428-9.
(28) SEILER, B. G., Anatomiae corporis humani senilis specimen, Erlangen, J. J. Palm, 1800.
(29) SEILER, B. G., Ueber die Zergliederung des menschlichen Koerpers im Alter, Arch. f. d. ges. Physiol., 6: 1-119, 1805.
(30) STEUDEL, J., Zur Geschichte der Lehre von den Greisenkrankheiten, Sudhoff's Archiv. f. Gesch. d. Med., 35: 1-27, 1942.
(31) PHILITES, C. A., Von dem Alter des Menschen, ueberhaupt ueber dem marasmus senilis insbesondere, Arch. t. d. physiol., 9: 1-128, 1809.
(32) SCHMITT, W. J., Ueber diejenigen Krankheiten der Harnblase, Vorsteherdruesen u. Harnroehre denen vorzueglich Maenner in hohem Alter ausgesetzt sind, Vienna, 1806.
(33) SOEMMERING, S. T., Abhandlung ueber die toedtlichen Krankheiten der Harnblase und Harnroehre alter Maenner, Frankfurt, 2nd. ed., 1822.

(34) Loos, R., Ueber den Gebrauch drastischer Purganzen bei hohem Alter, Archiv. t. med. Erfahrung, 12: 190-194, 1810.
(35) Mayer, L., Von den Veraenderung welche die weiblichen Genitalen namentlich der Uterus in hohem Alter erleiden, Bonn, 1825.
(36) Kruger, M., Naturheilkraft betrachtet in den verschiedenen Perioden des Lebens, Mitt. a.d.Gebiete d. Med., 5-6: 28-41. 1837-8.
(37) Garrison, F. H., op. cit., p. 421.
(38) Jameson, J., Essays on the changes of the human body at its different ages; the diseases to which it is predisposed in each period of life, London, 1811.
(39) Carlisle, Sir A., Essay on the Disorders of Old Age, Philadelphia Edward Earle, 1819.
(40) Sinclair, Sir John, The Code of Health and Longevity, Edinburgh, Constable, 1807, 2nd ed.
(41) Easton, J., Human Longevity, Salisbury, Easton, 1799.
(42) Johnson, J., The Economy of Health or the stream of Human Life, from the Cradle to the Grave, with Reflections, moral, physical and philosophical, on the septennial phases of human existence, New York, Harper, 1837.
(43) Hall, M., Commentaries on some of the more important diseases of females, London, Longman, 1827.
(44) Halford, Sir H., Essays and Orations, London, Murray, 1833.
(45) Van Oven, B., On the decline of life in health and disease; being an attempt to investigate the causes of longevity, and the best means of attaining a healthy old age, London, Churchill, 1853.
(46) Holland, H., Medical Notes and Reflections. See Chap 19: The Medical Treatment of Old Age, London, 1840.
(47) Symonds, J. A., Article on Age, Cyclopedia of Anatomy and Physiology, (Todd), London, 1835-6.
(48) Roget, P. M., Article on Age, Cyclopedia of Practical Medicine, revised ed., Philadelphia, Lea and Blanchard, 1845, vol. I.
(49) Day, G. E., A Practical Treatise on the Domestic Management and Most Important Diseases of Advanced Life, Philadelphia, Lea and Blanchard, 1849.
(50) Rush, B., An Account of the State of Body and Mind in Old Age, with observations on its diseases and their remedies. In "Medical Inquiries and Observations", Philadelphia, 1793, vol. II.
(51) Sinclair, Sir John, op. cit., vol. I, p. 23.
(52) Scudder, J., On the Diseases of Old Age as connected with a plethoric state of the system, New York, Van Winkle and Wiley, 1815.
(53) Pierson, A. L., Two cases of disease and dissection in old age. N. Y. Med. and Phys. J., 2: 67-74, 1829-30.
(54) Edward A. Holyoke, M.D., LL.D., Memoir of. Prepared in compliance with a vote of the Essex South District Medical Society and published by their request, Boston, 1829.
(55) McDaniel, W. B., Jr., "-your aged friend and fellow servant, John Redman", Tr. and Stud. Coll. Physicians, Philadelphia, 9: 35-41, April, 1941.
(56) Post-mortem examination of the body of a lady over 100 years old. Boston M & S. J., 16: 44-46, 1837. (No by-line; signed J. M. W.)
(57) Pennock, C. W., Note on frequency of pulse and respiration of the aged, Am. J. M. Sci., n.s. 14: 68-75, 1847.
(58) Jarrot, R., Amputation for gangrene of foot, successfully performed on a negro, at the age of 102. Charleston M.J. and Rev., 4: 301-303, 1849.
(59) Packard, F., History of Medicine in the United States, New York, Hoeber, 1932.

LIFE'S LATER YEARS

Studies in the Medical History of Old Age

FREDERIC D. ZEMAN, M.D.

[New York City]

Part XII

THE NINETEENTH CENTURY (CONTINUED)*

In the breathtaking advances of medical science in the second half of the nineteenth century one might well expect to find the study of old age submerged and neglected. Actually the discovery of the role of pathogenic organisms by Pasteur and the application of this knowledge to surgery by Lister brought inestimable benefits to old and young alike, in much the same way as had the first use of volatile anesthetic agents in the eighteen forties and fifties. Nor should we forget that the increasing accuracy of the methods of clinical study led to more refined diagnosis and more effective treatment in internal medicine, and to the extensive development of the specialties of neurology, psychiatry, dermatology, otology and laryngology. In the flood of medical publications resulting from this intensive study of diseases and their causes we find numerous contributions to old age which indicate that in France and Germany particularly, the subject continued to grow in importance with broader understanding of the basic sciences.

The stimulating and productive efforts of French medicine which had in the first years of the century drawn physicians from all over the world to Paris proceeded with undiminished activity. In addition to Pasteur we note such figures as Claude Bernard, Charcot, Brown-Séquard, Flourens, Nélaton, Broca, Huchard, Marie, Duchenne, and Déjerine. Many of these men attained their fame as members of the staffs of the Salpétrierè and the Bicêtre. In the bulletins of the *Societé Anatomique* of Paris one finds many reports of aged individuals studied both clinically and pathologically. In the 800 page volume for 1876 there are 63 reports of men and women over 60 years (1). Much of this material is worthy of more careful study but a few cases will be mentioned in detail later. Other sources of material on old age are the doctoral theses written by students but reflecting the views of their teachers, and the encyclopedias of medicine which have in all countries been favored by publishers and writers, and presumably by physicians seeking to catch up on missed reading.

In the supplement to the *Dictionnaire des dictionnaires de médecine* (2), published in 1851, we find the maladies of old age described at length by E. M. Gillette (1800–1859). He differentiated the age of decline, old age proper, and decrepitude, surveying the entire field thoroughly, giving full references to contemporary writers, and describing freely his own experiences at the Salpétrierè.

---

* This is the twelfth in a series of articles dealing with Studies in the Medical History of Old Age. Upon completion of their publication, the installments will be collected and reprinted in the form of a monograph.

The same volume contained an article on "Ages" by Durand Fardel, of whom more later.

The first edition of Bouchardat's (1806–1866) work on diabetes appeared in 1851 (3). Allen has termed him "the most brilliant clinician in the history of diabetes," and Magnus-Levy emphasized that Bouchardat's advice, "*manger le moins possible*," gave in four words a practical prescription for every case (4). The author discussed the age incidence of the disease and behavior of older diabetics under varying circumstances. In the second edition, published in 1875, this phase of the subject was treated in greater detail.

In 1853 J. H. Reveillé-Parise brought out his large volume on the hygiene of old age, described by Durand-Fardel as a gentle paraphrase of La Rochefoucauld's "*Peu des gens savent etre vieux*" (5). The subtitle is highly descriptive: "Researches on the physiologic state, the moral faculties, the diseases of advanced age, on the most certain means, the better tried ones, of sustaining and prolonging the vital activity at that epoch of existence." This is a gracefully written work embodying the best views of the day, but historically has its roots in the hygienic works of the Arab physicians of the Middle Ages.

Marie Jean Pierre Flourens (1799–1867), protegé of Cuvier, was professor of anatomy at the University of Paris, where he carried on fundamental studies of cerebral functions, establishing the vital center in the medulla, the function of the semicircular canals and the relation of the cerebral cortex to vision. His volume on *Human Longevity* depended greatly on the work of Buffon, and set forth the axiom that since it takes a man twenty years to grow, he should live five times that period or one hundred years (6). His views on old age were reminiscent of Bichat.

In 1854 Charles Louis-Maxime Durand-Fardel (1815–1899), who had been trained at the Salpétrierè and the Bicêtre, and practiced at Vichy, published his excellent practical treatise on the diseases of the old. In his preface he states that he "has lived a long time among the aged, has attached himself to their miseries and studied them with a profound interest without knowing only if some day he would have his share." The introduction is devoted to the changes of the aging process itself. The section on the central nervous system occupies 330 pages, the respiratory tract 307 pages, the circulatory system 80 pages, the abdomen including the genito-urinary tract, 116 pages. The appendix devotes 26 pages to gout and 5 pages to the diseases of the skin. The great merit of this work lies in the abundant case reports with postmortem correlations (7). The emphasis on the brain is to be explained by the author's own interest and previous publications (8) as well as the general background of French research. In the heart section we find no mention of the role of the coronary vessels, but excellent descriptions of both cardiac aneurysm and cardiac rupture which is considered a common cause of death in old age. Durand-Fardel in his preface acknowledged his debt to Canstatt, but had the obvious advantage of vast clinical experience over his German colleague. This French work has a sound basis in the actual observations of the author and his colleagues in the great Parisian institutions for the aged.

The importance of these special institutional influences cannot be overemphasized and is seen everywhere in French medical literature on old age. Inglessis, one of Charcot's students, in 1855 presented a thesis on cerebro-spinal meningitis as seen at the Salpêtrière (9). Cruveilhier, pathologist of this great combined hospice and hospital, at a meeting of the Anatomical Society (1856),

FIG. 1. MARIE JEAN-PIERRE FLOURENS (1799–1867)

discussed a case of congenital left sided diaphragmatic hernia in a new-born, and mentioned that he had observed a diaphragmatic hernia, probably congenital, in a woman aged 70 years, the strangulation of which caused death (10). G. S. Empis, physician to the home for female incurables, reported on progressive muscular weakness in the aged, pointing out that general muscular atrophy is associated with discoloration of the tissues and a tendency to vertigo, gastralgia, precordial oppression and palpitation (11). C. M. E. Potain, well known to Americans as an eponym, contributed two cases of interest in his capacity as physician to the *Hospice des Ménages*: one a man of 72 with progressive senile dementia who died of gangrene of the leg, and at autopsy showed ventricular aneurysm with closure of the left recurrent branch of the left coronary artery (12); and the other, a man of 73 who died with painless hepatic enlargement

FIG. 2. CHARLES LOUIS MAXIME DURAND-FARDEL (1815–1899)

and who showed at postmortem section a perforated carcinoma of the stomach with liver metastases and diffuse peritonitis (13).

An extremely important study of tuberculosis in the aged was published from the Salpétrière by L. Moureton (14), in which the author emphasized that the disease is less rare than generally thought, that it may continue to progress in old age although beginning much earlier, and that it may develop in old people who have had no previous infection. He pointed out how the diagnosis may be missed in old age because the usual signs are missing in the old. Furthermore, acute tuberculosis, noted heretofore as developing only in youth and adult life, may show up in old age and is not at all rare. The invasiveness of the disease was as marked in old age as in youth.

Regnard's case of senile dementia with subdural hemorrhage (15), Vulpian's study of senile fatty changes in the cerebral vessels of mammals (16), and Maindron's fusiform aneurysms of the terminal aorta with aortic rupture in a woman of 71 years (17), form a background for Marcé's (1828–1864) pathologic studies of senile dementia (18). As psychiatrist at the Bicêtre, he was able to describe some 40 cases, ranging from 50 to 84 years of age and to conclude that the mental changes of old age are not a distinct entity but may be associated with diverse organic affections of the brain, such as apoplexy and cerebral softening. The differentiation from general paralysis was made on clinical and pathologic grounds.

Along similar lines Legrand du Saulle described the position of the aged in relation to the law, the relation of mental states to criminal acts (19). He described physiologic, pathologic and mixed mental states. Age alone was no excuse for misdeeds. He discussed also the sexual transgressions of the senile dement, which at that time were not treated as criminal acts if the physician's opinion substantiated the diagnosis of mental disease.

Gosselin (1815–1887) in his surgical lectures stressed the influence of age upon the prognosis of surgical diseases and the consequence of operations (20). He believed that strangulated hernia may be operated at any age with equal chances of success (21). A. A. S. Verneuil (1823–1895) another distinguished Paris surgeon, discussed surgery in the aged and explained that bad results were due to acquired diseases rather than to years themselves. Not all the old are sick but precocious senility occurs in alcoholism, malaria and other intoxications (22). Dodeuil's studies on the pathology and symptomatology of prostatic disease comprised a treatise of 110 pages and yielded evidence of the surgical thinking of that time (23). In the same field A. Dieu studied the sperm of old men, reporting on the findings in 105 cases, ranging in age from 64 to 97 years, and stressing the medico-legal significance (24). Douaud, a student of Vulpian, published a thesis on the fatty degeneration of the muscles in old age (25).

The bright star of the Salpétrierè staff was for many years the brilliant neurologist, Jean Martin Charcot (1825–1893). A fascinating lecturer and stimulating thinker, he attracted large numbers of foreign physicians to his clinics at the old hospital. Thanks to translations by an Englishman and an American, his *Clinical Lectures on the Maladies of Old Age* (1867) have attained a reputation far beyond their actual worth, since of 22 lectures only three are devoted to old age, the others being concerned with gout and rheumatism, acute and chronic (26). The work does not purport to cover the entire field and cannot be compared with Durand-Fardel's masterpiece. Nevertheless the language of Charcot is so vivid even in translation that his work is eminently readable and entertaining as well as full of sound observation.

In describing the clinical picture of disease in old age, he stressed the unique character of the patients to be studied in the vast female population of the Salpêtrière. A brief historical review highlighted French contributions to the subject, although he paid his respects to Canstatt, Geist and Mettenheimer as representatives of "science beyond the Rhine." In his opinion "most of the medical works of the past century which touch, in a special manner, upon the senile period of life . . . are more or less ingenious paraphrases of the famous treatise *De Senectute* of the Roman orator." He recognized certain special diseases of old age, such as senile marasmus, senile osteomalacia, senile atrophy of the brain and arterial atheroma. Other diseases seen in all periods of life have special characteristics in the aged. Finally he explained the occurrence and the behavior of infections in the old, pointing out the observations of his student Inglessis on meningitis (9) and of Vulpian's student Moureton on tuberculosis (14), and concluded with the rhetorical question that neatly tied up the whole subject for a Frenchman.

"*And who besides, does not know that Louis XV died of smallpox at the age of sixty-five?*"

Pierre-Adolphe Piorry (1794–1879) is justly famed as the inventor of the pleximeter and the pioneer of mediate percussion in his relatively youthful days. When advanced in years, he held conferences on old age which were recorded by one of his students. He emphasized that the time to combat old age is in youth and deprecated the use of medicines. His conclusions are reminiscent of the wisdom of old men since the beginning of time (27).

"*Guard the activity of your spirit, the health of your body, the purity of your conscience, and your old age will be sweet, and death will be unable to frighten you.*"

Another example of an old physician writing about advanced age from personal experience is the contribution of Diday (1812–1894), the celebrated syphilologist, on senile disturbances of equilibrium (28), in which he discussed his own sensations six years after retirement. Here occurs, apparently for the first time, an epigram frequently quoted by later writers which sounds far better in French than in translation. Whether this was original with the writer is not known.

"*Pour la jeunesse vouloir, c'est pouvoir; pour la vieillesse, trop souvent, vouloir c'est douloir.*"

A contribution by Ferré on the often discussed symmetrical atrophy of the parietal bones of the skull in old age is of interest since it is based on the study of four skulls from the Salpêtrière, from women whose ages ranged from 79 to 88 years (29). In Ballet's contribution to the study of the senile kidney from the Salpêtrière, we find an excellent historical review of previous studies of the kidney in older individuals, emphasizing that the term "senile kidney" should no longer be used to designate a particular state of kidney peculiar to old age (30). The term is not to be taken in an anatomic sense but utilized in relation to cause in order to designate the interstitial nephritis with vascular sclerosis found in old people, just as in adults resulting from lead poisoning or gout. In Martin's study of visceral lesions due to arteriosclerosis we find this opinion confirmed (31). A. F. Voisin published in 1876 his *Clinical Lectures on Mental and Nervous*

Disorders given at the Salpêtrière, in which an excellent discussion of psychosis due to cerebral arteriosclerosis is found with particular emphasis on relation between symptoms and pathological lesions (32).

While Parisian physicians busied themselves in the study of old age, similar activities went on in Nancy, Montpellier and Marseille. In the medical journal of Marseille for 1878 we find several studies on old age from the anatomical and physiological points of view by J. Roux of Brignoles, one of the editors of the journal (33). Other papers treated of traumatic disorders and surgical conditions of the aged. These are well written reviews of current teachings containing little original material. Brousse, chief of the medical clinic at Montpellier, in a monograph on senile involution discussed the theories of senescence, and described the functional and organic changes of old age, concluding that senile involution, like death, is the result of living and is due to general and progressive weakening of the nutrition of the tissues (34).

In 1886 Emile Demange (1846–1904) of Nancy published a small volume of clinical and pathological studies on old age, based on his experience at the Hospice St. Julien where he had observed 500 necropsies (35). This remarkable work is really a study of the physiology and pathology of the senium, with only scant reference to symptomatology and therapy. It is well written with an excellent bibliography and based on the careful observations of a medical man who had already made contributions to the literature on obesity, diabetes, paraplegia, the senile kidney, senile osteomalacia and paralysis (36). The physician of today will feel a strong bond of fellowship on reading his preface in which he thanks "our eminent dean, M. Tourdes (37), in whom I have constantly found a strong support in the midst of the difficulties involved in setting up a clinical service in a home for the aged."

He was particularly interested in arteriosclerosis and believed that atheroma was due to obliterating endarteritis of the vasa vasorum. He stated that this endoperiarteritis was due to stress and strain and was the principal cause of the lesions of old age. His views on the relation of the coronary vessels to heart disease in the aged are likewise amazingly modern and are based on his personal technique of dissecting the finer branches of the coronaries. He found atheromatous changes in the coronaries of 22 out of 23 cases of old people who were not gouty, alcoholic, rheumatic or poisoned by lead, who died of pneumonia, erysipelas, diarrhea, brain hemorrhage or softening, or senile cachexia.

"*Up to now the close relations which unite the arteritic lesions of the coronaries to senility have not been sufficiently placed in relief; one has especially sought to explain certain maladies of the heart by lesions of these vessels; thus one has shown that fatty degeneration of the heart is related to atheroma of the coronaries; one knows infarction of the ventricular wall, recognizing as cause an obliteration of these vessels, and leading to degeneration and sometimes rupture of the heart; finally certain varieties of angina pectoris seem to be due to atheromatous alterations of the vessels.*" This represents an unusually clear conception of the role of the coronaries at a time when the views of most physicians in Europe and the United States were in a state of hopeless confusion. No reference to Demange's original observations is to be found in any of the histories of cardiology consulted. Huchard does not mention Demange nor does Demange list Huchard in his bibliography. In Cowdry's *Arteriosclerosis* Cobb and Blain quote Magliulo's review of the literature in which Demange's views on spinal cord arteriosclerosis are mentioned (38). The neglect of Demange's careful studies by contemporary and subsequent writers is to be explained in part by his location in a provincial city, in part by his differing from the prevailing view that angina pectoris was a nervous disorder, and finally by grouping him with Jenner, Parry and Hunter whose sound observations on the same subject were also disregarded by other physicians. Among contemporary writers on the heart that Demange quoted were Debove and Letulle (39), his own student, Haushalter (40), Robin and Jahel-Renoy (41), and Peter (42). In Romme's review of the senile heart we find Demange quoted as an authority on old age, and Haushalter's paper repeatedly referred to (43).

The turbulent life of Charles-Edward Brown-Séquard (1817–1894) had included professorships in the United States as well as in France, and had seen a great reputation securely founded on physiological research which had demonstrated the vasomotor nerves and the effects of transection of the spinal cord. At the age of 72 he undertook with the assistance of D'Arsonval to try out on himself the rejuvenating effect of extracts of animal testicles. He reported dramatically on the beneficial effects of the preparation before the *Société de Biologie*, June 1, 1889 (44). For a detailed account of his experiments and their startling effect on the world. the reader is referred to Dunbar's contemporary account and to Olmstead's excellent life (45). The remedy was tried out in every kind of hopeless case with reported benefit. "Before the end of the year more than twelve thousand physicians were administering the extract to their patients" (46). In a few years the furore died down, but the ideas of Brown-Séquard laid the foundation for modern endocrine therapy and stimulated the scientific study of the ductless glands. His testicular extract was science's latest answer to the folk-dream of an elixir of life.

In spite of the excitement caused by the demand for the panacea, physicians continued to treat old people according to established principles and from time to time recorded their results. Blum's study of surgery in the aged could be republished under a current date line. In reporting a series of successful operations, he laid emphasis on the preparation of the patient, avoidance of general anesthesia, keeping patient and operating room warm, minimizing loss of blood, rigid antisepsis, liberal feeding and early rising. In his opinion the success of an operation depended less on the age of the patient than on the previous state of health (47). The work of the great French masters of genito-urinary surgery, Felix Guyon (1831–1920) and Joaquin Albarran (1860–1912) contributed to growing understanding of disorders of the bladder and prostate.

In 1895 Jules Boy-Teissier (1858–1908) of Marseille, physician to the Hôpital St. Marguerite, a home for the aged, published his *Lectures on the Diseases of the Aged, given at the Marseille medical school* (48). This work by a clinician trained in the care of the aged is in the modern spirit and well deserves extended comment. He insisted on the study of old age from the biologic as well as the clinical and therapeutic viewpoints. Old age is not a sickness but a natural phase of life. The physician needs to know the period of senescence, by which one arrives at old age and not occupy himself with the already achieved senile involution. He criticized authors who have tried to explain old age by one lesion. He stressed the "coefficient of vital resistance," as being reduced with advancing years and depressed by secondary causes such as acute and chronic infections, intoxications and other acquired morbid states. The reaction against disease in the aged is

FIG. 3. JULES BOY-TEISSIER (1858–1908)

produced in the same way as in the adult, but is as much enfeebled as the coefficient of vital resistance is diminished.

Georges Marinesco (1863–1938) of Rumania (49), trained in Paris, collaborated with P. O. Blocq (1860–1896) in the first description of the brain lesions described later by Redlich as "miliary necroses" (50) and by Simchowicz as "senile plaques" (51). For an excellent discussion and historical bibliography of this important cerebral tissue change, the reader is referred to Critchley's thorough paper on the subject (52).

Magnus-Levy has called the second half of the nineteenth century the heroic age of German medicine and of the other sciences as well (53). The justification for this opinion is seen at once in the names of the leaders, Virchow, Helmholtz,

Bunsen, Gegenbaur, Waldeyer, Du Bois-Reymond, Ludwig, Erb, Billroth, Fraenkel, Cohnheim, Müller and Naunyn. Here as in France the rapid strides in the study and treatment of infectious diseases, in public health methods, and in basic anatomical and physiological concepts led to widereaching benefits for all segments of the population.

With the exception of Uhle's paper on typhoid fever in older people (54), the first important contribution to the subject after Canstatt was the *Klinik der Greisenkrankheiten* of Lorenz Geist published in 1860 (55). The author was a well trained clinician who had published careful studies on industrial phosphorus poisoning (56), and who had worked for 12 years at the Hospital of the Holy Gost, a sectarian institution for the aged in Nürnberg. The book is not only abundantly illustrated by case reports and postmortem findings, but contains many original findings based on Geist's chemical and physiological studies of metabolic processes. Spirometric measurement of the lung capacity based on Hutchinson (57) and analysis of the expired air for carbon dioxide are among the answers Geist was able to give to questions originally asked by Canstatt.

"*If I may summarize the status of the metabolism and intermediary metabolism, it appears from these findings that the age involution of the human body does not begin in one organ, and from this spread to the others. The involution which we recognized as an alteration of metabolism is simultaneous and general, the lungs being the organs in which the progressive involution of life can be measured by the products of their physiological activity. In the same relationship as the respiratory capacity diminishes, the changing metabolism will have manifested an increase of nitrogen excretion and a compensating retention of carbohydrates. Thereby intake and output, as long as relative health exists, are equalized but the metabolism in general diminishes from decade to decade.*"

Although a careful pathologist and trained by 500 autopsies on aged people, Geist showed the prevailing lack of understanding of the importance of the coronary arteries. In discussing stenocardia he states that this condition is combined with pathological conditions of the heart but that it would be erroneous to conclude from it a causal relationship. He quoted Virchow to the effect that only coronary emboli are able by themselves to cause acute paralysis of the heart, the severest form of angina. Geist's work is based on complete knowledge of German, French and English literature and ranks with Fischer, Canstatt and Durand-Fardel as a classical contribution.

Further studies of old age were made at the same time in Frankfurt a/M by Carl Friedrich Christian von Mettenheimer (1824–1898) who worked at the local home for the aged. In his *Sectiones Longaevorum* he has collected, translated and annotated reports of postmortem examinations of centenarians (58). In all he recorded seven cases, namely, Parr, reported by Harvey, Keill's John Bayles, J. H. Vopper reported by Scheuchzer, Haller's 100 year old woman, Poupart's 100 year old woman and Cheselden's two cases. His interest in pathological anatomy is reflected in his more ambitious work on nosologic and anatomic contributions to the study of the diseases of old age, in which are collected case reports and autopsy findings from the Frankfurt Home (59). He attempted to clarify thereby the whole picture of disease in old age. Although he became personal physician to the Archduke of Mecklenburg-Schwerin and was otherwise busily engaged, he continued to write on the subject from time to time. He was in close

FIG. 4. LORENZ GEIST (1807–1867)

touch with Geist but their plans to bring out a medical journal devoted to the problems of old age were terminated by Geist's death in 1867. Shortly after Mettenheimer's death in 1898 there appeared his *Viaticum*, made up of the experiences and counsels of an old physician for his son on his entry into practice

(60). Many years later (1910) the son published a large volume in tribute to his father called *The Development, Aims and Achievements of an Old Physician* (61). This is a rich source of biographical material not only on Mettenheimer but also on his contemporaries.

Two further studies in the pathologic anatomy of old age came from homes in Vienna. Chrastina reporting necropsies from the home at Alserbach laid stress on findings in so-called senile marasmus, describing tissue and vascular changes.

Fig. 5. Carl Friedrich Christian von Mettenheimer (1824–1898)

He also stressed organizing and unresolved pneumonia, denying that he had ever seen asthma of nervous origin (62). Engel reported on 500 postmortem sections in men and women of 60 years of age and over. He emphasized that while the home in Währingergasse admitted only poor infirm old people, the majority of the group suffered not only from the predisposition to illness that old age brings but also from certain definite diseases, often multiple. He referred to some individuals as being veritable storehouses of the most varied morbid processes. In concluding his statistical findings he stated that "the fragility of advanced age consists not so much in lessened resistance to external influences as in the presence of actual disease which is often enough together with minor external disturbances, to bring about death" (63).

In addition to Arnold's study of the cornea and the arcus senilis (64), we find two papers on the mental disorders of old age. Wille's paper was practical and full of clinical understanding (65). He warned of the danger of suicide in the milder cases. Some patients go downhill rapidly but others may last three to four years. Mental symptoms often follow a stroke. He described the nursing difficulties and emphasized cleanliness in order to prevent bedsores. Güntz stressed the need for careful differentiation of senile dementia from melancholia and mania (66). He described eight female patients. In one the mental state followed a stroke; in the others, after the death of their husbands. All were in reasonably good health. He told of one patient who entertained him with tales of Goethe and Schiller at the Weimar court 50 years previously but could not remember the examiner's name. These patients also suffered from mistrustfulness, and persecution manias, and frequently used foul language.

Beneke, distinguished pathologic anatomist of Marburg, contributed in 1879 an essay on age disposition as a contribution to the physiology and pathology of the various age levels of human beings (67) He emphasized the need for more anthropometric studies of the various anatomical systems at various periods in life. This is important since at different life periods the human machine possesses different constitutions, and on these differences indubitably depends the variation in vital manifestations. These changes occur as the necessary consequence of lawfully regulated developmental processes, of the work unavoidably demanded of separate parts of the machine and of the deterioration gradually brought on by work. He adduced abundant statistical material, some of it from reports of the New York City Health Department. He devoted considerable attention to the disposition to disease at various ages. He was certain that continuation of his work would ultimately bring pathologic anatomy and physiology together.

In the lectures of Julius Cohnheim (1839–1884) on general pathology we find a clear statement of his views on the nature of the aging process. He discussed age changes in the elasticity of arteries and ascribed senile atrophy to the effect of disease on tissues and cells combined with other changes which because of their frequency he considered physiological (68). Cohnheim further deserves attention for his experimental study of the effect of ligation of the coronary arteries leading to the erroneous conclusion that the coronaries are end-arteries, occlusion of which always caused death.

The papers of the distinguished neurologist P. J. Möbius on the pupillary reactions (69) and the knee jerk (70) in old age are of genuine clinical importance. He reported that narrowing of the pupils begins at an early age and ends with the pinpoint of the aged. Wide pupils over 50 years suggest a brain lesion. Of 83 patients examined, 60 were over 80 years. Of these 19 had extreme meiosis, 59 moderate; 5 with mydriasis were also blind due to cataract. In studying the knee jerk he found that weak or absent jerks occur in more decrepit individuals. He believed that this weakening is part of the aging process, and of no practical interest as one does not suspect tabes in 80 year old people. On the other hand it may appear prematurely as other senile changes do. In such a case this finding may substantiate a diagnosis of premature senility in the presence of other changes.

Seidel's work on the pathogenesis, complications and treatment of the diseases of old age appeared in Berlin in 1889 and one year later was translated and pub-

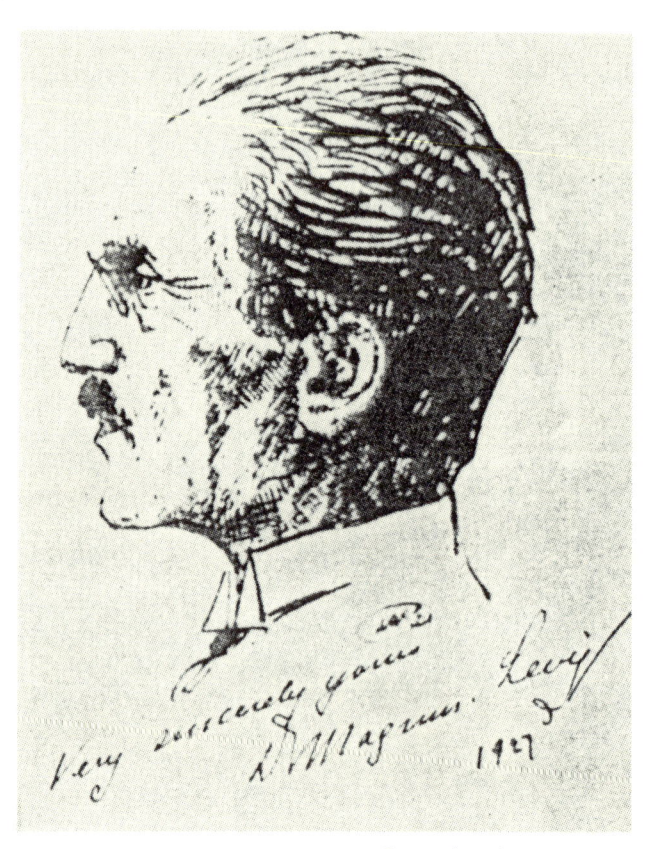

FIG. 6. ADOLF MAGNUS-LEVY (1865)

lished in New York, the first European work on old age to appear in the United States since that of Charcot (71). This is a sound review of existing knowledge presenting no original viewpoints but valuable for its excellent bibliography, and noteworthy for bringing European thinking to the attention of American physicians. Far more important than a book about old age was the actual accomplishment of Max Nitze (1848–1906) who developed the cystoscope in 1879, perfected it in 1886 with the addition of Edison's incandescent lamp and thereby laid the foundation for modern urology and its successful treatment of prostatic hypertrophy, bladder tumors, and calculous disease, in the aged.

Pflüger, the famous physiologist of Bonn (1829-1910), delivered an address in honor of the birthday of Kaiser Wilhelm II, January 27, 1890, on the topic, *The Art of Lengthening Human Life*. This is a good general review of the knowledge to the day, emphasizing the biological nature of death but still clinging to the old beliefs about the longevity of Parr and the others (72).

In 1899 Magnus-Levy established the fall of the basal metabolism with advancing age. In 1941 he, at that time 76 years of age, compared his own basal metabolism during the course of 50 years, showing a diminution in oxygen consumption of 24 per cent (73). In the same paper he quoted the basal metabolism figures of five other well known nutrition authorities in youth and age.

(To be continued)

LIFE'S LATER YEARS

Studies in the Medical History of Old Age

FREDERIC D. ZEMAN, M.D.

[*New York City*]

Part XII*

THE NINETEENTH CENTURY (CONCLUDED)

As we turn to examine the work of physicians in Great Britain we are once again reminded that information on old age must be sought not only in books and papers with self-explanatory titles but also in widely varied publications devoted to general medicine and surgery. In the course of long years devoted to the study of surgical pathology and to the practice of surgery, Sir James Paget (1814-1899), made many important observations on old age. We note first his study of fatty degeneration of the small bloodvessels of the brain and its relation to apoplexy (74), as well as his study of senile scrofula in which he pointed out that it is too often taken for granted that it is exclusively a disease of the earlier part of life, and that "the same error is in many minds respecting phthisis even though many clear accounts of phthisis in the aged have been written" (75). He had first described different types of aged individuals in his *Lectures on Nutrition, Hypertrophy and Atrophy* (76), characterizing one group in vivid words as the "wiry and tough, clinging to life and letting death have them, as it were, by small installments slowly paid". He returned to this theme in his *Various Risks of Operations* where he pointed out that among the old there are even greater differences than among the young in the ability to recover from operations (77).

"*Years, indeed, taken alone are a very fallacious mode of reckoning age; it is not the time, nor the quantity, of a man's past life that we have to reckon; and for this estimate, with a practised eye, looks are less deceptive than a tale of years. . . . They that are fat and bloated, pale with soft textures, flabby, torpid, wheezy, incapable of exercise, looking older than their years, are very bad. They that are fat, florid and plethoric, firm-skinned and with good muscular power, clear-headed and willing to work like younger men, are not indeed good subjects for surgical operations, yet they are scarcely bad. The old people that are thin and dry and tough, clear voiced and bright-eyed, with good stomachs and strong wills, muscular and active, are not bad; they bear all but the largest operations very well. But very few are they, who, looking somewhat like these are feeble and soft-skinned, with little pulses, and appetites, and weak digestive powers; so that they cannot in an emergency, be well nourished*".

In his memoirs and letters, edited by his son Stephen, we find references to his own old age that are extremely revealing and moving. In 1894 he gave his last address to students, advising that they should keep science and practice to-

---

* This is the second part of the twelfth in a series of articles dealing with the studies in the Medical History of old age. Upon completion of their publication, the installments will be collected and reprinted in the form of a monograph.

gether, and that those who said it could not be done were talking sheer nonsense (78).

Paget was well impressed by the work of Edwin Canton (1817-1885) on the arcus senilis and considered this ocular manifestation the best indication of the tendency to either general or partial fatty degeneration of the tissues (79). Originally published as a series of papers in the *Lancet*, starting in 1850, Canton's studies appeared in book form in 1863. Beginning with a general and microscopic account of the arcus, he also reviewed the literature, quoting among others, Virchow's observation that the eye muscles show marked fatty infiltration in the presence of the arcus. He considered the arcus as of hereditary occurrence and as the result of old age or injury to the eye, noting the occasional absence in advanced age. He described the associated fatty and calcareous degeneration of the costal and laryngeal cartilages, and suggested the influence of intemperance and gout on its development. In all he emphasized that it is an ocular sign of constitutional disorder, a point of view which has only recently been revived by studies on familial and acquired hypercholesterolemia in relation to arteriosclerosis.

In 1853 Henry Bence-Jones (1814–1873) published on diabetes in the aged, citing nine cases, all over 60 years, and differing from Dechambre who had made the statement that sugar was habitually present in the urine of old people (80). Surprised himself at the high incidence of the disease in old people, he stated that it was not universal, that it might occur in the aged without the marked symptoms which usually lead to the detection of the disease. He believed that this modified diabetes might at some time be the cause of the debility ascribed to age alone, and that more frequent urine examinations in the aged would lead to more correct diagnosis and subsequent improvement by use of an animal diet. In connection with this study it is timely to recall that in 1848 Bence-Jones had described the albumose that occurs in the urine of patients with multiple myeloma (81) and that the same year had seen Fehling's quantitative test for sugar in the urine first reported (82).

At this period we note briefly Hodgson's work on the prostate gland (83), Cummins' on the tenacity of life in old age, based on one case (84), and Bailey's uncritical records of longevity, enumerating all persons whose ages had reached 100 years and upwards (85). Garrod's work on gout appeared in 1859, and became the standard work for many years. In it he explained that he himself had never had the disease (86). At the age of 70 years he had his first attack which was accordingly recorded in the second edition. Murchison's classic volume on continued fevers stressed the measurable incidence of typhus, typhoid and relapsing fevers in old age. He described typhus in a man of 84 years (87).

Interest in the pathological anatomy of centenarians is shown in George Rolleston's notes on the postmortem examination of a man supposed to have been 106 years old (88), in Massey's report of the findings in the case of Thomas Geeran, aged 105 years (89), and in Sir G. Duncan Gibb's description of an autopsy of the Tring centenarian (90). These cases supplement those reported in von Mettenheimer's *Sectiones Longaevorum* (58).

The Chelsea Royal Hospital (fig. 7) for invalid soldiers was founded by Charles II and was opened in 1694, occupying a handsome building designed by Sir Christopher Wren and surrounded by extensive grounds including the old Ranelagh Gardens. The hospital accomodated about 500 men, many of whom were advanced in years. Physicians and surgeons attached to the institution have had ample opportunity to study normal and pathological aging. William Cheselden and John Hunter served the old pensioners in their time. Daniel Maclachlan (1807-1870), long an attending physician there, published in 1863, *A Practical Treatise on the Diseases and Infirmities of Advanced Life* (91). In 1932 Martin Lipscomb published his work on old age based on his service at Chelsea (92). More recently, during the Second World War, Dr. Trevor Howell was stationed there and published instructive studies of the old soldiers (93), as well as a description of the famous institution, including its severe punishment during the "Blitz".

FIG. 7. THE ROYAL HOSPITAL, CHELSEA (FROM FAULKNER)

Maclachlan discussed in his preface the neglect of the problem of the aged, emphasizing the insidious and chronic nature of the diseases, and pointed out that both rich and poor were afflicted. He appreciated "the great industry of French writers, the equal research and recondite reasoning of German authors", but inclined "more to the practical and sound sense of British and American observers, who in avoiding the trivial distinctions and refinements in description and diagnosis, never lost sight of the great objects of all medical inquiries,—the judicious appreciation of suffering and disease with a view to their amelioration, cure or prevention". He pointed to the paucity of papers on old age in English literature, but commended Floyer, Carlisle, Day, Halford, Holland, Van Oven and Roget. He expressed his debt to Canstatt, regretting that his great work was never translated by the Sydenham Society, and acknowledged his obligation to Durand-Fardel in recommending that his volume should be in the hands of every practitioner anxious to broaden his knowledge of the diseases of the old. In short, Maclachlan's work is an accurate reflection of Continental viewpoints with personal observation and common sense.

We note in passing brief contributions such as Fayrer's report of the rapid union of a fracture in a Hindoo aged 96 years (94), Sedgwick's discussion of the influence of age on hereditary disease (95), and Inman's advice on the preservation of health in old age, stressing the bad effects of overwork, and citing the influence of speed in reducing the average duration of life in America by ten years (6). F. E. Anstie discussed nervous affections in old persons expressing great hope for the new remedy, "chloral", and attempting to differentiate minor or constitutional causes for nervousness from real senile dementia (97), Crichton-Browne, one of the pioneer psychiatrists of Great Britain, later emphasized that senile dementia is not a pathological entity, and described three patients ranging from 74 to 86 years to illustrate the distinctions. He believed that the most stupid people are most prone to dementia, that brainwork does not cause brain degeneration, and that the cultivation of science and literature conduce to longevity (98). Woodman described the occurrence of the arcus senilis early in life (99). Annandale cited nine successful operations in aged patients, proving that age alone is no contraindication and that surgery on the old may be undertaken if the patient is in fair health, and the operation likely to prolong life or relieve suffering (100). A basic contribution to the understanding of kidney disease appeared in the classic paper of W. W. Gull and H. G. Sutton on arterio-capillary fibrosis (101). Sir William Gull was noted for his kindly attitude to patients and for his clinical aphorisms among which we find: "The young, the aged and the sick must always be helped" (102). In 1876 the remarkably versatile observer, Jonathan Hutchinson (1828–1913), reported on symmetrical central choroido-retinal disease in senile persons, of which he says, "I have failed to find in our standard works and atlases any description of similar cases. The disease is not improbably a well characterized and important form of senile amaurosis" (103). Ewens recorded operations performed successfully on aged persons, two patients who had the lower lip removed for epithelioma with cheiloplastic restoration, and a tippling female of 87 years who had a finger amputated for epithelioma. He believed that surgery in the aged should be encouraged (104).

From a distinguished scholar and antiquarian came the first application of the scientific method to the study of the records of longevity. William John Thoms (1803–1885), first a clerk in the secretary's office at the Royal Hospital, Chelsea, and later deputy librarian of the House of Lords, had founded the unique periodical, *Notes and Queries*, in 1849. Here for the first twelve or thirteen years after its inception he had inserted without question all the cases of exceptional longevity that were sent to him. Doubt as to the accuracy of these reports were cast by Sir George C. Lewis, in an article on centenarians published by that journal. Thoms' own studies soon convinced him that most of the cases accepted as having lived beyond 100 years were without basis in fact. His *Longevity of Man: Its Facts and Fictions* appeared in 1873 and created such a storm of adverse public opinion as to justify Thoms calling himself "one of the best abused men in England" (105). After discussing the background of popular belief in centenarianism and the views taken by medical men and naturalists of reputation, he laid down rules for the examination of the evidence in each case and then proceeded to take up the legendary tales of Henry Jenkins, old Parr, and the Countess of Desmond. Of Parr he says, "I really hardly know which is the more to be wondered at—the exceptionally great age of 152 attributed to Parr; or the fact that for upwards of two centuries nobody has appeared to doubt its accuracy, or to have taken the slightest trouble to ascertain upon what evidence it was founded". Most medical writers seem to have accepted Parr's age without question on the authority of Harvey. The appendix to Thoms' book contains Harvey's postmortem on Parr and also the text of the contemporary metrical life, *The Old, Old, Very Old Man*, by John Taylor, the Water Poet.

The evidence and the reasoning brought forward by Thoms was so irrefutable that many persons, scientifically trained and otherwise, reacted violently at the revelation of their own credulity. The controversy found place in the newspapers and medical journals as well as in *Notes and Queries*. Aside from such wordy dis-

"If you would fain know more
Of him whose photo here is—
He coined the word Folk-lore,
And started *Notes & Queries*."

FIG. 8. WILLIAM JOHN THOMS (1803–1885)

pute there were important results from Thoms' iconoclastic views. Most scientists had previously followed Haller's lead and assumed that with sufficient knowledge human life might be prolonged to 200 years. The modern concept of a maximum span of life determined biologically for man as for animals, stems from this disproof of popular wishful thinking. All subsequent work on longevity and on the possibility of extending the life span have depended entirely on Thoms' courageous and completely logical analysis. Later writers, such as Bailey (106) and Young (107) paid well deserved tribute to the pathfinder. Some later authors have misunderstood Thoms' opinion, in stating that he did not believe anyone could live to 100 years. Actually he was interested in getting at the truth, and stated that use of his method not only disclosed the impostor, but supported the case of the truly long-lived. In addition, the attention of the British Medical Association was focussed upon the problem and under the leadership of Sir

George Murray Humphrey (1820–1896) the Association set up a *Collective Investigation of Disease Committee* which addressed itself to *Old Age*, (108) as well as to many other medical problems. In Humphrey's words it constituted "a plan for the collection and utilization of the vast streams of experience which are daily allowed to flow away into the great abyss of waste". The magnitude of the project is evident in its organization which consisted of 54 committees including 800 to 1000 of the leading practitioners.

FIG. 9. SIR GEORGE MURRAY HUMPHREY (1820–1896)

Sir George had been professor of anatomy (1866–1883), and later of surgery (1893–1896) at Cambridge where he had achieved fame as a teacher and a builder of its modern medical school. In 1884 he published remarks on the repair of wounds and fractures in aged persons (109); in 1885, in the annual oration delivered before the Medical Society of London, he discussed *Old Age and Changes Incidental to It* (110); in 1886, described the power of recuperation in old age (111) and in 1889, assisted in preparing the reports of the committee of the British Medical Association (112). In 1889 he brought out *Old Age—the Results of Information received respecting nearly 900 persons who had attained the age of 80* years including 74 centenarians (113). The general tone of the report is optimistic stressing the importance of longevity, temperance, and the ability of old people to get over operations, injuries and brain affections. This work on old age is significant because it was based on real observation; indeed many of the cases were investigated by Sir George personally. The first chapter is a reprint of Humphrey's oration on the old to the Medical Society of London; the next four are devoted to analysis of the returns on the 74 centenarians as compared with findings of previous investigators. The next four chapters are concerned with men and women between 80 and 100 years, and with the maladies of old age.

This fascinating study of the English population suffers from the defects inherent in the questionnaire method and in the lack of uniformity of the approach of the individual medical examiner. Physicians experienced in the institutional care of the aged to-day are only too familiar with reports sent in by practitioners to the effect that a certain person is suffering only from the infirmities "to be expected with his years", and with the subsequent discovery of diseases ranging from congestive heart failure to senile psychosis. Review of the findings of this collective investigation makes clear that clinical studies of the aged must be correlated with postmortem observation to ensure that important changes may not be totally overlooked.

Of J. Milner Fothegill (1841–1888), who was not related to the famous John Fothergill (1712–1780), one gathers the impression of an able but badly adjusted individual. He engaged in quarrels with his colleagues, and was violent in his expression of opinion, a fact doubtless explained in part by his obesity, diabetes and gout. He had published *The Heart and Its Diseases* in 1872 in London and Philadelphia. The work included a novel chapter on the relation of heart and kidney disease. In 1885 his *Diseases of Sedentary and Advanced Life—a Work for Medical and Lay Readers*, appeared (114). In it we find many interesting opinions, as on the proper use of opium in hopeless malignant disease, the need for sympathetic understanding of the old, and particularly on the impairment of judgment in old age. He considered this "exemplified in self-electing oligarchies of senescent persons, as the Royal College of Physicians for instance—which is little removed from an intellectual mummy swathed in rags and cerate" That he was highly esteemed in the United States is indicated by his holding an honorary M.D. degree from Rush Medical College and his election as Foreign Associate Fellow of the College of Physicians of Philadelphia.

In his address at the opening session of the medical department of the Yorkshire College, Victoria University, Leeds, in 1891, Sir James Crichton-Browne pointed to the reduction of the death rate due to better housing, cleanliness and higher standards of living but drew attention to the fact that this improvement was chiefly in the first half of life (115). He attributed the increase in the death rate in the higher brackets to cancer and to diseases of the heart, nervous system and kidneys, resulting from the strain of modern life, as shown by the fact that women outlive men. He considered old age inevitable only in a sense, and that in spite of changes in the nerve centers with senescence, the freshness of youth may survive. In his opinion the natural span of life is 100 years. He suggested that the promotion of health in old age should be a branch of public health medicine and advocated old age insurance. The speaker was at that time only 51 years of age. Son of the first medical superintendent of the Crichton Royal Institution for mental disorders, he had helped in the establishment of research in neurology and psychiatry and was one of the founders of the periodical, *Brain*. As the Lord Chancellor's Visitor in Lunacy (1875-1922) he acquired wide experience in his specialty. He became a living proof of many of his ideas on longevity and old age, and on his 96th birthday prescribed "no fuss and no fads" as his own formula for a long life. He died in 1938, in his 98th year. He was an ex-

FIG. 10. SIR JAMES CRICHTON-BROWNE (1840-1938)

cellent speaker and wrote well. Especially remembered are his volumes of memoirs. In his *Prevention of Senility* address occurs the memorable dictum: "Old age begins in the cradle and youth still lingers in decrepitude" (116).

George William Balfour (1823-1903) of Edinburgh has been linked with Sir William Tennant Gairdner and Charles Hilton Fagge in London, as making the most important contributions of his generation to the clinical study of the affections of the circulation (117). He had published in 1876 *Clinical Lectures on Diseases of the Heart and Circulation*, and in 1894 his book, *The Senile Heart*, appeared and, according to his biographer, "at once took rank as a classic" (118). Thi work reflects the best thinking of its day, both English and European. The nutrition of the myocardium is emphasized, as are also the age changes in the vascular system. As to the role of the coronary arteries, he expressed what was the common error in the reasoning of most physicians for many years, namely, that while coronary sclerosis and angina are frequent concomitants, "coronary sclerosis is too often present where there has never been any angina to permit the circumstances to be looked upon as anything more than accidental". Balfour discussed *angina sine dolore*, first described by Gairdner and considered the senile heart similar to gouty heart of the English and to the *Luxusherz* of the Germans. His therapy was simple, depending chiefly on rest, but using digitalis as a cardiac tonic in the form of *Digitaline Nativelle*, a product that has in recent years again returned to favor.

In closing this section on the English studies of the aged, the reader must be reminded of the steps that had led to the improvement of public health referred to above by Sir James Crichton-Browne. According to Guthrie, credit for having drawn attention to the need for public health legislation belongs to the philosopher, Jeremy Bentham (1748–1832). Thomas Southwood Smith (1788–1861) coöperated with the lawyer, Sir Edwin Chadwick (1800–1890) in efforts to improve sanitation and to eliminate preventable sickness. Sir John Simon (1816–1904) became the first Medical Officer for London, and pushed sanitary reforms of all kinds with great vigor and outstanding success (119). The adoption of an aggressive policy in Great Britain and other civilized countries helped to bring about the profound changes in the age make-up of the population in the next century.

Samuel D. Gross (1805–1884) of Philadelphia was easily the greatest American surgeon of his time. In 1856 he published a *Report on the Causes which impede the progress of American medical literature* (120). He pointed out that the obstructions to the development of a national medical literature were four in number. The identity of the language of the United States with that of Great Britain made it easy for American publishers, in the absence of an international copyright law, to pirate English works and to sell them more cheaply than the originals. Likewise there was a strong disposition in the profession to patronize English rather than American works. Further, the medical press was lacking in independence, failed in its duty to provide constructive criticism, and was too subservient to the publishers of medical books. Lastly the physicians and surgeons of the country had failed to take advantage of the great opportunities offered in the hospitals and in their own practices to make scientific contributions as worthwhile as any emanating from European institutions.

As we proceed to study the work of American physicians in the field of old age we shall see that Gross' strictures are well borne out, with few exceptions. One of these is to be found in the works of the scholarly surgeon himself. Sir George Murray Humphrey writing in 1884 on the repair of wounds and fractures in aged persons (121), quoted from Gross' *System of Surgery* (1859) that age is no barrier to the union of fractures, citing his case of a woman of 100 years in whom union of a fractured humerus took place in the usual time, and that of a woman aged 93 years in whom a fracture of the upper third of the thigh united in seven weeks. In his treatise on the diseases and injuries of the urinary bladder, the prostate gland, and the urethra he discussed the question of the relationship of prostatic enlargement to old age (122). In his opinion, the fact that this condition occurred in men of advanced age meant that the condition probably originated much earlier, and only showed itself by appropriate symptoms after many years. He quoted Sir Benjamin Brodie's (1783-1862) often repeated remark: "When the hair becomes gray and scanty, when specks of earthy matter begin to be deposited in the tunics of the arteries, and when a white zone is formed at the margin of the cornea, at this same period the prostate gland usually, I might say invariably, becomes increased in size"; and then proceeded to deny the truth.

"*This view, I am inclined to think is more poetical than real. The belief I know is very general, even in the profession, that there is hardly a man of 50 who has not an enlarged prostate. My experience has supplied me with no facts in support of this opinion. The conclusion is too sweeping, the word 'old' is a relative one, and should be used in no other sense in reference to the present subject. Thus, one man is old at 40, another at 50, another at 60, and still another, perhaps, not until he is 70. Gray hair, earthy specks in the coats of the arteries, and a zone around the cornea, are no signs of old age, physiologically and philosophically considered*"

Nichols in his unusually discerning paper on old age stressed the neglect of the aged by physicians, and commended the aged to the attention of philanthropic reformers (123). He reviewed the physical changes and suggested the study of mental hygiene, since unsoundness of mind in the old should not be confused with insanity. Therapeutically he urged caution in the use of mild remedies, and dependence on nature and nursing, lest the patient be further enfeebled. Dutcher's lecture on age was of general character with no reference to actual observations (124). In a paper read before the Cincinnati Academy of Medicine, Dr. S. Gans mentioned the work of Durand-Fardel and of L. "Geis" of Nürnberg, the "latter being the most complete and comprehensive one ever published. I have made that work the principal basis of my report" (125). Geist's name is consistently misspelled throughout the essay which contains no original material.

Lee's study of the arcus senilis was based on 72 cases in negroes, from the Colored Home of New York City, which led him to support Canton's view of its relation to cardiac changes. The author believed that old age is synonymous with fatty degeneration (126). Haskins had previously taken the opposite point of view because he had seen 12 cases of arcus senilis in which there were no symptoms referable to the heart (127). In his opinion the arcus was of but little value to determine the seat and nature of obscure diseases.

Another supercentenarian was reported by "R.D." in the form of "John Gilley, who died in Augusta, Maine, at the age of 124 years". This account followed the familiar pattern including his marriage for the first time between 70 and 80 years to a girl of 18 years, by whom he had eight children. According to his wife, his virility ceased suddenly at 120 years. His only illness was a fracture of the leg. There was no postmortem examination (128).

Smith's and Griscom's essays on the physical indications of longevity were published by an insurance company, bound up with T. S. Lambert's discussion of longevity with relation to insurance rates (129). S. C. Chew (1808-1863) reported the case of a 97 year old lady with bladder symptoms which yielded to treatment quickly. He considered the case of physiological interest because of the age of the patient, and in view of the absence of signs of disease, wondered what would eventually cause her death. He assumed that it would be fatty degeneration of the heart (130). S. P. Cutler, writing on the physiology and chemistry of old age, stated that with age the cells become clogged with mineralized matter, thereby excluding a portion of the nutritive elements (131). The slow but constant change in hard tissues is proved by the teeth. The organs cool with age unless sustained by alcohol. He suggested limewater as a means of retarding the mineralizing process and the use of foods free of phosphates and a large percentage of vegetable acid. He believed that the scientific study of food might prolong youth indefinitely. Whitaker's study of a case of senile gangrene of both extremities led him only into theorizing (132). Bailey's report of senile prostatic hypertrophy was based on his own cases and reflected the reluctance and inability of surgeons to cope with this condition at that time (133). That the aged were on occasion being studied scientifically rather than theoretically, is shown by one of the rare publications of the famous New York physician, Edward G. Janeway (1841-1911). Discussing the need for postmortem examinations he cited a series of brain cases, many of whom were elderly, in which the diagnosis could only be made by the pathologist (134).

George Miller Beard (1839-1889) was a distinguished neurologist of New York City, who among other contributions is noted for his introduction of the word "neurasthenia" in his work in *American Nervousness with Its Causes and Consequences* (135). In his study of legal responsibility in age (1874) he was interested in the effect of age on the mental faculties, reviewing the work of many famous men (136). He believed that the acuity of the mind declined with age, listing the causes. In his opinion, 70 per cent of the work of the world was done before 45 years, and 90 per cent pefore 50 years. He cited many authorities who agreed with him and attempted to answer the objections of critics of his idea. These remarks of Beard, interesting in themselves, become more arresting in their reappearance some 30 odd years later in Sir William Osler's famous *Fixed Period* speech which was so horribly distorted by the newspapers. This relationship was apparent to the present writer when he first read Beard's paper several years ago. Only recently Sir James Crichton-Browne's address on the *Prevention of Senility* (116) came to hand in which he stated that Sir William Osler followed "close in the footsteps of the late Dr. George Beard", and in which he dissents vigorously from the viewpoint of both Beard and Osler. Beard's opinions on the decline of mental power with age formed the basis for his discussion of the legal responsibility of old men. This comes up in cases of crimes committed by the aged, in cases of wills that are disputed on the ground of senile incapacity, in fixation of the limit when important officials should be retired and of the age beyond which men should not be eligible to office, and in cases of contested priority in invention and discovery.

He admitted that there are definite exceptions to his rule but stated that great mental decline and grave cerebral disease are yet consistent with average responsibility. He had no great hope that his views would meet with easy acceptance, since they attacked "principles that are hoary with years, and treasured as heirlooms in the hearts of men; that it seeks to undermine doctrines that are sweeter than life, dear as heaven, and in defence of which many have joyfully gone down to die." He felt that it would be at least fifteen and probably twenty-five years before his theory was generally understood. Actually it has taken more than fifty, for only in the past two decades has modern psychology developed satisfactory methods for measuring accurately the decline of certain mental faculties in relation to age. Beard also wrote the *Longevity of Brain Workers* (137). According to Dana, Beard was very fond of his longevity and work thesis. He believed that brain work was the healthy defense against old age, and that brain workers lived 15 years longer than the average (138).

One of the distinguished practitioners of Louisville, Kentucky, was Lunsford P. Yandell (1805-1878), a pioneer in medical education in the Ohio Valley, an editor of several medical journals and an ardent collector of local fossils. The last paper he wrote was on *Old Age, Its Diseases and Hygiene* (139). The editor of the American Practitioner appended a note to the published article that news of the writer's death had just been received as the journal went to press. This is a general paper which indicates clearly the wide range of Yandell's reading and his clear understanding of the problems of older people. His grandson was Yandell Henderson (1874-1944) the well known director of the Yale Laboratory of Applied Psychology, who made such important contributions to our knowledge of the pharmacology and toxicology of gases. In a charming essay, written for the eightieth birthday of his friend, Simon Flexner, Dr. Henderson told of his own boyhood in Louisville, and paid tribute to his grandfather as "dean of the first medical school west of the Allegheny Mountains and a friend of the great McDowell. He was also a geologist of distinction, a writer on medical subjects whose works were highly prized, and a physician who was so much in advance of his time that he gave as small doses of as few drugs as his patients would permit."

The reader will recall that to the translation of the lectures of Charcot by Leigh Hunt, the publisher had added ten additional lectures by Dr. Alfred L. Loomis (1831-1895) of New York City (26). In his introduction to the book Loomis stated that these "embodied, in the main, the salient points in Diseases of Advanced Life which I have been accustomed to impress upon my classes at my clinic in Bellevue Hospital". The topics covered were senile pneumonia, senile chronic catarrh of the bronchi, asthma, atheroma and fatty heart, cerebral hemorrhage and apoplexy, cerebral softening, chronic gastric catarrh, senile constipation and senile hypertrophy of the prostate gland. These topics are discussed in a thoroughly practical manner, emphasizing the differences between the reactions of younger and older patients and devoting considerable attention to treatment. They constitute a good resumé of the medical teachings of that period, and indicate that the leading American physicians were familiar with European interest in older people and with scientific contributions to the subject

The case report of Frederick Winsor (1829-1889), of Massachusetts bears directly on the history of coronary heart disease. In 1880 he described a case of angina pectoris with cardiac rupture, in which on the basis of the postmortem findings he showed the sequence, coronary occlusion, myocardial infarction and rupture, constituting in the opinion of Benson, Hunter and Manlove, "the first entirely valid presentation of the etiology of cardiac rupture" (140). The patient was an obese merchant of 67 years who had suffered from anginal pain for two and one half years prior to the fatal attack.

In the increasing number of contributions to the topic of old age we note two large groups, general articles and case reports, none of which has the distinction of Winsor's crucial observation. In the first division may be recorded H. Wardner's report on diseases of old people (141), S. W. Caldwell's possible suspension of old age (142), H. C. Wood's hygiene of old age (143), F. C. Clarke's diseases of old age, leaning to Maclachlan (144), R. H. Grube's excellent pathology of old age, based on reports of five national military homes (145), W. J. Rothwell's lobar pneumonia in the aged (146), J. W. Bell's plea for more medical interest in the aged, showing a thorough knowledge of the literature (147), E. B. Montgomery's observations on prophylaxis and treatment (148), I. N. Love's needs and rights of old age, an address delivered at the commencement exercises of the Hospital College of Medicine, Louisville, Kentucky (149), and M. E. Nuckol's old age and the modifications in the course of ordinary diseases when they attack the aged (150).

Among the case reports are F. W. Stuart's case of embolism of the left vertebral artery in a man aged 62 years, with autopsy (151), C. A. Wood's unusual case of epilepsy in a male of 70 years (152), C. W. Hollister's senile gangrene complicated by encapheloid cancer of the face, with spontaneous amputation (153), an exceptional case of tabes in a man of 64 years, reported by N. E. Brill, the first to describe endemic typhus and whom the present writer served as house physician in 1921 at the Mt. Sinai Hospital, New York City (154), F. Ieuel's report on the use of moist heat after operations for senile gangrene (155), A. Hanchett's case of senile bronchitis in a female of 90 years (156), Van Harlingen's management of eczema in old people based on 40 personal cases (157), S. D. Lamb's postmortem report of senile hydrocephalus (158), Kammerer's case of sarcoma of the dura mater in a man of 65 years (159), S. M. Bennett's case of alexia in a man of 82 years (160), T. S. K. Morton's study of fractured ribs in the aged (161), and J. H. Emerson's group of aged patients (162). Cases of senile chorea were recorded by two distinguished Philadelphia practitioners. When Dr. J. M. Anders, in 1889, read his report before the Philadelphia County Medical Society, it was discussed by Dr. William Osler, who said, "Almost all cases of senile chorea are probably associated with organic changes, whereas the evidence is uniformly in favor of the view that the chorea of children very easily a functional disorder" (163). David Riesman (1867-1940) some years later, described senile chorea in a man aged 75 years and collected 65 additional cases from the literature (164). Pneumonia in the aged was discussed in an excellent paper by James B. Ayer, of Boston, who not only cited his own cases but also quoted the statistics for different countries, expressing the belief that the frequency of pneumonia in older people is underestimated (165). L. D White defended a different point of view (166). In his opinion the acute lung disorders in the aged generally termed pneumonia are in reality nearly always instances of pulmonary congestion resulting from a weakened circulation.

In general the surgeons of this period brought more tangible benefits to their older patients. Surgical exploration of the abdomen under aseptic conditions initiated by Billroth and his pupils was carried out in the United States by such men as Gerster, Halsted, McBurney, Fenger, Keen and Kelly. The descriptions of the clinical picture of acute appendicitis by Reginald Heber Fitz, of Boston in 1886, led to general interest in establishing early diagnosis in such cases. Two worthwhile studies of a common lesion in the aged are L. A. Stimson's (1844-1917) *On doubtful fractures of the neck of the femur and their identity with an alleged form of arthritis deformans* (167) and Nicholas Senn's (1844-1909) treatment of fractures of the neck of the femur by immediate reduction and permanent fixation (168). This paper was based on experimental work with cats. The author's group of eight cases included several of great age. "Patients suffering from this injury are with few exceptions advanced in years and liable to succumb to complications incident to long confinement in bed. The marantic changes in the tissues of the aged and in persons rendered prematurely old by hereditary or acquired causes are known to be antagonistic to a rapid repair while the anatomical conditions at the site of fracture are well calculated to retard if not prevent production of callus."

The prostate gland continued to challenge surgeons although there were many urologists who still were unwilling to admit that the enlargement of the gland was the only cause of urinary obstruction in older men. Senile weakness of the bladder muscles and a "sclerosis" of the bladder and urethra were considered the primary causes. The papers of Vance (169) and Wilson (170) were general reviews but D. Hays Agnew of Philadelphia urged "prostatotomy" (171) Actually suprapubic prostatectomy developed almost accidentally from operation on the bladder for stone, when it was found that the enlarged middle lobe could be removed without too much difficulty. Pioneers in this operative technique were von Dittel, of Vienna (172), McGill, of Leeds (173), Watson, of Boston (174), and Belfield, of Chicago (175). A. W. Mayo Robson was present at McGill's first operation and became an enthusiastic advocate. His paper is of added interest because the case reports were prepared by the house surgeon, Berkeley Moynihan (176).

At the meeting of the American Association for the Advancement of Science in 1890, Charles Sedgwick Minot (1852-1914), the distinguished anatomist and physiologist of Harvard, addressed the Section of Biology, *On certain phenomena of growing old* (177). This is the first approach to the subject by an American investigator from other than a strictly clinical viewpoint. On the basis of graphs showing the law of biological variations, Minot pointed out the effect of senescence in making the curves asymmetrical. He complained of the lack of vital statistics. He lamented the loss of a large colony of guinea pigs with which he had worked for five years and which were shaken to death in one night by a bull terrier. In Minot's opinion man's rate of growth diminished from birth to attainment of adult size because of the steady loss of vitality from birth onward.

FIG. 11. CHARLES SEDGWICK MINOT (1852-1914)

The body's power of continuing development steadily decreases. He compared young and adult tissues and found that the most characteristic change with advancing age is the growth in size of the cellular protoplasm in relation to the size of the nucleus. He believed that this development of the protoplasm is the cause of the loss of the power of growth and forms the physical basis of advancing decrepitude. He later gave to this process the name, "cytomorphosis", and elaborated his views in his book *The Problem of Age, Growth and Death* (178). Here he pointed out the difference in the growth of germ cells and those of adult tissues, which is expressed in the disproportionate bulk of the nucleus and cytoplasm. Death is the inevitable price that the organism must pay for the cytological differentiation on which all higher life depends.

These studies of the first American student of the fundamental cellular changes of senescence conclude our survey of the development of medical knowledge of old age in the nineteenth century. The increasing interest of physicians has gone hand in hand with the rapid growth of the fundamental sciences, with growing understanding of the causes of disease and with improved methods of controlling and treating infectious diseases. The old classical dictum, *senectus ipsa est morbus*, has given way to a concept of a biologically limited life span associated with degenerative tissue changes upon which a variety of disease processes are superimposed. A definite feeling of optimism is gradually pervading the thinking of physicians and surgeons as to the possibility of constructive aid to the aged, and has begun to replace the prevailing attitude of pessimism characteristic of the laity as well as of the profession. We have seen that even before the turn of the century an improved expectation of life was being observed for younger people and that an increase in the incidence of so-called degenerative diseases was anticipated. The actual achievement of unprecedented gains in life expectancy in the first three decades of the twentieth century brought about changes in the age make-up of the population of the civilized world that constituted the greatest challenge that society has ever faced regarding the problems of old age and made it necessary to multiply the methods of coping with them on medical, social and political levels.

AN INTRODUCTION TO LITERATURE ON THE HISTORY OF GERONTOLOGY

Gerald J. Gruman

NOTES AND COMMENTS

AN INTRODUCTION TO LITERATURE ON THE HISTORY OF GERONTOLOGY

GERALD GRUMAN

Interest in gerontology, the study of aging, has grown rapidly during the twentieth century. Progress in medicine and public health has increased the proportion of aged persons in the population. These persons require a vast program of support which has focused attention on the problem of senescence. Meanwhile, remarkable advances in such fields as cytology and biochemistry have revived the idea of prolongevity,[1] the hope that science may be able to extend greatly, perhaps indefinitely, the length of life.[2, 3, 4, 5]

Within the past decade gerontology has become a recognized and well-organized specialty in the United States. The American Gerontological Society was organized in 1945. The *Journal of Gerontology* began publication in 1946. In 1951, the federal government established a Committee on Aging which is now part of the Department of Health, Education, and Welfare. There are two Institutes of Gerontology in the United States, one at the University of Kansas and the other at the State University of Iowa.

Although it only recently has become an independent specialty, gerontology has deep roots in the past. Unfortunately, not enough systematic work has been done in tracing and evaluating these ties with the past. There is a great need for professional research in the history of gerontology. Such historical research would provide useful orientation on problems of aging; it also would throw light upon many now-hidden facets of the history of medicine.

---

[1] Gruman, G., C. A. Stephens (1844-1931)—Popular Author and Prophet of Gerontology. *New England J. of Med.* 1956, vol. 254, pp. 658-660. Idem, *Death and Progress: The Idea of Prolongevity in American Thought* (in progress).

[2] Stephens, C. A., *Natural Salvation*. Norway Lake, Maine: The Laboratory, 1903.

[3] Malisoff, W. M., *The Span of Life*. Philadelphia: Lippincott, 1937, pp. 188 and 265 ff.

[4] Shryock, R. H., *The Development of Modern Medicine*. N. Y.: Alfred Knopf, 1947, pp. 78 and 455-457.

[5] Thomson, George, *The Foreseeable Future*. Cambridge: Cambridge University Press, 1955, pp. 132-134.

Research in the history of gerontology is handicapped by the lack of a comprehensive full-length text on the subject.[6] The material is uneven in quality, and it is dispersed in numerous journals and books some of which are quite difficult to obtain. A number of essential sources have not yet been translated into English, French, or German.

A few years ago, N. W. Shock, Chief of the Section on Gerontology of the United States Public Health Service, prepared an extensive bibliography of gerontology and geriatrics. The work[7] was published in 1951 under a grant from the Forest Park Foundation which is devoted to the improvement of care for the aged. Since April 1950, Dr. Shock has continued his compilation in the bibliographical supplement accompanying each issue of the quarterly publication *Journal of Gerontology*. The classification system is designed in such a way that the bibliography can be kept up to date with the latest literature, while, at the same time, older works can be added as they come to the attention of the editor.

The Shock bibliographies are an invaluable contribution to the history of gerontology. However, it must be noted that in the 1951 publication not all the available material is to be found under the heading " History of Gerontology and Geriatrics."[8] For example, Zeman's important series of articles is listed under " Cultural Anthropology."[9] In the bibliographical supplements to the *Journal of Gerontology*, the history category, unfortunately, has been dropped entirely, and historical works are scattered through the " General Orientation " and " Miscellaneous " sections.

In my opinion, the three best historical works on gerontology as a whole are those of Freeman, Steudel, and Zeman. I will discuss these in turn. J. T. Freeman's article " The History of Geriatrics "[10] appeared in 1938. Freeman, a specialist in internal medicine in Philadelphia, helped to establish one of the first geriatrics clinics in the United States and has been a leader in the Geriatrics and Gerontological Societies. His 1938 article apparently was the first significant work on the subject. The word " geriatrics " in 1938 had not yet been restricted to its present

---

[6] There are, however, a number of book-length studies of special aspects of the history of gerontology, e. g., Simmons, L. W., *The Role of the Aged in Primitive Society*. New Haven: Yale Univ. Press, 1945, and Richardson, B. E., *Old Age Among the Ancient Greeks*. Baltimore: Johns Hopkins Press, 1933.

[7] Shock, N. W., *A Classified Bibliography of Gerontology and Geriatrics*. Stanford, Calif.: Stanford Univ. Press, 1951.

[8] *Ibid.*, p. 473.

[9] *Ibid.*, p. 449.

[10] Freeman, J. T., The History of Geriatrics. *Annals of Medical History*, 1938, vol. 10 (N. S.), pp. 324-335.

meaning, the medical treatment of the aged. Freeman's article is really as much a history of gerontology as of geriatrics. As must be expected of a pioneer effort, Freeman's article has several shortcomings. He relied entirely on sources available in English, and his treatment of ancient and medieval gerontology is inadequate.

Freeman's most important contribution, I believe, was his emphasis upon the history of gerontology as a rich and valuable field of research.[11] He tried to make his article more than a dry compendium of names and dates, and he succeeded in forming many of the data into a meaningful pattern. He felt that Roger Bacon was significant as a forerunner of the modern attitude towards old age, Cornaro for his rejection of alchemy and astrology, Floyer as the founder of modern geriatrics, Hufeland as the stimulator of public opinion, Canstatt for his professionalization of geriatrics, and Charcot as the symbol of the final shift of gerontology from the domain of philosophy to that of science. He singled out Rush, Franklin, and Caldwell as the originators of gerontology in America.

Steudel's article "Zur Geschichte der Lehre von den Greisenkrankheiten"[12] appeared in 1942. Johannes Steudel is Director of the Bonn Institute of Medical History and Associate Editor of *Sudhoffs Archiv für Geschichte der Medizin und der Naturwissenschaften*. His paper naturally is a thoroughly professional work of medical history.

There are, however, certain limitations which somewhat restrict the value of Steudel's article. It is disappointingly brief, and the author had to concentrate his attention on certain points in which he was most interested and ignore the rest. Thus, there is no discussion of pre-Greek gerontology nor any mention of Chinese or Indian theories of senescence, and the section on modern gerontology breaks off in the 1860's. As the title indicates, the author tended to be concerned primarily with the clinical side of gerontology. This probably is why he did not mention Aristotle, and why his analyses of the Hippocratic school and of Galen and Avicenna consist of detailed listings of their clinical observations and therapeutic recommendations rather than a penetrating inquiry into their theoretical formulations. Another bias in Steudel's paper is his emphasis on German contributions to gerontology. Nicholas of Cusa, J. B. Fischer, B. W. Seiler, and Carl Canstatt are the heroes of the piece.

Steudel's nationalism, while exaggerating the role of German scientists, on the other hand, stimulated the most interesting and original parts

[11] *Ibid.*, p. 324.
[12] Steudel, J., Zur Geschichte der Lehre von den Greisenkrankheiten. *Sudhoffs Archiv für Geschichte der Medizin und der Naturwissenschaften*, 1942, vol. 35 (N. S.), pp. 1-27.

of his article. He described the attempts of Nicholas of Cusa to establish an exact quantitative basis for gerontology by weighing the urine and the blood and by measuring pulse and respiratory rates.[13] He pointed out that Floyer, traditionally the founder of modern geriatrics, was essentially a Galenist,[14] whereas J. B. Fischer, a German physician serving as chief of the Russian medical service, published in 1754 a book reorganizing gerontology on the basis of Vesalian anatomy and Harveian physiology.[15] He discussed the relationship between Canstatt and nineteenth-century *Naturphilosophie*.[16]

Although German influences predominated in Steudel's article, he kept patriotic considerations within reasonable bounds. For example, he gave full recognition to the French lead in establishing special hospitals for the aged and exploiting the resulting abundance of clinical and post-mortem material.[17] He also mentioned American priority in organizing geriatrics as an independent medical specialty.[18]

Zeman's series of articles " Life's Later Years; Studies in the Medical History of Old Age "[19] appeared between 1942 and 1950. F. D. Zeman is a private medical practitioner in New York City. Since 1925 he has been chief of the medical staff of the Home for Aged and Infirm Hebrews, and he has written many papers on geriatrics and gerontology.

Dr. Zeman's work is on a comprehensive scale. He progressed in a methodical manner, article by article, from primitive societies to ancient Egypt, Israel, Greece, Rome, Islam, Medieval Europe, the Renaissance, the seventeenth century, the eighteenth century, and the nineteenth century. Upon completion, the series was to have been published as a monograph. Unfortunately, no new articles have appeared since the one in 1950 which carried the subject to the end of the nineteenth century.

Some of the early articles in Zeman's series rely rather heavily on secondary sources. However, as the author continued his work, he consulted more and more the primary sources and the foreign-language material. Many of the articles are excellent, and all are interesting and

[13] *Ibid.*, pp. 13-14.
[14] *Ibid.*, p. 12.
[15] *Ibid.*, pp. 15-17.
[16] *Ibid.*, pp. 20-22.
[17] *Ibid.*, pp. 22-24.
[18] *Ibid.*, p. 18.
[19] Zeman, F. D., Life's Later Years; Studies in the Medical History of Old Age. *J. Mt. Sinai Hospital* (N. Y.) 1942, vol. 8, pp. 1161-1165; 1944-45, vol. 11, pp. 45-52, 97-104, 224-231, 300-307, 339-344; 1945, vol. 12, pp. 783-791, 833-846, 890-901, 939-953; 1947, vol. 13, pp. 241-256; 1950, vol. 16, pp. 308-322; 1950, vol. 17, pp. 53-68.

beautifully illustrated. It is regrettable that Zeman's work has not yet been published in book form as an introductory history of gerontology.

The other historical papers on gerontology as a whole can be reviewed briefly. Kotsovsky [20] dismissed ancient, medieval and early modern gerontology in a few sentences and, thus having reached 1850, presented a lengthy list of investigators since that time together with laconic accounts of their gerontological theories. The article concludes with Kotsovsky's own theory and an extensive bibliography valuable for an historian of modern gerontology. The book by G. Stanley Hall,[21] the famous American psychologist, includes some interesting historical material. Hall's work was used by Freeman and Zeman and apparently helped to stimulate their research. S. R. Burstein's article in the *Post Graduate Medical Journal* [22] is helpful for its data on the gerontology movement in Great Britain. Her series in *Geriatrics* [23] is excellently illustrated but the text is rather brief and discontinuous. Price's misnamed article [24] is not really historical. Thewlis [25] and Nascher,[26] the latter of whom coined the term "geriatrics," each wrote brief historical essays useful as source material on the geriatrics movement in the United States just before and during World War I. Kafemann's misnamed article [27] is primarily a discussion of contemporaneous research on longevity.

In summary, it is desirable that medical historians give more attention to the history of gerontology. As yet no comprehensive book has been published on the subject and many important source materials have not been translated. However, the valuable studies by Freeman, Steudel, and Zeman can serve as an introduction to the field. The bibliographies of these authors and, above all, the splendid bibliographies compiled by Shock point the way to a mass of fascinating source material and list a

[20] Kotsovsky, D., Das Alter in der Geschichte der Wissenschaft. *Isis,* 1933, vol. 20 (N. S.), pp. 220-241.

[21] Hall, G. S., *Senescence: The Last Half of Life.* N. Y.: Appleton, 1922.

[22] Burstein, S. R., Gerontology: A Modern Science With a Long History. *Post Graduate Medical J.* (London), 1946, vol. 22, pp. 185-190.

[23] Burstein, S. R., The Historical Background of Gerontology. *Geriatrics,* 1955, vol. 10, pp. 189-193, 328-332, 536-540.

[24] Price, M. L., Ancient and Modern Theories of Age. *Maryland Medical J.* 1906, vol. 49, pp. 43-51.

[25] Thewlis, M. W., The History of Geriatrics. *Medical Review of Reviews* (N. Y.), 1918, vol. 24, pp. 285-288.

[26] Nascher, I. L., A History of Geriatrics. *Medical Review of Reviews* (N. Y.), 1926, vol. 32, pp. 281-284.

[27] Kafemann, R., Das Problem des langen Lebens von Gorgias bis Alexis Carrel. *Altersprobleme,* 1937, vol. 1, pp. 33-44.

large number of historical studies on special aspects of gerontology.[28] Using these pioneer works the medical historian should be able quite readily to orient himself in the history of gerontology.[29]

---

[28] Some examples of studies of special aspects of the history of gerontology are: Burstein, S. R., Care of the Aged in England. From Mediaeval Times to the End of the Sixteenth Century. *Bull. Hist. Med.*, 1948, vol. 22, pp. 738-746; Belt, E., Leonardo da Vinci's Studies of Aging Process. *Geriatrics*, 1952, vol. 7, pp. 205-210; and Angel, J. L., Length of Life in Ancient Greece. *J. Geront.*, 1947, vol. 2, pp. 18-24. There are many others.

[29] For a competent and provocative account of the present situation in gerontological research see Comfort, Alex., *The Biology of Senescence.* N. Y.: Rinehart, 1956.

REVIEW OF M. D. GRMEK'S ON AGING AND OLD AGE

Gerald J. Gruman

M. D. GRMEK. *On Ageing and Old Age,* Basic Problems and Historic Aspects of Gerontology and Geriatrics. (*Monographiae Biologicae,* 1958, Vol. V, No. 2). Den Haag: Uitgeverij Dr. W. Junk, 1958. 106 pp. Ill. 14 guilders.

This important little book appears at the best possible time. One of the most remarkable medical developments since World War II has been the enormous growth of interest in the care of the aged. Geriatrics has become a well-organized specialty, and gerontology, comprising the biology, psychology, and sociology of aging, is receiving major attention from the foundations, the government, and the public. The scientists and physicians working in these newly-recognized fields have felt a need for historical orientation; the Gerontological Society, for example, voted at its 1958-59 meeting to establish a committee on history. At the same time, historians have been taking more and more notice of the shift in medical emphasis from the problems of early and middle life to those of later years.

Actually, this is the second monograph-length history of geriatrics and gerontology. The first such study was by Frederic D. Zeman and was entitled *Life's Later Years: Studies in the Medical History of Old Age*. It was published as a series of 13 articles in the *Journal of the Mt. Sinai Hospital* (N. Y.) between 1942 and 1950. Dr. Zeman's work proceeded in a methodical manner through the chief periods of history from primitive societies to the end of the nineteenth century. Unfortunately, it has not as yet been issued in book form, but those able to consult the articles will find that the chronologic approach, the leisurely pace, and the numerous illustrations make them a pleasing introduction to the field.

Dr. Grmek's study, in contrast with Dr. Zeman's, is concise to an extraordinary degree and is more varied in format. In the 88 data-packed pages of the text proper there are eleven different chapters, all historical in nature but not consistently chronological: 1. Definitions, 2. Causes and Nature of Ageing, 3. Phases and Symptoms of Ageing, 4. Longevity, 5. Rejuvenation, 6. Geriatrics in Antiquity and the Middle Ages, 7. From the Renaissance to the end of the 18th Century, 8. Geriatrics in the 19th Century, 9. Remarks on the History of Arteriosclerosis, 10. Old Age as a Psychological and Social Problem, 11. The Modern (20th-Century) Geriatric Movement. Several chapters are only four or five pages long, but the work is weightier than size alone would indicate. Had it been written in a less laconic style, it easily might have been two or three times as long.

The most valuable feature of the book is Dr. Grmek's impressive grasp of a vast range of source material, both primary and secondary. The text is backed up with some fourteen pages of excellent footnotes which cite hundreds of separate works. Undoubtedly, this collection of footnotes represents the finest bibliography ever assembled on the history of geriatrics and gerontology, and it testifies to the author's previous experience with historical research. Working in Zagreb, Mirko Dražen Grmek has written in Croatian many studies of medical history, most notably a biography of Santorio Santorio and, as editor, a volume on the history of Croatian medicine. Of course, while praising the acumen of the author, one must not forget that the monumental bibliographies of N. W. Shock and the pioneering historical investigations of F. D. Zeman, J. Steudel, J. T. Freeman, S. R. Burstein, and many others helped to prepare the way for a work of this type.

Especially original and useful are the references to events in the medical history of Eastern Europe. The author's acquaintance with Yugoslav, Czech, Rumanian, and Russian material helps to map in a *terra incognita* of previous research in this field. At the same time, he shows a thorough conversance with West European and American sources. However, as in nearly all works of medical history, the discussion of Arabic, Far Eastern, and Medieval Latin medicine is based on inadequate data.

Although most of the material is so outstandingly good, the presentation of it falls short in certain respects. The text is so condensed and, in places, so abruptly didactic that it makes for slow and difficult reading. At the same time, the organization of the first five chapters on topical rather than chronological lines gives an impression of repetitiousness. The printing of names in capital letters, which might have been very serviceable, becomes self-defeating when applied in such a mechanical manner that, in a single paragraph, the name of Charcot appears in capitals seven different times. Finally, the usefulness of the footnote section as a bibliography is limited by the failure of the author to arrange it in a way that would have allowed easy access, either chronological or alphabetical.

The quality of the interpretation varies a good bit; at times the author is penetrating and creative, but then again he adopts a superficial tone and allows the data to escape from control. By and large, this is a study to be admired more for its wide-ranging scope than for its depth of analysis. The best-organized chapters are the one on the causes of aging and the one on geriatrics in the nineteenth century. Incidentally, for those who might be concerned that a doctrinaire quality might appear in this work from contemporary Yugoslavia, it may be said that the author has no ideological axe to grind; he discusses a great variety of concepts and hypotheses in an objective and impartial manner.

This is the first separately-published history of geriatrics and gerontology, and, despite some failings in editing and analysis, the author has succeeded in bringing together an invaluable collection of material on these subjects. The editors of the *Monographiae Biologicae* deserve commendation for issuing this much-needed study, and at a relatively modest price (about $3.78). The book, of course, is indispensable to anyone directly concerned with the problems of the aged. But it is more than a work for the specialist alone. Dr. Grmek has approached his subject from an unusually comprehensive point of view, and those concerned with the general history of medicine will find here much that is interesting and illuminating.

GERALD J. GRUMAN

THE HISTORY OF GERIATRICS

Joseph T. Freeman

THE HISTORY OF GERIATRICS

By JOSEPH T. FREEMAN, M.D.

PHILADELPHIA

THE history of the study of the diseases of the aged has been made venerable by the fact that almost every noteworthy clinician at some time in his career found occasion to note his reflections and observations on the subject. Although it was the rare individual essay that was novel, a sturdy literature grew in the warmth of genius applied to it. Yet many of these same contributors felt that the history of geriatrics was a barren one indeed. In 1863 Daniel Maclachlan[1] wrote that there was little in the English literature except some minor efforts which contained valuable information on the hygiene and diseases of old age. A half century later, C. S. Minot[2] stated that "from the time of Cicero to the time of Holmes, numerous authors have written on old age, yet among them all we shall scarcely find any one who had title to be considered a scientific writer upon the subject." Despite lengthening bibliographies, there is almost a humorous repetition of such plaints in the preface of each new work. As a matter of record, such statements are more blunt than correct, for old age has a notable lineage of students, as shall be observed. A brief inquiry seems necessary to refute these honest convictions. One generalization that emerges is that there have been two types of writers: first, those of past and recent date who philosophized and concluded from a personal viewpoint with little intent to be statistically exact, and second, those of a small but increasing number who avoided reflection for fact, aging reminiscence for scientific understanding. These parallel views will be seen to meet, as do train tracks, by eyes looking into the distance.

Outlining learnedly and logically, G. S. Hall, in 1922, wrote an ethnographic survey of old age from the vague eras of the past up to the time of defined history.[3] This study begins with many paraphrases from his book.

In the hazy periods of human culture, some of which persist today in those peoples whose level is but little above that of stone-age man, there were definite attitudes toward the aged which were almost ritualistic for the tribe. In such levels of civilization life is more obviously somatic, more clearly a matter of fears, food, and protection. The older half of society received accord in proportion to which of these basic tenets was predominant. When famine threatened, the aged were sacrificed for food, these meals usually being invested with solemn dignity. Where adequate burial was a problem, cannibalism served as a form of sanitation. In Fiji, self-immolation was not uncommon, sparing worthy persons from the degradation of a useless old age. Those who rose to high position were particularly aware of the privilege of self-destruction and were aided to a serene end by kin and friend. Darwin noted in Tierra del Fuego that the more noble organs of the body of such men were eaten in order that the survivors might tangibly participate in the good qualities of the deceased. Among the American Indians, the aged were revered on a par with the gods and the chief.

Very probably even in these stages of life, men who felt their physical powers beginning to abate—at least the more sagacious of them—had already hit upon some of the many devices by which the aging have very commonly contrived to maintain their position and even increase their importance in the community by developing wisdom in counsel, becoming repertories of tribal tradition and custom and representatives of feared supernatural forces of persons. . . .[3]

By utilizing the fruits of experience, the aged often became too valuable to destroy; religion gave them an aura, wisdom gave them a shield, and respect for accumulated surpluses extended their influence over possible heirs.

In ancient Greece, youth was the prize; age, in contrast, a matter of hatred. The feeble gray head found little respect from Homer's people despite notable exceptions cited in the classical literature. Strangely enough it was the Spartans, early seekers of the physical ideal for the masses, who alone realized the value of their older subjects. A council of twenty-eight men past sixty years of age and elected to office, the *gerousia*, held control over that city-state. As for the remainder of the peoples of that strange peninsula, "Greek writers take a very gloomy view of [old age], never calling it beautiful, peaceful, or mellow, but rather dismal and oppressive" (Hall). Some of the individual personalities that come to mind are Nestor, Socrates poisoned by his own hand at the age of seventy, Plato living to fourscore years, Plutarch who advised his aging contemporaries to "keep your head cool and your feet warm; instead of employing medicines for every indisposition rather fast a day; and while you attend to the body, never neglect the mind." His treatise on health and long life contains the essence of the best writers preceding him. Hippocrates made many observations on old age.[4] He noted that the aged as a rule complain less than do the young. His keen insight into disease postulated the severe conclusion that such chronic diseases as do occur in the aging body, rarely leave it. He tabulated the ailments of old age thus: "*to old people*, dyspnea, catarrhs accompanied by coughs, dysuria, pains in the joints, nephritis, vertigo, apoplexy, cachexia, pains in the whole body, insomnolency, defluxions of the bowels, of the eyes, and of the nose, dimness of sight, and dullness of hearing." He himself lived a long life, later much exaggerated in legend.

It is a commonplace that respect for the physical reached a high plane in the Egyptian civilization. The Egyptians practiced the art of lengthening life and insuring longevity by the routine use of emetics and sudorifics at definite intervals. As a rule, two emetics were taken each month. The stress placed on sudorifics was reflected in the customary form of greeting, "How do you perspire?"

As a key to antiquity probably more has been learned from the Bible than from Grecian columns or Egyptian masses. It yields some understanding of disease, sanitation, and attitudes of those distant times. In Genesis 5, there is the lineage of the generations of Adam naming ten men whose lives averaged eight hundred years, as reckoned then. The terrible disaster befalling the children who mocked the bald and senile Elisha is described in the second book of Kings. In Psalms 90:10 there is David's sonorous dirge which every generation has sung:

> The days of our years are threescore and ten,
> Or even by strength fourscore years;
> Yet is their pride but labor and sorrow;
> For it is soon gone, and we fly away.

THE
POURTRACT
OF
OLD AGE.
Wherein is contained a
SACRED ANATOMY
Both of Soul, and Body,
AND
A Perfect Account of the Infirmities of AGE Incident to them Both.

Being a Paraphrase upon the Six former Verses of the 12. Chapter of *Ecclesiastes*.

By *JOHN SMITH*, M.D.

The Second Edition Corrected.

Nam pernicitas deserit, Consitus sum Senectute, onustum gero Corpus, vires Reliquere; ut Ætas mala, mala merx est ergo. Plautus.

LONDON,
Printed by *J. Macock*, for *Walter Kettilby*, at the Bishops Head in St Pauls Church-Yard, MDCLXVI.

FIG. 1.

No more succinct and impressive description of aging has been preserved than that of Solomon in about two hundred words in the twelfth verse of Ecclesiastes[8] ending in that verbal saraband, "'Vanity of vanities,' saith the Preacher, 'all is vanity.'" The following scholars through their interpretations of the allegorical passages were led to other observations along the same lines: Andreas Laurentius 1599, Master Peter Lowe 1612, Bishop Hall 1633, John Smith 1665, Richard Mead 1755, and M. Jastrow 1919.[5-9]

Mead,[8] bearing the gold-headed cane from Radcliffe, physician at court, admired by Dr. Johnson, labored long for a satisfactory interpretation of meanings hidden in the lines inscribed in the chaste Hebrew language. He explained that the reference to the grasshopper belly full of eggs delicately indicated scrotal rupture, "a disease common to persons far advanced in years." His work was translated from the Latin by Thomas Stack, and the copy in the library of the College of Physicians of Philadelphia was at one time the possession of James Craik, physician to George Washington. Less than a century before, Dr. John Smith had written his "Pourtract of Old Age" in a far less dispassionate manner than that evident in Mead's "Medica Sacra." Smith, a young man, must have been a fierce fundamentalist crusader in the Restoration Period for he spins out pages of tirade, medical evangelism, and a complete acceptance of the truth of the Word regardless of all other considerations. The endless defenses of each poetic sigh of the ancient King are punctuated with keen perceptions: "Let none give over their patients when they come overburdened with the infirmities of Age, as though they were altogether incapable of having any good done unto them. Those that are negligent toward their Ancient Friends, are very near of kin to those inhuman Barbarians and Americans, who both kill and devour them." Sir Humphrey Rolleston[10] said that of the early writers, Smith alone lacked the qualification of mature age, which is in the light of praise rather than condemnation.

Ancient thoughts, Egyptian, Biblical, Grecian, and others flowed through Rome. Strong familial life was the basis of the world that grew around a great city, and this powerful unit created effectual protection for the aged. Unlike most of the Greeks but like the Spartans, the Romans were eager to benefit by the counsel of older leaders in all walks of life. The influence of their ruling body of older men, a Senate, has come unchanged unto this day. The most influential writing on the subject is in Cicero's "De Senectute" expressed through the medium of the central character, Cato Major. Benjamin Franklin commented on the wisdom of the observations. G. M. Humphry[11] felt that "from schoolboy-days, now fully fifty years ago, when the 'De Senectute' of the great Roman orator made a lasting impression upon me, the subject of old age has had some fascination for me." Minot refused to put the seal of biology on this work despite the fact that its value has been much greater than many lackadaisical texts in that field.

In 1744 J. H. Cohausen published his "Hermippus Redivivus or The Sage's Triumph Over Old Age and The Grave."[12] The whole imaginative work was built up on a single inscription (taken from Hufeland):

> To Æsculapius and Health
> Dedicated
> By L. Clodius Hermippus
> who lived CXV years V days
> By the breath of young maids

Cohausen hypothesized that this old citizen of Rome must have been a teacher in a school for young virgins in order to be blessed with the privilege of being constantly exposed to their supposed healthful and life-lengthening exhalations. This belief in the therapeutic value of the respirations of young people continues more figuratively today. However King David had tried it in his time, and the learned Boerhaave had ordered a patient of his, an old burgomaster of Amsterdam, to obtain the revivifying effects of sleeping between two young persons.

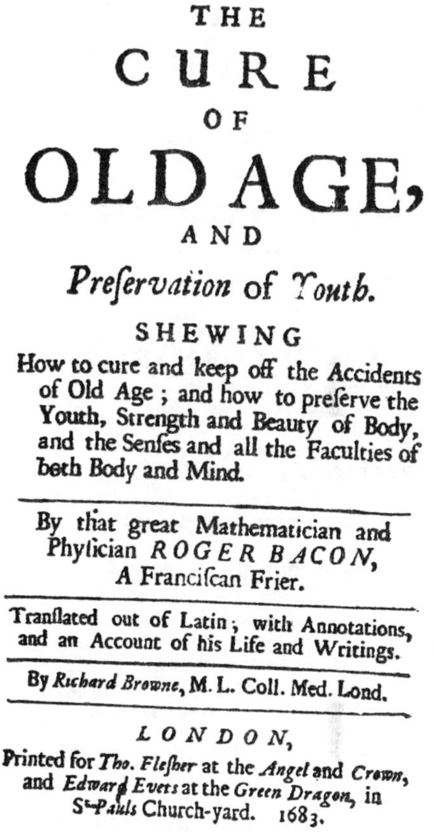

THE
CURE
OF
OLD AGE,
AND
Preservation of *Youth*.
SHEWING
How to cure and keep off the Accidents of Old Age ; and how to preserve the Youth, Strength and Beauty of Body, and the Senses and all the Faculties of both Body and Mind.

By that great Mathematician and Physician *ROGER BACON*, A Franciscan Frier.

Translated out of Latin ; with Annotations, and an Account of his Life and Writings.

By *Richard Browne*, M. L. Coll. Med. Lond.

LONDON,
Printed for *Tho. Flesher* at the *Angel* and *Crown*, and *Edward Evets* at the *Green Dragon*, in St *Pauls* Church-yard. 1683.

FIG. 2.

While Rome was fading, medical knowledge progressed in the hands of the Arabian physicians. The works of Isaac Beimiram, Hali Abbas, Avicenna, Averroes, Rhazes, Johannus Damascenus, and others, flower in the recognition extended by Bacon. Roger Bacon,[13] Franciscan friar, mathematician, physician, wrote on "The Cure of Old Age and the Preservation of Youth" in the thirteenth century. This work was translated into English by

Richard Brown in 1683. In that strange awakening age, this book emerges wonderfully prophetic with humanitarian understanding. Galen and Hippocrates are quoted with understanding, and not with obsequiousness. But it is a wistful tract, for in it one hears the cry of a man in a strange world sad because he could not be understood, fearful of recrimination lest he be understood. Science is neatly interwoven with fable and philosophy, and here are symptoms, signs, and treatment, much of which was liquidated from the frozen asset of old literature by Floyer in a more receptive time. Bacon's magnificent work presaged the modern attitude in geriatrics.

In the swashbuckling sixteenth century, the words of a gentle Venetian nobleman, Luigi Cornaro,[14] called the "Apostle of Senescence," spread like a soothing oil over the turbulent waves of humanity. The most quoted of the subjective works, his properly entitled book, "Sure and Certain Methods of Attaining a Long and Healthy Life with Means of Correcting a Bad Constitution," consists of four essays, the first of which was written at the age of eighty-three. The preface to the first American edition written by Joseph Addison in 1793 contained this writer's belief in the efficacy of proper exercising by the aging. Cornaro's work is a grandfatherly admonishment to temperance, modern in ideology and verbiage, remarkable for its sane evaluation of the methods he utilized to enjoy old age when so many others, desiring the same end, were being confounded by astrology and necromancy. Practically broken in health at forty, he forced himself to a summary of his mode of living, adopted certain principles, and reaped a reward of happiness in continuing age. He warned that those who would not partake of his "divine medicine, Temperance" would suffer from degenerative ailments. What Hippocrates wrote in the Thirteenth Aphorism, "old persons endure fasting most easily," Cornaro proved with great benefit. The unaffected and observant writings of this patriarch blessed with an unusual amount of common sense demand the pause of deserved admiration.

Inasmuch as Bacon's thoughts did not blossom in his own day, the writings of Sir John Floyer of Lichfield[15] in 1724 have generally been accredited as the beginning of modern geriatrics. Floyer is known also as the first to attempt accurate pulse readings by the

SURE AND CERTAIN
METHODS
OF
ATTAINING
A
LONG AND HEALTHY LIFE
WITH MEANS OF CORRECTING A
BAD CONSTITUTION.
WRITTEN BY
LEWIS CORNARO,
An Italian Nobleman, when he was near an Hundred Years of Age.

WITH A
RECOMMENDATORY PREFACE,
BY THE
Hon. JOSEPH ADDISON, Esq.

The First American Edition.

PHILADELPHIA:
REPRINTED FOR THE REV. *M. L. WEEMS,*
BY PARRY HALL, CHESNUT STREET:
M.DCC.XCIII.

FIG. 3.

watch which he described in the "Physician's Pulse Watch," and which ironically was passed over by his colleagues. Having knowledge of many of the masters of medicine ("I therefore reviewed my old Galen") and a native astuteness, Floyer elaborated the medical knowledge of the aged. With scant recognition of Bacon from whom he took much, he nevertheless expanded and clarified many views which is in itself an apology for possibly unconscious adaptation. His theme was moderation in all things with a liberal application of his favorite idea of cold or hot bathing depending on whether the patient was a thin hectical, or a fat florid, old person. This is recognition of the response of constitutional types to adapted therapy. Charcot considered this book as one of the early specific treatises because of the extensive therapeutics expounded. Elaborated drug therapy combined in a definite routine of treatment directly applicable to the complaints of the aged justifies this recognition. The title "Medicina Gerocomica or the Galenic Art of Preserving Old Men's Healths" emphasizes the feeling engendered by its perusal that there has been faithful adherence to the Galenic tradition. Evidently Floyer cherished the heritage of centuries more than Smith who expressed his feelings in the phrase, "Galenists and fools."

At the same time in England George Cheyne was publishing his views on the subject.[16] His book contained two unoriginal contributions: namely, that the aged should guard against the vagaries of the weather, which had been noted by Hippocrates, and second, that the diet of the old should be reduced to their actual needs, which was a commonplace even at that time. In this rather unnecessary collection of repetitious generalities the author's candor, "I know not what may be the fate and success of the performance; nor am I solicitous about it, being conscious the design was honest, the subject weighty, and the execution the best my time, my abilities, and my health would permit," is laudable.

It is apparent thus far that this subject has maintained a fixed, if minor, place in the medical mind. In each notable period there was at least one well-informed individual who did not permit a lapse, either by repeating much that was platitude, or by starting a new vein of thought. The failure of more rapid progress was not a peculiar sluggishness but a part of the general medical trend. With a quickening of the whole there was activity in each of its parts including geriatrics.

At a time when Dr. Guillotine's invention was falling on an era, Christoph Hufeland in Germany[17] was writing his book on the "Art of Prolonging Life." Translated into English as quickly as 1794, Hufeland's word, Macrobiotic, or the art by which life could be prolonged, had become generally known. He delved conscientiously into the past and made avowal of gratitude for Bacon's "Historia vitæ et mortis" with its ideas "bold and new." He also tells the story of gerocomic or the method of instilling strength and vigor into old bodies by contact with blooming youth, examples of which have already been cited. This gentle book from the pen of a philosopher-physician is so encouraging and compelling that it is easy to understand how it gave rise to that vulgar wave of enthusiasm to which has been applied the name of the Hufelandist Movement. Statistics, descriptions, general treatment, flow calmly and wisely in a philosophical channel recently deepened, widened, and perfected by Bergson. It is not medicine, nor pathology, nor physiology, but it is understanding, ingenuously debunking, exposing quackery, and sweeping the boards clean of much that had been carried along by inertia. The rapid progress of the next several decades can be traced to this impetus.

As the eighteenth century was ending, James Easton[18] collected the names of all those persons who had attained to the age of one hundred years or more from A.D. 66 to A.D. 1799, numbering seventeen hundred and twelve. The book was dedicated to the nameless oldest man alive. Although many of the names were cited without substantiation, it is of interest to note that he included St. Patrick, Attila the Red Hun, Thomas Parr, the Countess of Desmond, and Poor Joe All-Alone in his list.

In the 1805 edition of his "Medical Inquiries and Observations" Dr. Benjamin Rush has a chapter entitled "An Account of the State of the Body and Mind in Old Age, with Observations on its Diseases, and Their Remedies."[19] He expressed his belief in the following as the important factors in longevity: heredity, temperance, mental vigor, equanimity, and marriage,—"met with only one unmarried person beyond eighty years." His keen interpretations lifted the banal into the field of interest and speculation. With Benjamin Franklin, and later Charles Caldwell,[20] Rush is one of the earliest accredited American writers on this subject.

Meanwhile the thought of the surgeons was reaching a point of early crystallization expressed in Anthony Carlisle's little book printed in Philadelphia in 1819.[21] This strait-laced gentleman had strong tendencies toward therapeutic nihilism with the exception of his own potent list of favorite methods and drugs. He felt that the giving of opium at the close of a painful and fatal disease should be "reprobated, both from professional and moral considerations." Only extreme emergencies in the aged were considered in the surgeon's scope; corrective procedures for comfort or amelioration were condemned. However, these conclusions were only a bit more stringent than was applied to better physical subjects, in those difficult surgical times.

Late in the next decade Sir Henry Halford[22] shrewdly noted in a short lecture that the characteristics of aging often do not appear until some extreme change occurs. Thus illness of differing severity, the common cold, an accident, or mental anxiety, could so upset the balance between the internal and external that the mark of time in the physiognomy suddenly became as apparent as a hastily applied mask.

The name of Carl Canstatt emerged in 1839 with the publication of his work,[23] setting him on the highest level yet attained in geriatrics. Hailed as a "rich mine," "an excellent résumé of everything that had been written on the subject to its date," it is a thorough aggregation of all the facts logically considered that could be considered as contributory to the knowledge of old age. The debt to Canstatt began to be liquidated immediately by greater depth and sounder approach with fewer of the blasts of personalities which in the older literature were interesting but had ceased to be instructive. His theory of aging was that the death of individual cells was so much molecular death of the organism which was not replaced. Prior to this time, writers, unhindered by *precise* information, had outlined an excellent hygiene based on thoughtful observation. Canstatt erected a dam across that stream of thought, creating a vast reservoir into which it is refreshing to dip, but also enforcing newer channels for the newer currents. The following year, Prus, in France, completed a summary similar to that of his German colleague, underlining emphatically that the way back was blocked.

Within the next ten years, G. E. Day[24] produced an excellent compendium foreshadowing the more complete texts to follow. His grouping and discussion of the afflictions of the aged were modern for their day and complete in their time, though somewhat sketchy. Books such as this one were necessary to the evolution of the modern study. Van Oven[25] several years later made obeisance to Hufeland as his fellow Englishman, Day, had made to Canstatt. His paragraphs on the decline of life in health and in disease are general and pleasant and carry in balanced fashion the increased burden of a newer trend.

The issue is taken up in another language by Durand-Fardel in 1854,[26] "A péine existe-t-il quelques rares trâvaux sur la pathologie de la dernière période de la vie," despite the recent work of Prus and Canstatt, and while Charcot was beginning to elucidate incomparably those facts. His study takes up anatomical units, indicating thought in terms of physiology, with a discussion of the diseases of each, and the summation in a theory that life is a vital force of limited duration.

Those bits of knowledge that were of lasting value were beginning to be swept together leaving a chaff full of charm, but dated. Charcot said, "To constitute in reality a senile pathology, the scattered fragments must be brought together in a systematic manner." By the middle of the nineteenth century, subjective medical works became the literature of the laity, and geriatrics assumed its proper scientific niche, protected from ignorant criticism by intensifying specialization. Maclachlan's very solid work of medicine[1] written in 1863 is in the modern style of diagnosis, description, and treatment, but of its time, like the early pictures in a photograph album.

Every study is the subject of painstaking, and frequently aimless, accumulation of facts which some industrious and impatient person eventually condenses and classifies. These texts are a convenience, but in addition become a standard for comparison, perhaps envy, certainly criticism, the degree depending on the ability and standing of the original compiler. Similar books appear, and the pyramiding of texts is finally surmounted by a Colossus that bestrides the field until the next crest of knowledge is laboriously constructed. From the heights of Canstatt we have stepped up once more on the works of Day and Maclachlan to the high perspective created by Charcot.

In 1867 J. M. Charcot[27] wrote down some of the cream of his vast experiences at La Salpetrière which, translated by Leigh Hunt and rounded out by the lectures of Alfred Loomis, was published in 1881 as "Diseases of Old Age." The past is fully recognized in the words "Traditional ties are not sundered; the labor of times gone by is not lost; and we shall treasure up the immense heritage which our predecessors accumulated in the course of centuries. Still it must be confessed that new horizons have opened to us. . . ." The change from speculative philosophy to physiology is complete in Charcot. He did not see the aging body as an obsolescent physical machine, but sought to establish its type-physiology, hinted at by Floyer, as distinctive as that of other periods of life. It was clearly observed that the morphological changes of age sometimes progress to such a degree that there is almost a merging of physiological and pathological states. Although he lectured only on gout and other arthritic conditions, the lectures of Loomis amplified the subject matter in its complete and most learned form. The conclusion that "the importance of a special study of the diseases of old age cannot be contested at this day (1867)" waits fulfilment. Despite the signposts to the way of knowledge, geriatrics stands out as a field in which a certain type of medical work most persists, the school of furred tongue, cloudy urine, diet fads, and all those other common procedures which pass over new methods too lightly. To condemn an aging person to that traditional pat on the back is to return to that time when intelligent physicians struggled in the dark only now beginning to be illuminated by fitful light.

It is natural that insurance companies should take interest in longevity and the various factors entering into its attainment. In post-Civil War days in the United States, Smith and Griscom[28] wrote two essays on old age valuable to medicine because of the excellent preface by Clifford Allbutt. Statistics on old age have been collected by several notable physicians. Those of Easton have been quoted. In 1908 W. A. N. Dorland[29] wrote "Age of Mental Virility," which is a defense of old age supported by many figures. In 1888 J. Bailey[30] wrote his "Modern Methusalehs" and in the following year was published G. M. Humphry's "Old Age"[11] in which are the records of nine hundred persons over eighty years of age including seventy-four centenarians. His questionnaire covering almost every detail of life was received gracefully by the many colleagues who were requested to supply information. Humphry, attracted to old age because of its "calm interest in the present, and unshadowed by apprehension respecting the future" noted that "the aged body does not seem to be, on the whole, prone to disease," and also that healing frequently takes place as promptly as in the young. To express his dislike for human vegetation that simply grew old, he quoted Cowper:

For fourscore years this life Cleora led;
At morn she rose, at night she went to bed.

In 1886, J. M. Fothergill[32] published his work "to fill a gap in medical literature." It is simply the work of Machlachlan moved forward two decades. In 1890, A. Seidel's compact essays[33] appeared in Wood's Medical and Surgical Monographs. It is a model of concentration of facts, based on the pathology of the aged body, arriving at the conclusion that senile involution is an incurable disease. The newer attitude based on known observed changes in the organism and leading up to sensible therapy is splendidly exhibited.

After the turn of the century, C. S. Minot[34] outlined his theory of aging based on cytomorphosis and the rate of growth. The principles are supported by statistics and graphs, and his efforts were crowned with the encomium of "brilliant labors." The question as to why a man should grow old has been asked by every individual. Nascher[35] recorded ten, and Warthin, eleven, theories that had been advanced as an answer. Metchnikoff's conception[36] based on autointoxication dominated a generation of thought. Sir Victor Horsley[37] looked upon the thyroid gland as the keystone in the arch. A. Lorand,[38] following his lead, extended this conception to include the whole endocrine system. As a comprehensive book on the endocrines, his ideas contain much prophetic insight which bears up relatively well in the swift current of endocrine progress, but there is too much swerving of its tenets. That which was an important gain in endocrinology failed as a concept of geriatrics. The ductless glands are often surprisingly efficient in the aged, and nothing was adduced to explain why they should change except as the body changed, a coincidental rather than cause and effect occurrence.

Sanford Bennett's system for deferring age[39] depended on the routine exercising of the various muscle-groups of the body according to schemes which he laboriously tried and used. He professed to follow Cornaro who "proved the truth of his statements by his personal experiences." Sated with modern physical culture magazines pictorially idolizing over-developed bodies, this ancestor, adorned eighty-three times with the author's picture, is apt to be forgotten.

Stimulated by Lorand, guided by the pathologists, recognized by the state, knowledge moves forward in this century. The name Geriatrics, although it has been used throughout this study, was not invented until 1914 when I. L. Nascher applied it to his masterpiece.[35]

Believing that attention would be more readily concentrated upon this subject if it were considered entirely apart from maturity, the author suggested that it be studied as a special branch of medicine, to which he has applied the term geriatrics. This term, which has been generally adopted, is derived from the Greek, *geron*, old man, and *iatrikos*, medical treatment. The etymological construction is faulty but euphony and mnemonic expediency were considered of more importance than correct grammatical construction.

Jacobi, fathering pediatrics, foster-fathered this work, calling it the first modern comprehensive text on abnormal and normal old age. The defects evident today are apparent not because of its content then, but because knowledge has moved beyond it. The same is true of Robert Saundby's work[40] published about the same time in England, which recognized certain shortcomings in the English literature and proceeded to expound a "very competent clinical guide."

While the World War raged, Schlesinger published in Vienna a work in two volumes crowning, and worthy of, the best Germanic traditions. His conclusions were derived from experience directly applied to the aged, living, dead, sick, and well. Almost one hundred years after Canstatt, a small supplement of these two volumes was produced, ranking on a par with the earlier book. Its importance seems to have been overlooked somewhat.[41]

Thewlis' book[42] is advanced over that of his mentor, Nascher, just as the latter is pre-war, the former, post-war. Although much of the material is outmoded, the treatment is sympathetic and deserves attention. Floyer insisted on baths, Lorand, on the endocrines, Cornaro, on temperance, and Thewlis placed undue emphasis on the kidneys. There seemed to be no geriatric equation that could not be balanced by making the renal tract serve as X, for example, "a diet for nephritis will be satisfactory even though the patient may not have nephritis." This stress impairs the value of many discussions in addition to the fact that the therapy fails to live up to its times. However, criticism falls away in the gratitude for the book, and with an unintentional play on words, it may be said that in it, geriatrics comes of age. The bibliography is excellent. Thewlis continues to contribute new facts in this field in which he stands out as one of the most prominent workers.

The work of L. B. Williams[43] published in 1925 is a combination of endocrinology and autointoxication, its date of publication being its most modern feature. Despite a characteristic English charm of style, there is little of value or novel incorporated. The static tendency of the second decade of the twentieth century was cut short by A. S. Warthin's "Old Age."[44] The thesis is that "senescence is a normal involutionary process" and it continues to a logical, if depressing, end. The minor changes of the body are shown to be for the good of the individual; the major changes (including death), for the good of the species. The monkey-gland school is disposed of with honest scorn: "so-called rejuvenation produced by the sex-hormones of the transplanted testes, or by ligation of the vas, is no rejuvenation in any sense of the word, but is a re-erotisation wholly." However, the book is more valuable to the comprehension of the larger problems of biology than to the treatment of the ailing.

The glitterings in a handful of sand owe their occurrence to the point of view, differing in no respect from many of the names that emerge almost by chance in a chronology. Among the many that additionally deserve mention are Arnoldus de Villa Nova, Van Swieten, Richter, Louis, Scudder, Démange, Türck, Chaussard, Grisolle, Gillette, Ewald, Brossard-Ysabeau, Reveillé-Parise, Boy-Teissier, Quesnel, Weber, Holmes, Lipscomb, to mention but a few. Charcot dismissed far too many as "more or less ingenious paraphrases of the famous treatise 'De senectute.'"

We have come into the present wherein the application of new knowledge sifts down so that the aged benefit, although possibly at second-hand, and certainly more as individuals than as a group. Texts are less harmonious, journals are fuller, and more studies are being made both in routine and in particular reference to the aged. The illogical procedure of treating a child by Jacobi, an adult by Roentgen, and an old person by Galen is vanishing as Charcot had demanded. We have come through the subjective school, through empiricism, superstition, fads, undue emphasis, to the present; stepping off in a well-rounded view of the older individual as a thoughtful individual who must be handled ever so skillfully not because of any supposed defects in his aging mechanism, but because from a life of observation, he knows what is being done for him, and can evaluate his reactions almost from a distant plane. This individual realizes that "age is never chronological, except in a legal sense," knowing that there is a distinctive individuality of the aging body even as has been marked arbitrarily into other phases of the continuity of life. As Floyer wrote: "Every man is a fool, or becomes a physician, when age is upon him."

REFERENCES

1. MACLACHLAN, D. Practical Treatise on the Diseases and Infirmities of Advanced Life. London, Churchill, 1863.

2. MINOT, C. S. On the Nature and Cause of Old Age. Harvey Lectures, 1905-1906, vol. 1.

3. HALL, G. S. Senescence, the Last Half of Life. N. Y., Appleton, 1922.
4. The Genuine Works of Hippocrates. Tr. by Francis Adams. London, Sydenham Soc., 1849.
5. LAURENTIUS, A. Discourse of the Preservation of the Sight; of Melancholike Diseases; of Rheumes; and of Old Age. Tr. by Richard Surphlet. London, Jackson, 1599.
6. LOWE, P. Discourse of the Whole Art of Chyrurgerie. London, Purfoot, 1612.
7. SMITH, J. Pourtract of Old Age. London, Macock, 1666.
8. MEAD, R. Medica Sacra. Tr. by Thomas Stack. London, Brindley, 1755.
9. JASTROW, M. The Gentle Cynic. Phila., Lippincott, 1919.
10. ROLLESTON, SIR H. Some Medical Aspects of Old Age. Linacre Lecture 1922. London, Macmillan, 1922.
11. HUMPHRY, G. M. Old Age. Cambridge, Macmillan, 1889.
12. COHAUSEN, J. H. Hermippus Redivivus. Tr. by J. Campbell. London, Nourse, 1744.
13. BACON, R. The Cure of Old Age and the Preservation of Youth. Tr. by Richard Brown.
14. CORNARO, L. Sure and Certain Methods of Attaining a Long and Healthy Life. Tr. by Joseph Addison. First American Ed. Hall, 1793.
15. FLOYER, SIR J. Medicina Gerocomica. London, Isted, 1724.
16. CHEYNE, G. Essay on Health and Long Life. London, Strahan, 1725.
17. HUFELAND, C. W. Makrobiotik, oder die Kunst das Menschliche Leben zu Verlängen. Berlin, Wittich, 1805.
18. EASTON, J. Human Longevity. London, Salisbury, 1799.
19. RUSH, B. Medical Inquiries and Observations. Phila., Conrad, 1805, p. 426.
20. CALDWELL, C. Thoughts on the Effects of Age on the Human Constitution. Louisville, 1846.
21. CARLISLE, A. Essay on the Disorders of Old Age. Phila., Earle, 1819.
22. HALFORD, SIR H. Essays and Orations. London, Murray, 1833.
23. CANSTATT, C. Die Krankheiten des Höheren Alters und Ihre Heilung. Erlangen, Enke, 1839.
24. DAY, G. E. Practical Treatise on the Domestic Management and Most Important Diseases of Advanced Life. Phila., Lea, 1849.
25. VAN OVEN, B. On the Decline of Life in Health and Disease. London, Churchill, 1853.
26. DURAND-FARDEL, CH. L. Traité clinique et pratique des maladies des Vieillards. Paris, Germer-Balliere, 1854.
27. CHARCOT, J. M., and LOOMIS, A. L. Clinical Lectures on the Disease of Old Age. N. Y., Wood, 1881.
28. SMITH, J. V. C., and GRISCOM, J. H. Physical Indications of Longevity. With a preface by Clifford Allbutt. N. Y., Wood, 1869.
29. DORLAND, W. A. N. The Age of Mental Virility. N. Y., Century, 1908.
30. BAILEY, J. Modern Methusalehs. London, Chapman, 1888.
31. FRIEDMAN, H. M. Senility, premature senility, and longevity. *New York M. J.*, 102:65-71, 1915.
32. FOTHERGILL, J. M. Diseases of Sedentary and Advanced Life. N. Y., Appleton, 1886.
33. SEIDEL, A. Diseases of Old Age. In: Wood's Medical and Surgical Monographs, 5:636-665, 1890.
34. MINOT, C. S. The problem of age, growth, and death. *Popular Science Monthly*, 7:1907.
35. NASHER, I. L. Geriatrics. Phila., Blakiston, 1916.
36. METCHNIKOFF, E. Prolongation of Life. Eng. tr. by P. C. Mitchell. N. Y., Putnam, 1908.
37. HORSLEY, SIR V. On the functions of the thyroid gland. *Roy. Soc. Lond. Proc.*, vol. 38, 1884-85.
38. LORAND, A. Old Age Deferred. Tr. from German. Phila., Davis, 1911.
39. BENNETT, S. Old Age. N. Y., Phys. Cult. Publ., 1912.
40. SAUNDBY, R. Old Age. London, 1913.
41. SCHLESINGER, H. Krankheiten des höheren Lebensalters. Wien, Hölder, 1914-15. Klinik und Therapie der Alterskrankheiten. Leipzig, Thieme, 1930.
42. THEWLIS, M. Geriatrics. St. Louis, Mosby, 1919.
43. WILLIAMS, L. B. Middle Age and Old Age. Oxford Univ. Press, 1925.
44. WARTHIN, A. S. Old Age. N. Y., Hoeber, 1930.

ZUR GESCHICHTE DER LEHRE VON DEN GREISNKRANKHEITEN

Johannes Steudel

Aus dem Karl-Sudhoff-Institut für Geschichte der Medizin und der Naturwissenschaften an der Universität Leipzig. Direktor: Prof. W. von Brunn

Zur Geschichte der Lehre von den Greisenkrankheiten

Von Dr. med. et phil. Johannes Steudel

Einleitung

Die Lehre von den Greisenkrankheiten ist ein Stiefkind der Heilkunde. Sie hat sich nicht zu einer selbständigen Disziplin entwickelt, obwohl alle neueren Bearbeiter übereinstimmend den großen Unterschied betonen, der in Verlauf und Therapie zwischen den Erkrankungen des mittleren und denen des hohen Alters besteht. Fast jeder von ihnen blickt vergleichend auf die Pädiatrie und betont, daß die Verhütung und Behandlung der Erkrankungen des alternden Menschen ebensoviel Besonderheiten biete wie die Betreuung des kranken Kindes.

Die Antike hatte eine ausführliche, ins einzelne gehende Diätetik als Therapie des Alters geschaffen, das selbst nichts anderes als eine Krankheit sein sollte. Das Mittelalter und die folgenden Jahrhunderte haben die Galenischen Vorstellungen vom Altern übernommen und seine hygienisch-diätetischen Vorschriften in mannigfaltiger Abwandlung zur Grundlage ihres Schrifttums über das Alter gemacht. Die neuen Erkenntnisse der Anatomie, Physiologie und Pathologie kamen in dieser Literatur nur langsam zur Geltung. Erst im Jahre 1754 erklärte es Johann Bernhard Fischer für notwendig, der Darstellung der Krankheiten des Alters Untersuchungen über die morphologischen und funktionellen Veränderungen des alternden Organismus vorauszuschicken.

Vom Mittelalter bis in das schreibfreudige 18. Jhdt. ist das Alter in zahlreichen ärztlichen Schriften behandelt worden. Im 19. Jhdt., als sich aus der Anwendung naturwissenschaftlich exakter

Methoden auf die Medizin eine Fülle neuer Probleme ergab, hat es nur wenig Beachtung gefunden. Während die Kinderheilkunde in diesem Zeitraum zu einem selbständigen Fach mit einer umfangreichen Literatur heranwuchs, verloren Prophylaxe und Therapie der Alterserkrankungen den Raum, den sie früher im Denken der Ärzte eingenommen hatten.

Da Physiologie und Pathologie des Greisenalters jetzt wieder in das Blickfeld der Forschung rücken — das Gebiet besitzt seit 1938 in der Zeitschrift für Altersforschung auch ein eigenes Organ —, erscheint es angezeigt, einen Blick auf das zu werfen, was frühere Zeiten darüber gelehrt haben. Die Darstellung (1), die das wichtigste Material für eine Geschichte dieses Zweiges der Medizin zu sammeln versucht, beginnt mit den antiken Vorstellungen vom Alter und seinen Krankheiten, wendet sich dann den Altersregimina des Mittelalters zu und geht schließlich auf diejenigen Werke ein, die zu einer naturwissenschaftlich fundierten Lehre von den Greisenkrankheiten beigetragen haben.

Alterskrankheiten im Corpus Hippocraticum

Die Antike hat das abweichende Verhalten des alternden Organismus gut gekannt, wenn sie auch eine monographische Darstellung der Greisenkrankheiten nicht hinterlassen hat. Aus den Schriften des Corpus Hippocraticum läßt sich leicht das Bild wiedergewinnen, das die Hippokratiker vom alten Menschen gehabt haben. Haut und Muskulatur verändern sich (De morbis I, 22), das Blut wird dünn und wässerig, seine Menge stark vermindert (De morbo sacro 9), und der Tonus des jugendlichen Körpers geht verloren (De morbis I, 22). Aus dem abweichenden physiologischen Verhalten wird hergeleitet, daß auch der Krankheitsverlauf beim alten Menschen ein anderer ist: Infolge des Tonusverlustes treten die Krankheiten weniger heftig auf. Das Beispiel der Pneumonie und Pleuritis dient der Erläuterung, daß beim Greise die Schmerzen geringer und die Fieberanfälle leichter sind und sogar zeitweilig fehlen können (De morbis I, 22), Tatsachen, die seitdem dem ärztlichen Wissen nicht wieder verlorengegangen sind.

Neben der Geschlechtsdisposition und dem Einfluß der Jahreszeiten auf die Erkrankung ist den Hippokratikern auch eine vom Lebensalter abhängige Krankheitsbereitschaft bekannt. Jede Altersstufe ist zu bestimmten Krankheiten disponiert (Praenot. Coac. 502; Aph. III, 24—31). Für die Prognose ist es wichtig, zu ermitteln, ob die Erkrankung dem Alter des Patienten entspricht oder ob sie früher oder später hätte eintreten sollen (Epid. VI, 8, 11). Alte Menschen erkranken in der Regel nicht so oft wie jüngere; treten bei ihnen aber langwierige Krankheiten auf, so gehen sie meistens daran zugrunde (Aph. II, 39). Zum Tode führt dann in der Regel nicht das alte Leiden, sondern eine interkurrente Erkrankung (De morbis I, 22). Auch die Konstitution wird als wichtiger Faktor der Pathogenese geschildert. Phlegmatiker sind besonders im hohen Alter durch Krankheiten gefährdet, während sich Choleriker gerade dann bester Gesundheit erfreuen (De victu I, 32). Im Sommer und bis in den Herbst hinein fühlen sich alte Leute am wohlsten (Aph. III, 18).

Als Erkrankungen der Greise nennen die Aphorismen Dyspnöe, Husten und Schnupfen, die atypisch verlaufen, Nieren- und Blasenleiden, denen therapeutisch schwer beizukommen ist, Strangurie und Dysurie, Schwindel und Apoplexie, Gelenkschmerzen, Juckreiz, Schlaflosigkeit und anderes (Aph. III, 31; II, 40; VI, 6). Der Greis verträgt das Fasten am besten von allen Lebensaltern. Auch in gesunden Tagen ist es gut, ihn knapp zu ernähren, da die ihm innewohnende Wärme nur gering ist. Zu reichliche Ernährung kann sein Leben zum Erlöschen bringen (Aph. I, 13 u. 14).

Galens Gerokomia

In lebhaftem Kontrast zu der aphoristischen Kürze des Corpus Hippocraticum steht die selbstgefällige Weitschweifigkeit GALENS, die sich auch in seiner Darstellung der Alterserscheinungen und ihrer Verhütung breit macht. Die schlichte Beobachtung und Erfahrung am Krankenbett hat einen theoretisch-spekulativen Überbau bekommen, von dem aus physiologischen und pathologischen Vorgängen eine kausale Erklärung oder eine teleologische Deutung aufgezwungen wird. GALEN geht in seinem umfangreichen Werk an zahlreichen Stellen auf das Alter ein, am ausführlichsten im 5. Buche De sanitate tuenda (2).

Altern und Tod sind natürliche und notwendige Vorgänge (De marcore 2 — K VII, 672); kein Lebewesen kann sich ihnen entziehen. Τί γὰρ ἄλλο ἢ ὁδὸς ἐπὶ θάνατόν ἐστι τὸ γῆρας (De temp. II, 2 — K I, 582); GALEN wendet sich gegen die von anderen griechischen Ärzten vertretene Ansicht, daß das Alter selbst Krankheit sei (De san. t. I, 5, 32f. — K VI, 20f.). Er räumt aber ein, daß es nicht frei von Klagen ist, und daß sich seine Gesundheit, die Greisengesundheit, von der auf der Höhe des Lebens unterscheidet (ib. VI, 2, 22 — K VI, 388). Sie kann als ein Mittelding zwischen Gesundheit und Krankheit bezeichnet werden und ist in mancher Hinsicht der Rekonvaleszenz zu vergleichen (ib. V, 4, 3 — K VI, 330).

Physiologisch betrachtet ist der Prozeß des Alterns eine Verschiebung im Gleichgewicht der vier Elementarqualitäten. GALEN wird nicht müde, zu erörtern, daß im Alter das Warme und das Feuchte abnehmen, während das Kalte und das Trockene immer mehr zutage treten (De san. t. V, 9, 19 — K VI, 357 und an zahlreichen anderen Stellen). Alter läßt sich also durch Dyskrasie mit Überwiegen des Kalten und Trockenen umschreiben. Völliges Erlöschen der Wärme bedeutet Tod (De marcore 3 — K VII, 674).

Der im Corpus Hippocraticum vertretenen Anschauung, daß Greise kalt und feucht seien (De victu I, 33), kann sich GALEN nicht anschließen. Wenn auch das Alter durch seine reichlichen wässerigen oder schleimigen Absonderungen als überwiegend feucht erscheint, so soll man sich von diesem äußeren Bild nicht täuschen lassen; der Organismus selbst, Knochen, Muskeln, Bänder und Gefäße verlieren vielmehr zunehmend ihre Feuchtigkeit und sind im Alter trocken (De temp. II, 2 — K I, 580; in Hipp. de nat. hom. comm. III, 7 — MEWALDT 95f., K XV, 187f.). Moderne Laboratoriumsuntersuchungen bestätigen die Abnahme des Wassergehaltes im alternden Gewebe. Das Schwinden der eingeborenen Wärme zieht alle Lebensprozesse in Mitleidenschaft. Appetit, Verdauungsvorgänge, Ernährung der einzelnen Teile und der Ansatz sind geschädigt (De temp. II, 2 — K I, 582); die Blutbereitung ist so verlangsamt, daß Greise nur noch ganz wenig Blut in ihren Adern haben (ib.; Adv. Lycum 7 — K XVIII A, 238); Wahrnehmung und Bewegung sind erschwert (De temp. II, 2 — K I, 582).

Auch auf die Modifikation des Pulses durch das Alter kommt GALEN zu sprechen. Ist die Jugend durch einen pulsus frequens, celer und durus gekennzeichnet, so herrscht im höheren Alter ein pulsus rarus, tardus und mollis vor (De puls. ad tirones 9 — K VIII, 464). Am auffälligsten ist die Abnahme der Frequenz (De causis puls. III, 5 — K IX, 124). Diese so leicht nachzuprüfende Behauptung blieb bis in die Mitte des vorigen Jhdts. fast unwidersprochen. Erst CANSTATT erklärte eine Zunahme der Pulsfrequenz im Alter unter Hinweis auf die Beobachtungen von MITIVIÉ und LEURET aus dem Jahre 1832 für einleuchtender: „In dem Zustande von

Verknöcherung, Verdickung, Obliteration des arteriellen und Erweiterung des venösen Teiles liegt Grund genug, daß das Herz seine Anstrengungen und Kontraktionen vermehren müsse, um die Hindernisse des Kreislaufs zu überwinden" (Die Krankheiten des höheren Alters, Bd. 1, Erlangen 1839, S. 83).

Die Respiration ändert sich ebenfalls mit dem Alter. GALEN beschreibt sie als rara, parva und tarda (De diffic. respir. I, 7 — K VII, 771; De usu respir. 4 — K IV, 500). Die Haut wird schlaff und runzelig (De simpl. medic. temp. et facult. II, 19— K XI, 508) und fühlt sich kalt an (De temp. II, 2 — K I, 582). Die Cornea wird faltig, so daß der Greis nur noch schlecht oder gar nicht mehr sehen kann (De usu part. X, 5 — K III, 783f.). Auch Zahn und Alveole unterliegen dem Eintrocknungsprozeß. Die Gomphosis zwischen beiden erschlafft, die Zähne werden locker und fallen schließlich aus (De compos. medic. sec. locos V, 4 — K XII, 851).

Was GALEN über die Pathologie des Alters sagt, deckt sich im Kern zumeist mit den knappen Angaben der Hippokratischen Schriften. Es wird modifiziert durch sein Bedürfnis, die Krankheiten des Alters in Übereinstimmung mit seiner Theorie des Alternsvorganges zu bringen. Lehrt das Corpus Hippocraticum, daß der Greis von Blasensteinen verschont bleibe, so fügt GALEN begründend hinzu, daß er ja die zur Bildung eines Steines notwendige Wärme nicht mehr besitze (In Hipp. aph. comm. III, 26 — K XVII B, 634f.). Den Pruritus senilis erklärt er als Wirkung von Ausscheidungsprodukten, die die infolge Wärmeverlust dichter gewordene Haut nicht mehr passieren können (ib. III, 31 — K XVII B, 650). Neben solchen uns oft nicht mehr befriedigenden Deutungen finden sich vortreffliche Beobachtungen wie die, daß Unregelmäßigkeit des Pulses bei Greisen kein so alarmierendes Zeichen ist wie bei Jüngeren (De praesag. ex puls. II, 4 — K IX, 284).

In seiner Therapie verwertete GALEN das pharmazeutische Wissen aller seiner Vorgänger und entwickelte daraus eine medikamentöse Polypragmasie, die während des ganzen Mittelalters als vorbildlich angesehen wurde. Seine Diätetik ist fast bis in die Gegenwart lebendig geblieben. Als τὸ γηροκομικὸν ὀνομαζόμενον μέρος trennt er ein Gebiet von der Heilkunst ab, dem die Sorge für den alternden Menschen zukommt (De marcore 5 — K VII, 681). Nach dem Grundsatze Contraria contrariis vorgehend, verordnet er dem Greise alles, was warm und feucht macht (De san. t. V, 3, 3

— K VI, 319). Sein kaltes Temperament wird durch Weingenuß auf eine gemäßigte Wärme zurückgeführt (Quod animi mores corp. temp. sequ. 10 — K IV, 810), die Dyskrasie durch warme Süßwasserbäder und entsprechend ausgewählte Speisen bekämpft (De san. t. V, 3, 3 — K VI, 319). In weitschweifigen Erörterungen wird die zuträgliche Kost besprochen. Sie soll nahrhaft und leicht sein, damit sie der nur träge assimilierende Greisenorganismus verwerten kann (De marcore 9 — K VII, 700); besonders Fische mit zartem Fleisch bekommen alten Leuten gut (De aliment. facult. III, 29, 15 Helmreich — III, 30, K VI, 726). Auf die richtige Beschaffenheit des Brotes ist zu achten (De san. t. V, 7, 1 — K VI, 342), alles Stopfende zu meiden (ib. V, 6, 2f. — K VI, 339f.). Der Stuhlgang ist zu regeln, am besten durch Öl, das vor den Mahlzeiten genommen wird, oder durch Feigen und Pflaumen, die im Winter getrocknet gegeben werden können. Auf regelmäßige Harnentleerung ist zu sehen und nötigenfalls durch Sellerie, Honig oder entsprechende Weine nachzuhelfen (ib. V, 9, 1f. — K VI, 353). Den Aderlaß vertragen alte Leute schlecht (Ad Glauc. de med. meth. I, 15 — K XI, 46; In Hipp. de victu acut. comm. IV, 19 — Helmreich 287, K XV, 765). Da beim Greise geringe Ursachen große Wirkungen hervorbringen können, muß er sich beim Essen selbst vor geringen Überschreitungen des Zuträglichen sowohl der Qualität wie der Quantität nach hüten (De san. t. V, 4, 7 — K VI, 331).

Auch Bewegung, Gymnastik und Massage empfiehlt Galen dem Greise. Vollständige körperliche Ruhe tut ihm nicht gut, andererseits aber muß er sich bei seinen Übungen vor der geringsten Überanstrengung hüten (De san. t. V, 3, 6 — K VI, 320). Man lasse ihn nur Bewegungen ausführen, die ihm vertraut sind. Aktive Übungen beschränke man auf die gesunden Teile des Körpers, etwa geschädigte werden dabei unbemerkt vom Patienten mitbewegt und erhalten so wieder ihre volle Funktion (ib. V, 10, 10 — V, 3, K VI, 323).

Das in scharfsinnigem Eklektizismus errichtete Lehrgebäude Galens gelangte bereits in der Spätantike zu ungewöhnlich hohem Ansehen. Seine Gerokomia wurde in allen Epochen seines Nachwirkens eifrig benutzt. Sie gehört zu den Teilen seines Werkes, die sich bis in die Nähe unserer Zeit im Bewußtsein der Ärzte gehalten haben. In Galens Formulierung sind die antiken Vorstellungen vom Altern noch im 18. Jhdt. lebendig gewesen.

Altersregimina des Mittelalters

Der Zusammenbruch des weströmischen Reiches und die Wirren der Völkerwanderung setzten einer kontinuierlichen Weiterentwicklung der antiken Heilkunst ein Ende. GALENS System erhielt aus den Händen der arabisch schreibenden Ärzte die Autorität eines unumstößlichen Dogmas, das weit über 1000 Jahre lang das ärztliche Denken beherrschte. Seine Lehre vom Alter und seiner Pflege kehrt in zahlreichen arabischen Schriften wieder. Sie findet sich im Libellus de particularibus dietis des ISAAC IUDAEUS (z. B. Bl. 51 b und Bl. 56a des Paduaner Druckes von 1487). Sie gehört zu den Quellen der arabischen Kompendien der gesamten Medizin und begegnet uns im Malikî des HALI ABBAS (Pract. I, 23) ebenso wie im Werke AVICENNAS.

Im Kanon (liber I, fen 3, doctr. 3: Sermo universalis in regendo senes) gibt AVICENNA den breiten Ausführungen GALENS eine knappe, in ihrer praktischen Brauchbarkeit kaum angreifbare Fassung. Der Greis müsse durch die Wahl seiner Speisen und Getränke, durch Bäder, ausgedehnten Schlaf und viel Ruhe für Erwärmung und Durchfeuchtung seines Körpers sorgen. Er empfiehlt ihm eine vorwiegend laktovegetabilische Kost, bei der er neben die schon von GALEN gepriesene Ziegenmilch die Eselsmilch stellt, und bezeichnet als bekömmlichsten Wein den alten roten. Er nennt zahlreiche abführende Mittel verschieden starker Wirksamkeit; sie sollen je nach dem Grade der Verstopfung angewandt werden. Zur Tagesordnung des Greises gehört eine maßvolle Massage, an die sich körperliche Bewegung, ein Spaziergang oder ein Ritt, anschließen soll. Der Aderlaß (Cantica II, 99—105: Regimen senum) ist Greisen, die daran gewöhnt sind, nicht völlig zu untersagen; doch sollen Sechzigjährige nur zweimal, Siebzigjährige nur einmal im Jahre zur Ader gelassen werden.

Einzelne große Persönlichkeiten des Mittelalters strebten danach, sich der Herrschaft der mit überzeugender Selbstsicherheit vorgetragenen Lehren der alten Ärzte zu entziehen. Während sie aber versuchten, das überlieferte Gut durch selbständiges Denken, eigene Beobachtung und eigene Erfahrung zu überprüfen, verfielen sie in anderen Bezirken magischen Methoden der Therapie oder einer dem altbabylonisch-chaldäischen Kulturkreis entstammenden Iatromathematik. Es war ihr den Zurückschauenden lebhaft ergreifendes Schicksal, trotz aller Kühnheit ihrer Gedankengänge dem eigenen Jahrhundert nicht entfliehen zu können.

Gestalten wie ROGER BACON und ARNALD VON VILLANOVA, die beide dem 13. Jhdt. angehören, zeigen in einprägsamer Form diesen tiefen Zwiespalt des Mittelalters. Das erste große abendländische Regimen senum ist ROGER BACONS De retardatione accidentium senectutis et senii (3), das nach LITTLE (S. XXV) als Jugendarbeit zu gelten hat. In seinen philosophisch-naturwissenschaftlichen Werken wandte sich BACON gegen das Haften an überkommenen Denkgewohnheiten, bekämpfte den blinden Autoritätsglauben und trat für eine naturwissenschaftliche Behandlung derjenigen Probleme ein, die mit dialektischer Spekulation nicht zu lösen sind. Er setzte sich dadurch schwerer Anfeindung von seiten der Kirche aus. Trotzdem ist sein Alterstraktat nur eine gewissenhafte Kompilation aus den Handschriften der Araber — WITHINGTON (S. XXXIV) zählte etwa 100 Verweise allein auf AVICENNA —; aus eigenem Urteil und eigener Erfahrung hat der jugendliche Verfasser nichts hinzugefügt, wenn er sich auch gern den Anschein geben möchte, als ob ihm bisher verborgene Heilmittel bekannt geworden seien.

Schon im Prohemium spricht ROGER von den zwei Wegen, die man habe, um das Altern aufzuhalten. Der eine ist die Befolgung des Regimen sanitatis, alia est proprietas quarundam medicinarum quas antiqui occultaverunt (S. 3). Als Occulta umschreibt er in bilderreichen Wendungen Ambra, Schlangenfleisch, Rosmarinöl, den Herzknochen des Hirsches und anderes. Am ausführlichsten geht er auf etwas ein, dessen die alten Weisen ebenfalls nur tacite mentionem fecerunt (Cap. 7, S. 57ff.). Wie die Krankheit von einem Menschen auf den anderen übergeht, so ist es auch mit der Gesundheit. Mit geheimnisvoller Umständlichkeit deutet er an, daß die Ausdünstungen gesunder junger Menschen dem alternden Körper die verlorengegangene natürliche Wärme wiedergeben können. Seine Quellen sind im Umkreis der Geschichte von David und Abisag und des pseudo-aristotelischen Secretum secretorum zu suchen. Auf diese vermutlich syrische Schrift verweist er in seinem Alterstraktat mehr als zwanzigmal, ohne jedoch die Stelle heranzuziehen, an der empfohlen wird, bei Magenschmerzen ein warmes und hübsches Mädchen zu umarmen (4). Bei GALEN, der diese Methode der Lebensverlängerung bereits angegeben haben soll (5), läßt sich kein Beleg dafür finden. Er sagt lediglich, daß man sich bei gewissen Magenbeschwerden ein Kind oder einen kleinen Hund auf den Bauch legen soll, um das Defizit an Verdauungswärme von außen her zu decken (De simpl. medic. temp. et facult. V, 5 — K XI, 724).

Von ROGERS geheimen Mitteln hat sich diese später schlechtweg Gerokomie genannte Methode am längsten gehalten. SYDENHAM berichtet aus den 60er Jahren des 17. Jhdts., er habe durch langes Fieber erschöpfte Kranke, als kein Mittel mehr anschlagen wollte, mit der Ausdünstung gesunder, kräftiger Jünglinge geheilt. Das Auflegen erwärmter Tücher habe bei weitem nicht das gleiche geleistet wie der junge menschliche Körper (Obs. med. I, 4 — Bd. 1, S. 39 der Genfer Ausg. von 1749). BOERHAAVE hat nach einer Angabe HUFELANDS in seiner Makrobiotik einen greisen Amsterdamer Bürgermeister wieder zu Kräften gebracht, indem er ihn zwischen zwei jungen Leuten schlafen ließ. In das Bewußtsein des literarischen Publikums kam diese „Gerokomie" durch das erfolgreiche Büchlein eines westfälischen Arztes, des schreibgewandten JOHANN HEINRICH COHAUSEN, das 1742 unter dem Titel „Hermippus redivivus" erschien. Noch vor dem Ende des 18. Jhdts., im Paris MARIE ANTOINETTES, ist die mittelalterliche Geheimkur voll magischer Kraft zu einem lasziven Spiel geworden.

Wenige Jahre nach ROGERS Tode schrieb ARNALD VON VILLANOVA einen Traktat De conservanda iuventute et retardanda senectute (Sp. 813 der Basler Opera omnia von 1585). Es läßt sich fast mit Bestimmtheit sagen, daß ARNALD bei der Abfassung dieses Büchleins BACONS Schriften über das Alter nicht nur gekannt, sondern auch recht unbekümmert benutzt hat. WITHINGTON (6) betonte die weitgehende Übereinstimmung zwischen ARNALDS Traktat und einem kleineren Sermon ROGER BACONS De conservatione iuventutis, der an einen Frater E. gerichtet ist (7). Whole passages are verbally alike. In einer SUDHOFFschen Dissertation (8) wurde diese Behauptung zurückgewiesen und die Gleichheit der Formulierung aus der Benutzung derselben arabischen Quellen hergeleitet. Hätte die Verfasserin bei ihrem Vergleich auch den kleineren Alterstraktat ROGERS heranziehen können, würde sie zu einem ähnlichen Ergebnis wie WITHINGTON gekommen sein. Geistiges Eigentum ARNALDS sind aber zahlreiche praktische Winke, die Hinweise auf Medikamente und die Besprechung erprobter Rezepte und Vorschriften. Sie stammen aus seiner großen ärztlichen Erfahrung und fehlen bei ROGER, der selbst nie als Arzt praktisch tätig gewesen ist.

Bewährt sich ARNALD in seiner Therapie als der große Arzt,

der es wagt, unabhängig von der Macht der Tradition auch eigene Wege zu gehen, so zeigt ihn doch seine Stellung zur Astrologie als einen echten Sproß des 13. Jhdts. Astrologus quidem in multis dissentit a medico, tamen sermo eius non est vilipendendus (De conservanda iuv. 3 — Op. omn. 824 D). DIEPGEN hat in den Studien zu ARNALD VON VILLANOVA (9) dargelegt, daß sich ARNALD in seinen medizinisch-astrologischen Gedankengängen nicht von den iatromathematischen Vorstellungen seiner Zeit entfernt. Hier sei noch darauf hingewiesen, daß der Sermo super astrologiam, ein Abschnitt in ARNALDS Alterstraktat (Op. omn. 832 C), in der von ihm als Vorlage benutzten BACONschen Schrift nicht enthalten und ebenso wie die praktischen Ratschläge eine charakteristische Zutat ARNALDS ist.

Der früheste Druck, der der Betreuung des alten Menschen gewidmet ist, dürfte die Gerontokomia des italienischen Anatomen GABRIELE ZERBI sein: Bl. 1b (nicht 1a, wie HAIN 16284 angibt): GABRIELIS ZERBI VERONENSIS AD INNOCENTIUM. VIII. PON. MAX. GERENTOCOMIA FELICITER INCIPIT. Das gut gedruckte Buch erschien nach dem Kolophon im Jahre 1489, nicht viel später als die ersten Wiegendrucke auf dem Gebiete der Kinderheilkunde, und stammt aus der Offizin des in Rom tätigen Würzburgers EUCHARIUS SILBER alias FRANCK. ZERBI lehnt sich in seiner umfangreichen Gerokomie eng an GALEN an; zahlreich sind auch Verweise auf die Araber und auf römische Schriftsteller, besonders auf CELSUS. Die 57 Kapitel des Buches behandeln die Ursachen des Alters und seiner Erscheinungen, gehen auf die Hygiene des Alters ein, wobei auch Wohnung, Kleidung und Schlafstätte besprochen werden, erörtern ausführlich die für den Greis geeigneten Nahrungsmittel und Medikamente und geben die Indikation zu therapeutischen Maßnahmen wie Zur-Ader-lassen, Abführen und Erbrechen-machen an.

Antikes Gedankengut im Altersschrifttum des 16.—18. Jahrhunderts

Dem typographischen Erstling der Gerontokomie folgten in den nächsten Jahrhunderten zahlreiche Drucke gleicher oder verwandter Themastellung. LIPENIUS nennt in seiner gegen Ende des 17. Jhdts. erschienenen Bibliotheca realis medica unter Schlagwörtern wie Senum affectus, Senum regimen, Longaevitas etwa 30 Titel solcher Schriften; eine ähnlich große Anzahl ist ihm nicht bekannt geworden. In dieser Literatur blieben die Lehren GALENS von der Erhaltung und Wiederherstellung der Greisengesundheit lebendig, auch dann noch, als die jugendlich selbstbewußte Welt der Renaissance es wagte, der Unfehlbarkeit des Pergameners ein „Errores!" entgegenzurufen. Die neuen Erkenntnisse der Anatomie und Physiologie schoben sich nur sehr zögernd zwischen die Galenischen Vorstellungen vom Alter und seinen Beschwerden.

CANSTATT und GEIST nennen im Literaturverzeichnis ihrer Darstellungen der Greisenkrankheiten als zeitlich erstes Werk die Decreta aliquot medica (de senectute) STROMERS VON AUERBACH, die im Jahre 1536 erschienen und mehrfach nachgedruckt wurden. Sie sind noch völlig in der Tradition befangen, obwohl aus den Verweisen STROMERS deutlich wird, daß seine Quellen nicht nur die Araber, sondern auch die antiken Autoren sind. Er rühmt das Wirken LEONICENOS und seiner Schule für eine Erneuerung der Sprachen und Lehren, kennt seinen Kampf gegen die Barbari und betont, daß er HIPPOKRATES und GALEN fidelius traduxit (Bl. A 3b). STROMER ist auch dadurch bemerkenswert, daß er Dekan der Leipziger medizinischen Fakultät war, als durch einen in seinen Hintergründen noch nicht geklärten Einspruch von Leipzig aus die Drucklegung von HOHENHEIMS dritter Nürnberger Syphilis-Schrift verhindert wurde. Daß sein Name noch heute genannt wird, verdankt er GOETHE. Der rührige Mann hatte um 1530 ein großes Gebäude errichtet, in dessen Kellern er Wein einlagern und ausschenken ließ. Dort, in AUERBACHS Keller, spielt die Studentenszene im Faust.

Für medizinische Dissertationen und für Gelegenheitsschriften und Reden zu akademischen Feiern wurde das Alter bald ein beliebtes Thema. Die Epistola de longaevis (1664) des Helmstedter Anatomen HEINRICH MEIBOM ist eine historisch gehaltene Geburtstagsplauderei für den Landesherrn, GERHARD VAN SWIETENS De senum valetudine tuenda (10) eine an einem Festtage der Universität gehaltene Rede. VAN SWIETEN kennt die Altersveränderungen der Gefäße (S. 6) und beschreibt das Schrumpfen der Zwischenwirbelscheiben (S. 24); daneben stehen die seit mehr als tausend Jahren wiederholten Lehren: Senectus est nihil aliud quam siccum et frigidum corporis temperamentum, annorum multitudine proveniens (S. 24) und Liquida in frigidam et pituitosam degenerant Cacochymiam (S. 6). Diese humoralpathologischen Gedankengänge verleiten ihn jedoch nicht zu unfruchtbaren Spekulationen. Seine hygienisch-diätetischen Vorschriften für den alternden Menschen enthalten alles, was sich aus GALENS Gerokomie bewährt hat; Bäder, Massage, vorsichtig dosierte Bewegung und eine nicht zu reichliche Ernährung stehen auch bei VAN SWIETEN im Vordergrund. Er wendet sich gegen die betrügerischen Arcana zur Lebensverlängerung, sei es nun Zedernholz oder Gold, und spottet über die, die glauben, durch den Herzknochen des Hirsches oder Mumienfleisch das Altern aufhalten zu können (S. 21f.).

Daß der erfahrene Arzt aus GALENS Gerokomie eine in der Praxis sich bewährende Diätetik des Alters und Therapie seiner Erkrankungen entwickeln konnte, beweist das Buch des Engländers FLOYER, das im Jahre 1724 unter dem Titel Medicina gerocomica or the Galenic art of preserving old men's healths erschien (11). Von der antiken Krasenlehre und dem ebenso alten Begriff der Konstitution ausgehend, betont FLOYER, daß den Greisen charakteristische, voneinander abweichende Erkrankungsformen zukommen, according to their different constitutions and cacochymia's (S. 24f.). Jede Konstitution verlangt eine besonders auf sie eingestellte Therapie; no one method can be used to all old men to preserve their healths (S. 25). Unter Verwendung des Arzneimittelschatzes seiner Zeit gibt FLOYER eine fast verwirrend große Anzahl von Medikamenten, die nach Konstitutionen und damit auch nach den diesen zugehörigen Krankheitsgruppen in 14 Kapitel geordnet sind. Seine therapeutischen Vorschriften münden allzuoft in eine Apologie des kalten Bades (S. 108), was schon HALLER bei aller Anerkennung, die er dem Autor und seinen Büchern zollte, zu einem Ausruf des Erstaunens veranlaßt hat (Bibl. med. pract. IV, 10—14). Die Wasserheilkunde bewahrt ihm dafür als einem ihrer Pioniere ein ehrendes Andenken (12).

FLOYERS Vorstellungen von Alter und Krankheit stammen trotz aller Abwandlungen, die sie dem Jahrhundert VESALS und der Entdeckung HARVEYS verdanken, aus der Welt GALENS. Es scheint schwierig, wenn nicht fast unmöglich gewesen zu sein, von dem System des Pergameners einen Zugang zur Kenntnis der morphologischen und funktionellen Veränderungen des Alters zu finden. Das lassen die zahlreichen Schriften aus dieser Zeit vermuten, die sich, wie FLOYER, damit begnügten, in der Kakochymia, der schlechten Beschaffenheit der Säfte, die Ursache von Altern und Krankheit zu sehen.

Das Experiment in der Altersforschung

Dem 15. Jhdt. gehören die frühesten Bestrebungen an, die Medizin aus den Fesseln der arabischen und antiken Tradition zu lösen. In ihm begegnen wir auch dem ersten Beitrag zu unserem Thema, der sich, zunächst nur in Gedanken, in Neuland vorwagt. NIKOLAUS VON CUES — er starb 1464 als einflußreicher Kardinal und Bischof von Brixen — schlug in seiner Schrift De staticis experimentis (13) in einer großartigen Unabhängigkeit des Denkens vor, die exakte Methode des Wägens auch auf ärztliche Untersuchungen anzuwenden. Er erklärt, daß vor ihm noch niemand auf den Gedanken gekommen sei, naturwissenschaftliche oder biologische Probleme durch Gewichtsbestimmungen zu lösen (S. 119, 11). Aus den medizinischen Fragen gewidmeten Abschnitten sei hier nur auf diejenigen Stellen eingegangen, an denen er experimentelle Nachweise für das abweichende Verhalten des alten Menschen angibt.

NIKOLAUS VON CUES macht in seinen Versuchen mit der Waage den Vorschlag, den Harn nicht nur nach der trügerischen Farbe, sondern auch auf Grund des Gewichtes zu beurteilen. Eine Wägung des Harns werde gewißlich Unterschiede zwischen jungen und alten, gesunden und kranken Menschen ergeben und die Fixierung der gefundenen Werte (habere has omnes differentias annotatas) für den Arzt von größtem Vorteil sein (S. 120, 22ff.). Danach muß ihm eine Vergleichung des empirisch gefundenen Gewichts mit Normalwerten vorgeschwebt haben. Hier scheint vorweggenommen zu sein, was erst im vorigen Jahrhundert als diagnostische Methode Wirklichkeit wurde. Auch im Gewicht des Blutes erwartete der kühne Denker Unterschiede zwischen Jungen und Alten, Gesunden und Kranken zu finden.

Ferner schlug CUSANUS vor, aus dem engen Loch der Wasseruhr so lange Wasser in ein Becken tropfen zu lassen, bis man 100 Pulsschläge gefühlt habe, und sodann das Gewicht des ausgeflossenen Wassers zu bestimmen. Die in der Herophileerschule geübte Methode der Pulsmessung hat er offenbar nicht gekannt; sie war schon in der Antike in Vergessenheit geraten. Auch bei diesen Wägungen, so behauptet er, werden sich Unterschiede zwischen Gesunden und Kranken, Jungen und Alten ergeben (S. 121, 13ff.). Durch dieses Verfahren könne man zu einer genaueren Kenntnis der einzelnen Erkrankungen kommen, da man für sie je nach ihrer Art verschiedene Wassergewichte erwarten müsse. Die experimentelle

Ermittlung des Pulsäquivalents und des Harngewichts ermögliche eine vollkommenere Beurteilung als das Betasten der Pulsader und die Prüfung der Harnfarbe allein. Auch zur Bestimmung der Atemfrequenz zog Nikolaus von Cues seine wägende Zeitmessung heran. Man zähle 100 Atemzüge und lasse ebensolange Wasser aus der Wasseruhr in ein Becken tropfen. Es sei ausgeschlossen, daß diese Methode für einen Knaben und einen Greis gleiche Gewichtswerte liefere. Sobald man Normalwerte für die einzelnen Lebensalter ermittelt habe, werde die Durchführung dieses Versuchs schnell über Gesundheit oder Krankheit Auskunft geben (S. 122, 2ff.). Fände man z. B. bei einem gesunden Jüngling eine Maßzahl für die Atemfrequenz, die eigentlich einem hinfälligen Greise zukommt, so müsse man schließen, daß er bald sterben werde, und könne eine Bewunderung erweckende Prognose stellen.

Hier wird der Medizin zum ersten Mal die neue Aufgabe gezeigt, das funktionelle Anderssein des Greisenalters mit exakten Methoden zu untersuchen. Wenn auch Nikolaus von Cues seine physikalischen Versuche nicht auf den alten Menschen beschränken wollte, sondern damit ebensosehr das abweichende Verhalten des kranken messend erfassen zu können glaubte, so dürfen wir doch den Traktat De staticis experimentis, der im Jahre 1450 entstand, als den ersten Beitrag zu einer naturwissenschaftlich fundierten Physiologie des Greisenalters ansehen. Die Vorschläge des genialen Philosophen waren der Heilkunst ihrer Zeit um Jahrhunderte voraus. Sie blieben deshalb ohne Wirkung auf die Entwicklung der Medizin, obwohl die Versuche mit der Waage in der Zeit von 1488—1565 in fünf verschiedenen Drucken herauskamen. Ein ähnliches Schicksal hatte das Werk Theophrasts von Hohenheim, das, wie auf vielen Gebieten, auch auf dem der Greisenkrankheiten neuere Erkenntnisse vorweggenommen hat. In ihm finden sich nach einem Hinweis W. A. Leopold von Brunns (14) aus der ärztlichen Erfahrung gewonnene Anschauungen über die Behandlung der Greisenkrankheiten, die die Besonderheiten des alten Menschen berücksichtigen und für eine ihm angepaßte Therapie eintreten.

150 Jahre nach Nikolaus von Cues führte Santorio Santorio quantitative Bestimmungen zur Lösung biologischer Fragestellungen praktisch durch. Wie sein großer Vorgänger glaubte er, durch messende Methoden auch vom Alter und seinen Krankheiten bessere Kenntnis gewinnen zu können. Mit seiner gefeiertsten Leistung, dem wägenden Nachweis der Perspiratio insensibilis, hat

er der Physiologie das Tor zur physikalisch-experimentellen Forschung aufgestoßen. Darin liegt seine historische Bedeutung, nicht in der diagnostischen oder therapeutischen Anwendung seiner Experimente. In dieser folgt er zumeist Gedankengängen GALENS, dessen Herrschaft auch die Terminologie seiner Statica medicina noch deutlich erkennen läßt: Senes ob frequentia sputamina vitam protrahunt; retenta ut incapacia coctionis vel digestionis impediunt perspirationem; unde suffocatio et mors (15). Das Alter stellt sich ihm als eine zunehmende Erschwerung der Perspiratio insensibilis dar, die schließlich zu Erstickung und Tod führt. Es läßt sich hinausschieben, indem man den Körper durch regelmäßige Bäder und eine feucht machende Diät für die unmerkbare Atmung durchgängig (perspirabilis) erhält. Klinischer Wert kommt den Ergebnissen seiner Versuche trotz ihrer methodologischen Bedeutung nicht zu. Der Prozeß des Alterns war, ebenso wie eine Reihe anderer biologischer Vorgänge, denen SANTORIO auf der Spur zu sein glaubte, durch die Wägung der Perspiratio insensibilis nicht zu fassen.

Johann Bernhard Fischer

Das 17. Jhdt. hat trotz der großen Impulse, die HARVEYS Entdeckung der Physiologie erteilte, die Kenntnis der Altersveränderungen nicht mit bewußter Zielsetzung gefördert. Der hervorragende Beobachter SYDENHAM berührt in dem wenigen, was er an Aufzeichnungen hinterlassen hat, die Erkrankungen des Alters nicht. Noch BOERHAAVE dürfte ihnen wenig Aufmerksamkeit gezollt haben. Auch sein Schüler und Kommentator VAN SWIETEN scheint von einem therapeutischen Vorgehen gegen die Beschwerden des Alters keine Erfolge erwartet zu haben. Er sagt in seinem fünfbändigen Hauptwerk, den Commentaria in Hermanni Boerhaave aphorismos: Nulla spes est, marasmo iam tabescentes partes corporis in decrepita aetate denuo restitui posse (§ 1062). Wie in seiner Rede De senum valetudine tuenda verweist er den, der den Altersverfall aufhalten möchte, auf die Schriften GALENS (§ 128).

Der deutsch-baltische Arzt JOHANN BERNHARD FISCHER, unter ANNA IWANOWNA kaiserlich russischer Leibarzt und Chef des gesamten russischen Medizinalwesens, hat das Verdienst, diesem therapeutischen Skeptizismus in seinem Buche De senio eiusque gradibus et morbis (16) entgegengetreten zu sein. Er betont in der Einleitung (S. 12), daß, wie die Erfahrung lehre und er es selbst im Hauptteil seines Buches mit einprägsamen Fällen belegen werde, eine Behandlung der Greisenkrankheit keineswegs aussichtslos sei (in morbis senum non semper desperandum esse). Diese Anschauung durchzusetzen, scheint bis heute noch nicht völlig gelungen zu sein. Einer der neuesten Bearbeiter des Gebietes, A. MÜLLER-DEHAM (17), glaubt besonders ausführlich auf die Therapie der Greisenkrankheiten und ihre Erfolge eingehen zu müssen, „um dem vielfach vorherrschenden Nihilismus und Pessimismus entgegenzuarbeiten. Hier liegen die Dinge oft besser, als sie scheinen."

FISCHERS Buch De senio ist bei seiner Aufnahme in die Leopoldina geschrieben und im Jahre 1754 als Oktavband von 278 Seiten erschienen. Es verdient eine eingehendere Besprechung, da es einen neuen Typus in der Literatur verkörpert. Während die der Tradition folgenden Alterstraktate überwiegend prophylaktische Maßnahmen und hygienisch-diätetische Vorschriften enthalten, stehen hier die morphologischen und funktionellen Veränderungen des Alters und seine Krankheiten und ihre Behandlung im Mittelpunkt der Betrachtung. Das erste der drei Kapitel des Werkes, irreführend Recensio historica genannt, enthält als umfangreichsten und wichtigsten Abschnitt (S. 26—88) eine Darstellung der Anatomie und Physiologie des Greisenalters. In diesem macht es sich FISCHER zur Aufgabe, die eigentümliche Beschaffenheit des alten Menschen und die äußeren und inneren Veränderungen seines Körpers zu beschreiben (S. 15) oder, wie er an einer anderen Stelle wiederholt, formam senum ... primo externam, post internam, pro intimiore materiae examine ob oculos ponere, ut ex illo eo melius tam indicia senectutis quam rationes affectuum et incommodorum hauriamus (S. 26). Er betont die Notwendigkeit von Sektionen, um die Morphologie des gesunden Greisenorganismus (formam senilem internam) aufzuhellen (S. 38), und bildet sein Urteil nach eigenen Sektionen und der Literatur entnommenen Berichten. Als charakteristische Befunde, die das hohe Alter begleiten, bezeichnet er (S. 46f.) 1. die Erweiterung des Herzens und der Aorta (cordis et arteriae aortae enormis amplitudo), 2. die Verkalkung der absteigenden Arterien (arteriarum descendentium, quoad tunicam interiorem, ossificatio), 3. die Festigkeit des Gehirns und die Härte der Drüsen, für die er später als Beispiel die glandula pinealis anführt (cerebri densitas et glandularum durities), 4. das Fehlen von Veränderungen an der Lunge (pulmonum status incolumis), 5. die knorpelige Umhüllung der Milz (lienis cartilaginositas) und 6. die Umbildung der Knochen, an denen man saftlose Zerbrechlichkeit, bisweilen auch Neigung zu neuem Wachstum sehe (ossium nunc arida frangibilitas, nunc vegetativa virtus). Aus der Besprechung, die er jedem dieser Befunde widmet, geht hervor, daß er Spangenbildung zwischen Wirbelkörpern als neues Wachstum gedeutet hat (S. 57). Nach der Darstellung der Anatomie zieht FISCHER die noch im Bereich des Physiologischen liegenden funktionellen Veränderungen des Greisenalters (mutationes actionum, tam vitalium quam sensualium) in den Kreis seiner Untersuchungen. Er trennt diese lediglich aus der Zahl der Jahre zu erklärenden Abweichungen von denen ab, die er als Krankheiten erst später besprechen will (S. 62), und geht auf Atmung, Puls, Nahrungsaufnahme, Ausscheidung, Schlaf und anderes ein. Nach diesen anatomischen und physiologischen Ausführungen ist das zweite Kapitel, das umfangreichste des Werkes (S. 109—255), den Erkrankungen des Alters und ihrer Heilung gewidmet. FISCHER betont, daß ihm hier besonders an einer Darstellung der Therapie gelegen sei (S. 110). In dem kurzen dritten Kapitel bringt er allgemeine Vorschriften zur Lebensführung des Greises, die jeweils nach dem Habitus strictus oder laxus modifiziert werden. Auch in seiner Krankheitslehre begegnen wir diesem alten Erbgut aus der Methodikerschule.

Bei der Bewertung von FISCHERs Leistung ist zu berücksichtigen, daß ihm MORGAGNIS Beobachtungen und Sektionsberichte, die sich häufig auf das hohe Alter beziehen, noch nicht zur Verfügung standen. De sedibus et causis morborum kam erst 1761 heraus, sieben Jahre nach FISCHERs Buch. HALLER war zwar bereits von Göttingen in seine Schweizer Heimat zurückgekehrt; seine große, die eigenen Forschungen und die gesamte Literatur verarbeitende Darstellung seines bekanntesten Arbeitsgebietes, die Elementa physiologiae corporis humani, begannen aber erst 1757 zu erscheinen. Eine Zusammenstellung der zur Anatomie und Physiologie des Greisenalters bekannten Tatsachen brachte erst der 8. Band des riesigen Werkes vom Jahre 1766. FISCHERs Werk, in der Einsamkeit eines baltischen Gutshofes entstanden, darf deshalb als ein wichtiger, zu einem beträchtlichen Teil selbständiger Beitrag zu einer wissenschaftlichen Lehre von den Greisenkrankheiten gelten.

Im Jahre 1793 veröffentlichte BENJAMIN RUSH, bekannt als der amerikanische Vorkämpfer des Brownianismus, im 2. Bande seiner Medical inquiries and observations (Philadelphia 1793) eine kleine Abhandlung über das Alter und seine Krankheiten. Da sie zweimal ins Deutsche übersetzt wurde (18) und heute noch in der amerikanischen Literatur genannt wird, sei sie auch hier erwähnt. RUSH bezieht sich darin auf MORGAGNI und HALLER und ordnet den Stoff ähnlich wie FISCHER, ohne neue Gesichtspunkte zu bieten. Die Schrift steht für die Vereinigten Staaten am Anfang einer Entwicklung, die in neuester Zeit die Greisenheilkunde unter der Bezeichnung Geriatrics zu einem selbständigen Fach mit eigenen Lehrstühlen (19) erheben möchte.

Die Formulierung der Aufgaben

Am Ende des 18. Jhdts. erschien die erste monographische Darstellung der Anatomie des Greisenalters. Ihr Verfasser ist der Erlanger BURKHARD WILHELM SEILER. Er war später Professor der Anatomie und Chirurgie in Wittenberg und ist 1843 als Direktor der chirurgisch-medizinischen Akademie in Dresden gestorben. Seine 1799 als Dissertation gedruckte Anatomia corporis humani senilis ist eine sorgfältige und kritische Kompilation der Kenntnisse seiner Zeit, die in den folgenden Jahrzehnten viel benutzt worden ist; neue eigene Beobachtungen enthält sie nicht. Die programmatischen Gedanken jedoch, die sie zur Morphologie des Greises entwickelt, verdienen, als Formulierung der Aufgaben und Ziele künftiger Forschung beachtet zu werden: Unser anatomisches Bild vom Erwachsenen habe für den Greis nur beschränkte Gültigkeit. Jeder Organismus werde durch die langdauernde Funktion so sehr verändert, daß er im Alter als ein neues Gebilde anzusehen sei. Als solches verlange er seine eigene Betrachtung. Nova eius forma peculiarem contemplationem summo iure exigit (S. IX). SEILER forderte Reihenuntersuchungen und vergleichende Beobachtungen, um die dem Alter eigentümlichen Strukturänderungen zu ermitteln. Besonders die Anatomen, denen das Material der Altershospize zur Verfügung stehe, seien berufen, das noch der Bearbeitung harrende Gebiet systematisch zu durchforschen (S. X).

Für Untersuchungen zur Greisenanatomie stellte SEILER zehn Richtlinien auf. Die ersten sechs verlangen bei der Auswertung der Befunde Berücksichtigung des Grades des Alters, des Geschlechts, des Habitus, etwa angeborener Anomalien, der Lebensführung und der regionalen Einflüsse. Die folgenden vier sind fast Wort für Wort auch heute noch gültig:

7. Da die meisten Greise nicht an Altersschwäche, sondern an irgendeiner Krankheit sterben, muß man sich hüten, als Altersveränderung anzusehen, was die Wirkung einer lokalen oder all-

gemeinen Erkrankung ist (ne morbi alicuius, vel topici, vel universalis, effectus senectuti tribuamus). Es sind deshalb nur Sektionen solcher Greise verwertbar, die, ohne krank zu sein, gestorben sind (mortem sine morbo subierunt), solange nicht eine Norm entwickelt ist, nach der man entscheiden kann, was Alter, was Krankheit ist. SEILER dürfte als erster auf die Schwierigkeit hingewiesen haben, die beiden Zustände in jedem Falle scharf voneinander abzugrenzen.

8. Um ein vollständiges Bild des Greisenorganismus zu gewinnen, genügt die Methode des anatomischen Messers nicht. Injektionstechnik und Mikroskop sind zu Hilfe zu nehmen und Gewicht, Elastizität und Festigkeit der einzelnen Teile zu untersuchen. Flüssige wie feste Bestandteile des Körpers sind einer chemischen Analyse zu unterziehen, um festzustellen, inwieweit die Zusammensetzung des alten Organismus vom jugendlichen abweicht.

9. Ärzten, die Altershospize leiten, kommt die Aufgabe zu, Beobachtungen und Aufzeichnungen über die körperliche Beschaffenheit der Greise und ihre Wandlungen zu machen.

10. Nur was durch zahlreiche Beobachtungen bestätigt worden ist, kann als dem Alter eigentümliche Erscheinung angesehen werden (S. XVII—XIX).

Wie es SEILER auszeichnet, in seiner Anatomia corporis humani senilis Grundsätze für eine morphologische Altersforschung entwickelt zu haben, die uns selbstverständlicher Besitz geworden sind, so ist es das Verdienst CARL CANSTATTS, einer lehrbuchmäßigen Darstellung der Greisenkrankheiten die erste Form gegeben und auf zahlreiche noch ungelöste Fragen hingewiesen zu haben. CANSTATT, ein hochbegabter Schüler SCHÖNLEINs, hatte sich nach Abschluß seiner ärztlichen Ausbildung in Wien und Würzburg (1831) dem Studium der Cholera zugewandt, in Brüssel ein Cholerahospital geleitet und sich danach vorwiegend der Augenheilkunde gewidmet. Im Jahre 1838 erhielt er in Ansbach eine Anstellung als Gerichtsarzt mit der Erlaubnis, private Praxis auszuüben. 1844 wurde er als Professor der inneren Klinik nach Erlangen berufen, starb aber bald danach, noch nicht 43 Jahre alt. Sein Name ist verbunden mit dem von ihm gegründeten, später von VIRCHOW fortgesetzten Jahresbericht über die Fortschritte der gesamten Medizin. Obwohl er sich in Ansbach ex officio nicht mit den Erkrankungen des Alters zu befassen hatte, wagte er sich an die Bearbeitung dieses Gebiets, da es seit 85 Jahren, seit FISCHERS De senio eiusque gradibus et morbis, keine größere zusammenhängende Darstellung erfahren hatte. Sein zweibändiges Werk erschien 1839 in Erlangen unter dem Titel: Die Krankheiten des höheren Alters und ihre Heilung.

CANSTATT betont, daß dem Studium der Alterskrankheiten die Erforschung der Veränderungen vorausgehen müsse, ,,welche die verschiedenen Gewebe, Organe und Funktionen des Körpers während der Involutionsperiode erleiden" (Bd. I, S. IV). Er folgt darin der schon von FISCHER gewählten Einteilung des Stoffes und stellt eine Anatomie und Physiologie des Greises an den Anfang seines Werkes. ,,Hohes Alter ist identisch mit Involution" (I, 14). Sie beginnt bald in diesem, bald in jenem System, während die übrigen Organe noch unverändert sind. Es läßt sich kein Gesetz auffinden, durch das bestimmt wäre, ,,in welcher Sukzessionsreihe die rückschreitende Metamorphose sich über die übrigen Teile des Organismus fortpflanze" (I, 12). Grundsätzliche Gedanken zur Therapie der Alterskrankheiten schließen sich an. Er wendet sich hier gegen BROUSSAIS und seinen ,,blutgierigen Terrorismus" (I, 120) sowie gegen eine medikamentöse Polypragmasie, aber auch gegen ein allzu abwartendes Verhalten. ,,Der Arzt überlasse in Alterskrankheiten nicht zu viel den Kräften der Natur." Denn ,,die Lebensrichtung im Greise erfüllt an und für sich schon den Zweck der Krankheit, anstatt der letzteren eine die Individualität wahrende und schützende Reaktion entgegenzusetzen" (I, 129). Mehr als 100 Seiten nimmt die Besprechung des nur wenig abgewandelten SCHÖNLEINschen Systems der Krankheiten in seiner Anwendung auf das höhere Alter ein. Erst der zweite Band bringt die ,,spezielle Pathologie und Therapie der Involutionsperiode"; ihre Darstellung folgt jedoch nicht den Klassen und Familien des so ausführlich vorgetragenen nosologischen Systems, sondern der alten anatomischen Ordnung. Zur Besprechung kommen sowohl die ,,eigentlichen Involutionskrankheiten", die durch den Vorgang des Alterns ausgelöst werden, wie ,,die durch die Involution modifizierten Krankheiten", die in ihrer aus anderen Lebensaltern bekannten Erscheinungsform durch die Altersmetamorphose verändert sind (I, 15). Diese Trennung kehrt bei allen späteren Bearbeitern des Gebietes wieder.

CANSTATTS gedankenreiches Werk entstand in der Zeit der üppigsten Blüte naturphilosophischer Deduktionen. Es läßt wohl bisweilen an die abenteuerlichen Spekulationen denken, denen sich viele seiner ärztlichen Zeitgenossen hingaben, strebt aber selbst eine unbefangene Beobachtung der physiologischen und pathologischen Vorgänge an. Trotzdem ist die Kritik DURAND-FARDELS (20) nicht ganz unberechtigt, dem Buche fehle das Gepräge peinlich genauer, persönlicher Beobachtung: ce cachet d'observation rigoureuse et personnelle qui, seul, donne aux œuvres de ce genre une véritable autorité, et aux assertions qu'elles renferment un caractère de certitude. Man bedenke, wie beschränkt die Quellen waren, aus denen CANSTATTS Erfahrung floß. Es ist wenig wahrscheinlich, daß die Beschäftigung mit der Pathologie des Alters in die Würzburger Zeit zurückreicht; er bezieht sich nicht auf das Juliusspital, dessen Pfründnerbau 200 unbemittelte Greise aufnehmen konnte. Nach den Lehr- und Wanderjahren lieferte ihm aber nur die eigene Allgemeinpraxis das Material für seine Altersforschung. Zu der literarischen Neigung der Epoche gesellte sich dadurch der Zwang, sich oft mit Mutmaßungen zu begnügen oder gestellte Fragen offen zu lassen. DURAND-FARDEL dagegen standen für seine Untersuchungen die Salpêtrière und das Hospital in Bicêtre zur Verfügung, die zusammen etwa ebensoviel alte Menschen beherbergten, wie Ansbach Einwohner hatte. CHARCOT (21) machte CANSTATT den gleichen Vorwurf: Cet ouvrage ... a été composé sous l'influence de la doctrine de SCHELLING. ... L'imagination y tient une place énorme aux dépens de l'observation impartiale et positive. Obwohl nun CANSTATT als Schüler SCHÖNLEINS sicherlich zu Unrecht naturphilosophischer Befangenheit gegenüber exakten Untersuchungsmethoden verdächtigt wurde, so ist es doch leicht, bei ihm Gedanken zu finden, die den Einfluß SCHELLINGS nicht verleugnen. Wenn er „die Gravitation des Lebens zur organischen Individuellbildung ... das egoistische, organisierende Prinzip, die Gravitation des Individuums zur allgemeinen Natur ... das kosmische Prinzip" nennt und unter Krankheit „einen nach Überwindung trachtenden Kampf zwischen diesen beiden nach Alleinherrschaft geizenden Polen" versteht (I, 2), wenn er erklärt, daß egoistisches und kosmisches Prinzip sich im Involutionsmenschen wie 1 zu 2 verhalten (I, 66), so spüren wir das tiefe Bedürfnis der Zeit, Erfahrungstatsachen aus dem gedanklich gewonnenen Bild der Welt und der Wissenschaft zu deuten. Selbst von der phantastisch-verschrobenen Pathologie K. RICH. HOFFMANNS, der Krankheit als ein Abgleiten in niedrigere Formen organischen Lebens bezeichnete, lassen sich Spuren finden:

CANSTATT glaubt nachweisen zu können, daß der alternde Mensch „den niedrigeren Tierbildungen sich annähere" (I, 160). Unter anderem vergleicht er das Gerontoxon mit dem Knochenringe der Sklera bei Vögeln und Reptilien, die Xerosis conjunctivae mit der Bildung des Auges bei Insekten und Mollusken, den verknöcherten Altersthorax mit dem Brustkorb der Vögel und die Verschmelzung der Rückenwirbel mit dem Panzer der Schildkröte. Er hat jedoch selbst diesen Spekulationen keinen Wert beigelegt: „Einer weiteren Ausführung dieses Gegenstandes müssen wir uns enthalten, da sein praktisches Interesse ein geringes ist" (I, 163).

CANSTATTS Versuch, Gesundheit und Krankheit des hohen Alters zum Gegenstand einer spezialisierten Forschung zu machen, wie es für die kindliche Lebensperiode bereits geschehen war, schuf das Fundament für eine naturwissenschaftliche Lehre von den Greisenkrankheiten. Trotz aller Schwächen, die dem umfangreichen Werk aus seiner Zeit und aus dem Umstand anhaften, daß es fern von großen Kliniken und Altershospizen entstand, hat jeder spätere Bearbeiter des Gebiets die Leistung des zu früh verstorbenen Mannes anerkannt. Auch CHARCOT beschließt seine schon erwähnte Kritik mit den Worten: Nous trouvons dans l'ouvrage de CANSTATT des idées ingénieuses et souvent vraies qui lui assurent une place honorable dans la science.

Die Klinik der Greisenkrankheiten

Im Jahre 1799 hatte SEILER vorgeschlagen, die Möglichkeiten, die Altershospize zur Beobachtung gesunder und kranker Greise bieten, auszunützen und das Sektionsmaterial dieser Anstalten für eine wissenschaftliche Altersforschung zu verwerten. Während diese Anregungen von den deutschen Ärzten nicht beachtet wurden, führte die Entwicklung einer klinisch und pathologisch-anatomisch denkenden Medizin in Frankreich bald zu ihrer Verwirklichung. Nicht nur die Richtung des ärztlichen Denkens, auch äußere Umstände begünstigten in Paris die Ausbildung einer auf klinische und autoptische Beobachtungen gegründeten Lehre von den Greisenkrankheiten. Seit der Mitte des 17. Jhdts. war die große Salpeterfabrik auf dem linken Seineufer, die Salpêtrière, zum Altershospiz ausgebaut worden; zu CHARCOTS Zeiten beherbergte sie 2500 alte Frauen, die ebenfalls dort untergebrachten Geisteskranken nicht mitgerechnet. Etwa die gleiche Bettenzahl hatte das im Süden der Stadt gelegene Hospiz Bicêtre, das alte Männer aufnimmt und auch gleichzeitig Irrenhaus ist. Dieser einzigartigen Gelegenheit, Greisenkrankheiten in großen Reihen sowohl am Krankenbett wie am Sektionstisch zu studieren, verdankt die französische Medizin einige wertvolle Arbeiten. LEON ROSTAN, seit 1814 Arzt an der Salpêtrière, beschrieb 1817 das Asthma cardiale als Asthme des vieillards, wobei er eine nervöse Genese des Leidens ablehnte und behauptete, es sei ein Symptom einer organischen Erkrankung des Herzens. Im Jahre 1820 ließ er wichtige Untersuchungen zur Entstehung der Gehirnerweichung (22) folgen. R. PRUS, seit 1833 Arzt in Bicêtre und an der Salpêtrière, veröffentlichte 1840, ein Jahr nach CANSTATT, aber offenbar ohne dessen Buch zu kennen: Recherches sur les maladies de la vieillesse (23). Er hält es für geboten, dieses segenstiftende und dankbare Gebiet ärztlicher Tätigkeit endlich in Angriff zu nehmen. La médecine des vieillards est encore à faire. Bei der statistischen Auswertung seines Materials, der der größere Teil der Arbeit gewidmet ist, kommt er zu dem Ergebnis, daß Greise am meisten durch Krankheiten der Atmungsorgane gefährdet sind.

15 Jahre nach CANSTATTS Krankheiten des höheren Alters fand der Stoff die erste umfangreiche französische Darstellung im Traité clinique et pratique des maladies des vieillards von M. DURAND-FARDEL (Paris 1854). Auch diese Arbeit stammt aus den beiden Pariser Versorgungsanstalten; ihr Verfasser war dort über 15 Jahre lang ärztlich tätig. Anatomie und Physiologie des Greises behandelt er auf knapp 30 Seiten, die Pathologie dagegen umfaßt 867 Seiten. Seine Ausführungen belegt er mit zahlreichen Krankengeschichten und Sektionsprotokollen, die er zum größten Teil seiner eigenen Tätigkeit entnommen hat. Der Auseinandersetzung mit CANSTATT sind fast in jedem Kapitel mehrere Abschnitte vorbehalten. Auch DURAND-FARDEL fühlte sich als Pionier, der noch unerforschtes wissenschaftliches Neuland betreten muß, und beklagte wie sein deutscher Vorgänger das Fehlen von brauchbaren Vorarbeiten.

Auch die Leçons cliniques sur les maladies des vieillards des berühmten CHARCOT, die erstmals 1868 in Paris erschienen, gehören hierher. Sie verdanken ihre Entstehung klinischen Demonstrationen in der Salpêtrière, wollen aber nicht eine Darstellung des gesamten Gebietes geben, sondern besprechen bevorzugt Gicht und akuten und chronischen Gelenkrheumatismus. CHARCOT betont die Notwendigkeit genauer Temperaturmessungen beim kranken Greise. Am besten erfolgten sie wegen der Altersveränderungen der Haut rektal, ein Hinweis, den neuere Bearbeiter des Gebiets (SCHLESINGER, MÜLLER-DEHAM) wieder unterstreichen. CHARCOT hat zwischen axillärer und rektaler Messung Differenzen von über 3° beobachtet (2. éd., S. 253).

Erst in der 2. Hälfte des 19. Jhdts. begegnen wir einem deutsch geschriebenen Werke, das das Material eines Altershospitals wissenschaftlich verwertet. LORENZ GEIST, ein Altersgenosse CANSTATTS — sie sind beide 1807 geboren —, war seit 12 Jahren an der Pfründner-Anstalt zum Heiligen Geist in Nürnberg ärztlich tätig, als er sein überwiegend aus eigenen Untersuchungen und eigenen Erfahrungen erwachsenes Werk mit dem Titel: Klinik der Greisenkrankheiten (Erlangen 1860) herausbrachte. Es behandelt das in Deutschland seit CANSTATT nicht mehr zusammenfassend dargestellte Thema unter Einbeziehung der indessen gewonnenen Erkenntnisse. In der bereits bewährten Weise gliedert es den Stoff in einen physiologisch-anatomischen und einen pathologischen Teil. Wie DURAND-FARDEL, dessen Buch 1857 auch ins Deutsche übersetzt worden war, führt GEIST zahlreiche eigene klinische und autoptische Beobachtungen an. Vieles, was CANSTATT nur als Forderung aufzeigen konnte oder als Frage offen lassen mußte, ist hier erfüllt und beantwortet worden. Während CANSTATT es noch als wünschenswert bezeichnet, „zu wissen, ob die Quantität eingeatmeter Luft bei Greisen ebensoviel beträgt als bei Individuen anderer Lebensalter" (I, 75), berichtet GEIST über umfangreiche Untersuchungen mit dem inzwischen von JOHN HUTCHINSON erfundenen Spirometer (I, 102—117). CANSTATTS Frage, „wie sich bei ihnen die Menge des ausgeatmeten kohlensauren Gases verhalte" (I, 75), findet bei GEIST durch eine Reihe von Stoffwechselbilanzen ihre erste Beantwortung (I, 171—182). Beide Autoren legen ihrer Schilderung der Altersveränderungen des Respirationssystems die aus der Salpêtrière stammenden Untersuchungen der Atmungsorgane alter Frauen von HOURMANN und DECHAMBRE zugrunde; 500 eigene Greisensektionen (I, 95) ermöglichen es aber GEIST, die Befunde aus dem Pariser Versorgungshaus zu überprüfen und zu erweitern. Sein Werk hat nicht nur das Verdienst, als erste deutsche Arbeit das Material wissenschaftlich erschlossen zu haben, das in den Altershospizen verborgen lag; es erbringt gleichzeitig den Beweis, daß der Neubau der Klinik der Greisenkrankheiten auf der

Grundlage der pathologischen Anatomie auch in Deutschland vollzogen war.

GEIST blieb in seinem Bestreben, die Pathologie des Alters im Altershospital zu erforschen, nicht allein. Aus dem Frankfurter Versorgungshause veröffentlichte CARL METTENHEIMER: Nosologische und anatomische Beiträge zu der Lehre von den Greisenkrankheiten (Leipzig 1863). Sie enthalten Krankengeschichten und Sektionsprotokolle von Insassen des Frankfurter Spitals, das er vier Jahre lang betreute, und bringen pathologisch-anatomische Ergänzungen und Berichtigungen zu den systematischen Darstellungen des Gebietes. Obwohl METTENHEIMER später als Leibarzt des Großherzogs von Mecklenburg-Schwerin neue große Arbeitsgebiete fand, lieferte er in zahlreichen Zeitschriften-Aufsätzen Beiträge zur Kenntnis der Alterskrankheiten. Er stand mit GEIST in brieflicher Verbindung, um sich mit ihm über die gemeinsame Herausgabe einer Zeitschrift für die Physiologie und Pathologie des Greisenalters zu beraten (24). GEISTS Tod im Jahre 1867 setzte diesem ersten Plan einer Alterszeitschrift ein Ziel.

Seit dem letzten Drittel des 19. Jhdts. brachte die Weiterbildung der physikalischen und chemischen Methoden der Diagnostik auch auf dem Gebiet der Greisenkrankheiten neue Probleme und neue Erkenntnisse. Die Fortschritte der ätiologischen und physiologischen Forschung wirkten in der gleichen Richtung. In den ersten Jahrzehnten unseres Jahrhunderts fanden Physiologie und Pathologie des Alters bereits zahlreiche Bearbeiter; das vorwiegend französische und deutsche Schrifttum des Gebietes, das neben mannigfaltigen Spezialuntersuchungen auch einige neue Gesamtdarstellungen (RAUZIER, SCHWALBE, PIC und BONNAMOUR, SAUNDBY, SCHLESINGER) aufzuweisen hatte, erreichte einen ansehnlichen Umfang. Arbeiten der neuesten Zeit führen zu einer vertieften Kenntnis der Verhaltensweise des alternden Organismus in statischer wie in dynamischer Beziehung und werden befruchtend auf die Klinik der Greisenkrankheiten einwirken.

Wie die Alterstatistik zeigt, wächst das durchschnittliche Lebensalter des Menschen bei allen Kulturvölkern rasch an. Wir haben also, auch ohne die Einwirkung des Krieges, mit einer Zunahme der Greise im Bevölkerungsaufbau zu rechnen. Ihr prozentualer Anteil an den Beanspruchungen ärztlicher Hilfeleistungen dürfte mindestens ebenso groß sein wie ihr prozentualer Anteil an der Zusammensetzung der Bevölkerung. Das aber gibt der Altersforschung und den Bemühungen um eine klinische Lehre der Greisenkrankheiten ihren ärztlichen Sinn. Die Notwendigkeit, auch die Arbeitskraft des alten Menschen in der Wirtschaft nutzbar zu machen, vermittelt darüber hinaus diesen Forschungen einen großen praktischen Wert.

Schrifttum

(1) Mir ist nur eine einzige neuere Darstellung des Themas bekannt geworden: Jos. J. Freeman, The History of Geriatrics. Zu: Ann. med. History (Am.) N. S. 10 (1938) S. 324—335. Die Arbeit beschränkt sich fast ausschließlich auf die englisch geschriebene oder ins Englische übersetzte Literatur.

(2) Angabe der Kapitel und Paragraphen erfolgt nach der Kochschen Ausgabe in CMG V, 4, 2. Allen angeführten Galen-Stellen ist Band- und Seitenzahl der Kühnschen Ausgabe beigefügt; bei Schriften, die bereits im CMG editiert sind, ist auch darauf verwiesen. Untersuchungen über die Disposition des 5. Buches De san. t. und ihre abweichende Durchführung in: Hartlich, De Galeni ' $Tγιεινῶν$ libro quinto. Diss. Marpurgi 1913.

(3) Am besten zugänglich in der Ausgabe von Little und Withington in den Opera hactenus inedita Rogeri Baconi, fasc. 9. Oxonii 1928. Auf diese beziehen sich die Seitenangaben.

(4) Roger Bacon hat selbst das Secretum secretorum mit Anmerkungen versehen. Es ist in seiner Redaktion gedruckt in Opera hactenus inedita Rogeri Baconi, fasc. 5. Ed. R. Steele. Oxonii 1920. Die angeführte Stelle steht in II, 6 auf S. 73.

(5) Z. B. nach A. Beauvois: Un praticien allemand au XVIIIe siècle, Jean-Henri Cohausen. Thèse. Paris 1900. S. 84.

(6) Withington: Roger Bacon and medicine. S. 353. In: Roger Bacon Essays. Coll. and ed. by A. G. Little. Oxford 1914.

(7) Rogers De conservatione iuventutis ist von Little und Withington herausgegeben in: Opera hactenus inedita Rogeri Baconi, fasc. 9. Oxonii 1928. S. 120—143.

(8) Else Förster: Roger Bacons De retardandis senectutis accidentibus und Arnald von Villanovas De conservanda iuventute et retardanda senectute. Diss. Leipzig 1924. S. 17f. Dem Vergleich der zwei Werke lag ein Codex der Breslauer Stadtbibliothek zugrunde, der beide enthält.

(9) In P. Diepgen: Medizin und Kultur. Ges. Aufsätze. Stuttgart 1938. S. 150: Arnalds Stellung zur Magie, Astrologie und Oneiromantie.

(10) Gerhard van Swieten: Oratio de senum valetudine tuenda. Ed. J. Th. Känzler. Diss. Viennae 1778. Die Rede hielt van Swieten im Jahre 1763.

(11) John Floyer: Medicina gerocomica. 2. ed. London 1725. Auf diese Auflage beziehen sich die Seitenangaben.

(12) Z. B. ALFRED BRAUCHLE: Naturheilkunde in Lebensbildern. Leipzig (1937). S. 53 und 59.

(13) Am leichtesten zugänglich in der Heidelberger Gesamtausgabe: NICOLAUS DE CUSA, Opera omnia. Vol. 5. Ed. L. BAUR. Lipsiae 1937. S. 117: Idiota de staticis experimentis. Dazu: EDV. GOTFREDSEN, NICOLAUS CUSANUS und die Medizin. In: Münch. med. Wschr. 84 (1937) S. 1821. CREUTZ, Medizinisch-physikalisches Denken bei NIKOLAUS VON CUES. Heidelberg 1939. (S.ber. Heidelbg. Akad. Wiss., Phil.-hist. Kl. Jg. 1938/39) S. 5ff. DIEPGEN, Das physikalische Denken in der Geschichte der Medizin. Stuttgart 1939. S. 13f.

(14) WALTER A. LEOPOLD VON BRUNN: PARACELSUS und seine Schwindsuchtslehre. Leipzig 1941. S. 56.

(15) SANCT SANCTORIUS: De statica medicina aphorismi. Aph. 82. In der Ausgabe cum commentario MARTINI LISTER (Lugduni Bat. 1703) S. 43.

(16) JOHANN BERNHARD VON FISCHER: De senio eiusque gradibus et morbis. Erfordiae 1754. Auf diese Ausgabe beziehen sich die Seitenangaben. Eine 2. Auflage erschien ib. 1760, eine deutsche Übersetzung Leipzig 1777.

(17) A. MÜLLER-DEHAM: Die inneren Erkrankungen im Alter. Wien 1937. S. VI.

(18) In: Sammlung auserlesener Abhandlungen zum Gebrauche praktischer Ärzte, Bd. 17, 1 (Leipzig 1796) S. 109 und in: BENJAMIN RUSH, Neue medizinische Untersuchungen und Beobachtungen (Nürnberg 1797) S. 277.

(19) Nach MEYER GOLOB: Specialization in diseases of old age: Geriatrics. Zu: Med. Rec. (Am.) 147 (1938) S. 425—428.

(20) DURAND-FARDEL: Traité clinique et pratique des maladies des vieillards. Paris 1854. S. VI.

(21) CHARCOT: Leçons cliniques sur les maladies des vieillards. Paris 1874. S. 5f.

(22) LÉON ROSTAN: Mémoire sur cette question: L'asthme des vieillards est-il une affection nerveuse? Paris 1817. Auch in: Nouv. Journ. de Méd. 3 (1818) S. 3—30 (nach CALLISEN). Id., Recherches sur une maladie encore peu connue, qui a reçu le nom de Ramollissement du cerveau. Paris 1820.

(23) R. PRUS: Recherches sur les maladies de la vieillesse. In: Mém. Acad. royale Méd. 8 (1840) S. 1—27.

(24) H. VON METTENHEIM: CARL VON METTENHEIMER. Berlin 1940. S. 355.

Anschrift des Verf.: Karl-Sudhoff-Institut für Geschichte der Medizin
Leipzig C 1, Talstr. 33.

[Bei der Redaktion in Leipzig eingegangen am 9. Februar 1942]

A BRIEF HISTORY
OF THE PSYCHOLOGY
OF AGING

James E. Birren

A Brief History of the Psychology of Aging

James E. Birren[1]

PART I[2]

RESEARCH on the psychology of aging begins with the publication of a book in 1835 by Quetelet, *Sur l'Homme et le développement de ses Facultés*. The book opens with this provocative sentence, "Man is born, grows up, and dies, according to certain laws which have never been properly investigated, either as a whole or in the mode of their mutual reactions," (Quetelet, 1842, Edinburgh translation). Following this portentious beginning, the history of the subject may be divided into 3 phases: Early Period, from 1835 to 1918; Beginning Systematic Studies, 1918 to 1940; and Period of Expansion, 1946 to 1960. Between 1940 and 1946 is a gap due to World War II and its after-effects.

Many philosophers, of course, preceded Quetelet, and they often made profound observations which are still valid today. Not only early philosophers but reflective men in all periods have discussed psychological differences between men of different ages. Not the least known of these is Shakespeare, whose "seven ages of man" have been mounted in stained-glass windows above his tomb in the Collegiate Church of the Holy Trinity, Stratford-upon-Avon, England. Common man has been insightful also, and daily speech has embedded in it wise observations about aging by nameless observers.

A review of the early philosophers' ideas about aging would be a useful preface to the present brief history but it is a separate, although related topic, requiring the scholarship of a trained philosopher. Some of the philosophical views are discussed by Hall (1923) and are also mentioned by Von Mering and Weniger (1959), who have included a brief account of the philosophical background in their description of the social-cultural aspects of contemporary aging. The present concern is with the history of the psychology of aging as a research subject and thus begins in the early 19th century when the nature of aging came to be regarded as a problem to be solved by observation.

A simple definition of the history of the psychology of aging is that it is an account of the development of research on the changes in the behavior of adult organisms as they advance in age. This includes topics familiar in general psychology: sensation, perception, psychomotor skills, intelligence learning and memory, thinking and problem solving, personality, and social behavior. Perhaps to these we should add the study of psychopathological symptoms, for the conditions associated with or freedom from the appearance of psychopathology in relation to age is a joint interest of psychology and medicine.

Early Period, 1835-1918

Quetelet was a man of many accomplishments; he was a mathematician, statistician, and astronomer, and one might even call him a psychologist and a sociologist as well. He visited and corresponded widely with the leaders of science in Western Europe. He was both producing and actively participating in the science of the period. A biographer said of him, "Quetelet would then appear as the most conspicuous among the early workers in the field of exact social science, and as the first formulator of the quantitative method in the study of social phenomena," (Hankins, 1908, p. 105). It should be noted that this quotation appeared in a work about him as a statistician!

Quetelet was born in Ghent in 1796 and received the first doctorate in science from the University of Ghent in 1819 in mathematics. After his degree he became interested in probabilities and developed the concept of the average man around which values or measurements were distributed according to the law of accidental

---
[1] Chief, Section on Aging, National Institute of Mental Health, Bethesda, Md.
[2] Part II will be published in vol. 1, no. 3, of *The Gerontologist*.

causes. Simultaneous with his publications and teaching of probability he gathered information about "moral statistics." This latter work opened the way for investigation of the regularities in crimes, suicides, marriages, and other kinds of social data, with regard to age, sex, profession, season of year, latitude, and economic and religious institutions. He also reviewed available mortality data in relation to age, sex, and urban-rural and national differences. For Quetelet, little was beyond knowing if one attended to observation and statistical or mathematical relationships.

Perhaps he was more interested in probability and measurement properties than in the content of measurements, but this is difficult to tell. It is certain that he did not only make observations of human characteristics to obtain illustrative distributions or to test statistical concepts. He wrote too vigorously about the individual social implications of his observations for this to have been true.

In discussing the development of the intellect, he anticipates the later comprehensive work of Lehman (1953) by presenting a table of data which shows the relation of age to the creation of French and English dramas. He includes a column which shows the number of ". . . works [which] might have been produced, all things being equal, if the number of authors had not been reduced by death." He says (1842):

Now, if we proceed to examine the results which the table presents, we shall perceive that, both in England and in France, dramatic talent scarcely begins to be developed before the twenty-first year; between 25 and 30, it manifests itself very decidedly; it continues to increase, and continues vigorous, until towards the 50th and 55th years; then it gradually declines, especially if we consider the value of the works produced.

He also presented remarkably full data on the growth of men and women from birth. These data can be compared with contemporary results, since Quetelet not only gave the averages but also the maximum and minimum observed in each group. Also reported are data on strength of hands for 400 males and females from age 6 to age 60 years. In an addition to the Edinburgh Edition (1842), Forbes reports on the measurement of height, weight, and hand strength of students aged 14 to 25 years. This addition to the text presents data which led Forbes to conclude, "The tables incontestably prove the superior development of natives of this country over the Belgians. The difference is greatest in strength (one-fifth of the whole) and least in weight." I am not certain of Quetelet's reaction to this rather bold conclusion.

Although many persons are today unaware of Quetelet, the wide translation of his book shows the dissemination of his ideas in the period 1835-1850. The clarity of his ideas and expression was to a considerable extent responsible for the interest he aroused. For example, in discussing previous thinking he says:

Neither have they determined the relative value of his [man's] faculties at different epochs or periods of his life, nor the mode according to which they mutually influence each other, nor the modifying causes. In like manner, the progressive development of moral and intellectual man has scarcely occupied their attention: nor have they noted how the faculties of his mind are at every age influenced by those of the body, nor how his faculties mutually react.

In these words and the data presented, Quetelet clearly initiates the psychology of development and aging.

Quetelet was an enthusiastic and confident exponent of the value of the scientific approach to the study of all problems, including that of aging. His writings show that he recognized quite clearly the influences of both biological and social influences on how man develops and on how long and how well he lives. In this he is quite in step with contemporary views that the psychology of aging lies between the biological and social sciences and quite reasonably research may require collaboration between psychologists and biologists and with social scientists.

Quetelet was trained as a mathematician and helped to develop modern statistics. In this, he influenced Galton, who is credited with discovering the idea and a method of correlation. It is perhaps not surprising that the 2 great men who early had interest in the psychology of aging, Quetelet and Galton, were men of stature in statistics. Anyone concerned with aging of organisms must sooner or later come to face matters of individual differences, distributions, averages, and perhaps correlations, in arriving at conclusions or supporting inferences.

Galton was broadly trained, studying medicine in Birmingham and London and reading mathematics at Cambridge. This combination accounts in part for the breadth of his scientific interests; the more important part rises from his own intellect and personality. The latter might be more important considering the state of the experimental sciences in Cambridge in 1840, when Galton was a student in Trinity College. Galton's varied academic knowledge was mixed with a wide grasp of man's nature and habits gathered through his extensive travels. According to his biographer (Pearson, 1914), parental interest led Galton to be trained with a view to becoming a physician, but after his father's death, he became a geographer through his travels and intellectual efforts. His standing as a contributor to geographical studies is shown by his award of a gold medal by the Royal Geographical Society in 1854. He then evolved into an anthropologist with interests in heredity and then into a psychologist. It was in the later period that he gathered the data of special interest here. In 1883, he published a book, *Inquiries into Human Faculty and Its Development*, after, as Pearson points out, 7 years of work. Some of his notes were labelled "Psychometric Inquiries 1876."

It is quite possible that Galton' anthropometric studies did not lead to the predictions about man's psychological make-up he expected, and he was thus led to make more direct psychological measurements. If measurements of head size did not lead to predictions of intelligence, Galton was flexible enough to turn to more direct methods of assessing man's mental capacities. His willingness to turn to new sources of data, coupled with his interest in heredity and anthropology, resulted in a strong developmental vein in his work. An early statement (August, 1865) portends his later work. "The highest minds in the highest races seem to have been those who had the longest boyhood" (Pearson, vol. II, 1914). In 1883, he published a list of methods for " . . . measuring the quickness and the accuracy of the Higher Mental Processes."

A clear statement (Pearson, 1914, vol. II, p. 213) of his recognition of developmental psychology is shown in a request he made in 1884 to gather together an exhibit of

. . . means of defining and measuring personal peculiarities of Form and Faculty, more especially to test whether any given person, regarded as a human machine, was at the time of trial more or less effective than others of the same age and sex. Again, to show by means of testings repeated at intervals during life, whether the rate of his development and decay was normal.

From his statements it is clear that he was consciously concerned with development and aging as shown by measurements of an anthropometric nature, as well as of psychomotor, perceptual, and higher mental processes.

If we are looking for a second man and date following Quetelet who engaged in the purposeful gathering of psychological measurements of development and aging, Galton is, without question, the man, and the year is about 1880. The date is somewhat arbitrary, since he had been developing methods of psychological measurement for at least 4 years. By 1879, he had already gathered relevant data on the upper limits of hearing, using variable-pitch whistles, and made what is probably the first report of the late life decline in audibility of high frequency tones. Thus almost simultaneous with the founding, in 1879, by Wundt of the psychological laboratory at Leipzig in Germany, the experimental psychology of development and aging was established in Britain.

The long latency of subsequent work on the same subject is interesting. It seems to result from the fact that Galton was more interested in ideas than in training students or establishing departments. He was not interested in professionalizing science. By contrast, Wundt had a noticeably different kind of effect. Wundt trained many students, and since he was interested in the properties of the age-constant organism, his students acquired that outlook. It took almost a generation for Leipzig-trained students to become fully aware of the large differences in performance of subjects of different ages. For the early psychophysicists, large age differences in their experiments would have been an annoyance. For the contemporaneous Galton and for later psychologists differences between subjects were something to study and explain. Thus while he shared with Wundt an interest in psychophysical measurements, he was constantly aware that subjects of different ages showed different measurements. By the time Galton was making psychological measurements he had already been influenced by Quetelet's ideas about ranges of measured characteristics and of distributions of errors.

Galton used the term human machine, which is probably a reflection of his training in physiology and physics. He wanted to fit the facts of development and aging of the human machine into the broader framework of human evolution and heredity. Not only was he of the same period and culture as Darwin, but they were corresponding cousins as well. Galton regarded both mental and physical traits as inherited, and his earlier work led him to search for physiognomic indices of mental traits, which helped to contribute psychological and anthropometric characteristics. Nevertheless behind his psychological investigation of age is a point of view influenced by ideas of heredity and evolution. Unfortunately, perhaps, Galton did not dwell long with the psychology of aging but became concerned with eugenics. In the words of Pearson, Galton believed that "Man was to study the purpose of the universe in its past evolution, and by working to the same end, he was to make its progress less slow and less painful in the future" (Pearson, 1914, p. 291, vol. II). When we consider the fact that in the 1870's fellows of the colleges of Oxford and Cambridge were prohibited from marrying, perhaps Galton's interest in eugenics had some sympathetic contemporary ears.

The fundamental contribution of Galton to the study of aging is the data gathered by his Anthropometric Laboratory at the International Health Exhibition in London, 1884 (Galton, 1885). Over 9,337 males and females aged 5 to 80 years were measured in 17 different ways. Parts of this data were still in analysis 40 years afterward. Consideration of it fixed Galton's high estimate of the importance of statistical problems of correlation—the degree of association between 2 variables. On this subject Pearson believes Galton made his greatest contribution by evolving the concept of correlation and proposing the first index. Certainly without correlational methods later students of development and aging would be at a serious disadvantage, but then Pearson was a biometrician and he would be prone to give heavy weight to the statistical contribution. Many investigators now use methods of correlation, as in the correlation of some trait with age, without realizing that Galton had the idea of correlation as early as 1877 and he described an index of correlation in 1886 (see Pearson, 1914).

Galton was much impressed with the potential power of statistics and biometrics and left his personal fortune to establish the chair of biometrics of which Pearson was the first occupant. It is interesting to speculate what the consequences might have been had Galton chosen instead to endow the first chair of psychology in Great Britain. His action seems to have led to the prominence of British statistics throughout the world; the other action might have led to the prominence of British psychology with a strong developmental emphasis. He most likely would have had a more apparent if not more far-reaching effect than did Wundt, for he seems to have had a great mind. Boring said pointedly, "Galton was a genius" (Boring, 1929, p. 454). Also, "Wundt was erudite where Galton was original. Wundt had a school, a formal self-conscious school; Galton had friends, influence, and effects only" (Boring, 1929, p. 455).

Development and aging were for Galton not only a matter of measurement, and he mentions in an insightful manner the loss of criticism from his peers (Pearson, vol. III, p. 318):

Among the many things of which age deprives us, I regret few more than the loss of contemporaries. When I was young I felt diffident in the presence of my seniors, partly owing to a sense that the ideas of the young cannot be in complete sympathy with those of the old. Now that I myself am old it seems to me that my much younger friends keenly perceive the same difference, and I lose much of that outspoken criticism which is an invaluable help to all who investigate.

In many countries during the 19th century, physiologists and physicians were beginning to make observations about aging that had implications for an evolving psychology. In Russia, this early period culminated in the later work of Pavlov, who bridged the gap between physiology and psychology, between the nervous system and behavior (Nikitin, 1958), and he is thus of direct interest to psychologists as well as physiologists. Pavlov had many predecessors in earlier Russian ontophysiology (physiology of the lifespan which includes both childhood and old age) but his own work on aging as well as that of his students was mostly done after World War I. There is the impression that many of the metaphorical concepts of the late 19th and early 20th century did not lend themselves to research on aging, since they could not link the changing conscious and unconscious content and the altering capacities and physiology of the aging organism. By contrast, Pavlov's concepts, which were evolved at about the same time, implied observable connections between physiological and psychological variables, although Pavlov by no means solved the problem.

One of the continuing difficulties of the psychology of aging from Quetelet onward has been the lack of a series of concepts and a form of discourse to express the relations of the biological and social antecedents of the behavioral changes of aging. This is not only important for describing sequences of supposed events but perhaps more importantly for the planning of experiments.

Some people were made uneasy by the beginnings of the objective study of aging. Quetelet's explorations into social science and psychology caused him to be regarded as a fatalist in a period when people were made uneasy by the idea of subjecting man to objective physiological and psychological study. The term fatalist was a term of derision rather than a useful description of his ideas. While it was acceptable in his day to describe the physical world in terms of natural laws, man's behavior could not yet be acceptably looked upon as a consequence of identifiable biological and social determinants. One of the most significant contributions of the 19th century was the opening up of the psychology of aging for objective study. Much of the work of the period is essentially descriptive of the manner in which man's senses and faculties develop and change with advancing age. Unlike previous accounts, however, these were not descriptions based upon intuition, they were obtained from measurements and were reported quantitatively, using statistical methods. The great men of the 19th century made it legitimate, desirable, and possible to study man's psychological development and aging.

Beginning Systematic Studies, 1918-1940

While not yet a topic commonly found in elementary textbooks, after World War II the psychology of aging was showing evidence of systematic development. Hall brought attention to the subject by his book, *Senescence*, published in 1922, which is useful as a source of early ideas and references. Child psychology had undergone a period of considerable development between 1900 and 1914, and it was then tempting to regard the psychology of the second half of life as a mere regression along the same channels as development had occured. Hall (1922, p. 100) recognized the superficiality in regarding aging as the inverse of development and despite his specialization in child psychology struck an independent note:

As a psychologist I am convinced that the psychic states of old people have great significance. Senescence, like adolescence, has its own feeling, thought, and will, as well as its own psychology, and their regimen is important, as well as that of the body. Individual differences here are probably greater than in youth.

Another interesting departure Hall took from contemporary opinion concerned religious belief and fear of death. It had been commonly assumed that old people approaching death would become more fearful and hence become more religious to reconcile themselves to an uncertain future. Hall believed on the basis of questionnaire data that old people do not necessarily show an increase in religious interest nor are they more fearful of the idea of death. He thought that the opposite rather holds for the very old; fear of death seemed to be a young man's concern. One might contest the views of Hall as they were derived from an informal questionnaire study, yet he did touch upon fundamental points, some of which are still unsettled. The issues he raised are central to personality theories which regard fear and anxiety reduction as a cornerstone of explanation. If one believes that older persons show cognitive deficiency out of a fear-generated rigidity, then it is difficult to accept the idea that there can be an independent reduction in fear and anxiety toward the end of life. If there is a reduction of anxiety in later life, cognitive changes are unexplained in such theories. The whole explanatory pattern of personality theories is still challenged by consideration of the major independent variables of aging.

Hall was aware of the biologists of his day (e.g., Metchnikoff, Minot, Child, Pearl, and Weismann) who were writing rather prolifically about aging. Their writings seem to have sensitized him to the fact that the transformations of aging, while related to growth and development, had new or emergent features which required direct evidence. This committed him and others who followed to study aging rather than accept the rhetorical position that aging is regression to childhood.

In this period, studies of the spontaneous activity of rats suggested that there was a reduction in drive with age. Slonaker (1907) reported results which led to a systematic line of research added to by Richter (1922) Shirley (1928), and Stone (1929). The topic aroused less interest in the 30's, but more recently Anderson (1959) has reasserted the significance of studying age differences in activity level and suggested the roles of both acquired motivational influences and biological effects.

By 1920, methods of analysis of data showed a markedly increased sophistication. The article by Koga and Morant (1923) on age, reaction time, and visual and auditory reaction time, clearly shows in its multiple regression equations the advances made from the time of Galton, who gathered the data on which the analysis was based. This paper reported that reaction time was not correlated with visual or auditory acuity, an important point in aging. One of the suppositions about the slower performance of older subjects has been that they do not receive equivalent sensory input due to lower acuity. Although this article bears directly on the point, it has been often overlooked because of its statistical emphasis and perhaps to publication in *Biometrika*, more widely read by statisticians than psychologists.

Mental tests developed just prior to World War I were used to some extent in classifying recruits. Results showed age differences in test scores; such differences had to be explained if one were going to take seriously what such tests purported to measure (Brigham, 1921). These findings began a continuous line of research to the present day (Jones, 1959), a line of research which is showing increasing sophistication in the selection of subjects, statistical analysis, and observational methods. One of the more controversial aspects of this work is the extent to which cross-sectional studies show the same or different results as longitudinal studies of the same subjects. It now seems to be established that if one uses the same tests and the same type of subjects, longitudinal and cross-sectional studies will show essentially the same results, a tendency to increased verbal and decreased non-verbal aspects of intelligence over much of the adult lifespan.

One of the characteristics of research on developmental psychology in the U. S. A. during the period 1920-1940 was its emphasis on early childhood. It seems likely that the development of pediatrics and the encouragement given to the establishment of research centers for child development, by the philanthropies of the Laura Spelman Rockefeller Fund, led to the dominance of child psychology over the total field of developmental psychology or human development. Research on childhood needed and obtained special facilities like nursery schools, and research grants attracted young research workers. During this period, the psychology of aging was beginning to be systematically studied but studied on a much smaller scale. Also aging was studied by workers who had a different emphasis; they had more of an experimental approach and were perhaps more physiologically than socially oriented, in comparison with the child psychologists.

Pavlov and his students in the 1920's, and an occasional observation earlier, were finding that old animals conditioned differently from young ones and that the responses showed a different course of extinction. The extent of Pavlov's thoughts is shown by a quotation from a summary of Russian studies on aging (Nikitin, 1958):

On the basis of all the material at our disposal, we can say that the inhibition process is the first to succumb to old age, and after this, it would appear that the mobility of the nervous processes is affected. This is evident from the fact that a large percentage of our aging dogs ceased to tolerate the previous more complex conditioned-reflex system. The responses become chaotic, the effects fluctuate in an entirely irregular fashion, and good results can be obtained only by simplifying the scheme. I think that this can very legitimately be ascribed to the fact that mobility decreases with the years. If we have a distinct effect in a large system, this means that one stimulus does not interfere with another and does not spread its effect to the next nerve process. When a nerve process is delayed, however, the remaining traces of each stimulus become prolonged and influence the succeeding ones, i.e., we have a chaotic state and confusion.

The emphasis on the nervous system in Russia went further to the extent of assigning it a major role in aging. According to Petrova (quoted from Nikitin, 1958):

... In our dogs, we were able to observe both normal physiological and pathological old age. Our experimental findings indicated that the major and leading role in the process of aging of the organism is played by the central nervous system, and particularly by the cerebral cortex and the other systems associated with it.

Such an interpretive position is important for psychologists, for it places the nervous system in an active rather than a dependent position in aging and implies significant consequences of behavior upon the organism as a whole.

In Japan during the 1920's, Tachibana was becoming interested in the psychology of aging. He has summarized the development of the psychology of aging in his article, Trends in Gerontology in Japan, (1959). Although Tachibana is the first major contributor to the literature on the psychology of aging in Japan, he credits Matsumoto with the encouragement of this line of interest and research. Evidence of the early interests of Japanese in the psychology of aging is also shown in his book on senescence (1941) and as summarized in *Studies in Senescence* (1958). The Japanese interests seem to have been in mental testing, anthropometric changes, and in work. Jones (1959) has discussed the mental test work of Kubo (1938) and Kirihara (1934). Tachibana has offered a translation of the titles, which includes almost all papers written in Japanese on aging (Tachibana, 1959), but since not much of the Japanese work has been translated it is difficult to determine a major theoretical line of development. It would seem, however, that Japanese psychologists regard the study of senescence as a necessary part of developmental research.

Perhaps the first major research unit devoted to the study of the psychology of aging was established by Miles in 1928 at Stanford University in California. It is of interest to quote directly his statement (personal communications, Nov., 1960) about the background of the establishment of the Stanford studies of later maturity.

My interest in the ability of the older worker began and came to a focus in the latter part of 1927, when I learned that men over 40 were having difficulty in finding work with industry in California. I became interested to look up psychological measurements on oldsters and found but little. A study seemed to be needed. I assumed that subjects would have to be found and that therefore outside funds would be needed. I was in charge of the Psychological Laboratory at Stanford, and my colleague, L. M. Terman was chairman of the Psychology Department, so I spoke to him about the matter. He set up a committee which included Calvin P. Stone, Edwin K. Strong, L. M. Terman and W. R. Miles. I was chairman.

At first I planned to study a sample of people 50 years of age and older. I selected and trained a capable and attractive woman, age about 46, to canvass for subjects in Palo Alto and surrounds. We wanted to try out different measurements at the Stanford Psychological Laboratory. We had almost no success. People interviewed admitted there was a need to know but were not willing to come themselves for one dollar or more per hour. It was the wrong approach.

The second idea was to make use of students in Palo Alto High School. (a) Find out which students had parents and grandparents living in the community or near. (b) Use the student to persuade one or both parents and the grandparents to serve—all three generations would be tested with the same techniques. This was an improvement over the house to house canvass effort but not popular enough to produce adequate data.

In the meantime there was a little newspaper publicity in San Francisco area about the Stanford University Psychology Dept. having become interested in research on abilities in "later maturity." One prospective graduate student, Floyd Ruch, wrote and expressed interest in coming to Stanford to work in this field for his Doctor's thesis. We were given a big lift when on November 22, 1928, the Carnegie Corporation of New York granted $10,000 to Stanford University in support of a study of the psychology of later maturity.

About this time I had dreamed up the idea of making use of clubs, Sunday school classes, lodges, etc., as the channels through which to supply us with subjects. I met with the executive committee of each such group and explained our objective, and requirements, and that *the club would receive pay for each indivdual sent* to our testing center located conveniently in a Palo Alto cottage. Each individual tested came as a representative of some previously formed group and in coming made a contribution to that group. The plan worked well and through it we could control age and education in our population. We were able to offer partial support to a few graduate students; I was at Yale on a sabbatical during 1930-31 returning to Stanford for 1931-32, we had a heavy program. Some 8 doctor's theses resulted. I had hoped to publish them in one book but the World War II and moving to Yale frustrated that plan.

Miles gave his presidential address before the American Psychological Asociation in 1932, based upon the results of the Stanford Later Maturity project, and he published several articles on the psychology of aging in the period (Miles, 1931, 1933, 1935). His chapter in the first edition (1939) of Cowdry's *Problems of Aging* shows that the psychology of aging had become an appreciable area of knowledge, comparing favorably with contributions from other sciences.

In Vienna during the 1930's the work of Bühler (1933) and Frenkel-Brunswik (1936) was taking a more philosophical turn, an approach which considered man more hollistically than contemporary experimental studies. Man was considered over the lifespan by Bühler and her students and they studied age changes in values and the progression of individuals toward their life goals as revealed by biographical studies. Strong (1931) also broadened the scope of the psychology of aging with his studies of age changes in interests.

Thus by the mid-1930's the psychology of aging was showing both extensity and intensity of development. It was changing into a new phase, which was to follow, illustrated by the compilation of Cowdry's *Problems of Aging* (1939). Psychologists were beginning to see the desirability of a comprehensive subject as well as highly analytical experiments. The idea was also spreading that psychology and other aspects of aging, e.g., physiology, should not be considered as independent and unrelated.

The ideas and mood of this period are shown in a personal communication from Frank (Dec., 1960):

The Macy Foundation under the direction of Dr. Ludwig Kast supported a number of studies of the so-called degenerative diseases. About 1935 Dr. Kast was convinced that these studies should be included in a larger enterprise namely the study of aging. He invited the writer in 1936 to join the Macy Foundation to develop this interest in aging as an extension of his previous concerns with studies of childhood growth and development, first at the Laura Spelman Rockefeller Memorial and then at the General Education Board.

At this time Dr. Vincent Cowdry was urging the publication of a volume on aging and asked the Macy Foundation to sponsor and finance that publication. Cowdry's original proposal was for a volume dealing primarily with the medical aspects of aging. The foundation urged that he enlarge this conception to include some social, psychological and psychiatric approaches which he agreed to do.

In order to further the preparation of the chapters for the Problems of Aging, the Macy Foundation invited all those who were to contribute to the volume, to meet for a week at Woods Hole, Massachusetts, in 1937. At this meeting each participant outlined his proposed contribution, submitted it to a critical examination and obtained helpful suggestions from the others. These discussions were very lively and sometimes controversial as one specialist questioned another or cited findings that he felt should modify or supplement another presentation.

Cowdry, as a cytologist strongly criticized Cannon's concept of homeostasis, asserting that there were often local "disequilibria" in groups of cells and tissues. Oliver maintained that the kidney was basic to the functioning of all other organs and this led to similar assertions by various specialists pointing out that the organ system or functional process he represented was equally indispensable!

In these presentations the emphasis was upon the number and variety of pathological conditions found in the aged which then led to the question of how the organism is able to survive to old age if subject to such breakdowns and pathology. Considerable discussion took place on the question of whether the phylogenetically older or younger organ systems were more vulnerable to aging, and there was a general agreement that the younger organ systems were more likely to break down. Each participant asserted that his organ system was not responsible for death since he could show that at death his organ system was frequently intact and functionally effective. So, the question arose, how and why does anyone die?

The writer was insistent on recognizing the cultural, psychological and personality aspects of aging and persuaded Cowdry to invite Clark, Wissler, Louis Dublin, G. V. Hamilton and Walter Miles to participate and contribute chapters. Also John Dewey was invited to contribute an introduction in which he emphasized some of the social, psychological and humanistic aspect of aging. The writer contributed a Foreword emphasizing some aspects of the aging process which are still relevant. It is interesting to note that many of the contributors to this volume were at that time in the upper age brackets and were recognized as leading investigators in their several specialized fields.

About the time the volume was first published, Korenchevsky came to the U.S.A. from England and asked the Macy Foundation to sponsor the organization of The Club for Research on Ageing in the U.S. He explained that he had organized similar clubs in England and on the Continent and preferred that the name "Club" would emphasize that this was to be a group of gentlemen scholars and scientists who would meet and discuss and explore whatever aspects of aging seemed worth while considering. This Club was established with many of the contributors to the volume as members. The Club met under the auspices and with the financial assistance from the Macy Foundation at least twice a year and at these meetings discussed promising leads for the study of aging, some of which were undertaken by members of the Club or by others who were invited to do so. From this Club evolved the Conference on Aging which the Macy Foundation sponsored over a period of ten or more years. Some reports of these conferences were later published by the Macy Foundation.

In the late 1930's the writer negotiated with the Surgeon General of the U.S. Public Health Service for the establishment of a section on aging in Washington. The Foundation agreed to subsidize this Section until such time as the cost could be absorbed in the federal budget. Dr. Stieglitz became the first incumbent of this position and acted as secretary for the National Advisory Committee on Gerontology composed of members of the Club and contributors to the Cowdry volume. Funds were made available by USPHS for research projects recommended by this advisory group and a number of studies were financed in this way. When Stieglitz left the position after a year, his place was taken in December 1941 by Nathan Shock who acted as secretary for the Club and brought to that task a psychological as well as a physiological orientation.

One of the results of the trend of thought of the late 1930's was a conference organized by the Public Health Service in 1941 on the mental health aspects of late life. By the time the proceedings (U.S.A., 1942) were available, World War II had already started and men were directing their energies to the emergency. The war gap was so long that interest was not easily resumed; some of the men originally interested had taken new positions and were permanently diverted to other fields.

By 1940, thinking about problems of aging had become more systematic, and the psychology of aging was receiving at least a share of emphasis as one of a group of sciences. While child psychology dominated in the years between the wars, after World War II it was adult development and aging which was destined to come to the fore. In part, this was the consequence of large practical problems of older people but also it was the consequence of over 100 years of thinking initiated by Quetelet.

References

Anderson, J. E. The use of time and energy. In J. E. Birren (Ed.) *Handbook of aging and the individual.* Chicago: University of Chicago Press, 1959.

Boring, E. G. *A history of experimental psychology.* New York: Appleton-Century, 1929.

Brigham, C. C. *A study of American intelligence.* Washington, D. C.: Memoirs of the National Academy of Sciences, 1923.

Bühler, Charlotte. *Der menschliche Lebenslauf als psychologisches Problem.* Leipzig: Verlag von S. Hinze 1933.

Cowdry, E. V. (Ed.) *Problems of ageing.* Baltimore Williams & Wilkins, 1939.

Frenkel-Brunswik, Else. Studies in biographical psychology. *Character & Personality,* 1936, **5**, 1-34.

Galton, F. *Inquiries into human faculty and its development.* London: Macmillan & Co., 1883.

Galton, F. On the anthropometric laboratory at the late International Health Exhibition. *J. Anthropo Inst.* (London), 1885, **14**, 205-221; 275-287.

Hall, G. S. *Senescence.* New York: D. Appleton & Co 1922.

Hankins, F. H. *Adolphe Quetelet as statistician.* New York: Columbia University, Ph.D. dissertation, 190

Jones, H. E. Intelligence and problem solving. J. E. Birren (Ed.) *Handbook of aging and the individual.* Chicago: University of Chicago Press, 1959.

Koga, T., & Morant, G. M. On the degree of association between reaction times in the case of different senses. *Biometrika,* 1923, **14**, 346-372.

Lehman, H. D. *Age and achievement.* Princeton N. J.: Princeton University Press, 1953.

Miles, W. R. Measures of certain human abilities through the life span. *Proc. Nat. Acad. Sci., Wash.,* 1931, **17**, 627-633.

Miles, W. R. Age and human ability. *Psychol. Rev.,* 1933, **40**, 99-123.

Miles, W. R. Age in human society. In C. Murchison (Ed.) *Handbook of social psychology.* Worcester, Mass.: Clark University Press, 1935.

Nikitin, V. N. *Russian studies on age-associated physiology, biochemistry, and morphology. Historical sketch and bibliography.* Kharkov: A. M. Gorkiy Press, 1958.

Pearson, K. *The life, letters and labours of Francis Galton.* Cambridge: University of Cambridge Press, 4 vols., 1914.

Quetelet, A. *Sur l'homme et le développement de ses facultés.* Paris: Bachelier, 2 vols., 1835.

Quetelet, A. *A treatise on man and the development of his faculties.* Edinburgh: William and Robert Chambers, 1842.

Richter, C. P. A behavioristic study of the rat. *Comp. psychol. Monogr.,* 1922, **1**.

Shirley, M. Studies in activity. II. Activity rhythms; age and activity after rest. *J. comp. Psychol.,* 1928, **8**, 159-186.

Slonaker, J. R. The normal activity of the rat at different ages. *J. comp. Neurol. & Psychiat.,* 1907, **17**, 342-259.

Stone, C. P. The age factor in animal learning. I. Rats in the problem box and the maze. *Genet. psychol. Monogr.,* 1929, **5**, 1-130.

Strong, E. K. *Change of interest with age.* Stanford, Calif.: Stanford University Press, 1931.

Tachibana, K. Trends in gerontology in Japan. *Psychologia,* 1959, **2**, 150-156.

U.S.A. Proceedings of the Conference on Mental Health in Later Maturity, May 23-24, 1941. Washington, D.C.: Supplement 168 to *U.S. Public Health Reports,* Government Printing Office, 1942.

Von Mering, O., & Weniger, F. L. Social cultural background of the aging individual. In J. E. Birren (Ed.) *Handbook of aging and the individual.* Chicago: University of Chicago Press, 1959.

A Brief History of the Psychology of Aging

James E. Birren[1]

Part II[2]
The Period of Expansion, 1946-1960

Beginning in 1946, a rapid series of developments occurred which merit 1946-1960 being described as the period of expansion. Laboratories devoted to the study of aging were started, research societies were initiated, and many national and international conferences were held. A new kind of scientist began to be seen, one whose major career interest was that of studying developmental processes and aging. Centers of research whose students reflected certain main ideas or theoretical positions came to be recognized.

At the beginning and end of the period there was difficulty in conceiving how the exchange of information, teaching, and organization of research was to be effectively carried out. Aging was clearly a problem touching many disciplines, yet many investigators felt uncomfortable when talking across disciplines rather than within a small homogeneous group. A happy solution evolved for psychology. In 1945, a group headed by Pressey began to organize a Division on Maturity and Old Age of the American Psychological Association. In 1946, its first officers were elected and Pressey was the first president at its first meeting in Detroit in September, 1947 (Pressey, 1948). Here was the group to which psychologists could address themselves as a somewhat homogeneous division (now over 225 members). In his presidential address, Pressey makes these points in describing the new division (Pressey, 1948, p. 109).

We in this division are concerned with a range of years three times that of childhood and youth, during which there are changes probably in total more complex and more controllable, if means of control were known. They are the important years of life. They have been studied developmentally almost not at all. It seems not too much to hope that ours might be *the* field of most fruitful and distinctive psychological work of the next two decades.

[1] Chief, Section on Aging, National Institute of Mental Health, Bethesda, Md.
[2] Part I was published in vol. 1, no. 2, of *The Gerontologist*.

It [the Division] is indeed much concerned with old age, but no less with the other adult years, since it emphasizes that development and change go on throughout the adult period, which should be seen as a whole. Throughout the period there are problems—vocational, familial, social, economic—towards a better understanding of which we hope to contribute. The division believes that a true developmental psychology includes not simply the period of growth, but the entire sweep of the human life span. Ultimately, a union with that other developmental group concerned with the first two decades of life may therefore well be desirable. However, this division should continue until the major purposes have some assurances of accomplishment; until psychologists do think developmentally about the years after 20 as well as the years before, and until problems of adult life which much need study from that point of view are so dealt with. It has contributions to make, to psychology and to human welfare.

The multidisciplinary contacts for psychologists were provided through the meetings of the Gerontological Society, which was founded in 1945, and the Council and Corporation held its first meeting in June of that year in New York (Adler, 1958). The first issue of the Journal of Gerontology, sponsored by the Society, appeared in early 1946. Psychological research began to expand in the encouraging atmosphere. Perhaps it advanced more rapidly than even some of its closely associated disciplines, because it had both an independent organization as well as representation in a multidisciplinary society. Some emphasis of course had already been placed on psychological problems and research on aging by the Public Health Service's Conference on Mental Health in Later Maturity, May, 1941 (U.S.A., 1942).

In 1946, two developments occurred which significantly affected the course of events. Staffing was started of the Gerontological Unit of the National Institute of Health and of the Nuffield Unit for Research into Problems of Ageing at the Laboratory of Psychology at the University of Cambridge. The Unit on Gerontology had already been officially established in the National Institute of Health, Baltimore, as part of the division of

127

physiology in July, 1940. However, because of the war, the chief of the unit, Shock, had to delay major staffing of the unit until 1946. Birren joined this group in May of 1947 to initiate the psychological research.

Bartlett, professor of psychology at the Universit of Cambridge, was encouraged to submit plans for the development of a unit for research into the psychological aspects of aging in his department. He drafted suggestions for such a unit in the summer of 1945 in correspondence with Parkes of the Medical Research Council.

The proposals of Bartlett were forwarded by Parkes to the Nuffield Foundation, which approved the proposals and gave an initial grant for capital outlay and a recurrent grant for each of 3 successive years, with the possibility of renewal for a period not exceeding 3 years, making the grant for a total of 6 years. The Unit was to involve (quoted from Bartlett's personal records):

investigation by combined laboratory and field work, of the psychological and physiological differences between different age-groups with special reference to their industrial significance. For the investigations, two teams, each of three persons [under Professor Bartlett] are suggested:

(a) to develop methods for the accurate measurement of skills representative of a wide range of industrial operations (if possible, selecting some such types of operation as will bring out age-group differences, if any, in learning) with the emphasis upon the combined effects of a number of simultaneously operating functions;

(b) to determine what modifications of the above methods will make them applicable to field (industrial) conditions, and specifically to try to set up agreed standards of proficiency in selected industrial tasks, and to use those standards to validate the basic experimental measures.

Because of the crowded conditions at the University, there was difficulty in finding space for the new Unit and it was necessary to have a small temporary building erected to house the staff. Thus the actual work of the unit did not get under way until late 1946, when Welford, who was in the United States on a fellowship, returned to take an active role in the research and become the director of the Unit.

This Unit was one of the most productive ones to be established. It attracted a large number of alert research students, who by now have senior positions throughout many universities and industries of Great Britain. The first major account of the work done at the Unit is contained in the publication, *Skill and Age*, by Welford (1951). A final summary of the research of this Unit is

Sidney L. Pressey

contained in the volume, *Ageing and Human Skill* (Welford, 1958).

There were several characteristics of this unit— its high productivity, its emphasis on detailed analysis of the components of skilled behavior and on information theory as a series of concepts within which their results were discussed. It was a natural consequence of the limited-period grant that the Unit would exist for too short a period to have a significant institutional effect. Its main effect, aside from the published research results was in the training of researchers who have taken positions in various universities and can therefore introduce the concepts and facts in their teaching and thus ensure that a number of future research students will continue to be concerned with research into problems of aging.

The Gerontology Unit of the National Institute of Health had broad responsibilities. Psychology was and is currently part of a wide basic biological and medical research program. With the establishment of the National Heart Institute in 1948 the Gerontology Unit was transferred to it, and for an interval the Unit was designated as the Unit on Cardiovascular Diseases and Gerontology In 1958, it was established as the Gerontology Branch of the National Heart Institute. The Branch has an impressive productivity; and will supply a publication list on request (see also Shock, 1957).

Conference on the Pyschological Aspects of Aging, Bethesda, April, 1955.

Robert J. Havighurst, Harold E. Jones, John E. Anderson, and James E. Birren.

In 1953, the Section on Aging was formed in the National Institute of Mental Health with Birren as head. After a year it was transferred from the office of the Associate Director in Charge of Research to the newly formed Laboratory of Psychology for administrative reasons. Members of this Section collaborated with the Research Committee of the Division on Maturity and Old Age in planning and carrying out the Conference on the Psychological Aspects of Aging held in Bethesda in April, 1955. Anderson (1956), Committee Chairman, edited the proceedings of this conference, which had a significant effect by bringing together diverse interests and points of view about the psychology of aging.

In 1950, Welford and Birren met for the first time at the meeting of the American Psychological Association. It was at this meeting that Birren advanced the idea of a handbook on aging which would organize the scattered literature. A few years later, Anderson also lent encouragement to the evolution of a handbook on aging by pointing to the desirable effects of the first Handbook of Child Psychology. In 1956, an opportunity was provided to develop the handbook through a research subcommittee of the Gerontological Society, under the Chairmanship of Kleemeier, which took an interest in training. This interest in training was partly a natural outgrowth of current thinking in the Society and of ideas circulating at the National Institutes of Health and through which a training program for researchers in physiology had been instituted the previous year. The committee's activities were suported by a grant from the National Institutes of Health. Details of this background are given in the preface of the volume, Handbook of the Aging and the Individual (Birren, 1959).

The International Association of Gerontology has played an indirect role in encouraging training by fostering personal contacts between active workers in the field. While its first meeting, in Liège, was limited to biological and medical aspects of aging, its second meeting, in St. Louis in 1951, included a large number of research papers in the area of psychology. It was perhaps the next meeting of this Association, in London in 1954, which provided the first major opportunity for psychologists to exchange information on a truly international level. The proceedings of this well-attended congress showed a great variety of psychological research (Anon., 1955). Separate research committees of this Association began to be active, and in 1957 and 1960, research seminars were organized by a committee in the psychological and social sciences.

The Department of Psychology at the University of Ohio, under Pressey, trained more Ph.D. candidates in this subject than any other department in the U.S.A. On closely related subjects were the many students trained by the Committee on Human Development at the University of Chicago under the leadership of Havighurst, Henry, Hess, and Neugarten. In Great Britain, the largest and only training center was in the Nuffield Unit of the University of Cambridge's Psychological Laboratory where Bartlett and Welford made distinguished contributions.

Training of students has to some extent been facilitated in recent years by conference proceedings, handbooks (Birren, 1959; Tibbitts, 1960) and annual reviews (e.g., Birren, 1960) and also by the appearance of new journals and textbooks. Introductory textbooks are appearing which give a rather comprehensive view of the psychology of the lifespan. By the end of 1960, psychologists were coming to agree that the psychology of aging should be included in the teaching of a developmental psychology sequence.

While the period between 1946 and 1960 was particularly distinguished by the establishment of special research units of aging, there was much individual research effort in the U.S.A. and abroad. Certain names recur in the literature: McFarland, Lorge, Tuckman, Korchin, Braun, Kleemeier, Lehman, and many others, as primarily representative of individual research effort, as does the name of Donahue in connection with the organizations of the University of Michigan Conferences on Aging to discuss research.

The U.S.A. seems to have been the most active country in research, possibly because relative to the size of its population there are more trained psychologists. There are over 18,000 members of the American Psychological Association in addition to the larger number which function as psychologists without necessarily belonging to the Association or having a post-graduate degree. In Great Britain, more psychologists than in the U.S.A. have done research on aging relative to the number of psychologists, as a direct result of the Cambridge Unit. There are now few Western countries which do not have at least one psychologist or related scientist concerned with aging: Canada, Zubek; Denmark, Friis; Finland, Jala-Bourlière; Germany, Riegel, Thomae; Italy, Cesa-Bianchi; Netherlands, van Zonneveld; Norway, Beverfelt.

One unit seemingly destined to make a significant contribution is the Centre de Gérontologie Claude Bernard at Paris. Its director, Bourlière, is much interested in basic biological problems and is encouraging the development of psychological research in several areas: sleep, learning, and psychomotor skills. Another physiologist, Verzàr, who heads the Institut für Experimentelle Gerontologie, in Basle, has also encouraged psychological research in a broad context of basic research on aging. Such a facilitative and cooperative atmosphere cannot help but have desirable consequences for research in the coming years.

The German literature on the psychology of aging has been reviewed by Riegel (1958-1959); his comprehensive bibliography of 465 items includes not only German references but those from other countries as well. Such attention to cross-national publications helps to reduce the time lag in uptake of information from foreign sources, which when added to the lag due to preparation time, publication, and abstracting often makes the psychologist about 5 years late in his information. In commenting on the early research, Riegel (1958-1959) says, "The first empirical studies on the psychology of aging were conducted about 1925 in Germany. Before that there were large scale investigations of driving performance of middle-aged people in the German Army during World War I." He mentions in particular the early reviews of the literature by von Bracken and Hofstaetter. Riegel's own research began in 1956 on cognitive, social, and personality variables in aging; results are being prepared for publication.

Some of the most active contributors to social-psychological research have been Havighurst and his colleagues of the Committee on Human Development of the University of Chicago. He has expressed his own interest in this field in the following quotation from a personal communication (1960):

My own interest in aging developed around 1943 when I became Chairman of the Committee on Social Adjustment in Old Age, which was a subcommittee of the Committee on Social Adjustment of the Social Science Research Council. Ernest Burgess was chairman of the general committee, and he interested me in this general field of work. He and I and Ruth Cavan collaborated in the studies which resulted in the book, "Personal Adjustment in Old Age" [Cavan, Burgess, Havighurst, & Goldhamer, 1949]. In 1948 I started the study of older people in the midwestern community of Prairie City which resulted in the book by Havighurst and Albrecht entitled, "Older People" [1953]. At about that time I was a member of the committee which was responsible for the Community Project for the Welfare Council of Metropolitan Chicago. In 1950 Dr. Burgess and Dr. Ethel Shanas and I started a series of studies of retirement which involved a number of our graduate students and resulted in a number of journal articles, as well as two books "Effective Use of Older Workers" by Elizabeth L. Breckenridge, and "The Meaning of Work and Retirement" by Friedmann and Havighurst.

In 1951, we formed a faculty committee of the Committee on Human Development and secured funds from the Carnegie Corporation for the Kansas City Study of Adult Life. This project has continued in one form or another throughout that period and we will be doing field work in Kansas City for at least another year. There have been a number of publications from the Kansas City Study of Adult Life. After 1955 we commenced a new phase of the project with support from the National Institute of Mental Health and under the immediate direction of William E. Henry.

Probably the best examples of our work are the publications from the Kansas City Study. They show the range of our interests from the broad sociological to the specific individual psychological. There is now in press the book by Elaine Cummings and William E Henry entitled, "The Process of Growing Old," which presents the major results of the last four years of work. The earlier phase from 1951 to 1955 has been reported in a number of monographs and we are still working on a book to bring the major findings together in one place.

I think that my own approach to and interest in aging is best represented by the book, "Older People," by Havighurst and Albrecht [1953], and also more recently by the paper (in press) on "The Definition and Measurement of Successful Aging," which was given at the International Research Seminar in Berkeley, California in August, 1960.

In October, 1955, the Medical Research Council initiated at the University of Liverpool their Unit for Research on Occupational Aspects of Ageing. Despite this title, the work of the unit (under Heron) has been wide in scope. Apart from a 20-factory survey of aging effects among semi-skilled workers, 2 studies of industrial process change, and the launching of a scheme of retirement preparation for men aged 50 years, the unit has investigated rigidity, effects of hearing loss, immediate memory, and confidence. A noteworthy feature of the unit's activities is the creation of a panel of over 700 adult subjects, ranging in age from 20 to 75 years, from which samples can be drawn for both cross-sectional and longitudinal studies.

The Public Health Conference of 1941 (U.S.A., 1942) reinforced the fact that older people have a variety of mental problems which require research (see also, Roth, 1959). Psychiatry of later life, however, has been slow to develop, possibly because there were too few trained men who could consider entering into the systematic investigation of a relatively unexplored and difficult field. Despite the difficulties of developing a comprehensive geriatric psychiatry, the names of certain investigators are widely known for their contributions. In Great Britain, there are Post at the Maudsley Hospital and Roth at the University of Durham. In Italy, there is Cesa-Bianchi. In the U.S.A., there are also several: Rothschild, Simon, Weinberg, Goldfarb, and Busse.

Busse's interest in the psychiatric aspects of aging have led to the establishment of a significant research group. In the Department of Psychiatry at the Duke University Medical Center, there has been established an active research group involving both psychiatrists and psychologists. Since there have been so few units devoted to systematic research in this area, I asked Busse how he became interested. His reply was:

My interest in aging did not come from any particular person; rather, I was pushed into it because my interest in the functions of the temporal lobe and the chance findings of EEG abnormalities which are not infrequent in elderly persons and which resemble the seizure discharges found in epileptics. On the basis of this interest, I received my first research grant concerned with aging in the central nervous system in 1950.

Two papers published by Busse, Barnes, Silverman, Thale, & Frost (1954, 1955) describe their interests and the nature of their research.

Certain men like Terman had considerable effect, not so much through their own research on aging as in their encouragement of students in developmental psychology. Terman's studies of gifted children did of course turn into studies of adult development as the subjects were followed. He belonged to, or perhaps more correctly started, the California nucleus of interest in developmental psychology, which has included Jones, Miles, and Bayley, as well as others who were more specifically interested in child development. Shock was directly influenced in the direction of developmental research during his 10 years on the faculty at the University of California, as was Kaplan, who edited the significant book, *Mental Disorders of Later Life* (1945). Birren was also influenced by the California emphasis on development through Seashore as the vector. A biography of Jones (1960) reports some of the details about the University of California's developmental studies.

Publication of Research

More research seems to have been published in the decade of 1950-1959 than had been published in the entire preceding 115 years the subject may be said to have existed (table 1). The table is an approximation, since there may be a bias against a detailed search for and citation of the very earliest articles and also difficulties in locating articles may lead to an underestimate of the most recent publications. Location of articles published in the most recent 2 or 3 years requires a direct

TABLE 1. PUBLICATION OF RESEARCH ON THE PSYCHOLOGICAL ASPECTS OF AGING.

Date	Number of Publications A	B
1835	1	1
1884	1	0
1889	1	0
1900-09	1	0
1910-19	3	3
1920-29	24	28
1930-39	81	70
1940-49	121	102
1950-59	340	259

NOTE:—Based upon an analysis of psychological articles cited in col. A in the *Handbook of Aging and the Individual* (Birren, 1959) and in col. B the reviews by Riegel (1958-59). Each article was counted only once regardless of the number of times it was cited.

search of journals, which are not only often unbound in libraries but are also not yet abstracted and found in standard publication lists.

The actual tally of articles by year of publication as cited in Riegel's review (1958-1959) and in the *Handbook* (Birren, 1959) showed a decline between 1956 and 1959, which probably reflects authors' inability or difficulty in locating the very most current material. If one merely assumes a constant publication rate after 1956, then the estimate for the decade 1950-1959 is about 88 articles short. Furthermore if one allows a conservative estimated increase during this period, a total of about 500 articles represents the volume of publication of psychological research on aging during the period 1950-1959. A comparison of the growth of psychological research with physiological, biochemical, and other research could be made by an analysis of Shock's (1951) classified bibliography, and his later supplement (1957).

The *Handbook* (Birren, 1959) was of course selective in citation of published works. Aside from technical limitations in published research there are many other reasons for not citing works, e.g., articles verifying the same essential points. Experience in preparing the annual review for 1960 (Birren, 1960) suggests that about half of the articles located by searching journals and abstracts lists will currently be regarded as non-research in character, e.g., case histories, descriptions of programs, or semi-technical reviews. Such locating and sorting takes time, and it seems highly likely that if investigators and reviewers are going to master information in detail they will have to narrow their scope of reading about aging out of self-defense. The men with the broadest grasp of a subject for practical reasons are favored to come early in the history of a subject and the contemporary researcher in the psychology of aging will probably increasingly limit the scope of his subject matter; they will have to limit their grasp if they are to maintain an effective grip.

Some Conclusions

Aging is a subject which is difficult for an isolated investigator to study on a short-term basis; investigators need institutional support for a variety of things including the availability of subjects. While the concept of the lone scientist solving all problems by himself is sometimes appealing, perhaps as a reaction to the bustle of professional and scientific life, one cannot help but be impressed with increasing number of contributions to the psychology of aging coming from investigators working in organized research units.

If the psychologist is going to be inundated by publications and forced into a narrower specialization, a problem will face the investigator who wants to consider psychological functioning in the broad context of biological and social influences. It would seem that if this is a desirable position for some to retain, they will have to be aided by electronic library methods which will file, sort, and retrieve information. While much is gained for the individual investigator by articles and books which accidentally come into his hands, in a rapidly growing field it would seem that systematic searches will have to be facilitated by mechanical and electronic devices.

Should the study of the psychology of aging continue to grow at the rate shown by recent publications it will likely become a more specialized topic, and research units will be organized around selected aspects. How research on perception and aging, for example, will differ from past research done on perception is not apparent. One feature would seem to naturally follow, that the student of perception *per se*, in comparison with the student of aging, would be less interested in the interactions of perception with the rest of the organism. Perhaps this is merely saying that the developmental psychologist characteristically takes a more integrative position in psychology and that this will continue to be reflected in aging even as the subject becomes more compartmentalized. However, specialization may not only occur along scientific lines but also along the lines defined by the problems of older persons and a strong applied psychology of aging may develop with specialized activities in relation to medicine, public health, industry, and education.

The psychology of aging is beginning to be recognized as a sub-specialty of psychology. In a 1960 specialties list of scientific and technical personnel of the National Science Foundation, developmental psychology was divided into 3 parts: nursery and pre-school, childhood and adolescence and maturity and old age. Although the psychology of aging is part of developmental psychology, there is at present surprisingly little commonality of method and problems between it and child development. This seems partly explained by the type of training the investigators have received, with students of aging in greater number being more physiologically inclined. It has been said that students of early development have been over-disposed toward an emphasis o environmental causation, whereas students of late life have been given to "over organicity." If this observation is valid, then one might expect some correction in the years to come with students of child development coming to recognize more of the biological influences on behavior and the students of aging giving more attention to environmental influences. If this does evolve, then we will have a comprehensive lifespan developmental psychology.

The psychology of aging has for the most part borrowed methods, and if one regards method above all else, there is perhaps no separate psychology of aging. If content is also to be considered important, however, the psychology of aging is indeed by now a distinct entity. Advances in many fields of psychology are influencing the psychology of aging; however, there are, it seems, fewer strong "enthusiasms" in research on the psychology of aging than were involved in the growth of many facets of psychology. Perhaps the psychology of aging, now in its stage of rapid growth, learned something from the enthusiastic expansion of child psychology about 20 years earlier. Psychologists interested in aging seem less driven than some to categorical explanations. This may result from the fact that the student of aging is continually reminded that man's behavior is a result of combinations of biological and social forces plus a collection of unique circumstances, which either obscure the general or enhance the subject matter, depending upon one's views.

There are facts in the psychology of aging about which most psychologists now agree, but perhaps more important than the facts we have gained is the increased refinement in the many important questions being asked. The most comprehensive question facing the field is whether there is a general species pattern of aging which is expressed in behavioral characteristics as well as in longevity. Only evidence from research will tell us if there is a common thread running through phenomena associated with advancing age, a thread running through a somewhat orderly series of events, like beads on a string, with an end marker as well. Alternatively, research may tell us that aging results from consequences of events which accumulate like miscellaneous objects in a pile, toppling when it becomes over-balanced.

Implications of research on the psychology of aging are so extensive that encouragement of research has come from 3 rather different sources, industrial (occupational aspects of aging), medical (clinical problems), and educational (adult education and training). These 3 areas of application have formed a tripod of practical interest in research and provided the research worker with an audience eager for results. The noise level of public interest in the psychology of aging has risen in recent years, reflecting perhaps a change in society which has come to recognize that science may not only offer descriptions of aging but also eventual clues about how individuals can live better, if not longer as well. Not only the scholar and scientist but society has changed from 1835, when Quetelet first published, to 1961 when the White House Conference on Aging was held.

This brief history of the psychology of aging was not intended to be an exhaustive review, and in the process of writing many significant individuals and developments have had to be omitted for brevity. It is to be hoped, however, that this initial account will stimulate more detailed subsequent histories.

References

Adler, Marjorie. History of the Gerontological Society. *J. Gerontol.*, 1958, **13**, 94-100.

Anderson, J. E. (Ed.) *Psychological aspects of aging.* Washington, D. C.: American Psychological Association, 1956.

Anon. *Old age in the modern world; report of the Third Congress of the International Association of Gerontology, London, 1954.* Edinburgh: E. & S. Livingstone, 1955.

Birren, J. E. (Ed.) *Handbook of aging and the individual.* Chicago: University of Chicago Press, 1959.

Birren, J. E. Psychological aspects of aging. In *Ann. Rev. Psychol.* Stanford, Calif.: Annual Reviews, 1960.

Busse, E. W., Barnes, R. H., Silverman, A. J., Thaler, M. B., & Frost, L. L. Studies of processes of aging. VI. Factors that influence the psyche of elderly persons. *Amer. J. Psychiat.*, 1954, **110**, 897-903.

Busse, E. W., Barnes, R. H., Silverman, A. J., Thaler, M. B., & Frost, L. L. Studies of the processes of aging. X. The strengths and weaknesses of psychic functioning in the aged. *Amer. J. Psychiat.*, 1955, **111**, 896-901.

Cavan, Ruth, Burgess, E. W., Havighurst, R. J., & Goldhamer, H. *Personal adjustment in old age.* Chicago: Science Research Associates, 1949.

Havighurst, R. J., & Albrecht, Ruth. *Older people.* New York: Longmans, Green & Co., 1953.

Jones, H. E. (Obituary) *Child Develpm.*, 1960, **31**, 593-608.

Kaplan, O. J. (Ed.) *Mental disorders in later life.* Stanford, Calif.: Stanford University Press, 1945.

Pressey, S. L. The new division on maturity and old age. Its history and potential services. *Amer. Psychol.*, 1948, **3**, 107-109.

Riegel, K. F. Ergebnisse und Probleme der psychologischen Alternsforschung. *Vita Humana*, 1958-1959, **1**, 52-64, 111-127, 204-243; **2**, 213-237.

Roth, M. Mental health problems of ageing and the aged. *Bull. WHO*, 1959, **21**, 527-561.

Shock, N. W. *A classified bibliography of gerontology and geriatrics*. Stanford, Calif.: Stanford University Press, 1951. Also *Supplement One*, 1957.

Shock, N. W. *Trends in gerontology* (2nd ed.) Stanford, Calif.: Stanford University Press, 1957.

Tibbitts, C. (Ed.) *Social gerontology*. Chicago: University of Chicago Press, 1960.

U.S.A. *Proceedings of the Conference on Mental Health in Later Maturity, May 23-24, 1941*. Washington, D.C.: Supplement 168 to U. S. Pub. Health Rep., Government Printing Office, 1942.

Welford, A. T. *Skill and age*. London, Oxford University Press, 1951.

Welford, A. T. *Ageing and human skill*. London: Oxford University Press, 1958.

PERSPECTIVES IN AGING

Edited and Compiled as a Supplement

to

THE GERONTOLOGIST

by

JOSEPH T. FREEMAN, M.D.

and

IRVING L. WEBBER, Ph.D.

THE GERONTOLOGIST is a publication of the Gerontological Society, 660 South Euclid Avenue, St. Louis, Missouri. It is a quarterly journal of which the Editor-in-chief is Oscar J. Kaplan, Ph.D., and his assistant is Mrs. Marjorie Adler.

The Publications Committee consists of Dr. Morris Rockstein, Chairman, Thomas J. Moran, Ph.D., Raymond Harris, M.D., Jack Botwinick, Ph.D. and Robert Morris D.S.W.

The structure of the History of Gerontology Committee of the Society at the time of preparation of their Supplement consisted of the co-chairmen, Joseph T. Freeman and Irving L. Webber, and the following members: Joseph C. Aub, James E. Birren, Edmund V. Cowdry, Gerald J. Gruman, Robert J. Havighurst, William M. Krogman, and Clark Tibbitts.

Publication of this Supplement has been made possible in part by funds given to the Society by the Ford Foundation in 1961. Except for normal purposes, as in critical reviews and quotations, reproduction of the contents is permissible only upon written permission. All rights in THE GERONTOLOGIST and its Supplement are reserved under copyright held by the Gerontological Society.

THE GERONTOLOGIST

VOLUME 5 NUMBER 1
PART II
March, 1965

CONTENTS

Contributors iv

Foreword v

Introduction vii

Chapter

1. Medical Perspectives in Aging (12-19th Century) .... *Joseph T. Freeman* 1

2. The Historical Developments in the Biological Aspects of Aging and the Aged
   .... *Alfred H. Lawton* 25

3. Human Personality and Perpetuity .... *Walter R. Miles* 33

4. Some Historical Developments of Social Welfare Aspects of Aging .... *Ollie A. Randall* 40

Index

Subject Index 50

Author Index 53

iii

Joseph T. Freeman, Lecturer in Geriatrics, Graduate School of Medicine, University of Pennsylvania; Woman's Medical College of Pennsylvania; Consultant in Geriatrics, U. S. Veterans Administration Hospital, Coatesville, Pennsylvania; Lankenau Hospital.

Alfred H. Lawton, Director, Human Development Study and Center, National Institute of Child Health and Human Development, National Institutes of Health, Public Health Service, U. S. Department of Health, Education and Welfare, St. Petersburg, Florida.

Walter R. Miles, Scientific Director, Submarine Medical Research Division, U. S. Naval Submarine Medical Center, New London Submarine Base, Groton, Connecticut.

Ollie A. Randall, Vice president, National Council on the Aging, New York City, New York.

Foreword

GERONTOLOGY cannot afford to ignore its history. Certainly it cannot do so if its achievements are to be distinctive and visible to both the scientific and the general community. The four papers in this supplement issue of THE GERONTOLOGIST demonstrate clearly that it is not the intent of gerontology to deny to its history a significant place among its many and varied constituent activities.

These are not the first papers or monographs to be written on the history of gerontology, nor are they the first to appear in this journal. What is of unusual significance, however, is that this is the first supplementary publication of the Gerontological Society to be devoted exclusively to this area. Furthermore, these papers represent the tangible result of a determined Society activity directed toward the development of historical interests in gerontology.

With the support of the Ford Foundation, the Gerontological Society's History of Gerontology Committee organized a symposium on the history of gerontology under the joint direction of Dr. Irving L. Webber and Dr. Joseph T. Freeman. This symposium was presented at the Society's scientific meeting in Boston in 1963. The papers now published in this supplement were originally presented in abbreviated form at this annual meeting. The authors of these papers are singularly well equipped to carry out these assignments. The abiding interest of Dr. Freeman and Dr. Webber in the history of gerontology and geriatrics sparked the initiation of the symposium and provided the persistence which brought it to this culmination. Alfred H. Lawton's training and experience in medicine, biology, and public health, and his research in aging and development, gave him a broad base upon which to approach the historical developments in the biological aspects of aging. Walter R. Miles' classic research in the psychology of aging, carried out in the early 1930's, provides a place for him as a significant figure in his own right in the history of gerontology. Ollie A. Randall's preeminent and pioneering work in the social welfare of the aged is well attested by the unique citation which she was awarded at the first national conference on aging called by the U. S. government in 1950.

This publication will not be the last evidence of interest in gerontology's history. The History of Gerontology Committee has major plans for future activity of this body. These include the encouragement of interest in this special area in the International Association of Gerontology in order that the world-wide growth of gerontology will not go unnoticed in the history of science. Publication of this symposium must be considered as a significant step in this direction.

Robert W. Kleemeier, Ph.D.
President
Gerontological Society

St. Louis, Missouri
March 6, 1965

Introduction

IN ITS role as a major research-oriented organization of multidisciplinary content, the Gerontological Society has concerned itself with historical factors which deal with aging in all of its aspects. Within its History of Gerontology Committee, a number of discussions were initiated to determine the responsibility of the committee, and through it, of the Society, to this special area. Two major questions were found. How much effort should be made to classify the annals of aging in historical array? How much effort should be given to an analysis of this composite science in a medical, biological, sociological, and economic perspective of aging as part of an historical design?

Preliminary conversations took cognizance of what had been accomplished, and the long-term decision was based on this identification. There was ready awareness of the fact that the two conjoined and organic features of aging, which could not be separated and which contributed to mutual development, had to be met in catalogued chronological fashion.

On the one hand, there was the straight biographical citation, the common aspects of history, or the *annalistic* component of an organic body of thought. Historical documentation of the science of aging has consisted of a series of overlapping episodes. Usually these have been eponymic and often little more than anecdotal. Still, in the over-all sense, the record has been surprisingly comprehensive and virile. The way was to be paved for interpretations in which the study of this phase of human development was known to be essential if all states of living were to be understood in their full biological range.

On the other hand, there was that part of the historical discipline involving an understanding of trends in which *analytic* components had to be assayed. This was interpretative of historical data and applicable as the foundation on which current thought is based.

Obviously this double approach is a device rather than a fact. It is a didactic division which intimated, quite unjustly, that these methods could be pursued separately without damage. Such implications were known from the start but had to be risked to find a practical approach to an unwieldy problem. In the presentation, there is awareness of the shortcomings with the hope that what was done would compensate for that which, in full knowledge, was not done.

In the deliberations it soon became apparent that historical reviews are not paginated monuments; they are involved inextricably with current gerontological investigations and thought. An encyclopedic analysis of aging in all of its contours was indicated as the ultimate goal. This concept far exceeded the number of scholars known at the time to be qualified to make the effort and to perform it in proper fashion. The evaluative phase has not, and possibly will not have, adequately involved scholars for a while. The outlines are being prepared in anticipation of the time when it will be possible to see the mass of gerontological material in the round. In brief, this part of the project has been in deferment, but the grand design has not been abandoned. Meanwhile, it may be possible to direct the attention of requisite investigators into channels which have strangely been somewhat neglected, with a few very notable exceptions.

To initiate the effort and to give bibliographical structure to future studies, understanding in depth finally was received. Through the efforts of Dr. Robert Morris of Brandeis University, the opportunity was made available to invite some essayists to classify and analyze some historical data for presentation at the annual meeting of the Gerontological Society. Four papers were woven into the Boston meeting held in November, 1963. The civic arrangements were under the direction of Dr. Hugh Cabot of the New England Center for Aging, and the scientific program was arranged by Dr. Morris. Summaries of four papers presented at the meeting make up in expanded form the substance of this Supplement to *The Gerontologist*.

Possibly in no other matured science does the ratio of useful to useless information appear to more disadvantage than in gerontology. The number of contributions to aging made by empiricists, pragmatists, and authoritative dignitaries, whose opinions were self-designated as worthy of distribution to others, has complicated the problem immeasurably through the centuries. Fortunately, throughout the recorded bibliography, there have been major items of lasting value.

There is almost a sense of violence implied to a population which has been described as burgeoning. There is a rather hectic type of scientific reference to the various adjustments made by men to their times, to their environments, and to themselves. Only in aging, irrevocable, implicit, and inevitable, there is an air of timeliness (due to time) and of continuity (earned but not secured as yet). Those who have noted these facts in the scientific world are those who must interpret. Those are the names which historical documentation must acknowledge, with respect and with insight.

Opinions differ whether men direct or follow historical movements; often it is impossible to determine the order of precedence. The arbitrary selection of the chronological method for the selection of topics and their protagonists is justified by expedience. Such methods need not have obvious and uniform relations to historical movements, to factual changes in the evolution of ideas, or to any form of sequential reality except for calendar progression. This method by chance and in-gathering can point out the constancy and growth of incontrovertible ideas without regard to eras. A truth in fourth century pre-Christian Greece is just as absolute 2500 years later. Another reasonable conclusion is the fact that it would be unlikely for any man to rise high in his century, or to continue in the esteem of later times, if his thought and products were not significant.

Many influences flowed out of the eastern Mediterranean basin, along both shores and particularly in Greece, to find a focus in Spain from the eighth to the twelfth century. Western Europe accepted and projected the ideas in momentous scientific moves. In both static and dynamic cultures, the aging became a matter of special issue because of the attainment of an increase in average individual life span and expanded expectancies of survival. Despite a number of contributions to the clinical science, in geriatrics, it was not until the late nineteenth century that the spread between genetic and ecological potentials began to be closed. Prior to that time most reflections on aging had been summarized in Renaissance man's views as part of his humanistic inheritance. Later, specificity in the studies of aging produced a different type of literature.

While biologists struggled with theories with regard to the causation of aging, physicians endeavored to bring order into clinical management. Both approaches tended to be tampered with by emotions and uncritical material. Clinical clarity appeared in a number of works from the middle of the nineteenth century. By 1867 Charcot had been able to demonstrate in his wards and autopsy studies certain conclusions about senescence of which physicians were beginning to become informed. Concurrently, an occasional definitive study of physiological mechanisms in contrasting age groups began to appear. Annotations and documentation followed the lead of von Ranke into the twentieth century. A dazzling list of great students pointed to this time and gave impetus to forces which are still in acceleration.

The changing economic and social structures added their share. By the time of the second World War, all of the accumulated needs for objective understanding of aging as a biological process, and of its clinical counterparts which required identification and proper management, came to the fore. This modern era in gerontology dates to 1940. This was not a fully matured goddess sprung from the head of a geratic Zeus. It was the culmination of a great deal of effort which was novel only to those who did not bother to investigate the gathering lines of influence which led to this point of departure. These are the influences which warrant formal identification.

In the meantime, the Committee plans to continue its thoughts to a definition of the major perspectives in aging, to the manner in which the aging and aged of the population are influenced by all of the business of a complicated and evolving social community, as well as the influences on this community of its older people. It has been appreciated from the very start that the divisions in the projects, as cited, were artificial, and that it would be impossible to separate them, but it was believed possible to help to trace the progress of the future with some historical notes as a stencil. With the publication of these four papers, the first half of the project can, in a limited sense, be considered to be completed. The long-range procedure will require optimism even to approximate a completion of the second part of the envisioned objective. If gerontological science is to get beyond the age of homilies, still unfortunately influential, it will do so by way of a variety of efforts already apparent in outline. Those in the field accept each addition to the literature critically—but as a natural event. Others may stumble on things which they never suspected, and unexpectedly may broaden the syndromes of their knowledge.

Works such as this Supplement are undertaken

with caution, fully cognizant that at best it is but a transitional marker. Many people have been involved personally and by their accumulated influences. To cite them would but leave many others without just identification. Those who are in gerontology would be aware of such contributors to whom the co-editors are obligated. Those who are unknowing may acquire this information by a charitable, and hopefully a useful, scan of the pages.

To the structure and authorities of the Gerontological Society, including its central office in St. Louis, to *The Gerontologist* and its editor, and to many others, special thanks are given for kindnesses and assistance. Miss Ollie Randall, Dr. Lawton, and Dr. Miles have been gracious and understanding of editorial urgencies. For those bothered by the many omissions, their judgment may be softened a little by the following which Dr. Miles has used in his paper as a quotation from the humanist, Erasmus:

"There are more Saints than are found in our Catalogue."

We knew this of course or we would not have undertaken the project. There was a point of view to get expressed; there were contingencies to be met. Perhaps it will suffice to say in temporary conclusion that there is more, much more, yet to come.

Joseph T. Freeman
Irving L. Webber

Medical Perspectives in Aging (12th-19th Century)

Joseph T. Freeman, M.D., F.A.C.P.[1]

How to identify, or what to recognize, in man's literate history are matters of delicate choice. As a rule, a medical bibliography starts with lists of distinguished names, the "parade of personalities," and then creates awareness of those historical forces which come to a focus in certain individuals. In the field of aging, the medical figures who stand out of the calendar have forged a solid line of understanding from the fanciful to the factual. In larger measure, in every age, they are the archetypes of that person ultimately personified as Renaissance man even before there were such epitomes of universal ideas motivated in some manner by humanism. For the most part, such is the historical manner, there has been undue emphasis on men almost as if they could be free of their origins, their times, or the accumulations of thought by which emergent cultures were molded first into regional responses, then into national programs, and finally, into universal acceptance.

In aging, the medical views of these men partook of their entire world. Their observations were accepted on the basis of the totality of their stature. Some records survive in incunabula and early books or in the commentaries on the works of others by which modern medicine has been shaped. From pre-literate times to the Greeks, the Arabians, and post-Crusader Europe, lines of medical communication remained open. Human values became established in social forms and in the process lost some of their promise in their time. The amulets, ceremony, caste, myth, taboo, social order, emblems of authority, and power of customs have restraints on man's capacities.

Collective experiences attain accepted form through the repetition of verbally transmitted citations. These become a force in social integration and direction. The first stages were the documentary recording of the complete tribal recall.

This acquires the status of a Code. The story of the past, usually recounted by the elderly tribal historians, becomes a formal guide to the society's direction. The recited catalog of classified events is formalized as an edifice which can become a source of enrichment or enslavement of the society of which it is the record. In clear language or, more often, in symbolical terms, such codes had incorporated into them the great matters endured by the tribe. Cycles of food problems, waves of disease, catastrophic natural events, flux of spiritual ideas, deifications, collective experiences in battle, rigidity in inter-personal relationships, trials of therapeutic substances, and all the minutiae of successive generations become stratified in a hereditary ruling class, a priestly authority, and in an almost irrevocable set of rules usually recalled, recounted, and relayed by the elders.

These records or codes tend to become static in time, fixed in geography, and possessive for the group.

Ancient civilization bore the hallmarks of their patriarchs. Aging personified achievement. From China, India, and Chaldea, there flowed a number of attitudes toward aging in which were reflected a relatively stable and unchanging civilization which absorbed rather than underwent variations with the passage of millenia. Major Chinese and Indian influences in the care of the old remained largely local, unadaptable, and almost unexportable.

In Hebraic and Greek thought, some universality in an approach to the old began to develop. Even the likelihood of survival to any reasonably adult stage, let alone to old age, was more a matter of chance than of biological capacity. Distinctions between life and death were accepted as less acute or cataclysmic than in modern times and tended to put emphasis on methods by which dead bodies could be preserved into eternity. In China, disturbances in physiological balance were deemed responsible for disease, and aging in the Taoistic

1

views was caused by opposing Yin and Yang principles. In India, in addition to a classification as disease, aging was accepted as a natural part of life which possibly could be arrested or even reversed. Old age was a time when morbid and mortal susceptibilities seemed to increase (Grant, 1963). Elsewhere, records such as the Palestinian scrolls, the citations chiseled into the stone bases at Delos and Delphi, the tablets of Rome, inkings on the parchments of North Africa (Bryan, 1931), the papyri (Breasted, 1930) of the Islamic world of the Eastern and Western Caliphates, and finally the manuscripts of Europe with an irreparable loss linked forever to the destruction of the bibliographical monuments in Alexandria—all of these indicate that the elaboration of men's thoughts and their forms of preservation were unceasing.

Medical citations in the Bible are representative of unusual excellence in historical continuity in which the experiences of tribal and early state forms achieved authoritative form as social hygiene crystallized from human experience. Biblical medical concepts were of very little specific value in individual care, but public hygiene compensated for such deficiencies. Biblical dogma ultimately formed a union with the unique and explosive developments of Greek thought manifested in every discipline which ingenious and able men could bring to systematic direction. Despite, and possibly because of, the local significance of Greek value, particularly from Solon's sixth century B.C., this particular brand of Grecian colloquialism became an expression of the universality of man for all ages. Early biblical concepts contained the germ of that which became known as humanism. The full flowering, however, was Grecian. The basis on which the Christian ethic developed, cleared of the superstructure of hierarchy, was a clear expression of the primary importance of man. Aging in perspective is an essential part of this humanistic philosophy.

In those early days, aging for the most part had no special attributes in the minds of thinkers nor in the compilation of social experience except as part of group and personal aspirations. Individual value was subordinated to traditions. Attitudes of respect normally accorded to long survival contained esteem for that acquired status as if long life attainment were a special trait in itself. The need for the experiences of older people, reliance on their recollections as well as their interpretations of accumulations of law, the usefulness of the old verbal stories, as repositories of tribal history, as advisors, as centers for family cohesion, as well as sources of amassed capital, gave elders a position which seemed to be justified. Some of them attained privileges as former warriors. Many customs became fixed in personal rules or laws. Later, food surpluses and increasing tribal security added a dimension to survival. In some civilizations, such as the Chinese, veneration for the aging went beyond actual survival. In other civilizations, such as the Egyptian, efforts were made to perpetuate the body of the deceased. In India, destruction of the body by fire did not terminate family respect or memory. Reverence for aging was enshrined in practically every religion and a number of them utilized the Father Abraham concept. Possibly the first setback occurred in Greece when youth was identified as the acme and old age as the nadir of life.

Rome was more pragmatic. It put aside priestly parts in the medical world. Its physicians were assigned an important part in public health and in the expression of the *res Romanae*. Explorations

MEDICAL PERSPECTIVES IN AGING

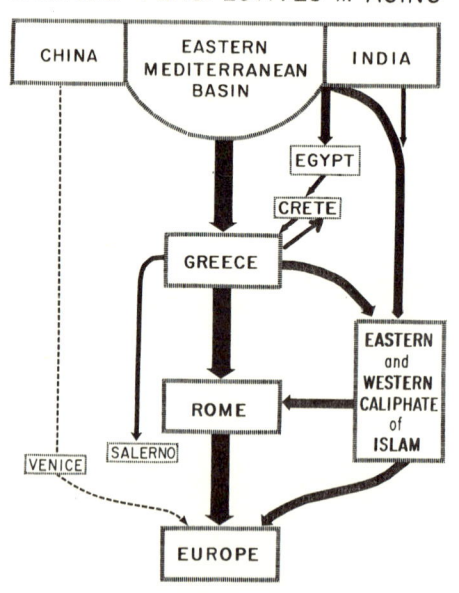

Fig. 1. A schema of a number of major developments in the history of the scientific study of aging. Many later influences have been omitted. Only major trends, designated by lines of different thickness to indicate importance, have been placed in the diagram.

of purely scientific nature were limited. The function of the Roman physician in the community was subservient to his place in the total political organization. Even at that, it was better than the position of the Egyptian physician, who was a state officer of particular technical training and not much more in standing. By the very complacency of its attitude toward medicine, Rome became responsible for the rigidity of medical thinking which developed during feudal times. Later, such views made it easy to accept the religious dogmatism of the growing Christian thought. But Rome never was to escape the Greek influence.

As early as the fourth century B.C., Hippocratic theory "voiced the spirit of an entire epoch" and began to separate medicine from the religious influences and the mysticism of the past. The shapes of truths based on observations were becoming identified. A humoral theory of aging within the context of the total life span began to take shape. The nature of senescence was thought to be caused by the progressive diminution of the store of innate heat or vitality in the lifelong normal course of events. Those diminutions were accountable for diseases which are seen more commonly in the older body. There was an awareness of the increasing degrees of vulnerability to forces by which life could be terminated. A century later, Aristotle expressed his views on old age.

He had a burning curiosity about facts. . . . Mystery Aristotle rejected and he took this Hippocratic need to combine observation and experience with logical reasoning and intuitive knowledge which Hippocrates applied to illness but Aristotle tried to apply to everything.

In an all-encompassing mind attuned to Plato and sharpened by his tutelage of Alexander the Great, it has been said in aging that "since Aristotle, we may just have been marking time" (Grant, 1963).

The third Greek was Galen who practiced medicine in Rome. He reviewed and venerated Hippocrates but followed his own lines of development (Garrison, 1960). To him, old age was an inherent property as well as a process continuous with living (Linacre, 1517). Until the Renaissance, these ideas generally were unchallenged. Galen indeed is fortunate not to have had an Aristotle in his circle, or the medicine of the millenium after him would have been different.

However, the benign thought of Grecian freedom did not include more than a token appreciation of the aging. "Fundamental to everything that the Greeks achieved," said Hamilton (1930, 1957),

was their conviction that good for humanity was possible only if man was free, body, mind and spirit, and if each man limited his own freedom.

Applying such dicta rather ruthlessly, Aristotle knew that freedom was relative and never more so than in the confines of the body (Taylor, 1808). In his *Rhetoric*, he limned quite distinctly the selfishness, loquacity, defensiveness and egocentricity of the old. "Apparently there was no golden age for the aged in Greece" (Haynes, 1962). Plato had to make idyllic laws for the protection of the old, but Aristotle expressed himself in cynical and percipient terms.

Attitudes toward old age derive from the full nature of things, from the totality of social and familial man in the full pattern of his existence, under the influence of the past, in concurrence with the privileges and pressures of the present, and possibly clothed with the hopes of the future. In the field of aging, physicians wrote with consistency based on observations which did not contain any particular originality and possibly were of no more use than the views of those who commented directly or in their translations of previous observers.

There was an enormous literature on all aspects of aging by the year 1200 A.D. It came from a variety of sources but was singularly repetitious. It was the rare student of the time, physician or philosopher, who did not feel an urgency to include his views on rejuvenation or survival to old age, on the diseases in aging, or even on the nature of aging itself. Their literary forms, as a rule, were more original than their ideas, which came to consist of comments on comments sanctified by allusions to the Greeks based on translations which had a variable degree of purity. The physicians who wrote *Opuscula Medica* were significant of their times and their works. By the end of the 12th century, the outline of modern man was apparent.

The history of geriatrics began to assume some degree of authority. When Galenic views predominated, speculative and experimental concepts languished. Much of the detail of the science was yet to be revealed and much more was in need of identification and interpretation. A scientific discipline which deals with man's basic drives, the urge to live, the fear of death, the desire for youth, the quest for rejuvenation, the distaste for old age, and the care of illness in the old, is involved in human forces which have not, nor are they likely to be, changed.

12th Century

The twelfth century bore the full impact of all of man's past and directed it into the future in more orderly fashion. The learned men of the twelfth century certainly did not act or write as if their period in history was dark. They had ample sources of authoritative literature. Their minds scanned a thousand years of recorded wisdom as if time moved in a slow deep stream rather than a foaming tidal race. Values had an opportunity to be enriched, to be savored and tested, to eliminate the spurious, and to receive the stamp of acknowledgement. The groping for authority and its attainment in various forms by personages, in books, and in structures either of institutions or stone, were the type of solidity which twelfth century man had to have and could accept. The aging, fewer in numbers, less protected and generally less secure, participated by their acquiescence to formal authority. The Church clothed itself in inviolability. Social forms became organized in orders, customs, rules, respect for that which was ordained, the fiat of status, and the unquestioned subservience to dreadful, usually premature, biological inevitabilities. These did not seem to arouse the bitterness of soul that a more demanding and rebellious society expressed in such implacable upheavals as the French Revolution five hundred years in the future. The Peasants' Revolt of a nearer time showed that man knew the way. He just did not use it as yet.

The Arab World

The authorities which flowed into this vivid area were established and accepted without question. Later, when society was more fluid and personalities flourished, the ancient thoughts of Greece could be appreciated and reinforced. China, India, Egypt, Palestine, Greece, Rome, and the Christian traditions of the centuries from St. Augustine to the Council of Clermont and the Crusades came to a sharp focus in the twelfth century. Just as 600 A.D. marked the beginning of the spread of monastic and cloistered thought in widening circles, 1200 A.D. signified the focus of ideas by which the centuries of such seclusion came to an end. All that had been latent, from Greece, from Rome, from the triangle of the East which pointed to the easternmost extremity of the Mediterranean, and even from other lands and cultures, broke over the growing population. The Arabian surge had borne with it not so much of the novel as of the unclassified debris of the lands where the Islamic tide had touched. It was a channel by which Grecian, Jewish, Roman, and even Oriental cultures were transmitted almost unchanged. And it was at this time, in this place, on the Iberian Peninsula, from the apex of the Adriatic, in Marseilles and from Rome, that the ideas spread. They were stirred by that surgent miracle of the Crusades whose dreadful reality was terrifying in retrospect.

The eastern and western moieties of the Islamic Arabian world, as heir and cupbearer of more ancient civilizations, preserved and extended lines of human communication. From the time of Charlemagne in the ninth century to the last of the Crusades, for four hundred years the Arabians pruned, preserved, and lived with a high note of intelligence in a span from Cordova to Bagdad geographically and a spectrum from Rhazes to Averroes intellectually. Inadvertently, the Crusades opened the doors. From the deadly serious, inspirited waves of these many thousands in their bloody treks to their destruction until the end of the chivalric age whose epitaph was written in a Spanish prison cell, a man can only stand in awe, secure in the attainment of the current privileges of his body and soul.

The closing of the 12th century was that point in time, if ever, when most of man's established efforts converged, not as an end but as a beginning. The huge static societies of the Far East continued to revolve slowly around their elaborate and unchanging rites. The aspirations of the eastern Mediterranean nations were memorialized in the South by rules governing the dead, in the eastern basin by an inspired book of faith, and in the unique cumulus of Grecian thought to the North. The headless Roman structure had been toppled between pagan despotism and dogmatic Christianity. In Venice, Spain, and other areas of this restless European peninsula, society had been imbued with dissatisfaction. There were signs everywhere that man was on the move and in this motility, new desires and new attitudes became apparent. Challenge replaced acceptance. Parochial and regional beliefs were stirred first by physical needs and then by the intellectual urgencies of inquiry and curiosity. Traditional ways and values were not discarded. They were beginning to be weighed against the presence of constant misery, the hopelessness of plagues, the daily concern with hunger, and the perpetuation of an unquestioned rigid ruling system. The growth of population which was almost held in check, (and this was condoned as a salutary effect) by war, famine, and disease, was associated with the longer survival of more individuals. Aging was only an occasional by-product. The old were participants rather than objectives of the society in which they lived.

The monastic Christian world of this period was fearful of the vigor of the Arabian and Jewish intellectual urgency. Grecian studies entered the era as an active force to which scholastic rigidity and secular thinking had to bow. The Arabian physicians quoted Aristotle and questioned Galen. Their rules of health sounded of the past and served as models for the future but were primarily subjective in origin. They were written in categories of inspirational medicine in which Aristotle was quoted but not served. In such times, aging's problems found no particular solution.

Medicine had been fairly regional, a matter of feudal communities, battlefield surgery, homilies, and nebulous repetitions. It was not that the old had been forgotten but there was so little about or for them which was new. In a small group of Arabian physicians, the works of the Greeks and more important the questioning approach of Aristotle became asserted once more. The inherent curiosities of intelligent men were breaking away from social and religious disciplines in which every diurnal act and every nocturnal deed was a prescribed and imposed routine. In a sense, their challenges were prorated as a hand raised against everything which had been accepted instead of being identified as a proper, even laudable, evidence of an inquiring spirit.

The Arabian Physicians

The high level sophistication and energy of the Arabian physicians of both the Eastern and Western Caliphate cannot be dismissed as a five-century holding tactic (9th to the 14th century). These great men, like most great men, always had their champions and their bibliographers. They have become standard, almost classical, figures in medical histories. Their chronological citation would serve only to refresh memory. Their published works are sources of permanent reference, although some have been buried under strata of medical repetition.

Their era shaped their reactions, but their perceptions helped to direct their world. In those areas in which they were universal, they diluted their mortal abilities and achieved a measure which transcended their own period despite obstructions of minor and major nature. Their limitations are equivalent to their stature in their own centuries. These learned travelers, astute observers, and medical veterans, brought with them their civilized concepts of what was identified once again as the humanistic school. The physicians of Islamic and Jewish faith had a continuity which was political in affiliation and Islamic in discipline. In addition, it was universal in an unswerving adherence to the works of the Greeks. Although they may not have advanced these universal thoughts, and this is not a just criticism, they did translate, if at times inaccurately, as they studied the great body of preserved thought, albeit in a scholastic rather than critical fashion.

The Arabian scholiasts avoided the restraints of Christian monasticism, which was a form also utilized in their own faith. Still, they served the humanistic concept more in form than in substance. If they did not vitalize it, at least they did not let it die of neglect. Some of them gloried in the role of Aristotelians, Platonists, or variables of both. These distinguished turbanned and unbane men were linguists, students, and free observers, who served as a strong framework for a remarkable civilization. It is no wonder that they pondered on life and death, on disease and old age, and they did it fully, in the framework of their times and within the limits of its capacities.

Unlike those Egyptian physicians whose service to the crown was a cross between a modern health officer and a state social medicine employee (Soubiran, 1963), the Arabian physicians served from Persia to Spain at the high level of a fairly free society. It would not be meet to select any one of these great physicians for signal attention. In a sense, a composite would be a better reflection of the fact. To choose one because he questioned some of Galen's thoughts (Maimonides), which was daring enough, or another because his works were standard texts for centuries (Avicenna) even in the face of disparagement by a famous physician, or one who stood on the threshold of the Renaissance (Arnoldus de Villanova), or still another because his texts of surgical principles were used in the European medical schools for 500 years (Averroes), or a fifth for his standards of therapeutics (Avenzoar), would be to neglect many of great and almost equal stature (Garrison, 1960). The fact is that many of these men saw, recorded, treated, and sought confirmation of their ideas in their intellectual predecessors, the Greeks (Gordon, 1959). That which was called the "Arabic repository" certainly was not a vacuum.

Probably the major issue in the transition from aging as a part of the humanistic tradition to aging in its own specific context is in itself the proper description of what was occurring. The ultimate achievement of a scientific status for studies of old age was an affirmation of earlier impulses to be able to categorize old age medically in an era when such distinctions were blunted by the actualities imposed by the unrestricted spread of lethal infectious diseases.

A reasonably accurate picture can be drawn of the influence of the men of Arabian medicine through the medieval period. Monasticism had become entrenched in northern Europe. The great medical schools were coming into being. Nations were forging boundaries, languages, and customs. The Christian order was showing its strength in crusades, inquisitions, the imposition of an all-embracing and inviolate theology based on a life after death and an acceptance of physical suffering and limitations in the present as payment for original sin.

The Arabian physicians, many of whom were of the Jewish faith, were cosmopolites, adaptable men, and experts versed in many cultures. Persecution drove some of the Jews into living lives in Islam, writing in Arabic. In their thoughts they helped to link both wings of Arabian thought. Skilled in rhetoric, versed in Greek, (Rhazes was called "the Arabian Hippocrates"), and other thought, they tended to be Galenists in their anatomical ideas and Aristotelians, at least from a literary point of view, in their challenges and concepts of experimental approaches. They resolved their issues by increasing rejection of Galen, recorded a number of superb clinical observations, and flowered in a profusion of writings and translations in which they maintained an unchanging loyalty to the men of the Aegean world. Physicians of the later period of western Europe leaned on these works and found in them the values of Grecian medicine, either with commentaries, or in direct translations similar to the fragments of values picked up from the eastern Mediterranean Basin, Palestine, and India. Arabic thought was the light from which the European Renaissance took some of its flame and much of its fuel.

Avicenna (981—1037) (1930) was said to have known all of Aristotle by heart. His *Canon*, which was Galenic in its anatomy and Hippocratic in its theory, was authoritative for hundreds of years. It served as a text, for example, at the University of Montpellier until 1650. Albucasis (c. 931—1110) wrote a masterful surgical text based on Galen's erroneous anatomical studies, and it served as a surgical authority for 500 years. The derogation of surgery blocked medical progress in medieval times and this had to be corrected.

The principal interest of the medieval period, therefore lies not in its internal medicine, for there was precious little of it, but in the gradual development of surgery from the ground up . . . (Garrison, 1960).

Another Arabian Galenist, although somewhat more eclectic, was Avenzoar, a master clinician. The apocryphal statement was made about him that he may have lived 135 years. A century later, Averroes (c. 1126—1198) was more of an Aristotelian. Apparently there was one major issue for the Arabic physicians, namely, to try to be loyal to the best of Galen, to understand Hippocrates, and to live by Aristotle.

About the same period, the great Rambam, Maimonides (c. 1135—1204), physician to the Vizier of Saladin in Cairo and a man great enough to be able to refuse a bid to serve as physician to the King of England, made himself thoroughly informed in an Aristotelian cast of medical thought (Zeitlin, 1955). Like all of the others, this was primarily a literary rather than a scientific device. More important, he, like a few others, voiced specific criticism of Galen and enumerated more than 40 objections in his own collection of medical aphorisms written in the popular manner. Maimonides is a good example of the Arabian physican. Born of an old and distinguished Jewish family in Cordova, he was forced to flee to Fez in Morocco by the religious violence of an Islamic sect. He wandered all around that wonderful world of the Mediterranean basin. To him, the works of Averroes were sovereign, due in particular to that great clinician's interpretation of Aristotle. Maimonides himself was authoritative in many fields, certain of his opinion and judgments, prolific in his writings, sure of his inspiration, and secure in his place as an aristocratic intellectual who made decisions without much thought of critical opposition. As was to be expected, "he never wrote a prescription unless its efficacy was warranted by the great masters of medicine." He advised older people to see their physicians frequently. He favored the use of bleeding and purges in emergencies but was opposed to the use of strong drugs. Moderation was the prime virtue. He warned his aged as well as his cardiac patients of the dangers of excesses in marital relations. Wine was useful for the aged as was cleanliness. He wrote books on poisons, asthma, diet, drugs, hemorrhoids, constipation, and tabulated long lists of hygienic rules. For his time, these were the expressions expected of men who dwelled in the high planes of thought.

The Knight, the monk, and the Arabian physician march back into the pages of history. . . . Looking back from the vantage point of A.D. 1925, we are tempted to look upon the Middle Ages as one of ignorance, superstition, bigotry and lawlessness, while fighting and religion occupied the whole attention of the great men of these ages, and standing amid the galaxy of the great leaders of the misty past, we see the great figures looking down upon us from the visor of the Knight and the cowl of the monk. But the Arabist tradition of Medieval Europe brings to our minds yet another figure, that of the Arab physician-philosopher with his gold and silver brocaded turban and his halo of intellectual curiosity and broad tolerance. . . . (Campbell, 1926)

Fig. 2. Maimonides, otherwise known as Moses Ben Maimon or Rambam, a Spaniard of Jewish faith of whom it was said that this religion had two great men named Moses. He lived 1135-1204 A.D.; was one of the greatest physicians of his day as well as a noted commentator on the Old Testament. (Photograph courtesy National Library of Medicine)

After the Arabs: Christian Monasticism

The fall of the Roman Empire saw the development of three disciplines, monasticism, scholasticism, and humanism, each of which had obvious forerunners and descendants that predominated in particular periods. Monasteries spread throughout Europe from the 5th-6th centuries until the Crusades. The idea of a "monk, alone" was not new but it achieved levels beyond the concepts of a hermit or a small group of religious recluses. The cloistered orders were oriented primarily to preparation for a life in eternity. They served as training areas of discipline and as religious repositories in which there was a constant refinement of established thought and dogma, unfortunately in a rather circular and unproductive way, if secular judgment is correct. Monasticism saw the spread of a militant organization and the establishment of the authority of a dominant church which replaced the militant organization of political and pagan Rome. The monastic centers served as static, almost timeless, units suspended in sanctified living. Dating formally from St. Benedict, members of this Order were studying the Greek physicians as early as the 9th century.

The new monasticism reflected the needs of the recently developed cities. The orders of St. Francis and St. Dominic were designed in quite a different manner from the old Benedictine monasticism, consonant to the needs of the new non-feudal society. The Franciscans were mostly devoted to social services in hospitals, especially for leprosy, while the Dominicans devoted themselves primarily to learning and preaching. (Beaumont, 1964)

By the 12th century, military orders were developed to oppose the spread of Mohammedanism. Furthermore, they were useful as refuges and hospices as well as sites of rigid disciplinary training for a number of somewhat circumscribed and unquestioned religious activities. The advancement of thought derived little from them. The preservation of manuscripts had the value of buried gold with as little alteration in values. No particular aspects of aging aside from charitable meals, some nursing care, teaching, medical advice, and religious guidance could be expected from the monasteries.

The medicine of this era was said to be "stereotyped, dogmatic, and devoid of any lofty outlook" (Gordon, 1959). During the 11th and 12th centuries, with the strengthening of the Christian force and structure throughout the West, these theological centers served as walled lyceums for the exercise of logic. Monasteries reached their peak before the 13th century and then entered the cycle which led to the changes of the Reformation and establishment of the militant response of the Jesuitical corps. In some ways, they assisted in the next important development in man's education, the era of scholasticism.

Scholasticism

Overlapping the monasteries and potent from the 11th to the 14th centuries, scholasticism was considered to be "the most typical product of medieval thought." Initiated in the 9th century by Charlemagne, who demanded fertile activity, abbey schools were founded as centers of repetitive and later speculative and questioning learning. Such distinguished students as Linacre (1517), Rabelais (Putnam, 1928), and Erasmus were outstanding among the scholiasts. The endless discussions became as sharp as a pin in their focus on a variety of ideas. Possibly the *form* of discussion was more important than the *product* but the acuity of discussion led to valid inquiries. At first the ecclesiastical structure dominated the sessions but, possibly unconscious, reactions against such restraints resulted in centrifugal forces as the likely to be anticipated products of unending questions.

Because of the requirement to mold all answers to questions into logical defenses of the nature and thought of Catholic theology and theocracy, ideas seemingly had to conform. The cynical fable of the traveler in the inn who had to fit a bed of fixed length was more often than not factual in religious inquiries. In a sense, the questions were rigged because the answers just had to be "correct." In other words, the answers were parents to the questions and this was never to be forgotten. The rigors of the Inquisition were the measures of conformity. The monasteries were gestational for new thoughts which were at first repetitive but ultimately were the nidus for inquisitive minds. When the monks and later the scholars began to take an Aristotelian bent, the unbroken continuity of humanism became apparent. Aristotle's ideas were used on an *a priori* as well as *post hoc* basis but it would take a longer period and more than words to make the old Greek logician and experimentalist seem to conform to this rigid faith.

All of the ideas which were burgeoning in Europe had earlier counterparts in the Islamic renaissance. Withal, these medieval European physicians were compilers and not innovators. They made little inquiry into medical or disease causes and their new publications were but later versions of old works. Only the inquiries of the Greeks, now a thousand years back, could stir up their imagination but unfortunately not to the investigations which were needed. These led only to more venerable and venerated commentaries.

Through all of these times and trends, the aging were re-identified in endless repetitions of ideas taken directly from the Hippocratic aphorisms, the thoughts of Plato, the ideas of Aristotle, and the cold reality of those few in number who were able to survive the variety of biological harassments as well as man-induced lethal situations to reach the full content of old age.

Salerno

Athough the culture which started in the cities and on the shores of eastern countries crossed into Europe on the crest of Arabian learning, there was one small corner in which an almost undiluted Greek effort persisted. This was the medical center of Salerno whose origins are somewhat undefined. It probably was an ancient health center which was serviced by Greek physicians, around whom a teaching center developed into a school. It possibly may have started as a spa or as a Roman vacation area. It catered to Roman patricians. Emulating the hospital, hospice, and medical clinics of Epidauros on the Salonikan Gulf near Grecian Nauplia, Salerno taught medicine in the Greek manner. Although touched by the thoughts from all corners of the Mediterranean world, it continued in its serene way with a purity that was Greece. Its school was in a little town, Salerno, near Naples, and its hospital dated back at least to the 9th century. Although the date of the founding of its school is not known, its teachings and its language certainly were Grecian. Its health regimen in all likelihood was a verbal record of the school's customs.

About the middle of the 13th century, the Catalan diplomat and physician, Arnoldus de Villanova a one-man bridge from Arabic to late medieval medicine, put 362 of these aphorisms into verse form. Later these were expanded tenfold and published until 1846 in repeated editions which exceeded 240. These rules, which were regulations of diet and other hygiene, were entitled "Compendium Salernitanum" or the *Regimen Sanitatis Salernitatum* and, at different times, quite diplomatically, were dedicated to major rulers.

With the emergence of other medical schools on the Italian peninsula, that of Salerno began to lose its influence. It declined with grace. After a distinguished role served with dignity, it was abolished in 1811 by Napoleon I. Like the works of Homer, the aphorisms of this school were the product of many authors in time, just as its medical school served as an example of what clinicians needed. Sudhoff (1926), who traced this school to Aristotle, said that "Salerno was never anything else but a medical school" in which medical science received its due but the belief in a more gradual evolution of the teaching center had its advocates. Tired and wounded Crusaders found haven here from 1096 to 1270 A.D. Part of the Regimen found a traditional use in the medical direction of the aging.

The following lines from Harington's translation, published in London in 1608, are of interest as giving an idea of the introduction to the Regimen:

The Salerne Schoole doth by these lines impart
All health to England's King, and doth aduise
From care his head to keepe, from wrath his heart,
Drink not much wine, sup light, and soone arise,
When meate is gone, long sitting breedth smart;
And after-noone still waking keepe your eyes.
When mou'd you find your selfe to Nature's Needs,
Forbeare them not, for that much danger breeds,
Use three Physicians still; Doctor Quiet,
Next Doctor Merry-man, and Doctor Dyet.

13th Century

Arnoldus de Villanova, that man of Spain and compendium of the Arabic science, was a graduate of medicine at Naples, an internationalist who practiced medicine in Montpellier, Barcelona, Rome, and Paris, and was a personage of many parts (Burstein, 1955). Born about 1235, he acquired an encyclopedic knowledge of his times. He was a diplomat, social reformer, linguist, author, translator, and student both of astrology and alchemy. Although protected by Pope Boniface VIII, some of his statements made him subject to the Court of Inquisition by whom he was forced to recant. Aside from his early collection of the Salernitan Regimen, his own monograph on old age offered ideas on diet as well as advice on rejuvenation. In the full bloom of this Arabic scholastic era, he turned to chemical experiments. The use of alcohol in medications was one of his favorites.

His book was translated by Drummond in 1544 (Villanova, 1912). This "famous clarke and ryght experte medycyne," said his English translator, knew the medicine of his day and added to it a knowledge of chemistry. Since he "lived to old age . . . he must have been a very clever man." In his works, Arnoldus followed the Galenic idea that age was due to an increase in cold dry humors which could be treated with moist humors. Occasional sharp restrictions in diet, seasonal use of drugs, the maintenance of a good hygiene, bathing, remedies made from vegetables, medicinal wines, a secret remedy called gold water (Eau d'or) which contained no gold, and moderation in all things summarized his views.

Fig. 3. Arnoldus de Villanova of whom it was said "an inquiring mind, a keen observer, and a practical physician, who, while still imbued with Arabian theory was not afraid to set forth his own views and to defend them." He was a Catalan whose years were 1235 to 1311 A.D. He followed Hippocratic methods, advised the use of recorded clinical notes, and is credited with having written at least a part of the Regimen of Salerno. (Photograph courtesy National Library of Medicine)

The special interest of the treatise of Arnoldus lies in its being the matured advice of an erudite experienced and popular physician of the thirteenth, sometimes called the greatest of centuries.

In evidence of his cultural background, this Spanish physician quoted Galen, Aristotle, and "a certain Saracen." The last is a confirmation of the influence of the Arabic physicians on his thought (Sudhoff, 1926). Obviously he was of his age, witty, diplomatic, capable, learned, expressive, and undoubtedly courageous. His books were burned by religious authorities and on one occasion he was imprisoned by the ecclesiastics but only for a day. The punishments were imposed because his works broke out of the circular verbal sterile structure of the scholasticism of his time. Although he may have made no contributions in fact, he was a force by which those to come would be more likely to be able to follow lines of acceptable reality. He was one of those who grafted Arabic to European medicine and in this effort almost singlehandedly he accomplished more than the vigorous armies of Moslems.

Roger Bacon

In the north of Europe, another great physician was emerging about the same time. Just as Villanova was a product of the Arabian scholiasts, Roger Bacon was a product of monasticism. "He represented a new monasticism reflecting the needs of the recently developed cities." The monastic, dynastic, and scholastic phases of human development occurred in the expanding Arabic culture and in its counterpart in that part of Europe above the Iberian peninsula. The former seemed to thrive in the warm yellow light of the Mediterranean world, whereas the latter culture emerged in the cool blue-white light of northern Europe. The Islamic world imposed less rigidities and constrictions and was characterized by less of the guilts and fears which the Christianized North underwent. Even with their unfailing reverence for the Greeks, the Arabic physicians were representative of their urbane culture. With the militant spread of Catholic dogma, Catholic scientists too often seemed to have to go counter to the Church. In that crucial 13th century, there were bridges between the two salients. Villanova with his ties in Spain, Salerno, Greece, and his travels in southern Europe was one, just as Roger Bacon in England was another.

This Doctor Mirabilis, who studied at Oxford, was an eminent scientist and philosopher (Woodruff, 1938) His life seemed to vacillate between Oxford and Paris. He taught at both universities. As a Franciscan friar he was subject to strict discipline for his views and ultimately he was imprisoned in Paris from 1278 until the last year of his life in 1292, when he was permitted to return to Oxford, where he died and was buried. Bacon knew the Arabs and the Greeks. He exhibited a great deal of concern about the faulty Greek translations and undertook the preparation of a Greek grammar by which others could have proper

Fig. 4. This is the title page of Arnoldus de Villanova's book as translated by Drummond in 1544.

Fig. 5. Roger Bacon, a Franciscan friar, of English origin, c.1214-1292 A.D., who studied at the university of Paris and later at Oxford. Of him it was said that "his originality lies not so much on any positive contribution to the sum of knowledge as in his insistance of fruitful lines of research and methods of experimental study." The death of Clement IV ended Bacon's hope of placing sciences in the university curriculum. (Photograph courtesy of National Library of Medicine)

direction in that classical field. He insisted on the experimental method, yet treated medically by methods of logic, and resorted to astrological interpretations. In a sense, he opened the door of the medieval world to the European renaissance.

Scholasticism enveloped this monastic Bacon and colored his efforts. In his knowledge of the world's literature he was a humanist; in his training he was a monk; in his activities he was a scholiast. He quoted authorities in some areas and denied those in others. It was this type of complex and courageous mind which could permit a renewal of man's development. It was said of him that it was not so much his new contributions to knowledge but his insistence on research and experiments which showed his greatness. As a disciple of Aristotle, and in a sense one who turned from Avicenna, he dreamed of placing science in the university curriculum. Such was the man who might be called the fulcrum of the Renaissance.

In his studies of old age, Roger Bacon (1683) wrote: *Retardation of Old Age, the Cure of Old Age, and the Preservation of Youth.* Although he followed the Galenic thought that aging was due to the loss of innate heat from infection, negligence, and ignorance by which natural moisture is lost and extraneous moisture increased, he taught that capacities to survive could be at least 80 years. Couched in terms of his century and clouded by ecclesiastical obscurantism, the fact is that all of the theory of aging is here—of inherent hereditary properties, of the ability to alter these capacities by a proper health program, of extrinsic influences, and of the lessened likelihood of control over those forces whose effects, while accidental, were also allied to inevitable morbid and mortal results. This book is a collection of astute as well as colorful and unreal ideas. It was definitive in its following of the Greek thought "that the process of aging is wholly pathologic" (Burstein, 1955).

In another work, his major study, Bacon (1928) said quite dryly that "in regard to the prolongation of human life . . . medical art has nothing to offer except the regimen of health." Like Aristotle, however, he held to the possibility of prolonging life. In a proper program, old age and senility can be retarded, moderated, or mitigated. None can exceed the limitations of the species. Although little that he said was new (he quoted Pliny, Avicenna, Aristotle, Galen, Hippocrates, and others), how and when he said it were important. Although not fully appreciated until the Elizabethan era, 300 years later, such was his perspicacity that he saw that the products of secular schlolasticism were clever and ingenuous rather than contributory and ingenious. Novelty was to be avoided because of a fear of conflict with theological principles which were as binding as those geographical assumptions which dictated to sailors that the world ended beyond certain defined areas. In an age of theocracy which was served by a militant wing, it was a brave consideration to see the other side of the picture. Like many of the others (Cuffe, 1607; Ficinus, 1547), Bacon was a pioneer in his efforts but his times were not ready to accept him.

In the translation by Browne in the 17th century, Bacon was revealed to state that every day was a step toward old age and this progression could be accelerated by diseases.

I am persuaded were men as careful in preserving their Health as they are solicitous for the recovery of it, they might often multiply the summ of their years, live the Product without a Disease.

When it became a matter of citation of specific agents by which to alter age, aside from his major emphasis on diet, he did as so many others did, he resorted to mysticism and evasion. He barred himself from spelling out his particular panacea for the aging in order, as he excused himself, to keep it out of the hands of the unfaithful by whom it could be used improperly.

14th Century

Complex as Villanova and Bacon were, sometimes a poet can simplify the work of their lives. In the *Canterbury Tales,* Chaucer (1340-1400) wrote verses in his description of the doctor with full awareness of Greek and Arabic influences.

With us ther was a Doctour of Phisyk,
In al this world ne was ther noon him lyk
To speke of phisik and of surgerye;
For he was grounded in astronomye.
He kepte his pacient a ful greet del
In houres, by his magik naturel.
Wel coude he fortunen the ascendent
Of his images for his pacient.
He knew the cause of everich maladye,
Were it of hoot or cold, or moiste, or drye,
And where engendred, and of what humour;
He was a verrey parfit practisour.
The cause y-knowe, and of his harm the rote,
Anon he yaf the seke man his bote.
Full redy hadde he his apothecaries,
To send him drogges and his lectuaries,

For ech of hem made other for to winne,
Hir frendschipe, was nat newe to begine.
Wel knew he the old Esculapius,
And Deiscordies, and eek Rufus,
Old Ypocras, Haly, and Galien;
Serapion, Razis, and Avicen;
Averrios, Damascien, and Constantyn;
Bernard, and Gatesden, and Gilbertyn.
Of his diete mesuarble was he,
For it was no superfluitee,
But of greet norissing and digestable.
His studie was but litel on the bible.
In sangwin and in pers he clad was al,
Lyned with taffata and with sendal;
And yet he was but esy of dispence;
He kept that he wan in pestilence.
For gold in phisik is a cordial,
Therefore he lovede gold in special.

At this time, Petrarch, traditionally called Father of the Renaissance, denounced scholasticism and asked physicians to free themselves from the Arabists who had their own restricting scholastic tradition and almost inadvertently had subverted humanism. With the passing of monastic influences and the competence achieved by scholastic methods, it was to be expected that once again humanism would emerge. This required a more rigid and classical interpretation of the compilations of the Arabs on their Greek mentors. In the writings of the Arabian physicians, resentment against the positivity of Galen had appeared frequently. This was associated with a sense of need for the forthright, if disconcerting, methods of Aristotle. In aging particularly, Aristotle was nothing if not blunt and yet to the Arabs he was "the summit of Greek philosophers."

In summary, monasticism had its own level of medicine, which was primarily preservative and even museum-like, but it was influenced by the environment of the times in which it existed. In an atmosphere of religious piety, veneration of relics, dependence unquestioned on faith, in a life lived on a wholly spiritual plane, it would be natural to see an escape into visions, forms of faith-healing, and confirmation of miracles. What else could avail when Death was Black and Diseases were Kings, when malnutrition was the courtier and poverty the field of battle? The old could account for little in such desperate circles. Who could talk of the living and the old when the signature of that epidemic-ridden century was death, decimating, intrusive, inescapable, plague death? Even the term decimating is a kindness. In the plague of 1381, almost a quarter of the population of Europe succumbed.

The Renaissance

The three forms of thought overlapped in the 13th and 14th centuries. With the rise of the universities in the 13th century, primarily as successors to the abbey schools of Charlemagne, the three intellectual dogmas met. If any one of them had been dominant, it would have stultified the atmosphere of the university. The interplay of their methods and ideas was stimulating. Even at the present, universities in a sense are monastic, scholastic, and humanistic; but only insomuch as they serve for excursions of fresh thought do they serve the future.

The University of Padua added medicine to its curriculum in the latter part of the 13th century. From the 10th century on there had been medical teachers at Montpellier. The University of Naples had overshadowed Salerno. Roger Bacon studied at Oxford and at the University of Paris.

The desperate concept of the Crusades announced at the Council of Clermont in 1096 was, in a sense, a diversion from the misery of the present by a holy assignment of the cause of European ills to the defilement of the Holy Land by the Moslems. The succession of these was a recurring international phenomenon born out of the desperation of disease, nourished by misconceptions, and parent to untold misery and death.

In 1348, Europe was violated by a severe plague. Tuberculosis, smallpox, malaria, leprosy, plague, to say nothing of nutritional problems, personal violence, and other threats lurked over the population as an ever-present warning of mortality. It was a rare place from hut to palace which did not have its pock-marked individuals, its victims of infections, and its deaths among young and old from acute catastrophic diseases.

The Renaissance started with the universities. Petrarch was pacing off the future. It was an age of discovery. When the Turks failed in their assault on Constantinople and later, Vienna, Greek scholars, artists and teachers swarmed over Europe. European printing had its beginning. Copernicus widened the astronomical horizons that he scanned. The precursors of the Reformation, the spiritual ancestors of Luther, were appearing. One could attack the Church and survive. Humanism, never dead, rose again.

The 14th century was odd, difficult, unhappy, and a time best characterized as transitional. Scholasticism was declining. The extension of monastic thought beyond the cloister was marked for decease. Universities were rebellious children of staid and conforming parents; they broke their bonds. When facts were forced to bend to an *a priori* system, that system wrote its own doom. The men of theological schools could not suppress questions forever no matter how many questioners were suppressed in the process.

In aging, Arnoldus de Villanova, the Arabist and yet European physician, and Roger Bacon, the Franciscan and experimentalist, were those two who carried the knowledge of aging from the great era of the 13th century into the turbulence of the 14th century.

15th Century; 16th Century

By the 15th century, events were moving fast. The study of man in his humanistic sense came to the fore. Humanism

is the term especially applied to the movement which in the 15th century broke through the medieval tradition of scholastic theology and philosophy in Western Europe and devoted itself to the rediscovery and direct study of ancient classics.

It was a direct offspring of the successful revolt against the superimposed ecclesiastical authority (Johnson, 1835). Linacre (1517) translated the Greeks into Latin. Rabelais, the physician, was a foremost French humanist (Putnam, 1928; Rabelais, 1532).

It was the medical humanists who largely effected the liberation of medicine from the domination of Galen and Avicenna as they began to study Hippocrates and other Greek texts in the original and with an open mind.

Since humanism must involve man in his entire cycle free of the artificialities of abnormal social and religious forces, aging naturally shared in the process. America had been discovered. There was a route around Africa to India. Knighthood in armor was deflowered. Men began to distinguish themselves with school insignia and degrees instead of heralds and shield markings. The Reformation had started. It still awaited that particular signal when Luther attached his protest, the Ninety-five Theses, to a church door in Wittenberg in 1517. This was not an isolated act but the crest of a wave which broke at the end of a long swell.

In this century, too, old age had its champion, an Italian, Gabriele Zerbi (1489). To him is given the credit of having written the first monograph on old age which was put into print (Rome, 1489). This work was dedicated to Pope Innocent VIII, and although it relied on the tried and true authorities in the same sense as Roger Bacon and the others, it used a word descriptive of physicians who were to be known as specialists in old age, namely the gerontocomi.

Zerbi was born in Corgné, near Verona, in 1468. He practiced medicine in Padua and Venice and taught philosophy at Padua and in Bologna. Subsequently he was called to Rome as professor of medicine. He received a flattering and substantially better offer, left this post where he taught medical history, and returned to Padua in 1495 to teach medicine. His work on old age was a product of his earlier period, written when he was just 21, if his given natal date of 1468 is cor-

Fig. 6. Gabriele Zerbi published his work on older age medical affairs in Rome, 1489. He lived from 1468 to 1505, and his worthwhile career was terminated by his assassination in Dalmatia. Mr. Richard J. Durling, History of Medicine Division, National Library of Medicine discovered that Zerbi's portrait "is found in the only copy of Zerbi's work to be printed on vellum, now held by the Vatican Library. The book is a presentation copy dedicated to Pope Sixtus IV, and shows the Pope seated on his throne. Of the two kneeling figures before him, the figure on the right, shown in profile, is probably Zerbi himself; the other figure may be the artist." (Courtesy, Department of Photography, Vatican Library)

rect. The book *Gerontocomica Scillicet de Senum Cura atque Victu* (Zerbi, 1489) contains a good deal of information on the general hygiene of old age. As is to be expected, he summarized the work of the Arabic physicians, made reference to astrological influences, and gave, as Zeman (1945) said, a very clear picture of the medical features of old age. This was a factual approach to these problems and reflected the change in attitude from the past to such masters of the 16th century as André du Laurens (1599).

In the prologue of the book, the Galenic concept was reviewed and 300 diseases seen commonly in the old were noted. The work was substantiated by Hippocratic descriptions of the clinical aspects of older age diseases. In the subsequent 57 chapters, means for the retardation of old age were outlined. The years from 30 to 60 are described as the precursors, and those after 60, as the veritable state of old age. In systematic order, the causes and characteristics of old age, the duration of life, the influence of astrological forces, proper sites for homes for the aged, regimens of health, and the usual bizarre, even baroque remedies were described. In the last chapter the inevitability of death is discussed. "Old age," Zerbi wrote, "is inevitable, but its end is uncertain." Only through the practice of a special study of old age along Galenic lines would it be possible to retard the natural changes of age.[2]

In 1505, Zerbi had become so well known that when the Doge of Venice was asked to recommend a physician to treat a dropsical pasha in Turkey, the name of the Paduan professor was proposed. Zerbi took his son with him on the trip. The patient under treatment responded so satisfactorily that Zerbi was recompensed in a most liberal fashion and permitted to start for home. While traveling to Dalmatia, his erstwhile patient died, quite suddenly. Thinking that this was due to the delayed action of poisons purposely administered, agents of the defunct ruler pursued Zerbi, killed his son in his presence in an atrocious manner, and then did the same to the father and luckless physician. This brought to an end a life of less than 50 years duration in which great promise and ability were terminated in a manner of violence which somehow tells more of this period of time than more formal studies.

Zerbi, famous for his anatomical studies, had lived when Leonardo da Vinci was enacting the role of Renaissance man. The Vatican Library had been founded and the first medical work had been published in print in 1457. Copernicus, Michelangelo, Julius II, the *auto da fé* of Spain, epidemics in England (bubonic plague) and Germany (smallpox) were concurrent. Syphilis had its very first notations. In 1509 Henry VIII came to the English throne. Vesalius was working at his anatomical text. Magellan went around the world, or at least part of his fleet did, in 1519 and 1520. Great medical and surgical minds, such as Paracelsus, Paré, and Jerome Cardan were at work. Hospitals were founded throughout the known world.

In 1464 there was born in Venice to the distinguished Cornaro family, a son named Luigi. He traced his lineage to the ancient Roman line of the Cornelii who were among the early settlers of Venice. Although he came to be known as the Centenarian of Venice, he left that city and lived most of his life in Padua. This migration was due to family connivances in which he had lost some of the prerogatives of his noble birth. He lived the profligate life of the nobleman of his times, which had a weakening impact on his poor constitution. By the age of 35 he was able to list that he had stomach trouble, colic, gout, fever, extreme thirst, and a number of other conditions. Convinced that all of these problems were due to his intemperance, particularly in nutritional matters, he altered his life's program arbitrarily and regained his health by rigid discipline. Although he had no medical degree, he was sure of his health methods and their results and wrote of them for the enlightenment of others.

He married a lady of noble family by whom he had one daughter and ultimately 11 grandchildren in whom he took great pride. On every side, he received much acclaim for his successful survival, for his architectural works, and just about everything else that a man could want.

About a half century after he had instituted his plan of health, he decided to write a brief essay about it. He said from what he had learned from observations of himself that his constitution required 12 ounces of solid food and 14 ounces of fluid daily, primarily as fresh wine. He learned to avoid extremes of temperature, violent exercise, and the like. He called this chapter: *La Vita Sobria*. It was a pleasantly emotional and per-

---

[2] The discovery of this special feature of geriatric history was the result of the scholarly investigation of Dr. Frederic D. Zeman (1945). During a review of the literature of aging, Dr. Zeman found the reference to the work of Zerbi. He was able to locate a copy in the then Army Medical Library and made arrangements for its translation, which, as he says, "reveals Zerbi's clear understanding of the problems of old age, and his remarkably realistic approach to their alleviation."

sonal description of his illnesses and methods of treatment. He said that he had been warned by physicians of his excesses. He experimented on himself for those foods, drinks, and methods best suited to his own nature. He enjoyed rest, good ventilation, avoided extremes of exposures to sun and wind, refused bleedings and purgings, even when his life was endangered in an accident, and always lectured on the values of temperance. In a way, he had come to a program much like that of Galen, who, 1200 years earlier, had adapted a rigorous scheme of living because of delicate health and also had profited with long life. The essay of Cornaro was a little on the prideful side in which his home, country place, villa, habits, daughter, grandchildren, singing talent, work, architectural feats, and even a comedy written at the age of 83 came in for favorable mention. All of this was done in such a nice self-centered way with a Tom Thumb pulled-out-a-plum air that it is rather hard to do any more in the way of criticism than to like what he wrote.

Possibly surprised by his literary and vital successes, Cornaro wrote a commentary on his original essay three years later. In it he said that the natural term of life is 100 years and that survival is subject to some astrological influences. Proper eating was a method of restoring the natural moisture. On page 87 of this essay he gave the details of his own diet.

Five years later, a third discourse was written in the form of a letter in which Cornaro said with some complacency that his ability to sing and to write was such that professors from a nearby university said "that I could by no means be considered an old man." In this chapter, which is a commentary and defense of his original ideas, he judged himself to be an ordinary mortal composed of the routine four elements, earth, water, fire, and air. In the context, this might have been a concession on his part. Finally, at age 91, he wrote a brief final essay in which he stated that "the orderly and temperate life has the power and strength to remove the causes of illness." In this penultimate panegyric of praise and thanks, somehow Cornaro again avoided giving offense. In defense of the brevity of his four contributions with their broad implications, he said that "long discourses are read by a few only, but brief ones are read by many." History has borne him out.

Up to this time, all references to aging had consisted of variations on the Grecian themes that it was inevitable, that a general regimen of health could influence the rate of progression of what was otherwise the inevitable force of senescence, and that there were some unusual remedies to assist in rejuvenation. The greatness of the little gray-bearded Venetian, also called the Apostle of Senescence, is the fact that he rejected the mystery about aging by the exposition of practical and obvious methods of influencing it and its diseases. He did not resort to gold water, "eau d'or," or remedies which could not be put into print because the unfaithful might benefit thereby, or noxious mixtures of viper's blood, dung, chemicals, and all other remedies more suitable to fable than to fact. Simply and ingenuously, he offered a nutritional method of altering the nature of the life cycle as well as the time of onset and rate of impairment of chronic diseases.

Fig. 7. Luigi Cornaro was known as the Apostle of Senescence on the basis of the four essays which he wrote over a number of years and in which he related his personal habits and the rules which he observed through a very long life. His rules of diet were promulgated in a period of dietary catch-as-catch-can, which had an instant as well as a long-term effect. This portrait, which has been ascribed to Tintoretto, is in the Pitti Palace Gallery in Florence and the photograph was obtained from the Alinari Brothers of that city.

The unreality of the catch phrases about the retardation of age and the maintenance of youth (its counterpart in appeal), faded into the medieval mist. Concepts of caloric restriction having a 20th century stamp have a matter-of-factness which exposed the illusionary nature of unwarranted therapeutic concepts. In his evaluation of the proportions of foods and liquids in a recommended dietary approach to health which has been shown to compare favorably with most modern diets, Cornaro gave mankind the first practical method of altering aging. He offered his own life and works as examples and lived what he preached. Scientists prior to him had advised temperance but never with quantitive outlines by which the scheme could be followed.

Cornaro's life was evidence that his methods were applicable to the well being and survival of the human species. When his Galenic and astrological references are overlooked, when his deep religious devotion and various tender little prideful recitations are put aside, the fact remains that he had made a momentous discovery. In that time, when the whole world was opening and expanding before the mind of inquiring man, six years before the birth of Shakespeare, and when the heavy-ringed and authoritative hand of ecclesiastical Rome was being lifted by a number of forces, the tiny Italian text printed in Padua in 1558 received its identification.

Weary of words, epidemics, church indulgences, and in pursuit of physical as well as spiritual relief, such as that promised by the Reformation, and as the world that was known became doubled, trebled, and quadrupled by the men of science in astronomy, navigation, and the arts, a gentle little man told the toiling and moiling and expanding populus of his world that there was a method in each man's hands by which he might, just might with luck, change his personal susceptibility to premature senility and the superimposed strata of diseases. Removed from the platitudes of the old quoted regimens of health, freed of the odors and impossibilities of the secret remedies and unbelievable concoctions of medical authorities, this was a tidy, clean, and brave new work in a brave new world. It gave courage to those who believed and broke bonds which a fixed social, religious, economic, and medical world had placed literally, liturgically and figuratively on mankind. The 16th century effort placed a détente against any possibility of a relapse to the old ways. The furred and gowned professors and teachers are just about forgotten, except by historians and painters, or those who deal in the esoterics of an interesting era. Luigi Cornaro, exemplary of his age, wrote a little book and changed his world.

17th Century

The 17th century opened to phrases such as this:
> Let me embrace thee, good old chronicle,
> That hast so long walk'd hand in hand with time.
> Hector, *The Tragedy of Troilus and Cressida,*
> by Shakespeare (1602)

This type of understanding of the old was new. This age had in it some of the qualities of the 4th century pre-Christian Greece. There was such exuberance in the opening of the era that even a simple tabulation of names and events is exciting. It was the time of Shakespeare and F. Bacon, Harvey, Raleigh, Elizabeth I, Essex, Hawk and Drake, Copernicus and Rembrandt, Galileo and Leeuwenhoek, Louis XIV and Sir Christopher Wren, Peter the Great and Sir Edward Coke—in short, a time of the great doing wonderful things. Into the most luxurious of this odoriferous and luxuriant society there was born on January 22, 1561, one of those minds of such content as to be forever contemporary (Bowen, 1963).

Francis Bacon lived two lives. In one he was a gentleman and knight who lived by all the rules of his times by which to aggrandize himself, and he succeeded. Born in a great house on the Thames not far from the Tower of London where he was to spend a few days ultimately in the time of his disgrace, he had been courtier to the Virgin Queen and adviser to her successor, James I. He played prominent parts in many of the dramas of his day and became Lord Chancellor of England like his father, Nicholas. From this post he was thrown down to live the final years of his life in disgrace.

It was during this period that his second and parallel life came to fruition. From his early years, after an education at Cambridge's Trinity College, and the attainment of the position of barrister in 1582, subsequent to readings at Gray's Inn, he attempted in a variety of ways to rise high in the kingdom. At the same time, he was trying to find a sphere big enough for his imagination, a stage broad enough for his entrances. Between the courtier and the scholar, the former a figure in Elizabeth's land of 5 million people and the latter a scholar whose mind encompassed all thinking from original sin to the indefinite present, no common ground could be found.

By the age of 36 he had written the first ten of his famous essays and followed with a succession of works, the *Advancement of Learning* in 1605, the *Novum Organum* in 1620, and in 1623 his *Historia Vitae et Mortis*. His grand scheme was the *Instauratio Magna* in which he conceived of a way to know "the order of nature and error of man." This mind dared to put itself up against all that had gone before it. Whereas Plato aimed to find and encourage the best minds of the state to the benefit of individual liberty, Bacon apparently felt that mankind had to make a fresh start from the errors which dated to the fall of man. So great were his questions, so penetrating were his phrases to which posterity gave the term "Baconian" that he almost bypassed other fine minds of his time.

Nevertheless, in his master plan, with its endless works in bits and pieces, he encompassed nothing less than a new inquisitive start by mankind to be tabulated in a rigid review of all facts. He planned to explore all possibilities. In his lifetime there was much that he left incompleted but nothing that he did was dull. What he touched he changed. What he distilled, others saw as if for the first time. His mind exceeded the possibilities of his age. He knew some of the sterility of scholasticism and pointed the way to the experimental. In writing of Plato, Scott Buchanan said that

The first and most obvious symptom that (education) is taking effect is an incorruptible urge to question things that have always been taken for granted.

This is what Bacon certainly did in a grand way. In his work on aging, *Historia Vitae et Mortis*, Bacon started as follows:

To the Present Age, and Posterity. Greeting

and goes to the theme that the inquiry into truth, the knowledge of truth and the belief in truth are sovereign for man.

Is was but natural that one who took all of man in all of time as his experimental material should have had something to say about old age. He noted many things about it.

Repair of tissue in older age is effected unsatisfactorily.

Death is due to loss of inner spirit and inability to effect repair.

Age is nothing of itself, being only the measure of time . . . and the cause of the manifestations of aging is the dryness of body moisture.

He believed that three things were necessary to life, namely, adequate motion, body coolness, and proper nutrition. Like Cornaro, whose work he knew, he believed in moderation in all things, and especially in diet. As to exercise, he thought it to be useful but added that

exercise, if it be much, is no friend to prolongation of life, which is one reason why women live longer than men, because they stir less.

Personally, Bacon was a bit of a hypochondriac who stuffed himself with varieties of evil tasting drugs, quoted a number of platitudes (incidentally, many current platitudes were the sprightly phrases of Bacon originally), and proposed a complete program of good hygiene for old age. This included fresh air, adequate sleep, temperance, pleasant activities, happy memories of a satisfactory childhood, which is a thought which he had derived from Marsilio Ficino (1498) the Platonist, the avoidance of extreme changes, the adherence (this man above all) to a calm approach to things, and the like.

Withal, he ended by saying that "age will not be defied."

Fig. 8. Francis Bacon, Lord Verulam, lived from 1561-1626 A.D. He was the scion of a distinguished English family and was born in one of England's most famous mansions, York House in London. After studies at Trinity College, Cambridge, he was recognized for his abilities in philosophy as early as his 16th year. One of England's greatest minds, his life was one of successes and tragedies and his thought has been preserved in his works as part of the inheritance of Western culture. (Photograph courtesy National Library of Medicine)

It was in this vein that this the last of the great medievalists wrote. His phrases have little in them of his urge to re-examine everything and to subject questions to answers by the experimental method. Although he spoke of old age in blunt endpoints, he made no particular contributions to its knowledge nor much to its literature beyond his aphorisms. As a man, he knew from his salutations to posterity that the world scene in which he was a courtier bore no reality to the world scene that he had in his mind. He knew that the timing was wrong. He knew that techniques were not available. But his thoughts could throw a beam into the unknowing future. Relatively speaking, he was enmired in his age. He tried to project himself forward by the force of ideas, and he came nearer than anyone to succeed in this Faustian-like tragedy in which fresh and buoyant knowledge was his Margaret.

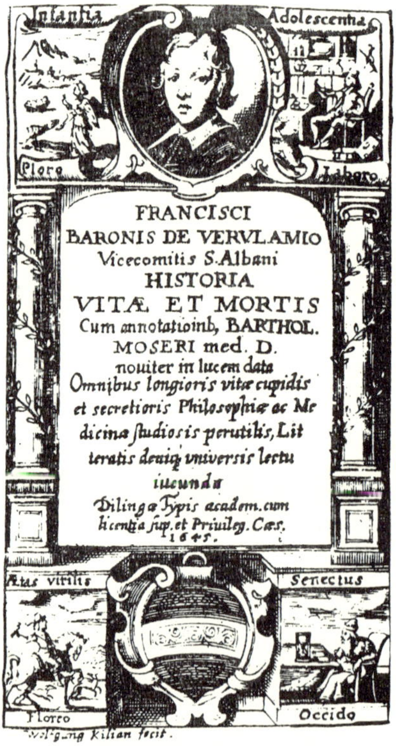
Infantia
Adolescentia
Ploro
Laboro
FRANCISCI
BARONIS DE VERVLAMIO
Vicecomitis S. Albani
HISTORIA
VITÆ ET MORTIS
Cum annotationib. BARTHOL.
MOSERI med. D.
nouiter in lucem data
Omnibus longioris vitae cupidis
et secretioris Philosophiae ac Me
dicinae studiosis perutilis, Lit
teratis deniq; universis lectu
iucunda
Dilingae Typis academ. cum
licentia sup. et Priuileg. Caes.
1645.
Ætas virilis
Senectus
Floreo
Occido
Wolfgang Kilian fecit.

Fig. 9. Title page of Sir Francis Bacon's book, *Historia Vitae et Mortis*, 1645. In the four corners of this small page there is an engraving of the four major stages of life interpreted by the activities of each period. The pictures signify the era as Infancy, Adolescence, Virility, and Old Age.

Son of the Elizabethan period, contemporary of all great minds, dweller in a time of savage epidemics, he died in 1626 of pneumonia. He was an aristocrat in body and mind. These in him may have been incompatible. The palaces of Whitehall are gone. The mansions along the Thames and the fields around the City of London are changed. Bacon's works and words are still fresh.

In general, those who accepted the scholarly responsibility of defining the role of man in his times for all time of necessity had to extend their observations into all phases of life. This included potentials for survival and the nature of the senescent process. Such views on aging as part of the humanistic involvement belong in every historical summary and can contribute to it. In aiming at a universality of concept which included all of man in his life span, the scientist *cum* philosopher (or the reverse) would have aimed poorly if he had failed in his effort to relate man to his aging as part of the totality of his thought. He had to make reflections on all human potentials. This included specific capacities for natural survival, the nature of individual old age, and the components of man in a social world. The variance between that which the preoccupied observer could offer in his own time and his certain understanding of what man could be were constricted in each era. The man under observation was promethean and his studies became equally bound. The scientist's limitations were never more evident than when he attempted to challenge human inevitabilities in each period with man's obvious possibilities. Francis Bacon for one knew both range and restrictions. No conjunction of words gave better evidence of this than the title he gave to his work on old age, *The History of Life and Death*.

In the founding of a gerontological science, as part of all biological effort, the practical issue was to determine methods within the limits of sound hypotheses. This was the way to take the measure of what things are, as essential steps in finding out what they mean. Both being and meaning are absolute values, seemingly distinct, but are seen invariably to emerge from a common root. This unity has always been known, but technical abilities had to progress slowly. At times there was the danger that technical methods would conceal rather than reveal the true significance of things. At such times, men like Bacon set the record in proper order again.

When Bacon died, the population of London had swelled beyond the 200,000 mark despite wars, floods of diseases, hunger, social inequities, and all other limitations. Men lived, and lived longer. The concepts of old age became a part of the normal reflection (Santorio, 1728). The colonists reached Virginia. The Pilgrims stepped off at Plymouth. Rembrandt was painting, and Louis XIV became the pox'd Sun King of France. Lisbon had an epidemic of smallpox. London followed suit with the malignant Great Plague of 1665 followed by the Great Fire of 1666 in which St. Paul's Church burned and Sir Christopher Wren, possibly in his pleasant house on the Thames, planned a new London. The ages of microscopy, histology, and chemistry succeeded to the sound anatomical efforts of Vesalius. Sydenham was England's master's clinician. Peter the Great ruled Russia. John Sebastian Bach was born, and England had its revolution in 1688. This was the world that left Bacon and his self-imposed task behind to enter the period of the 18th century.

18th Century

In aging there were many studies. From the great and confusing heights of the Elizabethan era, the world embarked on the more settled times of the new 18th century. At Hintes Hall near Lichfield in Staffordshire, John Floyer was born April 25, 1649 (Gunn, 1936). He graduated in medicine at Oxford after 12 years at that university, where the courses in medical education were scholarly and inadequate. The Regius Professor of Medicine, to which chair a Canadian-American, William Osler, was to succeed 200 years later, read to his class twice a week from Hippocrates and Galen.

Floyer was a good classical student and learned his early medicine from his reading, which gave his work a strong Galenical slant. At his time at Oxford there were many great men, such as Sydenham, Boyle, Lower, Willis, Mayow, and others. Floyer went back to Lichfield, where he practiced medicine until he died in 1734. In the interim he had been knighted in 1686, possibly for some political service rendered to James II. His friend and patient, Dr. Samuel Johnson, was touched by the King for scrofula, doubtless on the advice of Floyer. Both of these men suffered from asthma. Floyer wrote on this subject in addition to his views on emphysema and some experiments on respiration, and it is quite likely that the works were published by Johnson's father. Floyer invented a watch for accurate recording of the pulse, tried to determine blood volume precisely, advised on the values of cold bathing, and published a book on old age. With unconscious irony, it was said of him: "There is no record of any other notable events in his life, except the publication of his several books." Despite a limited medical education, Floyer studied the natural history of diseases with acuity and acquired a fine reputation in his locale. He was an original observer in a world peopled with great minds. "His works show independence of thought and the spirit of research." One example was his observations on a dyspneic mare outlined in his excellent account on emphysema.

His book: *Medicina Gerocomica, or the Galenic Art of Preserving Old Men's Healths*, was published in London in 1724. Like his other works, this book was well received and soon went into other editions as well as into translations. Not very novel in observations, the title and the specificity of application made this little work a major landmark in the scientific inquiry into aging. Its title was a measure of its true limitations. In an appendix, Floyer advised on the use of unctions

Fig. 10. Sir John Floyer lived his life in England, 1649-1734. Despite the inadequate facilities for education in medicine at Oxford at that time, he became an excellent observer and projected his skill in his text on aging. This drawing is his only known likeness and was found by chance in a volume in the Bodleian Library at Oxford.

and added a letter on a regimen for the maintenance of youth. The traditional ideas of old age are repeated and the particular observations made by the author in his own daily clinical rounds were offered as a program of treatment.

Other aspects of this violent and exciting century had much more to hold attention than this gentle book by a doctor from a county shire in England. When Floyer was practicing, there was a pandemic of dysentery in Europe. London was swept with a massive epidemic of smallpox in 1719. Marseilles once again had its visitation of the plague. Peru was swept by influenza. In Russia, Catherine the Great opened a Secret Hospital for Venereal Diseases in St. Petersburg. Linnaeus was undertaking his great classification, which led to the work of Wallace and Darwin. Boerhaave was such a distinguished physician that his mailing address on at least one occasion was simply: Europe.

Medicina Gerocomica :
OR, THE
Galenic ART
Of PRESERVING
Old Men's Healths,
EXPLAIN'D:
In Twenty CHAPTERS.

To which is added an APPENDIX, concerning the Use of Oyls and Unction, in the Prevention and Cure of some Diseases. As also a Method, from a *Florentine Physician*, of curing *Convulsions* and *Epilepsies*, by external Operation.

By Sir JOHN FLOYER, Kt. of *Lichfield*, M.D.

Pugnandum tanquam contra morbum, sic contra Senectutem. Cicero de Senectute.
Calida lavatio & pueris & Senibus apta est vinum dilutius puer s, Senibus meracius. Celf. de re Medi. lib. 2

LONDON:
Printed for J. Ifted, at the Golden-Ball, between St Dunstan's Church and Chancery Lane End, in Fleet-street. MDCCXXIV. Price stitcht 2 s.

Fig. 11. This is a reproduction of the title page of Floyer's book.

Goethe was at work in his life struggle with Faust. The world was torn by that political geographical contest to which has been given the name the Seven Years' War. While smallpox was destroying 3 million people in India in one year, the United States was coming into being. Benjamin Franklin and Benjamin Rush made their cultured contributions to the knowledge of old age, among many other things. Charles Willson Peale wrote an 18th century tract on old age that was more artless than Cornaro's. As the century came to a close there was a sudden interest in longevity by Easton, Christian Hoffman, Hufeland (1797) and others (Bichat, 1800). France was torn by revolution and Napoleon led his world into the 19th century. To the sound of Beethoven's *Eroica*, Europe groaned and bled and died and lived. In 1815 there was a great battle near the little town of Waterloo in Belgium and modern times had arrived.

19th Century

Ten years after that battle, in November, 1825, Jean-Martin Charcot was born in France. Reticent and withdrawn, he became a superb teacher and clinician. His talents of observation were bolstered by his ability to sketch. After graduation in medicine, he entered the rigorous gauntlet of the French faculty methods of promotion. By the age of 37 he had identified the unusual values of La Salpêtrière and lectured there on diseases of the aged, joint disorders, neurological problems, and all of that vast array of material which waited for discernment and classification.

It would be impossible to write of Charcot without mention of the hospital associated with his name. For four centuries La Salpêtrière had been an asylum for the old as well as for those with neurological and psychiatric disorders. It was founded by royal edict in 1656 as a refuge for the beggars, infirm, insane, and aging of Paris. Over the years it became transformed and most of this change was due to the clinicians who served on its faculty.

Through the Franco-Prussian War of 1870, Charcot continued his clinical studies and finally achieved the chair of what was the first full professorship of neurology as an independent discipline. Reserved, brilliant, unsparing, resourceful, and energetic, he went from one level of success to another. When elected to the French Academy of Science in 1883, he observed:

I believe that the practice of medicine does not have a real autonomy but that it lives on borrowed discoveries and applications; and without a continuous scientific renovation it would become decadent. A physician is only as good a clinician as he is a pathologist.

Aside from his basic efforts and responsibilities in medicine, he traveled widely, loved music, painted, gloried in museums, read Seneca and Plato, as well as Shakespeare, who was among his favorites. His love of animals was so intense that he could not approve of vivisection. His Tuesday soirées and dinners were lavish and popular. All of this was in conformity with his motto: *nihil humanum à me alienum puto.*

From the very first, Charcot showed interest in the aging. Between the years of 1862 and 1870, he gave a series of lectures on the diseases of the aged, chronic ailments, and neurological disorders. He prepared his lectures with intensity and used various teaching devices, which included his ability as a draftsman to express his concept in clear visual demonstrations. He knew that certain

Fig. 12. Jean-Martin Charcot, the master French clinician, who lived from 1825 to 1893. Of him it is said that "Each year at Salpêtrière in a small ward, which had been provisionally vacated, he lectured on diseases of the aged, rheumatism, gout . . ." His works contain many quotable statements and his stature is unquestioned in a number of areas of which gerontology has been a particular one. (Photograph courtesy of the National Library of Medicine)

diseases in the old have a long period of latency in the formation of the ultimate pathological picture. He observed also that the nature of the medical situation promoted the greater likelihood of failure in diagnosis of a number of serious lesions in the deceptive old bodies.

Thermometry received impetus from him and he found its application useful in the diagnosis of diseases in the old.

He had strong opinions, such as the fact that senile tremors are not so common as had been stated. He said

Often playwrights depicted in their comedies, old people as having tremors of the head and limbs. This is a mistake that Shakespeare, a scrupulous observer in addition to being a great poet, knew how to avoid.

The study of aging as a property of the compilers and the commentators should have come to an end in Charcot's clear remarks. He drew a line as clear as his drawing between the last remnants of the empirical age and the first decades of the scientific one. As this austere, industrious, and illustrious scientist worked, he expressed himself with the type of lucidity that knows identification in every century. The science of aging emerged from the old rooms of his hospital, which in itself was a social outcast that blossomed into a major source of medical fact. The merger of social and medical interests had many battles to face, but to Charcot there was never any doubt of the result. When he died in August, 1893, he had given substance to scientific visions which are still in the process of completion.

His book, *Clinical Lectures on the Diseases of Old Age*, translated by Leigh Hunt, contained additional lectures by A. L. Loomis. It was published in this form in 1881 although the original French edition of lesser coverage was published in Paris in 1867. The longer English edition had 31 chapters, of which Charcot wrote the first 21 and Loomis the remainder. The book opened with a chapter on senile pathology followed by a number on gout, arthritis, an appendix on thermometry, and some observations on fevers. It was introduced as follows

The course which we today inaugurate is proposed to acquaint you with the general characteristics that distinguish the pathology of old age from that of adult life and to fix your attention on some of those diseases which are more especially met with in hospitals for the aged.

It was he who said that medicine of the past "has always been deficient in those elements necessary to the construction of a positive theory," in contrast to his views of the possibilities of the medicine of his own day. He knew that a radical revolution was occurring in his medical world and he ascribed it to the studies of the great anatomists, the observations of the Greek physiologists, and the emergence of studies in pathology. These definitive views were in contrast to the sterile emphasis formerly placed on the uncorrelated study of symptoms. Charcot was very much aware of the fact that "ideas are more stubborn than facts" and this is a phrase which could reach from Hippocrates through Galen to Francis Bacon.

When these lectures were being given on those aging females who, from the nature of their social world, had the least expectancies of survival, the American Civil War was engaged in a land with a population of 35 million. The Italian state was beginning to emerge. Prussia and Austria had fought a war. The Reconstruction Era in the South was to get under way. New machines were multiplying. The Atlantic cable, the cotton gin, balloons, heavier than air machines, uses of steam, discovery of oil, mass immigrations to the United States, expansion of the British Empire, and the growth of the era of colonialism, were only a few of those changes in the world of Darwin, Ehrlich, Koch, and so many others. Charcot's work was part of these vibrant times.

Populations were growing. Men had shown more likelihood of living to the human species' capacities. The great cities of Europe were built. The outlines of nations seemed to acquire permanence. The nature of future times of peace and of struggle had been defined. Those who lived into old age received identification with Charcot. He knew that

most of the medical works of the past century which touch, in a special manner, upon the senile period of life have a literary or a philosophical bearing; they are more or less ingenious paraphrases of the famous treatise 'De Senectute' of the Roman orator.

In an early lecture he pointed out what all of that band which had preceded him on this quest for knowledge of the medical aspects of old age could have said in their respective centuries, "The importance of a special study of the diseases of old age cannot be contested at this date." Modern medicine was yet to be born, but one of its greatest students had seen in aging a key to many of the problems of living and had tried to offer a valid hypothesis for its explicit exploration. The industrial and social facts of the times were major forces in the creation of an aging salient in the population. Having done so, it was necessary to find the men and the means in every field, which included medicine, to cope with the new issues.

In the 19th century those like Charcot had begun to be wary of the grand designs for the prevention of old age. These had been the invention of shrewd men based on authority and hope rather than substantive knowledge. One might have expected as much merit from King David's Abishag or Zerbi's favorite remedy of human milk, at its natural source. In Charcot there was a cold, almost implacable, desire to know, to identify, to classify, so that the management of aging and the aged should be based on an established pathological physiology.

His integrity put a halt to much but not all of the nonsense and divided the studies of aging into two permanent lines of inquiry. One consisted of the investigation of the *facts* of age; to describe its effects and to measure its capacities. This, to a degree, is a logical derivation of the best of the Galenical approach. The other looked for *principles* in aging, for causes, for a central theme such as autointoxication or for a humoral basis. This is more basically derivative from the Hippocratic concept.

The former is a descriptive procedure. The latter, when achieved, will touch on the basis of the whole organic pattern in which aging is an unbroken part whose occurrence is not a property to be manipulated in the aged but a method to alter the rate of progression of those limitations associated with long survival. Both lines of study are of ancient lineage. These two great divisions in which progress is being made are challenged and alternately joined or set asunder by the unrelenting inquisition and ruthlessness of the Aristotelian approach. Until the full story is known, these are times for modesty and humility in gerontology.

It was only natural that those who ventured to comment on the great scientific themes of life did not hesitate, and even felt a responsibility, to include their observations on aging. This was a realistic and expected part of their personal scientific equity. Their comments, primarily opinions and interpretations of the Greeks, and often from unsatisfactory translations, were all that they could be. The views of the classicists, which had the fine edge of a humanistic orientation, by chance were their greatest contribution to the knowledge of aging. It could not be expected to be more than that in view of the poverty of experiments and the quality of techniques available. As has been said in many ages and ways, there is certain timeliness in events. The world can wait much more than the span between the unnoticed Mendel of 1866 and the re-discovery by deVries in 1903. The true humanist is geared to this ultimacy and to this period of expectancy. Charcot quoted Graves to say: "Individuals take rest, but the general intelligence of mankind is forever sleepless." What the students of the past did generally was dignified, even if certain rare exceptions must be made for the out-and-out alchemistic charlatans like "Sir" John Hall, satirists like Cohausen, or experts in mass sex psychology like London's Graham.

The clinical pictures were acute and sound. The status of bedside and experimental observations slowly acquired a quantitative base in step-like fashion from Francis Bacon to the studies of the Belgian mathematician Quetelet in 1836 and observations of vital capacity by age made by Hutchinson in 1846. Clinging obsequiously to these pioneer and honest efforts, and always adding distortion to the picture, there were the unsupported flights of imagination of the quacksalvers who tempted belief by attractive if unsupported assertions of methods by which the senescent nature could be altered either in its progression or in its culmination. Roger Bacon's hidden remedy did no more and no less. Fortunately, the scientific era from 1750 learned to live rather tolerantly with these claims and to progress in ever-narrowing effective channels of investigations to the endpoint that aging should be understood in all of its aspects. Truth is not a declamation, no matter how boldly made or how loudly sounded. It is a state of actuality whose revelation is inevitable and absolute.

Conclusions

There is no core of mystery nor is there a hidden remedy in the medical care of the aging and the aged. The esoteric writings of the learned men of the 12th through the 19th centuries, and even those before and after, particularly in nonclinical areas, often partook of the nature of a plagiarized dream in which healthy *aging* was the goal. The confusion of aims and terms about aging, such as they were and are, made their objectives actually *non-aging*. Clinicians have always been more practical. Like Napoleon's grenadiers, they grumbled, but they always marched. Their functions as physicians have always been in the present, and in this regard they have changed very little through the centuries. When the dream of aging reached the stratum of a fantasy, the goal became greater and also less likely to obtain success since it was Elysian. Its aim seemed to be to attain to a method by which to retard old age on one hand and to restore youth on the other. At this point there was just no link to reality.

Efforts in aging of the human species consist of the constant attempt to close the gap between average species inherency to age (Hippocrates: Aging is inevitable) and environmental permissibility for longer survival (Diseases seek young men; old men seek diseases). Factual ways of retarding age and restoring youth remain remote and intangible. Once the full potentialities of human individual survival as a species and the environmental assistance thereto overlap, it will be a foregone conclusion that efforts will be brought to bear to alter this total span as well as to control the rate of loss of diminishing capacities (see George Bernard Shaw, *Back to Methuselah*). As a matter of fact, of course, these efforts have long been in effect, although to date they are almost wholly premature, with some very slight exceptions. At what age should retardation be started? What point will indicate that the regulation of environment and genetics has been successful? Although Hippocrates was quite pragmatic in his fatalism about ultimate senility, he made no such categorical statements about the rate of progression of senescence, nor did the very authoritative Galen. The truism, then, is that aging is inevitable but that the rate of its progression and some of its pathological counterparts may be modified.

Meanwhile the clinician, like the turbanned Arab, like the certaine clarke and ryght medycyne, the staffed and gowned physician, the laced and peruked Restoration figure, the top-hatted and tail-coated physician, and his very businesslike modern counterpart have incorporated in their duties the care of an increasing number of those successful in aging. "The scientific discipline in aging is beginning to acquire a collective identity as part of (humanistic) philosophy" (Freeman, 1961). Changes in rural life, the Industrial Revolution, the production of food surpluses, the benefits of social hygiene, the creation of concepts of public health—these are the methods. Physicians through the centuries were untrammelled by *causes* of aging since *their* special prerogatives were *results*. By and large, the clinical records of the medical perspectives in aging have been adequate.

References

Avicenna: *A treatise of the Canon of Avicenna*. O. C. Grunes, translator. Lerzac & Co., London, 1930.

Bacon, F.: *Historia vitae et mortis*. Dilligen, London, 1645; or History natural and experimental of life and death or the prolongation of life. W. Rawley, translator. W. Lee & H. Moreley. London, 1658.

Bacon, R.: *Opus magnus*. R. B. Burke, translator. Univ. Pa. Press, Philadelphia, 1928.

Bacon, R.: *The care of old age and preservation of youth*. R. Browne, translator. T. Flesher, London, 1683.

Beaumont, A.: Personal communication, 1964.

Bichat, X: *Recherches physiologiques sur la vie et la mort*. Brosson, Gabonet Cie., Paris, 1800.

Bowen, C. D.: *Francis Bacon, the temper of a man*. Little Brown & Co., Boston, 1963.

Breasted, J. H. (Editor): *The Edwin Smith Surgical Papyrus*. Chicago Univ. Press, Chicago, 1930.

Bryan, C. P. (translator): *The Papyrus Ebers*. Appleton & Co., New York, 1931.

Burstein, S.: The historical background of gerontology. *Geriatrics,* 10: 189-193 (Part I); 10: 328-332 (Part II); 10: 536-540 (Part III), 1955.

Campbell, D.: *Arabian medicine and its influence on the Middle Ages*. Kegan Paul, Frence, Trubner & Co., London, 1926.

Charcot, J. M.: *Clinical lectures on diseases of old age*. L. W. Hunt, translator. With additional lectures by A. L. Loomis. W. Wood & Co., N.Y., 1881.

Cornaro, L.: *Trattato de la vita sobria*. Gratioso Perchacino, Padua, 1558.

Cuffe, H.: *The differences of the ages of man's life; together with the original causes, progress, and end thereof*. A. Hatfield, London, 1607.

Ficinus, Marsilus: *De triplica vita (libri tres): De vita sana, de vita longa, and de vita coelitus comparandi*. Poncetus, Paris, 1547.

Floyer, J.: *Medicina gerocomica, or the Galenic art of preserving old men's healths*. F. Isted, London, 1724.

Freeman, J. T.: Gerontology and the Gerontological Society. *Gerontologist,* 1: 162-167, 1961.

Galen, C.: *De sanitate tuenda*. M. Green, translator. Charles C Thomas, Springfield, Ill., 1951.

Garrison, F. H.: *History of medicine* (reprinted). W. B. Saunders, Philadelphia, 7th Ed., 1960.

Gordon, B. L.: *Medieval and renaissance medicine*. Philosophical Library, London, 1959.

Grant, R. L.: Concepts of aging: a historical review. *Persp. Med. Biol.,* 6: 443-478, 1963.

Guillain, G.: *J. M. Charcot, his life—his work*. P. Bailey, Editor and translator. P. B. Hoeber, New York, N. Y., 1959.

Gunn, J. A.: *British masters of medicine, Sir John Floyer*. Med. Press & Circular, London, Oct. 3, 1934, 297-299. Also Power, Sir D'Arcy: Sir John Floyer, British Masters of Medicine, Med. Press & Circular, 17-23, London, 1936.

Hamilton, E.: *Echo of Greece*. W. W. Norton & Co., New York, 1930.

Harington, Sir J.: *The School of Salernum, the English version*. John Holme and John Press, London, 1607.

Haynes, M. S.: The supposedly Golden Age for the aged in Ancient Greece (a study of literary concepts of old age). *Gerontologist,* 2: 93-98, 1962.

Hufeland, C. W.: *Die Kunst das menschliche Leben zu verlängern*. F. Hass, Vienna and Prague, 1797.

Johnson, J. N.: *Life of Thomas Linacre*. Lumley (Publ.), London, 1835.

Laurens, A. du: *A discourse on the preservation of the sight: of melancholick diseases; of rheum, and of old age*. R. Surphlet, translator. F. Kingston, London, 1599.

Linacre, T.: (translator) *Galen's de sanitate tuenda*. Paris, 1517.

Putman, S.: *François Rabelais; man of the Renaissance*. Kape & H. Smith, N.Y., 1928.

Rabelais, F. (Editor): *Aphorisms of Hippocrates*. Printed for S. Gryphius, Lugduni, 1532.

Regimen (sanitatis) Salernitanum or Flos medicinae. —see Harington, Sir J.

Santorio Santorio: *medicina statica; being the aphorisms of Sanctorius*. J. Quincy, translator. Osborn, Longman, Newton, London, 1728.

Shakespeare, W.: *The tragedy of Croilus and Cressida*.

Soubiran, A.: Medical services under the Pharaohs. *Abbottempo.* 1: 19-23, 1963.

Sudhoff, K.: *Arnoldus de Villanova and Salerno, from Essays in the history of medicine*. F. H. Garrison, Editor & translator. Metrop. Life Press, New York, 1926.

Taylor, T. L.: *The Treatises of Aristotle*, translated from the Greek, On length of life and death. R. Wilks, London, 1808, p. 464.

Villanova, A. de: *De conservatione juventutis et retardatione senectutis*, written for King James of Spain and translated by J. Drummond, 1544, with additions from the *Breviarium of Arnaldus*. C. Dana, Editor. Elm Tree Press, Woodstock, Vt., 1912.

Woodruff, F. M.: *Roger Bacon, a biography*. J. Clarke & Co., London, 1938.

Zeitlin, S.: *Maimonides, a biography*. Bloch Publ. Co., New York, 1955.

Zeman, F. D.: Life's later years. *J. Mt. Sinai Hosp.,* 11: 339-334, 1945; 12: 783-791, 890-901, 939-953, 1945.

Zerbi, G.: *Gerontocomica, scilicet de senum cura, atque victu*. Ad Innocentam VIII, Pont. Max. Prologus, Rome, 1489.

The Historical Developments in the Biological Aspects of Aging and the Aged

Alfred H. Lawton, M.D., Ph.D.[1,2]

"Thus all the days of Methuselah were nine hundred and sixty-nine years and he died." (Genesis 5:27). For many this biblical citation has been the first acquaintance with the notion of aging and ultimate death. It has always been rather trite and certainly troublesome, since it presents an ultimate goal of an increasing life expectancy. It could serve as a text for social action, inasmuch as it implies uselessness of an extremely long life and justifies such slogans and catch phrases that urge the addition of life to years as well as years to life. As a matter of historical fact, the statement may be dismissed as a very primitive effort to account for the period between creation and the beginning of recorded history.

Methuselah and the other Biblical patriarchs probably represented in allegory the same epochs from dawn man to the diluvial period as the Sumerians recorded in their "list of kings." The Sumerian historians estimated that the period from creation to the flood was 465,000 years. Their calculations correspond well with the 500,000 years that modern anthropologists assume to have elapsed between the first true man and the first use of metal. According to the Sumerian chronology, each of their 10 rulers attained an average age of 45,000 years (Wendt, 1963). Truly, there were giants in those days.

Current ideas and concepts of aging arise from several cultural sources but are dominated by Judeo-Christian and classical Greek thoughts. The Bible stresses that age should bring reverence, status, and prestige. In Exodus, it is stated that whoever curses his father or his mother shall be put to death, and the fifth commandment of Moses is "Honor your father and your mother that your days may be long in the land which the Lord your God gives you." Even today, the middle-eastern view is that old age is the summit of life (Potai, 1959). The title of "sheik" literally means "old man," for great age is viewed as a sign of virtue and of divine blessing.

Although the Hebrews tended to believe that the good live long lives, the Greeks said that those whom the gods love die young. They viewed aging as a misfortune. The seventh century Ionian poet, Mimnermos of Kolophon, lamented (Guthrie, 1946),

> Brief is the fruit of youth
> No longer than the daily spread of sunlight
>   over the earth;
> But when the springtime of life is passed,
> Then verily to die is better than life,
> For many are the ills that invade the heart.

In Rome, too, it was felt generally that old age was burdensome, for it brought not only loss of physical health but also a weakening of mental powers. An old man was admired if he ended his own life when it became wearisome (Haynes, 1963).

In all of these civilizations, however, the opinions about aging were confused. Among the Hebrews the Psalmist pleaded: "Do not cast me off in the time of old age," and in the wise literature of Ecclesiastes, a philosopher observed with deep disillusionment that all things are fleeting and there is no lasting joy save in death. In Rome (Layman, 1960), conversely, the position of paterfamilias obligated the young to assume an attitude of worshipful behavior to the old, who retained control of the family fortune.

The treatment of the aging always has ranged from profound respect to callous rejection. The prestige of the aged is highest in those societies in the mid-range of cultural development. In primitive societies, living at bare subsistence levels, abandonment or killings of the aged may occur. At the opposite extreme of the economic

25

scale, affluent societies often show disregard for the aged, although they provide for their basic maintenance and care (Simmons, 1945). Ultimately, the value of the aged in any society has been dependent upon the number of important functions they perform.

The necessity to produce always emphasizes the value of youth and vigor and steadily directs the focus of interest of that society away from the problems of the aged. In terms of the eons of the past, the human being only recently has developed any interest in his own structure and function. The generations of complacency suddenly culminated in an intense self-examination known as scientific research (Hoffman, 1957). Aging is superimposed on maturity so imperceptibly that it remains unnoticed until most of the pressing problems of interest to youth have been examined.

It has been pointed out that the mixed heritages tended to emphasize youth; that society demanded youthful vigor and productivity, and that much of beginning science was focused on the phenomena of youth. This explains why the studies of aging were to bear fruit late on the vigorously growing tree of science, although hints of the bud appeared early. Science is as old as perception, with no real beginning in written history (Boring, 1957). This is true of concerns with the problems of aging. The first preserved statement about the treatment of the aged dates from 3000 B.C. (Breasted, 1930).

Biological science had its beginnings in medical science, which in turn originated in philosophy. Hippocrates, living in Greece from c.460 to 370 B.C., usually is revered as the founder of medical and, therefore, of biological sciences. Many of his aphorisms make mention of the changes with age and the problems of the old (Adams, 1939).

The great scientific genius, Aristotle, 384-322 B.C., was not only a profound philosopher, but his writing indicates that he well deserves to be called the first great biologist (Guthrie, 1952). A contemporary, Erasistratus, 8th century B.C., may be regarded as the founder of human physiology. Inadvertently he may also have founded another cult which has always been troublesome to biologists. He was accused by Celsus, who has been cited as the first major medical historian, of practicing vivisection, and worse, even human vivisection (Dobson, 1927). Two hundred years later, a Greek migrant to Rome, Asclepiades, became the society physician of his day, in the second century B.C., through his successes with the treatment of chronic diseases (Guthrie, 1946). Mention should also be made of Galen, the clinical observer and experimenter, of Vesalius the anatomist, of Harvey the physiologist, of Leeuwenhoek the microscopist, of Linnaeus the classifier, and of Bichat the histologist. All were in the direct biological family lineage.

Albrecht von Haller and Johännes Müller each have been credited with siring modern experimental physiology. They were followed by Charles Bell, Claude Bernard, Johannes Evangelista Purkinje (1787-1869), and many others who lived and worked during the eighteenth and nineteenth centuries. A review of the work of many of these scientists provides little indication of a primary interest in the problems of aging or of the aged.

In spite of the preoccupation of beginning science with growth, development, acute disease processes, and other youthful subjects, people have always speculated about death and longevity. Primitive man soon learned how long animals could be expected to survive and be useful. Fabulous stories arose about the great ages attained by some creatures. Even today there are persistent rumors of vertebrates, such as parrots and elephants, living to be over one hundred years of age. The only proved centenarians are tortoises and man.

It is reasonably accurate that Pierre Jourbert, a Canadian, lived 133 years. More dubious are the reports that Christian Drakenburg, a Dane, lived to be 146 years of age, that recently, an African lived to be 120 to 130 years of age, and a South American attained an age of 130 to 140 years. Cited often in the literature of centenarians are Henry Jenkins, purported to have died at age 169, Katherine, Countess Desmond, who died at age 140, and Thomas Parr, who was reputed to have died in 1635 at the age of 152 years (Weyer, 1958).

This super centenarian, Thomas Parr, is said to have committed a sexual offense when he was 102 and to have married a widow when he was 120 years of age, with what is reported to have been complete marital bliss. Fanciful as this record may seem, it has another special fascination. A post-morten examination was performed on Thomas Parr, by order of the King, by none other than William Harvey, who discovered the circulation of the blood. This physician-physiologist studied pathology as an important branch of physiology (Lorand, 1928). His autopsy report of the old man was significant only in that the organs and tissues he examined seemed to be compatible with those of a much younger man. Parr was buried in Westminster Abbey and legends that his age actually was the sum of his own and his father's years have been offered in explanation of the dates on his memorial plaque.

Modern science was developed as recently as the sixteenth century by Copernicus, Kepler, Galileo, Newton, Harvey, and the others. It was during this era that philosophy was separated into the physical sciences and the life sciences. The rapid fragmentation of the studies of nature into special scientific disciplines may be dated as starting in 1819, with the appearance of Sir William Lawrence's book, *On the Physiology, Zoology, and Natural History of Man*. The word "biology" was introduced in 1837 by S. T. Treviranus in the title of his book, *Biologie oder die Philosophie der lebenden Natur*.

The growth of knowledge in biology was explosive. For a time, biology and medicine remained confluent, with mutual anticipation for rapid answers to the questions about normal and diseased life processes. After Virchow, this commonality disappeared. Biologists progressed from the study of cells to a concern with the cellular components. While studies of disease continued to be concerned with cellular pathology, the understanding of biological processes depended upon the knowledge of molecular events (Valee, 1963).

The history of studies of aging has been divided into an Early Period from 1835 to 1918, a Period of Beginning Systemic Studies from 1918 to 1940, and a Period of Expansion since 1946 (Birren, 1961a & b). Prior to the beginning of this Early Period, many scientists were discussing their concern with the problems of death and of growing old. Roger Bacon, 1214(?)-1292, wrote several books, including *On the Retardation of Old Age* and *The Cure of Old Age, and Preservation of Youth* (Castiglione, 1958). André du Laurens, known better as Laurentius, 1558-1609, wrote the first work in geriatrics published in French; Benjamin Rush, 1745-1813, prepared an American physiological study of the aged entitled *Account of the State of the Body and Mind in Old Age: With Observation of Its Diseases, and Their Remedies* (Grant, 1963).

During the Early Period, the Russian biologist, Ilya Metchnikoff, remembered chiefly as a Nobel Prize winner for Medicine in 1908, wrote prolifically on aging. He advanced the intoxication theory and blamed poisons from intestinal putrefaction for the onset of aging (Lansing, 1952a). Also in this period, the drift of many scientists from their studies of growth and development to investigation concerned with aging, the aged, and death, is typified by the American biologist, Raymond Pearl. During his mature years, Pearl progressed from studies of heredity and organismal variations to write such articles as "The Biology of Death," "Alcohol and Longevity," "The Rate of Living," and "The Biology of Population Growth."

Early in this same period, Quetelet introduced the study of probabilities and statistics into the studies of aging. Simultaneously, several Germans, notably Weismann, Weber, Wagner, Herman, and Nagel, were making detailed studies and writing prolifically in the new science of physiology. They amassed into "Handbooks" the information on which the future systemic studies of aging were to be based.

During the transition between the so-called Early Period and that of the Beginning Systemic Studies, a disconcerting series of events developed which have had serious impact on modern gerontology. Even in the old kingdom of Egypt, 3000-2500 B.C., man was interested in recovering his lost or waning youth, just as he is today (Breasted, 1930). Unfortunately, these persistent desires of mankind to maintain sexual prowess and to live forever became mixed with the beginning of the specialty of endocrinology.

As early as 1776, de Bordeu had clearly stated the function of the ductless glands in his book *Analyse Médicinale du Sang* (Garrison, 1922). This theoretical pronouncement was verified scientifically in 1856 by Brown-Séquard during his studies of the adrenal capsule, and by Moritz-Schiff during his research on the thyroid.

There is little doubt that Brown-Séquard was a brilliant physiologist, although today his name is rarely mentioned. In 1889, when he was 72 years of age, he reported that following the subcutaneous injection of extracts of crushed animal testicles into his arms and legs, he was rejuvenated in health, muscular power, mental activity, and ability to work without fatigue. The scientific report was acceptable, but his disrepute arose because he began at once to apply this new-found knowledge to restoring youth to the aged.

While Brown-Séquard was attempting to rejuvenate people by injecting them with testicular extracts, a Russian, Voronoff, was trying to reinvigorate the aging by grafting them with the glands from monkeys, and Eugen Steinach became confused between his honest attempts to isolate and test sex hormones and the renewal of eroticism in the aging by chemical means (Wendt, 1963). The low point in this development was reached in the early 1920's when John R. Brinkley became a millionaire by performing transplant operations of goat and other animal glands on thousands of the innocent old (Gardner, 1957). This subject of rejuvenation has not only had a long and insane history but is still manifest today.

Fortunately, there was much of worth in the early studies on the endocrine organs. Robert Battey, in 1872, excised both ovaries from a female patient and noted that he had produced an artificial menopause. Although the indications for his surgery, to cure a neurosis, were in error, his observations were useful. In 1890, Victor Horsley, famed as a neurologist, pointed out the similarities between senility and myxedema. He ascribed old age to degeneration of the thyroid gland because he had observed an increase in connective tissue, a shrinkage in follicular contents, and fatty degeneration of the epithelium in the thyroid from older individuals (Lorand, 1928).

Animal experimentation became important during this era of endocrine interest. Related observations gave rise to the first laboratory studies on atherosclerosis, for Eiselsberg noted that atheromata formed rapidly in the aorta, coronaries, and other vessels of dogs from which the thyroid had been extirpated, and Josue was able to produce arteriosclerotic changes in rabbits by the injection of adrenal extracts (Lorand, 1928).

By 1907, Slonaker (1907) was studying the spontaneous activity of rats and reported a reduction of their drive with age. Goodpasture, in 1918, reported his detailed observations on the changes incident to senescence (Hoskins, 1922). From his work based upon studies of 50 dogs, he formulated a concept that there was a continuing increase in cellular structural intricacy with aging, until finally the body cells lost their equilibrium. The ultimate result of this progressive cellular differentiation was death.

Laurentius, in 1599, reported the first pathological observations from autopsies done specifically in old men to study the problem of aging. He firmly eradicated the long-held view that the heart grew in size until the age of 50, and then diminished gradually to cause old age, for he found that the hearts of old men were as heavy as those of the young men (Grant, 1963). However, laboratory studies on the elderly were not done commonly until much later.

In 1885, Galton (1885) published extensive statistical studies on 9,337 males and females aged 5 to 80 years, measured in 17 different ways. Hall (1922), presented in his book on senescence further epidemiological data, especially relevant to death and religiosity of the aged. This book is particularly valuable because it reviews the earlier theories of aging. This resumé, in addition to the comprehensive summation of studies on aging found in a famous system of endocrinology which also appeared in 1922, indicates a surprisingly modern understanding of the biology of aging (Barker, 1922).

Although Gabriele Zerbi wrote in 1489 the first printed monograph devoted expressly and exclusively to aging and entitled it *Gerontocomia*

Fig. 1. Gabriele Zerbi, an enlargement of the figure presumably Zerbi of Verona, kneeling before the Pope, as described in the photograph on p. 13 made available through the same sources. Appreciation is expressed to Professor L. R. Lind of the Department of Classics and Classical Archaeology of the University of Kansas, Lawrence, Kansas, for his advice with regard to this source of Zerbi's book and portrait.

(Grant, 1963), the word "geriatrics" was apparently not introduced until 1909 and also was popularized in 1914 by its coiner, Nascher (1914), in a text using *Geriatrics* as its full title. However, such an august publication as the Encyclopaedia Britannica did not recognize the specialty until much later. In the yearbook of 1957, a section devoted to gerontology first appeared, and not until 1959 was there a separate heading for geriatrics. American dictionaries began to include the term "geriatrics" by 1923.

Meanwhile, Stieglitz was championing the need for the pursuit of these special fields of interest. In the late 1930's he became the first chairman of the U.S. Public Health Service Section on Aging and he was Secretary of the National Advisory Committee on Gerontology until 1944, when Dr. Nathan Shock succeeded to this position.

In 1933, a book edited by Edmund V. Cowdry (1933) entitled *Arteriosclerosis: A Survey of the Problem* appeared. This volume was the forerunner which resulted in the book *Problems of Ageing* published in 1938, with subsequent editions of this work still in use as a standard text (Cowdry, 1942; Lansing 1952).

Early in 1937, there was a Conference on Aging at Woods Hole. Less than a year later, the growth of interest was such that it was necessary to convene a Conference of Committees on the Biological Process of Aging, in Washington, D.C.; the subject of aging was becoming popular. In that year, the Medical Society of Pennsylvania had considered the subject for the first time in its annual meeting under the title, "The Status of Geriatrics."

In rapid succession during 1940, symposia were printed in the *Medical Clinics of North America* and the *American Journal of Orthopsychiatry*. Meetings were held at the University of Pennsylvania Centennial Celebration and were assembled by the Massachusetts Society for Research in Psychiatry, the Public Health Service, the American Chemical Society, and the Chicago Medical Society.

During this same active year, Surgeon General Thomas Parran, of the U.S. Public Health Service, appointed a National Advisory Committee on Gerontology and authorized a survey of investigations on aging. Almost simultaneously, a Unit on Gerontology was established in the Division of Physiology in the National Institutes of Health. Meanwhile, the National Research Council's Committee on Aging was reorganized under Dr. A. J. Carlson. Drs. V. Korenchevsky and William de B. MacNider were working to organize an American Branch of the International Club for Research in Aging.

On December 7, 1941, the Period of Beginning Systemic Studies ended abruptly with the attack on Pearl Harbor and the citizens of the United States were confronted with more urgent problems than those of understanding the biology of aging and senescence.

In the long literate scientific history of aging, 1909 is a special date; Nascher of New York as noted had invented the word *geriatrics* and followed it with a publication (1914) of a comprehensive text on the subject under that title five years later. In 1919, M. W. Thewlis (1919), his friend and student, published the first edition of his own book *The Care of the Aged (Geriatrics)*. After the economic upheaval of 1929, a number of students of biology and medicine were drawn to the field of aging.

Monroe in Boston was working on the material which eventuated in his book: *Diseases of Old Age* (1957). Zeman (1945) in New York had initiated his authoritative historical series in aging and was working actively to bring accepted ideas of aging in custodial facilities into the modern focus of medicine. Freeman (1938) in Philadelphia had published his "History of Geriatrics," had given an age-definition to a specific disease in a study of tuberculosis, founded his clinic and ward service in geriatrics, and started a medical lecture course in an undergraduate medical school in 1944 (Freeman, 1938, 1941, 1960).

In 1942, the American Geriatrics Society had been founded. Shortly thereafter the Gerontological Society was incorporated as a successsor to the Club for Research in Aging.

Early in 1945, the current Period of Expansion was evident. Dr. Edward J. Stieglitz (1954) had published the first edition of his *Geriatric Medicine*. Dr. Nathan Shock was steering the National Advisory Committee on Gerontology. Within a few months, staffing of the Gerontological Unit of the National Institutes of Health began, although it was not until 1948 that this unit became a full Branch of the National Heart Institute.

Likewise in 1945, the Division on Maturity and Old Age of the American Psychological Association was formed. The first issue of the Journal of Gerontology appeared in 1946.

In 1949 the International Association of Gerontology had its first meeting in Liège. Korenchevsky had proselytized with vigor in his efforts to obtain this international understanding. Ernst Boas (1947) *(The Patient Past 50)*, Albert Mueller-Deham (1942) *(Internal Medicine in Old Age)*, Louis Dublin, and many others were reporting observations and publishing results in substantial texts.

In 1951, the Philadelphia County Medical Society created its first Committee on Geriatrics, which initiated the Commission on Geriatrics of the Medical Society of the State of Pennsylvania. This organized medical group in turn proposed the creation of a similar committee in the American Medical Association, which came to be known as its Committee on Aging. At the White House Conference on Aging in 1950 and again in 1961, successive levels of discussion of these problems came to better understanding. At the latter meeting, the Gerontological Society proposed an Institute of Gerontology to the delegates. The biolgy of aging had left behind the indefinite but hopeful aspects of the past and had entered an era of scientific precision.

Dr. E. W. Busse of Duke University received his first grant for Studies on the Aging Central Nervous System in 1950, but it was not until 1952 that grants were being made regularly for specific research in the biological and medical aspects of aging. These were first given by the National Heart Institute through the National Heart Council, then chaired by Dr. Paul Dudley White.

That same year, 1952, Oscar R. Ewing, Federal Security Administrator, appointed a Committee on Geriatrics and Gerontology with Clark Tibbitts as Chairman. This committee was charged with the responsibility of integrating the activities in the field of aging which had developed in various branches of the Federal government, as well as under various non-Federal sponsorships. The next year, the Section on Aging was established in the National Institute of Mental Health; it is in this section that Birren had been so productive. Meanwhile, symposia and local, national and international meetings devoted to reports from studies in aging, such as those underwritten by the Josiah Macy Foundation, became almost commonplace.

In spite of these developments, Lansing (1952b) felt compelled to sound a note of pessimism; he stated that, in 1952, research on the biology of aging was almost at a standstill with scarcely a handful of workers in the area. He pointed out that research on cardiovascular diseases, specifically on arteriosclerosis, was receiving proper emphasis, but that otherwise support for studies on the biology of aging was inadequate.

Fortunately, the studies of aging began to receive strong support and flourished. To attest to this is such evidence as the recent appearance of several works and many multivolumed sets of books reporting the results of studies on aging, and the listing of 18,000 entries from the published literature during 1956 to 1961 by Shock in the third volume (1963) of *A Classified Bibliography of Gerontology and Geriatrics*. Perhaps to the biologist the full maturity of studies in the biology of aging was evidenced when the 1963 program of the Federation of American Societies for Experimental Biology included a full session of aging sponsored by the American Physiological Society.

In 1954, national consideration of financing medical care of an increasing number of aging in a highly developed free-enterprise system (United States) had been proposed. This led to a long and rigorous debate because of actual and assumed implications. The background is the fact that a society effective in the promotion of an environment of longevity must accept some degree of responsibility for these results and do so within the context of its economic pattern.

In 1952, Lansing (1952a) reviewed the theories of the causes of aging which had been propounded during the first half of the twentieth century. Cell intoxication, changing relationships between cell volume and cell surface area, cellular ultradifferentiation, and colloid aging were those which were receiving the most research attention. Ten years later, another review article indicated that there was still no unanimity among scientists as to the biological factors of aging (Anon, 1963). It was stated that there were at least 120 theories of the cause of aging receiving serious study. Cellular changes primarily were suspected, but there was virtually no agreement as to what specifically produces the cellular changes observed. Today, the only unanimities are that no one ever dies from aging, although it increases the chance that an individual may die, and that aging dulls the excitement of existence at the end of a long life.

The foundations of biology, physiology, and pathology were established prior to 1900. The cell theory, the nature of cellular division, the cellular basis of reproduction, evolution, and the germ theory of disease were well known. Yet the biological texts of that date contained little that is included in today's books. Since the beginning of the present century there has been an exponential increase in all scientific knowledge. The studies of chronic diseases and of the aging processes are special products of these recent scientific advances (Glass, 1963).

The studies of the biology of aging have progressed from the unity of science to diversity. From philosophy arose the physical and the natural sciences, and from the latter developed biology, physiology, biochemistry, and numerous other specialties. As the biologists became increasingly adept, these special fields in turn were subdivided into detailed studies of molecules, and, then, of atoms. The more deeply the biologist analyzed, the further he seemed to remove himself from the problem he meant to solve. The details he studied prevent the recapture of a concept of the unified problem (Du Nouy, 1947).

As soon as gerontology matured as a true subspeciality of biology, there developed those inevitable geniuses, the super-specialists. The very nature of their preoccupation with engrossing detail tends to cause them to lose sight of the total problem of understanding aging. Biological research in aging is now characterized by the same fragmentation engendered by the available variety of technical approaches that has developed in all rapidly advancing sciences. Fortunately, "the resulting data may well turn out to be amenable to integration which cuts across all technically defined areas" (Sidman, 1961).

Aging is a natural process that must be studied intensively, for it remains one of the most agonizing problems in all biology. Not only must the gerontologists continue to concentrate on performing the research necessary to understand aging, but they must assume an increasing role in the application of their knowledge for betterment of the status of the aged. Self-analysis, as represented by the appearance of historical essays, represents an important step toward the integration and applications of the findings of a maturing science of gerontology.

The history of science is a new discipline, not yet well organized, and, unfortunately, attractive to "amateurs, dilettanti, and cranks" (Sarton, 1927). A defense for the temerity of this amateur may be found in the words of Thoreau:

Most that is first written on any subject is a mere groping after it, mere rubble stone and foundation. It is only when the observations of different periods have been brought together that he (the writer) begins to grasp his subject and can make one pertinent and just observation (Stapleton, 1960).

References

Adams, F.: *The genuine works of Hippocrates*. Williams & Wilkins, Baltimore, 1939. Aphorisms 299-330.

Anon: The enigma of human aging. *Chem. Enginr-News*, 40: 138-146, Feb. 12, and 104-112, Feb. 19, 1963.

Barker, L. F.: *Endocrinology and metabolism*. D. Appleton & Co., New York, 1922.

Birren, J. E.: A brief history of the psychology of aging. Part I. *Gerontologist*, 1: 69-77, 1961. (a)

Birren, J. E.: A brief history of the psychology of aging. Part II. *Gerontologist*, 1: 127-134, 1961. (b)

Boas, E.: *The patient past 50*, Year Book Publ., Chicago, 3rd ed., 1947.

Boring, E. G.: *A history of experimental psychology*, 2nd ed., Chpt. I. The rise of modern science. Appleton-Century-Crofts, New York, 1957.

Breasted, J. H. (Trans.): *The Edwin Smith Surgical Papyrus, Vol. I*. Univ. of Chicago Press, Chicago, 498, 1930. Cited by Grant, 1963.

Castiglioni, A.: *A history of medicine*. Krumbhaar, E. B., translator, Alfred A. Knopf, New York, 351, 352, 510, 1958.

Cowdry, E. V. (Editor): *Arteriosclerosis: a survey of the problem*. Macmillan Co., New York, 1933.

Cowdry, E. V.: Preface to the Second Edition, July 15, 1942. In: A. I. Lansing (Editor) *Cowdry's Problems of Ageing* (3rd Ed.) Williams & Wilkins, Baltimore, ix-x, 1952.

Dobson, J. F.: Erasistratus. *Proc. roy. Soc. Med.*, 20: 825, 1927.

DuNouy, L.: *Human destiny*. Mentor Book, New York, 1947.

Freeman, J. T.: The history of geriatrics. *Ann. med. hist.*, 10: 324-355, 1938.

Freeman, J. T.: Financing medical costs after age 65. *Pa. med. J.*, 63: 847-851, 1960.

Freeman, J. T., and C. A. Heiken: The geriatric aspect of pulmonary tuberculosis. *Amer. J. med. Sci.*, 202: 29-38, 1941.

Galton, F.: On the anthropometric laboratory at the late international health exhibition. *J. R. Anthrop. Inst.*, 14: 205-221, & 275-287, 1885.

Gardner, M.: *Fads and fallacies in the name of science*. Dover Publications, New York, 1957.

Garrison, F. H.: History of endocrine doctrine. In: L. B. Barker (Editor) *Endocrinology and Metabolism*. D. Appleton & Co., New York, Vol. 1, 45-78, 1922.

Glass, H. B.: Evolution in biology. In: H. J. Deason (Editor) *A Guide to Science Reading*. Signet Science Library Books, New York, 15-24, 1963.

Grant, R. L.: Concepts of aging: an historical review. *Perspect. Biol. Med.*, 4: 443-478, 1963.

Guthrie, D.: *A history of medicine*. J. B. Lippincott Co., Philadelphia, 60-61, 1946.

Guthrie, W. K. C.: *Orpheus and Greek religion*. Methuen, London, 148-150, 1952.

Hall, G. S.: *Senescence*. D. Appleton & Co., New York, 1922.

Haynes, M. S.: The supposedly golden age for the aged in Ancient Rome (a study of literary concept of old age). *Gerontologist*, 3: 26-35, 1963.

Hoffman, J. G.: *The life and death of cells*. Dolphin Books, Doubleday & Co., Garden City, N. Y., 21-29, 1957.

Hoskins, R. G. (citing Goodpasture): The endocrine organs and old age. In: L. F. Barker (Editor) *Endocrinology and Metabolism*. Vol. I. D. Appleton & Co., New York, 22-25, 1922.

Lansing, A. I.: General physiology. *In:* A. I. Lansing (Editor) *Cowdry's Problems of Ageing.* Williams & Wilkins, Baltimore, Chpt. I, 3-22, 1952. (a)

Lansing, A. I.: Preface to the third edition. *Cowdry's Problems of Ageing.* Williams & Wilkins, Baltimore, vii-viii, 1952. (b)

Layman, C. M.: *The message of the Bible.* Graded Press, Nashville, Tenn., 44, 1960.

Lorand, A.: *Old age deferred.* F. A. Davis Co., Philadelphia, 1928. (Same as 1st Edition, 1910, plus one chapter).

Monroe, R. T.: *Diseases in old age,* Harvard Univ. Press, Cambridge, Mass., 1957.

Mueller-Deham, A.: Internal medicine in old age (S. M. Rabson, translator.) Williams & Wilkins Co., Baltimore, 1942.

Nascher, I. L.: *Geriatrics.* P. Blakiston's & Son, Philadelphia, 1914.

Potai, R.: *Sex and family in the Bible and the Middle East.* Doubleday Dolphin Books, 229-233, 1959.

Sarton, G.: *Introduction to the history of science.* Vol. I. Carnegie Institution, Washington, 1927.

Shock, N. W.: *A classified bibliography of gerontology and geriatrics,* Stanford Univ. Press, Stanford, Calif., 1963.

Sidman, M.: *Tactics of Scientific Research.* Chpt. I. The Scientific Importance of Experimental Data. Basic Books, New York, 1961.

Simmons, L.: *The role of the aged in a primitive society.* Yale Univ. Press, New Haven, 1945.

Slonaker, J. R.: The Normal Activity of the Rat at Different Ages. *J. comp. Neurol. Psychiat., 17:* 342-359, 1907.

Stapleton, L.-Ed., and H. D. Thoreau.: *A writer's journal.* Dover Publications, New York, 196-197, 1960.

Stieglitz, E. J.: *Geriatric medicine: medical care of later maturity.* J. B. Lippincott Co., Philadelphia, (3rd Ed.), 1954.

Thewlis, M. W.: *The care of the aged (geriatrics).* C. V. Mosby Co., St. Louis, 1919.

Valee, B. L., and W. E. C. Wacker: Medical biology: a perspective. *J. Amer. med. Ass., 184:* 485-489, (May 11) 1963.

Wendt, H.: *In search for Adam.* Colier Books, New York, 153, 1963.

Weyer, E. M. (Editor): *The illustrated library of the natural sciences.* Simon & Schuster, New York, 1958.

Zeman, F. D.: Life's later years. *J. Mt. Sinai Hosp., N.Y., 11:* 339-344, 1945; *12:* 783-791, 890-901, 939-953, 1945.

Human Personality and Perpetuity

Walter R. Miles, Ph.D., Sc.D.[1]

Traditional Views of Old Age

IN THE FIFTH Egyptian dynasty, 2750-2625 B.C. there lived a learned and energetic man who was chief physician to his king. The name of this royal physician was Nenekhsekhmet (Breasted, 1907). Knowing full well that even a physician cannot escape death, he had already prepared his tomb, which had been cut into the rock, but it was cold and uninviting. Of a sudden one day he thought of a way to redeem this tomb from its prospective atmosphere of despair. When there was a suitable opportunity he spoke to his king and said,

May thy person, beloved of Re, command that there be given to me a false door of stone for this my tomb of the cemetery.

His majesty answered this request with royal generosity. Two great stone slabs were brought and placed in the audience hall so that the work by the artisans might be done in the presence of the king. Each day there was an inspection of the work. Finally after the false doors had been painted blue, his majesty considered them completed and said to the chief physician,

As these my nostrils enjoy breath, as the Gods love me, mayest thou depart into the cemetery at an advanced old age as one revered.

As the chief physician performed his duties and grew older it may be surmised that the prospect of departing this life was somewhat brightened by the knowledge that he would rest behind these royal doors.

Not only planning places of burial but also the elaboration of burial customs and the association of religious services with these customs have operated to ameliorate in a measure the dark and gruesome prospect of death.

Cicero's brilliant defense of the capabilities, accomplishments, and satisfactions of old age, set forth in his well-known essay, *Cato Major*, or *De Senectute* (Cato, 1773; Edmonds, 1956), for many centuries has been one of the most universally popular of all the Latin classics. The famous orator, in addressing this essay to his friend Atticus, did not hesitate to refer to old age as a burden which they have in common but he was quite unwilling to admit the necessity for the pessimism and gloom which frequently accompany this period of life and influence society's attitude toward old age. In the rich variety of human interests and occupations Cicero found ample opportunity for every combination of physical and mental make-up to reap substantial life satisfactions. He has the settled conviction that the intellectual powers are quite capable of being retained in the old, irrespective of whether a man be of high endowment or average ability, provided these mental functions are exercised and kept fit. With copious illustrations from history, from his own very broad personal acquaintance, and from a great store of observations, he controverted one after another the four more common unfavorable charges made against age and its influence on adult performance. These accusations are (a) that age produces exclusion from active life, (b) enfeebles the bodily powers, (c) deprives the individual of sensual pleasure, and (d) through the realization of approaching death, destroys mental buoyancy and hope. Does age isolate men from the active duties of life? Cicero answered,

From which, from those which are performed by youth and strength? Are there, then, no concerns of old age, which even when our bodies are feeble, are yet carried on by the mind?——Great actions are not achieved by exertions of strength, or speed, or by quick movements of bodies, but by talent, authority, judgment; of which faculties old age is usually so far from being deprived, that it is even improved in them; unless, indeed, I, who both as soldier and tribune, and lieutenant-general, and consul, have been employed in various kinds of wars,—now seem to you to be idle when I am not engaged in wars. (Edmonds, 1946)

In a similar manner he takes exception to the charge of impairment of memory by age and pleads that older people can "remember all the things which they care about: e.g. who are indebted to them, and to whom they are indebted." This hopeful, confident, and at some points rather

---
[1] U.S. Naval Submarine Medical Center, New London, Connecticut.

defiant attitude which the entire *Cato Major* conveys fits it to be a book that should be known, as it has been for centuries, and it has well filled an important place in popular pre-scientific literature. It has had, and still has, deserved popularity. The high esteem in which it has been held and the commonsense view middle-aged adults especially have taken toward the essay have perhaps never been better expressed in combination than by Erasmus (1680), the humanist, in one of his colloquies, "The Religious Treat." The conversation runs as follows:

> Erasmus . . . There are more Saints than we find in our Catalogue. To confess my self now among my Friends, I cannot read *Tully, of Old Age; of Friendship; his Offices;* or his *Tusculane Questions,* without kissing the Book; without a veneration for the Soul of that *Divine Heathen;* and then on the contrary, when I read some of our Modern Authors, their *Politique, Oeconomics,* and *Ethiques;* Good God! how Jejune, and Cold they are? And so insensible, compar'd with the other, that I had rather lose *all Scotus,* and twenty more such as he, than *one Cicero* or *Plutarch.*

Thus Cicero's portrayal of age, its capacities, and even its incapacities, has been generally welcome, cheering, and as fascinating as a colorful sunset, which, even though it be but the lateral play of refracted light on clouds, is universally preferable to the grey evening mists of Ecclesiastes,

> Then shall the dust return to the earth as it was; and the spirit shall return to God who gave it. Vanity of vanities, saith the Preacher, all is vanity. (Ecclesiastes, 1881)

Humans are given to personal boasting and the old often have overstated their achievements in contending against time. Luigi Cornaro, a Venetian nobleman, 1464-1566, established his health claims for old age in a way that won him much attention and an outstandingly good reputation. His disclosures of the Advantages of a Temperate Life claimed much public attention. The small treatise was widely translated and often reprinted. (See Chapter I, Medical Perspectives in Aging). Joseph Addison in "The Spectator," October 13, 1711, gave Cornaro (1558) and his prescription for health and long life a decided nod of approval. Cornaro was so successful in reaching an interested responsive public by his first discourse that he published three others at intervals of three to five years in which he progressively expanded his theme of Divine Sobriety.

A man or a woman in middle life frequently looks back on past days and finds them crowded with memories, some of which are so clear they can be "relived" in much detail. The process of living leaves deep traces in the mental self from days and nights that are past. This rich experience of memory generates expectations of experiences to come, some that may take place tomorrow, others that may occur next week or some later time in the future. "There certainly will be a future"; human hope cannot tolerate the negative of this proposition. Therefore, growing out of the experience of being an inhabitant of the earth, man in all climes and ages has listened to the magic man, prophet, or seer who tells of an eternal life after earthly death.

Religious prophets and leaders the world over recognize man's zest for life and its perpetuity and that this zest might involve him in antisocial behavior and have called him to worship and to believe in something greater and more lasting

Fig. 1. Title page of the major views of Cornaro in the form of four essays collected almost inadvertently into one volume. Cornaro was so pleased with the reception of his original views that he expounded on them in subsequent years. One of the essays actually is a commentary in the form of a very self-satisfied letter.

than himself. Religion, prescribing a way of life, promises salvation to man. The Ten Commandments which according to sacred tradition God gave to Moses on Mount Sinai prescribed types of behavior both positive and negative that should characterize those who profess to believe in the Divine Principle. In the Book of Proverbs, third chapter, we read

My son, forget not my law; but let thy heart keep my commandments for length of days and years of life and peace will they add to thee.

Again in the 91st Psalm the security of him who trusts in Jehovah is promised. Speaking in the first person, God is made to say of the worshiper,

I will be with him in trouble, I will deliver him and honor him. With long life will I satisfy him and show him my salvation.

The Capitulary of Charlemagne issued in the year 802 A.D. records that

the most serene and most Christian emperor Charles did choose from among his nobles the most prudent, and venerable abbots, and pious laymen—and did send them over his whole kingdom; and did grant through them, by means of all the following provisions, that men should live according to law and right. And, [the Lord Emperor] ordained that every man in his whole kingdom—ecclesiastic or layman, each according to his vow and calling—who had previously promised fealty to him as king should now make this promise to him as emperor; and that those who had hitherto not made this promise should all, down to those under 12 years of age do likewise.—But all should know that the oath comprises in itself the following meaning. Firstly, that everyone of his own accord should strive, according to his intelligence and strength, wholly to keep himself in the holy service of God according to the precept of God and to his own promise—inasmuch as the emperor can not exhibit the necessary care and discipline to each man singly.

The Capitulary was strict in reference to the habits and recreation of the bishops, abbots, priests, and deacons. No one who belonged to the clergy might presume to have hunting dogs or hawks, falcons or sparrow-hawks,

but each one shall keep himself wholly in his proper sphere, according to the canons, or according to the rule. Any one who presumes to do this (have hunting dogs, etc.) shall know that he loses his standing. Furthermore he shall suffer such punishment for this that others shall fear to wrongfully do likewise.

No. 14 in the Capitulary of Charlemagne uses the phrase that rings like a great, distant bell through the ages.

The bishops, abbots, and abbesses, and counts shall be mutually in accord, agreeing with all charity and unity of peace, in wielding the law and in finding a right judgment; and that they shall faithfully live according to the will of God, so that everywhere and always, through them and among them, just judgments may be carried out. The poor, widows, orphans and pilgrims shall have consolation and protection from them; so that we, through their good will, may merit, rather than punishment, the rewards of eternal life (Henderson, 1892).

William Tyndale translated the Hebrew Bible into English and, against intense opposition from Cardinal Wolsey and King Henry VIII, succeeded in introducing printed copies into England shortly after 1525. He wrote and circulated religious tracts which were related to the English Reformation. For personal safety he was compelled to live in hiding outside England. He was captured in 1535, tried, and condemned for heresy. He was executed by strangulation and his body was burned.

To Benjamin Franklin we are indebted for an account which shows how one British family valued the English Bible. "Our humble family," Franklin relates, "early embraced the reformation. They remained faithfully attached during the reign of Queen Mary (1553-1558) when they were in danger of being molested on account of their zeal against Popery. They had an English Bible, and to conceal it the more securely, they conceived the project of fastening it, open, with pack-threads across the leaves, on the inside of the lid of a close-stool. When my great-grand father wished to read to his family, he reversed the lid of the close-stool upon his knees, and passed the leaves from one side to the other, which were held down on each by the pack-thread. One of the children was stationed at the door to give notice if he saw the proctor, an officer of the spiritual court, make his appearance; in that case, the lid was restored to its place, with the Bible concealed under it as before. I had this anecdote from my uncle Benjamin" (Ruger & Stoessiger, 1927).

Tyndale loved his country and fellow countryman and by his devotion and self-sacrifice succeeded in bequeathing to them what has been termed "the most valuable thing that this world affords"—the Bible in the mother tongue. What we may call Tyndale's Program to help provide moral support and hope to young and old has gone on and on. The British Bible Society was founded in 1804. By that time the Scriptures, or parts of them had been translated into more than 60 different languages. In 1936, when four centuries had passed since Tyndale's martyrdom, this Society could report translations into more than 700 languages, and that annually more than ten million volumes of Holy Writ were circulated throughout the world. The wide acceptance of the Bible as a psychological or spiritual guide to assist man in preparing for and entering a perpetual existence beyond the event of mortal death is a fact of human behavior of vast import (Pollak, 1948). Furthermore, not only Christians but the devotees of most other religions are or have been urged to have faith in the prospect of an everlasting future life. The way to achieve it may not be easy, but it has been promised to the faithful.

Various social organizations have been devised as means to assist the individual in conducting his life in accordance with the precepts of his adopted religion. As example, the Prologue for The Rule of St. Benedict states that a school for the Lord's service is about to be founded

in the organization of which we trust that we shall ordain nothing severe and nothing burdensome. But even if, the demands of justice dictating it, something a little irksome shall be the result, for the purpose of amending vices or preserving charity;—thou shalt not therefore, struck by fear, flee the way of salvation, which can not be entered upon except through a narrow entrance. But as one's way of life and one's faith progresses, the heart becomes broadened, and, with the unutterable sweetness of love, the way of the mandates of the Lord is traversed. Thus, never departing from His guidance, continuing in the monastery in His teaching until death, through patience we are made partakers in Christ's passion, in order that we may merit to be companions in His kingdom (Henderson, 1892, p. 274).

A living concept of individual immortality was not a fundamental belief for many thoughtful critical minds of the past centuries and such doubters are still more numerous today. High ethical standards and behavior have their more immediate spheres of value and usefulness in human society and also in respect to the life forms with which men share the Earth as their rightful home. A man can throw his body away, as by jumping off a high building, but his ego must accompany his body and be crushed in the wreckage. He is culpable as a destroyer of society's valuable assets. A martyr, through his faith in some principles or truth he regards as constructive for Society, surrenders his body as social fertilizer that the seed may grow and bear fruit. He may be regarded as a creative hero, a man who won historical immortality through self-sacrifice.

All the major religions of the world are united in their basic ethical admonitions, e.g. Brahmanism, "This is the sum of duty: Do naught unto others which would cause you pain if done to you" (Mahabharata, 5, 1517).

Buddhism: "Hurt not others in ways that you yourself would find hurtful" (Analects, 15, 23).

Taoism: "Regard your neighbor's gain as your own gain, and your neighbor's loss as your loss."

These representative quotations are eloquent evidence of man's ideals for human life on Earth (Browne, 1961).

The Discovery of Senectitude

A beehive may experience such a multiplication of its living units that a swarm must leave and occupy a new locality. However long the old hive and the new one may persist as working colonies, other swarms will develop even though individual bees in these colonies have relatively short sweet lives. If, for example, everyone born in Boston in the relatively short span of 333 years since this city was founded had continued to survive and live there, bearing children, having grandchildren, and x numbers of great great greats, it would be difficult to imagine the population content and social conditions that would have resulted. Cotton Mather, born in Boston in 1663, is credited as being one of the first Americans to write about aging and might have had some later thoughts to communicate. Benjamin Franklin, whose mother, Abiah Folger came from Nantucket, was born in Boston in 1706. Doubtless, he could have had some sage advice to supplement his oft-quoted words, "Against diseases known, the strongest fence is the defensive virtue, abstinence." Still another fine philosophical poem could have come from Oliver Wendell Holmes, born 1809. Such flights of fancy must come to earth with the realization that individual man must pass life on rather than be a hoarder of it.

In all cultures that have had long settled communities, man's life from birth to death has enjoyed the close scrutiny of physicians and others devoted to curbing his ills and adjusting him to his recognized handicaps. Senectitude, nevertheless, has always been a part of the puzzling picture. Physicians and philosophers among the Greeks considered that man's decline was due to the loss of innate heat. Medical writers in Arabia surmised that the loss of body moisture produced shrinking and hardening of the tissues. At a much later date Sydenham coined the line, "Man is as old as his arteries." Other tissues have at times been considered the weak link. Dr. C. S. Minot, in a famous address delivered at Indianapolis in 1890, tentatively diagnosed old age and death as the result of a continuous loss of growth energy throughout individual life (Minot, 1890). Dr. Minot, addressing the Section of Biology, made a strong plea for institutional financial support of research in this field. August Weismann (1834-1914) is credited as the first biologist to recognize the intrinsic nature of biologic death and to interpret senility and natural death as having been acquired through natural selection as characters of advantage to the species as a whole.

Psychology Awakens to Opportunity

Psychologists and sociologists looked with admiration on what had come to pass largely through the advances of medicine and public hygiene in extending the average span of man's life. However, they have had some part in this great venture and achievement. Furthermore these sciences as such are much younger, have had fewer workers and less financial support, and have had to discover ways and means applicable to this complex problem. The prescriptions of these disciplines are not such as are sold in apothecary shops. Clinics to deal with aging and the aged have been slow to develop. The research path of choice has seemed to be that of measuring individual differences and in this way achieving information about changes in function or capacity among those who are past middle life. Such a program has seemed feasible as a means of characterizing different decades or semi-decades.

It has seemed desirable to measure individuals who have no special complaint, are ambient, and will perform some type of behavior rather than have something done on them. A great majority of individuals who are 50 to 70, or older, feel no need of having such measures perpetrated on them and S population samples are distorted by being composed of volunteers.

A classical attempt of this nature was undertaken in London by Francis Galton in 1884. He arranged what was called an "Anthropometric Laboratory" and set it up in connection with the Health Exhibition at South Kensington. Galton had a keen interest in measuring and testing people and in this undertaking in 1884 he measured seventeen traits. Seven thousand males from among those attending the Exhibition were enticed to cooperate. The measures included strength-type tests, sensory perceptions, and others. His Ss ranged in age from 6 to 81 years. There were only 38 cases 70 years or older, 172 in the age range 6 to 69, and 380 in the range 50 to 59. It seems that Galton, in correspondence with the American psychologist. James McKeen Cattell, informed him that the Ss who came to the South Kensington Laboratory "were so mixed that no homogeneous group can be extracted out of them that is both large and interesting." Ruger and Stoessiger (1927) secured Galton's data and provided a modern statistical work-up of this early material. Galton's visual acuity test results for ages 25 to 80, which included 3,250 cases, gave a Pearson $r = -.512 \pm .008$. The correlation for perception of highest audible pitch with age was $r = -.482 \pm .008$. It seems probable that strength tests were more easily motivated than some of the others. Galton used five such tests; all of them showed minus correlations. The range was $-.25$ to $-.39$ in a population of 3800 plus.

Cattell, after receiving his doctor's degree at Leipzig, worked with Galton in England. In fact Cattell was interested in individual differences while he was a student in Germany. At Columbia University he was very active in promoting this field of investigation, not from the standpoint of working on old age but in terms of individual differences at the college or university level. He began collecting data on physical and mental measurements of students at Cambridge University, and later at the University of Pennsylvania, and Bryn Mawr College in 1887-1888. He published a description of these tests in 1890 (Galton, 1890). The methods were gradually revised and were used on students at Columbia University in 1894-1895 and 1895-1896. At a Philadelphia meeting of the American Psychological Association in December, 1895, a committee was appointed to consider the feasibility of cooperation among the various psychological laboratories in the collection of "mental and physical statistics." The members of this committee were Professors Cattell, Baldwin, Jastro, Sanford, and Witmer. There were stirrings of this same nature in Europe; Kraepelin in Germany and Binet in France were interested and put students to work in this general field. The Ss of these tests were usually young people who were available as student material who could be called upon for this purpose. It was a scientific development that captured the interest of many capable people with different kinds of scientific training.

The Mental Test Movement

Before the development of mental tests of the Galton-Cattell-Binet type there had been publications, such as that of G. M. Beard (1874), "Legal Responsibility in Old Age," and by R. A.

Proctor, (1873), "Growth and Decay of Mind." Both these men proposed testing the capacity for appreciating one of Shakespeare's plays as a kind of mental dynamometer. Actually it was the Army Mental Tests used at the time of the first World War that advanced and popularized the idea of mental testing of adults. Robert M. Yerkes (1921) prepared the very extensive report published as a National Academy of Science memoir under the title "Psychological Examining in the United States Army." Chapter fourteen especially is germane to our interest. Quite a number of trail-blazing publications in psychological journals, monographs, and books appeared in the decade 1920-1930. As examples, there were contributions by Beeson, Bunch, Grace, Hollingsworth, Jones, Conrad and Horn, Sorenson, Thorndike and associates, Nicholson, and Willoughby, to name a few. In this same period came the large volume by G. Stanley Hall with the title "Senescence; the Last Half of Life." This volume is not based on experimental data but nonetheless is filled with very interesting and erudite observations and comments. It is worthy of perusal. Contributions resulting from the work on Later Maturity at Stanford University, aided by two grants made by the Carnegie Corporation of New York, might be cited (Miles, 1931, 1932). There is one study associated with that research which is particularly worthy of notice. It is a book by Professor Edward K. Strong entitled "Change of Interests with Age." It is based on a very large population of results and contains much information that remains of interest to those working in this general field. The gerontological bibliographies which resulted from the labors of Dr. Nathan W. Shock indicate that the Stanford University Press is greatly interested in this field. Stanford University may also take some credit for what has been accomplished by one of her emeritus professors, Dr. Lillian J. Martin, who, when she retired from her Professorship in Psychology in the University at age 65, founded and carried on a Mental Hygiene Center and Clinic in San Francisco for 27 years. This work resulted in a number of publications, one of which appeared when she was 79 under the title "Salvaging Old Age," published in 1930. It is still a vital document (Martin & de Gruchy, 1930).

Zoologists and other students of animal form are banding or otherwise marking creatures that they wish to study from the standpoint of migration or life duration. Fish have sometimes been marked this way by bright metal tags, but it happens that the bright metal serves to make them bait for other fish. The obvious lesson is that older men and women, both the researchers and the researched, must be on the alert to avoid predators.

Man's Opinion of Man Develops

In 1882, an Illinois newspaper, commenting on the illness of a certain gentleman, said: "He is 50 years of age, and his ailment is simply old age." In 1957, a magazine report on an American businessman of 90 years, quoted him as saying "Some people talk nowadays as if work is just something to be endured for the leisure it buys us. I look at it just the opposite, I would be willing to endure quite a bit of leisure, if I had to, for the pleasure of working."

President John F. Kennedy on February 21, 1963, delivered a notable message before the House of Representatives. He entitled that address: "Elderly Citizens of Our Nation" and in his first sentence quoted Toynbee to the effect that, "A society's quality and durability can best be measured by the respect and care given to its elderly citizens." In the House of Representatives and in the Nation many were surprised by our current population statistics quoted by the President. Age 65 is the most widely adopted retirement rule and the population at the time he spoke included 17.5 million people of that age or older. This number was said to be increasing by about 1,000 per day.

The President in a most gracious manner said, in part, "our senior citizens present this Nation with increasing opportunity to draw upon their skill and sagacity and the opportunity to provide the respect and recognition they have earned. It is not enough for a great nation merely to have added new years to life—our objective must also be to add new life to those years."

This is a well-known call to rally gerontology, psychology, and all the sciences of man to a united effort for achievement of a deeper understanding of man and his place and future in the universe.

Postscript: Some who peruse this address will think of the importance of conferences on aging, such as were organized by the Macy Foundation three decades ago. There are also individual names and publications that are perhaps just as worthy as those that have been mentioned. The author shares this attitude and suggests Walter B. Cannon's "The Way of an Investigator."

References

Addison, J.: (Translator) Trattato de la vita sobria, by L. Cornaro, The Spectator, Oct. 13, 1711.
Beard, G. M.: Legal responsibility in old age. Russell, New York, 1874.

Bible: Pictorial family Bible containing the Old and New Testaments, together with the Apocrypha. Walden & Stone Publications, Cincinnati, 1881; *Eccl., 12:* 7-8.

Breasted, J. H.: *Tomb Stele of Nenkhsekhmet. Ancient records of Egypt.* Historical Documents, Univ. Chicago, 1907, Vol, 108-109.

Browne, L.: The world's great Scriptures. Macmillan Co., New York, 1961, pp. xvi + 559, see p. xv.

Butler, W. F.: The art of living long. Privately arranged and printed in Milwaukee, Minn. Undated. Butler wrote a preface to this collection of reprinted essays by Cornaro, Addison, Bacon, and Temple.

Cannon, W. B.: *The way of an investigator. A scientist's experience in medical research.* Norton, New York, 1945, pp. 229, see pp. 219-223.

Cato: or an essay on old age by Marcus Tullius Cicero with remarks. Printed for J. Dodsley, London, 1773, pp. 319.

Cattell, J. McK.: Mental tests and measurements. *Mind,* 15: 373-381, 1890.

Cicero's three books of offices or moral duties, literally translated by C. R. Edmonds. H. G. Bohn, London, 1856, pp. 213-262.

Erasmus, D.: *Select colloquies,* L'Estrange, translator, London, 1680, pp. 264, see p. 91.

Franklin, B.: *The works of Benjamin Franklin,* consisting of essays, humorous, moral, and literary: with his life, written by himself. S. Andrus & Son, Hartford, 1850, pp. 304, see p. 13.

Hall, G. S.: *Senescence: the last half of life.* Appleton, New York, 1923, pp. xxvii + 525.

Henderson, E. F.: (Editor and translator); *Select historical documents of the middle ages.* Bell & Sons, London & New York, 1892, pp. xiv + 477, see pp. 189-201 & p. 274.

Kennedy, J. F.: *Elderly citizens of our nation,* 88th Congress, 1st Session, House of Representatives, Document No. 72, Feb. 21, 1963, pp. 10, U. S. Gov't Print. Office, Washington, D. C.

Martin, L. J., and C. deGruchy: *Salvaging old age.* Macmillan, New York, 1930, pp. 173.

Miles, C. C., and W. R. Miles: The correlation of intelligence scores and chronological age from early age to late maturity. *Amer. J. Psychol.,* 44: 44-78, 1932.

Miles, W. R.: Measures of certain abilities throughout the life span. *Proc. nat. Acad. Sci., Wash.,* 17: 627-633, 1931.

Minot, C. S.: On certain phenomena of growing old. *Proc. Amer. Ass. Adv. Sci.,* 39: 1890; also offprinted with special cover by Salem Press Publ. & Prt. Co., Salem, Mass., 1891, pp. 21.

Pollak, O.: Social adjustment in old age. A research planning report. *Soc. Sci. Res. Council, Bull.,* 59: see p. 161, 1948.

Ruger, H. A., and B. Stoessiger: On the growth curves of certain characters in man (males). *Ann. Eugen.,* Pts. I & II, 1927, pp. 76-110.

Sherrington, C.: *Man on his nature.* The Gifford Lectures, Edinburgh, 1937-1938. Penguin Books, Harmondsworth, Middlesex, 1955, pp. 312, see sections on "zest-to-live."

Strong, E. K.: *Change of interests with age.* Stanford Univ. Press, 1931, pp. 235.

Yerkes, R. M. (Editor): Psychological examining in the United States Army. *Mem. nat. Acad. Sci.,* Washington, D. C., No. 15, 1921, see Chapt. 14.

Some Historical Developments of Social Welfare Aspects of Aging

Ollie A. Randall, A.B., Hon. A.M. and Ph.D.[1]

It is clearly evident that a statement of social welfare developments in the field of aging as that is thought of today, in this seventh decade of the 20th century, to be comprehensive and historically accurate in detail would require several well-documented tomes in order to do justice to the topic or to give it coverage with any degree of accuracy. "Social welfare" in its fullest meaning is all-inclusive, embracing as it does all the factors, economic, cultural, scientific, religious, or spiritual, which have an impact on the well-being of a human being and upon the social organizations of which he is an integral part—his family, his local, state, and national communities, and such subdivisions of them of which he is a functioning member.

There is a very real and unavoidable *interdependence* between the character of the basic economy of man's environment and his ability to function within it in his own behalf or that of others, between the actual existence and kinds of measures for the preservation of health and their availability to him, between his heritage of social and cultural mores of a racial, national, and religious nature and his attitudes toward himself and toward others of any age, and between the geography and climate of the place in which he lives and his behavior toward his fellow men. All of these factors weight the degree of their interdependence, especially when the situations of older people of a given society are at stake. Therefore for the purposes of this résumé, the primary focus must be limited and directed to those fairly recent developments in the United States which have either promoted or prevented improvements in the status of people, either as individual members of society or as members of an age group. Like population curves, the historical acceleration is a development of the 20th century. The past has its markers which changed slowly because needs emerged slowly and were met readily.

Early History

Social concern for the aging and the aged antedates Biblical days and the early Christian era. This is recorded in the history of those nations or racial groups which reached a stage of social and civil organization in which the individual was accorded status as a person in that organization. It took the teachings of the Judeo-Christian faiths to bring this concern to a tangible flowering to which both the Old and the New Testaments bear eloquent witness. True, the numbers of those who survived birth, infancy, adolescence, and early adulthood were comparatively few indeed, but those few were as a rule greatly respected and honored, not only for their age but for the wisdom of their years.

Provisions for the care of the survivors of the very real hazards of life usually were accepted as the logical responsibility of the family, immediate or not so immediate. This fact, rooted in religious philosophy as it is, accounts for many legal requirements with regard to family obligations, as well as for many of the emotional or psychological difficulties created for families by such rapid social change that it seems to make events revolutionary rather than evolutionary. So-called "social provisions," those made by the community, whatever their nature, for the elderly as well as other "misfits" generally were institutional. Concern for the individual as a person and for his needs as a human being within an institutional environment were non-existent or at least have not been plainly evident.

It is interesting to note that in southern Europe, where institutions or "homes for the aged" were established many centuries ago and are still in operation, what seemed to be public responsibility, in the beginning, in reality was an expression of

[1] National Council on the Aging, 20 West 45 St., New York, New York, 10036.

concern on the part of public-spirited citizens. Both government and the church engaged in the operation of these homes only when forced to do so either by the pressures of increasing costs of the care of increasing numbers or the uncomfortable pressures of religious conscience when the kind of care given could no longer be tolerated. Some homes for aging persons established in Yugoslavia in the 14th and 15th centuries, for example, are still in use, in the original buildings. Their direction and programs are completely modern in scope. Similar old structures with advanced methods are to be found in practically every country in the Western civilization. History is said to repeat itself, and the historical development of social concern and its practical expression in America parallels that of Europe.

Early American Development

In America the social, moral, and economic responsibility for an older person has been vested primarily in the individual himself for himself (the rugged individualism of pioneer days) or in his family, if there was one. This ethic still exists with a strength that has diminished very little. From it stems much of the overt and unspoken intent of the social legislation which is the basis of public social welfare programs. Such intents are even more important for the individual whose circumstances force him to become a beneficiary; and, upon this concept depends the interpretation of that intent *in practice*.

Roman law established basic responsibility for self and family. As later incorporated and interpreted in Elizabethan laws, it in turn forms the basis of *most* (Napoleonic law is given this role in some areas of the South) of the laws of the United States that govern personal and social responsibility, that is, for whom and by whom. The tradition and statutory effect of such law still dictates in large measure both private and public methods of meeting that responsibility. Today's struggles with filial, familial, and personal responsibility are modern evidence of the slow pace of legislative adjustment to social change and are even more cogent evidence of the lag in attitudinal changes required for an adjustment of cultural mores in a new world.

Public responsibility for the homeless, the sick, the "poor," or the "paupers," including the old, helpless, and infirm, was accepted in Elizabethan days as a matter of necessity for government, when those who required such care proved too great in number to be cared for any other way. In his biography of William Shakespeare, Rowse (1963) pointed out that the dramatist lived in Cripplegate ward north of St. Paul's Catheral in 1602.

Two foundations of almshouses testified to civic spirit: one in neighboring Wood Street of the previous century, the other of recent foundation, 1575, "wherein be placed twelve poor and aged people rent free, having of them seven pence the week, and once a year each of them five sacks of charcoals, and one quarter of an hundred of faggots." (from Stow). These almshouses Shakespeare could see as he went up the street on the right...

Early developments in American colonies, and later in the United States of America, saw "public homes," "poor farms," and "asylums," which housed a heterogeneous group of people who were acknowledged to be socially disadvantaged for a variety of reasons. These followed the pattern of service as it existed in the major mother country.

Philadelphia is an example typical of 18th century United States, possibly influenced by the particular energies and public-minded innovations of a city with a strong Quaker tradition. In 1712, the Philadelphia Almshouse was proposed. The money was appropriated 17 years later, and the structure completed in 2 years. The ordinance of 1712 read:

The poor of this city Dayly Increasing it is ye opinion of this Council that a Workhouse be hired immediately to imploy poor P'rsons and sufficient P'rsons be appointed to keep them at work.

In 1728, the Almshouse was proposed, with 1000 pounds appropriated to purchase the site and 2000 pounds to build the structure. A green meadow bounded by Third, Fourth, Spruce, and Pine Streets was bought for 200 pounds and the brick building erected in 1731 or 1732. It had 14 rooms. By 1751 it had 48 inmates of whom 8 were receiving medical care (the Pennsylvania Hospital was founded in that year). The sectarian Friends' Almshouse was already in existence (1713). The poor, old, foundlings, lunatics, sick, and out-pensioners were the inmates. By 1767, the Almshouse census was 368. Paid physicians in attendance were selected by 1769. In the following year a new almshouse was built

having a colonnade walk (like the monastery at Capistrano) so that the aged could get out in the open in inclement weather.

Such was the early history of what was to become the Philadelphia General Hospital (Hunter, 1955).

As the country grew in geographical size and in numbers of the population, as well as in experi-

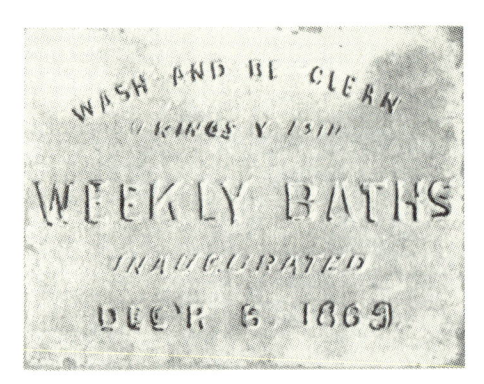

Fig. 1. Bath sign of new policy initiated at the Philadelphia General Hospital (Philadelphia Almshouse, 1869). The biblical admonition is typical.

ence in a democracy founded on the concept that "all men are created equal," the practice of herding together the transient or vagrant, the beggar, the civil offender, the feebleminded and the insane, the sick of all ages, and the old created grave doubts with regard to its soundness or desirability. In fact it became such a cause of concern on the part of religious and fraternal orders, as well as of socially- and philanthropically-minded persons, that "homes for the aged" under church and other private sponsorship began to come into being in greater numbers. These were operated by voluntary, independent management and were supported by voluntary or charitable financing. Public participation usually was limited to the waiving of taxes on land and buildings. This type of participation exists today, but because of the great expansion of voluntary and non-profit enterprises and the burgeoning needs, it is undergoing very close scrutiny with an eye to possible revision if not discontinuance.

Privately or charitably sponsored homes began to acquire a place in the community as a substantial social resource. They provided also a practical method of easing the twinges of social conscience. This occurred at about the same time in the 19th century that voluntary social agencies began to be organized. This dual development was in its early stages in the 1840's and 1850's—with little or no relationship between the two. Social agencies recognized no ties with, and no responsibility for, homes for the aged, which were independently incorporated and which functioned in their own fashion without much regard to social trends. The agencies represented the beginnings of organized "secular" social service as distinguished from church service. However, this was not considered a "professional" function, for the major emphasis was on volunteer service, which consisted mainly of relief in kind to families. Some individuals (the unattached or detached and the elderly) were, as a matter of course, relegated to the public home or to whatever church-sponsored home for which they might prove eligible—when it was clearly demonstrable they could no longer care for themselves or had no one upon whom they could depend for care.

In the nursing profession, the concept of dedication and service of volitional nature by highly-motivated persons was personified in Florence Nightingale, who was trained at Kaiserswerth in Germany. She took her group of religious sisters, practical nurses, and well-born volunteers for nursing service to British troops in the Crimean War. Within a decade, ladies from Germany came to the United States to serve as nurses in a hospital, albeit as deaconesses of the Lutheran Church, but equally motivated by discipline, soap, and prayer.

In a few communities, among them Boston, at the end of 19th and the early years of the 20th century, there is a record of efforts to improve the daily lives of elderly persons outside of institutions, and even to improve the management of the institutions themselves, by moving children, people with infectious or communicable diseases, civil offenders, the feebleminded and insane to places equipped to deal with the special needs. But the institution persisted until the late 1920's and early 1930's as the major solution for the care of the sick or poverty-stricken elderly. The typical family agency felt, and assumed, no obligation for doing anything more than referring them to whatever place could, or would, provide them with shelter, food, and clothing. It is only fair to say that there were several agencies, notably in Boston and New York, which were exceptions to this rule.

Faint stirrings of social conscience were reflected in the few sporadic efforts made by members of the settlement movement, by those neighborhood centers where people were known as neighbors and persons, where there were workers who tried to ease the troubles of those among whom they had chosen to live. Leaders of the stature of Jane Addams, John L. Elliott, William H. Matthews, Mary K. Simkhovitch, and Lillian Wald did much to point the way for non-institutional services, through local clubs, through direct service given when and as needed. In New York City, the interest and financial support of Cornelius N. Bliss and

John D. Rockefeller, Jr., made possible the initiation and maintenance of a "sheltered work" program for elderly men and women. The main purpose was to enable them to enjoy the dignity of "earning" at least part of their cost of living. More important was experimentation with a regular monthly allowance system as a preventive of institutionalization, a visiting nurse and housekeeper plan, and well-developed relationships with public and private hospital social services, and a vacation service which was almost unique in its day.[2] These programs, administered by a voluntary family agency, proved a valuable source of experience when plans for a public old age assistance program were under consideration. They proved a capacity for a high degree of self-management on the part of most of the elderly (and they were elderly!) when given the financial and moral support of a stable, interested organization. Life might be a struggle, but it was infinitely preferable to the "living death" of the institution.

A Broader Social Approach

The statistics of changes in the age composition of the population need not be cited here. Following World War I, during the inflation and short hard depression of the roaring, prosperous 20's, the growing numbers of the elderly *not* sharing in that temporary prosperity began to plague communities which had given little or no thought to their plight, its causes, or its possible remedies. Communities which thought that independent sporadic efforts and after-thoughts of charitable bequests were sufficient were brought up short by the size of the problem which began to enter more homes more directly as life span and aging numbers increased. The elderly of those days, so careless of the future, and of today, can be grateful to the foresight and the dynamic leadership of Abraham Epstein. He was wise enough to anticipate that programs, no matter how well motivated their sponsors and supporters were, would soon be far from adequate to meet the social and economic demands of those older people whose own resources proved insufficient for decent living and for whom community resources were equally in very short supply or non-existent. His unremitting personal drive and that of his organization, the American Association for Social Security, for a public program of social insurance and assistance coverage put the problems of the elderly in their proper perspective, although the timing and the climate of opinion were not conducive to open-mindedness or to ready acceptance.

In 1922, his book, *Facing Old Age—A Study of Old Age Dependency in the United States and Old Age Pensions* (1922), followed by another in 1928, *The Challenge of the Aged*, were an irrefutable call for action by people who admitted a responsibility for their fellows, regardless of citizenship or age status. It was both startling and humiliating to be reminded that the United States was one of three large nations of the world that had taken no action on the matter of old age pensions or dependency support. The other two were China and India! A number of individual states had made studies, a number of associations had taken private action for members. Studies revealed an urgent need for insurance coverage for workmen's compensation, for unemployment, for sickness, and for old age or retirement. The main hurdles were those of estimating costs and the development of sound funding; with increasing longevity the casual estimates of the Iron Chancellor, Bismarck, were shown to be completely erroneous. The placement of management in a nation with unbounded faith in the capacity of private enterprise to deal competently with these social issues posed further problems.

In New York State, to use one example, several social agencies (including an informal association of homes for the aged) organized a group concerned with the social welfare of the aged in its Welfare Council in 1925-1926. This group endorsed and promoted the appointment of a State Commission by Governor Alfred E. Smith to study the needs of older people and to make recommendations for state action. Meantime Mr. Henry G. Barbey planned and built one of the first, if not the first, specially designed rental apartment house for elderly people as an experiment and a demonstration that this type of living was practical and desirable. Serious concern was expressed by many that such housing, with a relief or pension system that would enable people to live in it, would empty almshouses and make homes for the aged unnecessary. Experience has proved the fallacy of this thinking.

The Commission's report (Old Age Security, 1930) recommended a program of public assistance for the elderly, persons 70 or over, and, thanks to a well-administered public program of widows' and mothers' allowances, favorable legislative action was taken in 1930. That this enactment coincided with the beginnings of a cata-

---

[2] The then New York Association for Improving the Condition of the Poor, one of the two parent organizations of the present Community Service Society of New York.

strophic economic depression of overwhelming national proportions had much to do with the "crisis" or "emergency" nature of policy development and the stringent restrictions imposed on the administration of old age assistance at the local, state, and ultimately the national level from which public welfare never recovered in the succeeding 30 or more years. The depression economy brought into being the Social Security program of the federal government with its financial participation in state programs. This has had a lasting influence on the philosophy and practice in social welfare services, administered by either public or voluntary agencies, at state and local levels. The agency controlling the purse strings has much to say about policies, and the gradual shift in the balance of expenditures from private and public funds has both directly and indirectly determined the manner in which funds from both sources are used.

With unemployment the precipitating factor of the depression, the immediate effect of old age assistance was to remove persons 70 or over from the labor market. When this plan proved to be an ineffective measure, the eligibility age for assistance was reduced in 1937 to 65—the age established as the "normal" retirement age. Its normality was determined by the economic requirements of the day rather than individual qualifications for leaving the active labor market. The problems of employment and retirement of the older worker (defined more or less precisely as being a person 45 or over) were emerging even in the 20's. They have seesawed ever since; they were sharply aggravated in the 30's, very much diminished in the war years, and again sharply aggravated in the 20 years since the conclusion of the war actions of World War II and Korea. They still constitute an almost insoluble element in the huge unemployment situation of the 60's, with the consequent movement to lower the normal retirement age from 65 to 62 or to 60. This has been regarded as a solution not for the elderly but for the young workers coming into the labor market.

The quarter of a century of the existence of the several social security programs and the almost phenomenal increase in private pension programs has put a financial floor under old age, flimsy and spotty though it is. The constant improvement in social security insurance coverage is encouraging. Unemployment insurance has proved itself an important factor in the stability of income, but the tremendous numbers of the unemployed (among whom the older and the elderly form what is known as the "hard core"), with the changes in industrial organization resulting from automation or technological developments, present a very bleak future so far as work opportunities are concerned, especially for those 60 and over. There are even more serious problems of morale and status for the workless people in a prosperous or affluent society that is still "work oriented." The dilemma of a shortened work life and an extended biological life doubtless is one of the most serious human problems facing the country today. War no longer provides the right answer, if it ever did.

Family Culture and Housing

The family is the smallest and most important social unit of which a person is a member. There are the unchangeable ties of kinship, those of culture, and of affection which are generally apt to be binding. Much is being written of the weakening of the family structure, of the irresponsibility (chiefly in terms of economic support) of one generation for another. Actual acquaintance with families often reveals that this so-called weakening of family fiber is more superficial than real. The demands of living and working conditions of the modern world necessitate the separation of generations in their living arrangements. The availability of income for the elderly just as often makes this a welcome possibility for each generation. Studies show that many older people live in the households of younger members of the family; it is not known with accuracy how many do this from preference and how many from an ethical or publicly enforced plan. The historical fact is that economic security, mobility, better health, and better education have altered living patterns, in most instances without destroying family relationships, and even with an actual strengthening of bonds.

What does this mean for housing, for living arrangements? In the 20's and the 30's there was limited experimentation by both voluntary and public agencies in New York City and Cleveland. As public housing for low income families became a federal as well as a state and local program, a few elderly persons were included, although it was not until the 1956 amendments to the Federal Housing Act that single persons were eligible for accommodation, despite the fact that they far outnumbered the elderly couples. A decade after the slow start of the 30's and 40's builders and realtors discovered a growing market for housing among retired elderly people. By the 60's provision of "housing for the elderly" by private enterprise became a major activity in most communities, large or small. The true co-operative, the simulated co-operative financed by founders' fees, the condominium, the houses for sale in "retirement towns" increased phenomenally after the passage of the 1956 Housing amendments. Already emerging are the genuine problems of providing personal and social service inevitably required by all groups of persons, and especially by those who are older. Should these be organized and administered by the community at large, or should they be, as they sometimes are, a direct service of the management of the specialized housing developments? For the elderly buyers, as it should be for developers and management, or tenants, this is a question which should be answered before completion of arrangements.

Institutional care, public and private, also has undergone radical change since 1940. From being well-intentioned custodial homes, poorly equipped or staffed to meet the new types of situations that greater longevity has created, institutions have found themselves unable to continue the kind of independent operation and social isolation they once enjoyed. Official inspection and approval by local and state authorities as well as formal accreditation became requisite. Standards for buildings, personnel, and service were introduced. Costs soared and the philanthropic dollar was increasingly hard to come by. Institutions were forced to abandon life-care contracts and had to establish boarding rates on a cost or less than cost basis to maintain "charitable status." This meant that persons in receipt of public assistance could be admitted for an amount mutually agreed upon by the public agency and the home. It also meant the introduction of a fairly powerful "third party" in the decision as to what the payment bought in accommodations and service. It removed the stigma of "non-payment" from the resident, even though funds were from the public coffer. The greatest change has been in the marked advance in the average age of those seeking admission and of the resident population; the first hovers around 80 and second around the middle 80's. It takes no imagination to realize that under these circumstances the character of service of necessity changes from the traditional board, room, and casual supervision to one in which the major component is medical and nursing service. Long-term chronic invalidism under good nursing with the purpose of maintaining fairly good physical functioning is a common characteristic of the health status of residents of current homes for the aged. Rates for care have increased enormously, but so have standards. Homes for the aged, public and private, are, if they are responding to community needs, in large measure residences in which nursing supervision of rehabilitative as well as therapeutic quality is a major aspect of the programs.

Health Services

Without touching upon medical advances and the changing attitudes of the health profession toward the potential for positive results in work with elderly people, it is essential, in a discussion of the history of social welfare developments in the field of aging, to point out the "indivisibility of health and welfare," as indicated by Dr. C. E-A. Winslow, the public health leader. As acute illness became treatable and modified, if not always actually curable, the patient survived to become the host of the chronic sequelae of his illnesses. Elderly people continued to go to hospitals, remained a long time, but a new era has dawned for them. The majority no longer go to die. Their hospital stay often was and still is lengthened, not necessarily by the need of hospitalization itself, but also by the paucity of alternative arrangements. Visiting nurse programs, visiting housekeeper services, and subsequent home care programs were invented and organized in the 30's and 40's, with the patient's home, when suitable, as the base for care.

Nursing homes under proprietary auspices sprang into being almost overnight to house for pay those whose own homes were not appropriate or for whom visiting services did not exist or were not available. Patients who could afford to do so paid, and the public agencies paid for those who could not, with federal, state, and local tax funds. The inability to build hospital beds during World War II contributed much to the development of home visiting services, but even more so to the extraordinary growth in the number of profit-making nursing homes. This has become a big business. While waiting for the establishment of standards of quality of service and responsible agencies to enforce those in existence, there has been created a real standard-setting and enforcement program for both official and voluntary agencies concerned with quality of care and with what happens to older people, already an integer of nursing home care. How this will be solved by the several national and state bodies involved is being debated in the hope that a plan satisfactory to all can be delineated.

Improvement in medical knowledge, the discovery of the capacity of older as well as younger patients to respond successfully to rehabilitative treatment, the gradually growing interest of psychiatrists in the mental, physical, and psychological aspects of aging have contributed to a major change in the organization of services. Restorative nursing, the treatment of disorientation and mental infirmity in the elderly through renewed social involvement, has meant both the release of many persons from unnecessary hospitalization in institutions for the mentally ill, as well as blocked their unnecessary and uneconomic admission. (And this is historically an old issue.) One of the greatest community problems in the so-called "mental health area" is to organize enough appropriate "protective services" for the many older persons who are not wholly able to manage themselves or their affairs and who are without anyone legally responsible to do this for them. The hospital for the mentally ill is ceasing to be the dumping ground, for lack of any other alternative, for this person or his refuge from the age-altered pressure of community living. With the difficulties of health maintenance, this is the traditional and growing social and health problem for elderly individuals, families, agencies, and communities. Prevention of isolation from social contacts and the natural lapse of interest in the affairs of a retreating and narrowing world by many of the elderly, for whom society provides too few opportunities for association with others of all age levels, has been demonstrated to be practical and possible, if people can be aroused to care and to do something about it.

Leisure

Time, any amount of it, can be an asset when there is a use for it. Nothing is so precious. If there be awareness of it, it is, after all, the assurance that there is still possession of life itself, no matter how painful, how sordid, or difficult it may be. For many elderly people living has been a progression through a period of practically no free time, no leisure, to a period when in a sense there seems to be "time unlimited," chronologically and unfortunately circumscribed by the lessened number of days and years left. As industrial society has cut off more older workers earlier in the life span, with more years left with nothing of importance to do with them, various measures for meeting the emergent needs for interests or occupation of the already retired have been devised. As yet too little has been done for those who will follow to prepare them for a retirement which they will enter with better health, better income, and better education than their predecessors had, but with little improvement in knowledge of how to spend uncommitted time wisely.

The most successful and prevalent development has been that of clubs and centers for the elderly which have been poorly and inaccurately nominated as "golden age clubs." These grew in number after the imaginative concern of Harry Levine of New York launched and nurtured the first center under quasi-public auspices. These have been called the only new social invention of this period. Centers and clubs grew in numbers and in quality of program with the introduction of professional leadership. The influence of adult education on program development has been marked, especially in New York State, where state aid through the Adult Education Division of the State Education Department is available to programs or centers operated and supported by municipalities, towns, and villages.

Nationally, centers across the country, under all types of sponsorships, voluntary, religious, and public, have sensed a need for a means of exchanging experience in order to improve standards and to make programs effective outlets for the skills and abilities of the older persons who comprise their membership. This takes not only time and good organization but also genuine skill; few people, particularly the elderly of today, have had either experience or training in the satisfying use of leisure. Fewer still realize that out of the 24 hours in a day there must be time allocated by plan for the chores of daily living and time for rest and quiet, hopefully so long as this does not become true isolation.

Volunteer work constantly is under discussion as a possibility for the elderly or retired, but recent studies and experiences reveal that in practice this has many hurdles to overcome, such as inexperience, the same age discrimination in the use of the older volunteer as that which operates in regular employment, and the costs of giving such service that the fixed income of elderly people often does not permit. This is another dilemma for the individual and the community toward which center and club personnel are groping for solutions. It too is not new but an adaptation of neighborliness which becomes diluted as urban complexes become more concentrated.

The Church and the Elderly

There is no denying that the church almost always has been the agency with a traditional and openly expressed concern for the elderly. In every denomination, in almost every era, fortified by a variety of dogmas, the aging have been the beneficiaries of religious practices and expressions. This traditional concern has carried into modern times and is manifest both in structures and traditions. The hospice, refuge, asylum, home for the aged, and long-term hospital have benefited from religious concern as well as its coffers. It is the natural place to turn for counseling, for giving and receiving service. But it is just not as simple as this in the highly organized sectarian and denominational groups of today. Church leaders, the clergy, often are preoccupied with the heavy administrative demands made upon them, with holding and improving the place of the church in the community, and with the active involvement of youth, as the guarantee of the future. However, within the past two decades there seems once again to be a growing sense of church responsibility for older people other than that which finds its tangible expression in institutional care.

The leadership in all faiths has been giving much closer attention than ever to the social and health needs of their members and their non-member neighbors. They are renewing active relationships with secular social service agencies and also are organizing their own services with professionally trained leadership. They have opened their doors and given use of their buildings to clubs. They have urged their institutions to examine their programs and to raise standards to meet modern requirements. There is more provision in the curricula of seminaries for training in pastoral counseling of the elderly, for chaplaincy especially related to homes and hospitals. All this, which is rooted in the past, augurs well for the older people of tomorrow. It indicates a willingness and an ability to adjust to modern society within highly organized or structured groups that are, with the secular world, struggling with such vital issues of segregation based on age. The force of religious organization has always been potent; it must acquire elasticity to cope as well in the future as it has in the past with its aging members.

Educational Development for Social Welfare

The need for training to be useful and helpful, for special training in understanding the older person and the forces which make him what he is, was recognized by a very few some 40 or more years ago. The road to acceptance of this philosophy has been hard and long. Some progress in understanding has been made recently, although it must be admitted that more has been achieved with the lay leaders of the community and practitioners than with educators.

Grants by foundations (that modern adaptation of the old beneficent philanthropist) have made studies and demonstrations possible. These have endorsed the principles of generic approaches, but they have also indicated the special characteristics of the personal, social, and health problems of older people. It has been found that a clear understanding of what has created or formed the personality of the older person, or his abilities to handle his own situation, is as important for a worker in any of the professional disciplines as is that understanding in work with young people, if not more so. The doctor, the psychiatrist, the nurse, the therapist, and the reluctant social case worker (the social group workers and community organizers have responded much more readily) are finding new potential in a new generation of the elderly which was never suspected and seldom sought in earlier days.

Schools officials, faculties, and universities in several departments are experimenting with courses, seminars, and institutes designed to explore the special aspects of the process of aging and of its results, the aging and the aged. Many universities are undertaking applied research in the field. Social research, which is still regarded as "unpure," has received abundant support from private and governmental resources. The fundamental factor which makes this explosive situation possible is that there is no phase of personal or organized living which is not in some way affected by the processes of aging. Historically speaking, the record of education for social welfare activities and action in aging has been very disappointing, although the outlook is now brighter. There is the hope that both educational developments and research findings can be effective in practice in the professions, at least for persons now in their middle years. For those already elderly, there is a slim hope that some modest use of what is already known can be made in their behalf.

Organizational Developments

From 1925-1926, which saw the first Division for the Aged in a Welfare Council, to 1964, developments in many types of organizations have been constant, although extremely spotty and variable in effectiveness. Organization of programs for the elderly in community councils, by whatever name known, has been very slow. As has been noted, usually this has been at the behest of lay leaders rather than members of the professions. However, as public programs in insurance, assistance, housing, and health of the aging grew in size and importance, the degree of participation by councils in planning policies was regrettably small. The results of this habit of non-participation are plaguing both public and voluntary groups at the present time.

State developments, especially in New York, under the energetic and able leadership of Senator Thomas Desmond, Chairman of New York State's Joint Legislative Committee on Problems of the Aging, and his Committee's Director, Albert J. Abrams, from 1948 on gave a steady stimulus to support of improving and of initiating programs in employment, insurance, health, housing, education, recreation, and institutional care. Other states found this an excellent device. Some followed suit.

The organization of the American Geriatrics Society, of the Gerontological Society with its interdisciplinary research approach to aging, and the first "White House Conference on Aging" in 1950 was a series of important historical events. Creation of the National Committee on Aging as a standing committee of the National Social Welfare Assembly, and, since 1960, as the autonomous National Council on the Aging, occurred in 1949 and 1950. At this time the topic of the aging and the aged became a particular phenomenon in programs of national, state, and local forums of a number of professional groups. Since 1950, the proliferation of publications on the many aspects of the topic has become marked. Thus from very limited bibliographies there are now many volumes of references. The most important are those prepared and edited by Dr. Nathan Shock of the U.S. Public Health Service in the quarterly issues of the *Journal of Gerontology*, since 1946, one of the official publications of the Gerontological Society. From time to time Dr. Shock published these as bound volumes. There are also the quarterly listings published by the National Council on the Aging.

Federal, state, and municipal governments have established offices or commissions on aging. Governors and mayors have had conferences on the topic. The American Public Welfare Association established a standing Committee on Aging. The American Association of Retired Persons under the leadership of Dr. Ethel Andrus, the American Association of Senior Citizens dedicated to the development of a sound national medical care program for the elderly and its support, and numerous others came into being on the national scene. In 1951, the Philadelphia County Medical Society established a Committee on Geriatrics under the chairmanship of Dr. Joseph T. Freeman. In the following year, the Pennsylvania Medical Society initiated its Commission on Geriatrics which proposed to the American Medical Association what was to be its Committee on Aging under the current direction of Dr. Frederick C. Swartz of Lansing, Michigan.

Influential unions, such as the UAW-AFL-CIO and the United Steel Workers, set up staffs and departments to work with retirees and older workers. All of these and many more joined with the Staff on Aging of the Department of Health, Education, and Welfare to hold the 1961 President's Conference on Aging of several thousand participants. This was organized through the adoption of Congressional legislation introduced by the Hon. John Fogarty, Rhode Island member of the House of Representatives, who was unflagging in his concern and work in behalf of the elderly. The U.S. Senate has its Special Committee on Aging under the Chairmanship of Senator George A. Smathers of Florida, in 1964.

The organization of the Department of Health, Education, and Welfare, with Mr. Robert Ball as Social Security Commissioner (a constant friend of the elderly) and Dr. Ellen Winston as Social Welfare Commissioner and Executive Chairman of the President's Council on Aging, has in it promise of active relationships between voluntary and public programs. The panel of advisors to the Secretary of Health, Education, and Welfare on the aging from across the nation and a well balanced group of disciplines has a potential for service not yet fully realized.

Conclusion

As the country moves into the mid-60's the grave question of half the 18 million elderly living on incomes below the figure established as the "poverty" line is a disturbing one. The anti-poverty program, at least so far, has ignored this group. The even graver question of the provision of adequate medical care, both preventive and therapeutic, and of decent housing for more than half of them cannot but arouse concern. This is particularly true of the current elderly and those who will be included among them before measures adopted in this decade can be effective. There is the gigantic task of education, of keeping ahead rather than behind in action, and of recognizing that the measures of yesterday let alone today do not serve the changing needs of a changing society and a changed people.

All the elderly do not now require help from the community nor will all the elderly need it tomorrow. But the community which should develop historically is one in which there is a climate of opinion congenial to the maintenance of personal and social competence and opportunities for the exercise of this competence. If anything really has been learned in the years of this century, it is that society cannot ignore the older people in its midst, no matter by what chronological age they are identified.

It is good to conclude that the country is moving, albeit slowly, to the point at which its progress can be judged favorably by the way in which it treats its aging and aged. It is a long road from the management of older persons in the families, tribes, clans, and simple social organizations of the past. Despite increasing complexity and vexing problems, the objective remains the same—the aging and the aged with the identical needs and aspirations. The individual has not been erased by the greater expectancy of survival by more persons. The successful community in the final analysis is measured by its success with its old.

References

Epstein, A.: *Facing old age; a study of old age dependency in the United States and old age pensions.* A. A. Knopf, New York, 1922.

Epstein, A.: *The challenge of the aged.* Vanguard Press, New York, 1928.

Hunter, R. J.: *The origin of the Philadelphia General Hospital.* Rittenhouse Press, Philadelphia, 1955.

Photograph of old Philadelphia General Hospital bath plaque made of marble; now in the Osler Museum of that institution. Photograph courtesy of Dr. Hunter.

Old Age Security—State of New York—Report of New York Commission, 1930. (Act signed April 10, 1930). Chairman, S. C. Mastick. Members: C. N. Bliss, Mrs. S. Borg, S. Barkin, L, Gulick, Director.

Rowse, A. L.: *William Shakespeare.* Harper and Row, New York, 1963.

Source Material:

Annual Reports of New York State Joint Legislative Committee on the Aging. 1949-1963.

Kaiser, P. (Special Assistant on Aging): *Charter for the aging, 1955.* New York State Governor's Conference on Aging.

Man and his years: Report of 1950 White House Conference.

The Nation and its older people: Report of 1961 President's Conference.

Publications of the President's Council on Aging and the Office of Aging, Dept. Health, Education, & Welfare.

Schneider, D. (Editor): *Personality in nature, society, and culture.* A. A. Knopf, New York, 1953.

Unpublished and published papers and bibliographies of the National Council on the Aging. 1950-1964.

Subject Index

A

Abbey schools of Charlemagne	8, 12
Abishag	22
Adrenal capsule	27
Aging	11, 23
biological aspects	25
facts (Galenical)	22
Galenic concept	11
history of studies	27
early period (1835-1918)	27
beginning of systematic studies (1918-1940)	27
period of expansion (1946-)	27
killings in primitive societies	25
"non-aging"	23
principles (Hippocratic)	22
studies	26
theories	11, 27, 30
colloid aging	30
humoral	3
intoxication	27, 30
ultradifferentiation of cells	30
treatment	25
initial historical citation	26
Albucasis	6
Alexander the Great	3
American Association of Retired Persons	48
American Association of Senior Citizens	48
American Association for Social Security	43
American Geriatrics Society	28, 48
American Psychological Association	37
American Public Welfare Association	48
Apostle of Senescence *See Luigi Cornaro*	
Arabians	1
physicians *See under individual citation*	5-7
scholiasts	5, 10
World	4-5
Aristotle	3, 5, 26
Aristotelians among the Arabians	6
Army Mental Tests in adult testing	38
Arnold de Villanova *See portrait P. 9*	5, 8, 9-10
Asclepiades	26
Asthma *See J. Floyer and S. Johnson*	19
Astrological influences in longevity	15
Atherosclerosis, initial laboratory studies	28
Avenzoar	5, 6
Averroes	4, 5, 6
Avicenna	5, 6

B

Bacon, Francis *See portrait P. 17*	16-18
Bacon, Roger *See portrait P. 10*	10-11
Bible	2
Book of Proverbs, 3rd Chapter	35
Ecclesiastes compared with *De Senectute*	34
Hebrew, translated by Tyndale into English	35
Holy Writ, world circulation	35
Psalms, 91st	35
Ten commandments and Divine Principle	35
Biological aspects of aging and the aged	25-32
Biological life span	44
British Bible Society (1804)	35
Boerhaave, Herman	20
Brahmanism, ethical concepts	36
Buddhism, ethical concepts	36
Burial customs and death	33

C

Caliphates, Eastern and Western *See Schema P. 2*	2, 5
Canterbury Tales of Chaucer	11-12
Catherine the Great of Russia	20
Cellular structure, intricacy and aging	28
Celsus	26

Centenarians *See by individual citation*	26
Centers for the elderly	46
Chaldea *See Schema, P. 2*	1
Charcot, Jean-Martin *See portrait P. 21*	20-23
Neurology *See J.-M. Charcot*	20
Charlemagne *See Abbey Schools*	4, 8
Capitulary (802 A.D.)	35
Chaucer, Geoffrey *See Canterbury Tales*	11
China *See Schema, P. 2*	1
Christianity, ethic and thought *See Bible*	2, 3
church and the elderly	46-47
Clinics for the aging	37
Club for Research in Aging	29
Cold bathing	19
Compendium Salernitanum	8
Copernicus	12
Cornaro, Luigi *See portrait P. 15; title-page, P. 34*	14-16
Council of Clermont and the Crusades	4, 12
Crimean War and Florence Nightingale	42
Crusades	4, 6
Custodial homes for the aging *See Homes*	45

D

Darwin, Charles and natural selection *see also Wallace*	20
Da Vinci, Leonardo	14
Death, biologic	37
natural and natural selection	37
Delos, inscribed tables	2
Delphi, inscribed tables	2
Divine Principle in types of behavior	35
Doctor Mirabilis *See Roger Bacon*	10
Dynanometer, "mental"	38
Dysentery, pandemic	20

E

Eau d'or or gold water as remedy for aging	9
Ecclesiastes *See Bible*	25
Ego and survival	36
Egypt *See Schema, P. 2*	
physicians	3, 5
Eighteenth century	19-20
Elizabethan era	11, 19
Emphysema *See John Floyer*	19
Employment and retirement of older workers	44
Endocrinology *See under individual citation*	27-28
Endocrine organs *See under individual citation*	28
English Reformation	35
Erasistratus	26
Eroticism and programs of rejuvenation	28
Ethical standards in human society	36
Europe, *See Schema, P. 2*	6
medicine	10
renaissance	6
Exercise, Baconian concept	17
Experimental method of Bacon	18

F

Family	40
culture and housing	44-45
obligations	40
structure and culture	44
voluntary family agency and the aging	43
Father Abraham concept	2
Faust	20
Fifteenth and sixteenth century	13-16
Financing medical care of the aging	30
Floyer, Sir John, *See portrait P. 19; title page of book, P. 20*	19
Fourteenth century	11-12
Franco-Prussian War	20
Franklin, Benjamin	20
French Academy of Science, election of Charcot	20
Revolution	4

SUBJECT INDEX 51

G

Galen, Claudius 3, 5
   views and thoughts on aging 3, 11
Galenists among Arabian scientists 6
Geriatrics 3, 29
Gerontocomi, specialists in old age 13
Gerontology 18
   Gerontological Society 29, 48
   Journal of Gerontology (1946) 29, 48
Gerontology Branch of the National Institutes of Health;
   National Heart Institute 29
Golden Age Clubs 46
Greek thought see Schema P. 2 .... 1, 25
   Grecian influences 1-3
   physicians and scientists 2
Growth energy, loss through life 37

H

Hall, "Sir" John 23
Harvey, William 17
Health services to the old 45-46
Hippocrates 26
   theory of Hippocrates 3
Historià Vitae et Mortis See title page P. 18 18
Homes for the aging 40, 42
   custodial 45
   nursing 45
   public housing 44
      housing for the elderly 45
      Federal housing act 44
   rental apartments for elderly people 43
Home care programs 45
   visiting housekeeper services 45
Human personality and perpetuity 33-39
Humanism 1, 7, 13
   definition 13
   medical 13
   philosophy 2
   tradition 5
Humoral theory of aging 3
Humors and degrees of health (Galenic) 9
   the four elements 15

I

Iberian peninsula 4
Immortality 36
India See Schema, P. 2 1
Industrial revolution 23
Influenza in 18th century period 20
Inquisition, Spanish 6
Institutional care of the aging 45
   institutional environment, attitudes 40
International Association of Gerontology (1949) 29

J

Jesuitical corps and the Reformation 8
Johnson, Dr. Samuel See Sir John Floyer 19
Judeo-Christian faiths 40

L

La Salpêtrière See J.-M. Charcot 20
Law: Elizabethan, Napoleonic, Roman 41
Leisure for the aging 46
Leprosy and monastic orders 7
Life sciences as contrasted with physical sciences 27
Linacre, Thomas, English humanist 13
Longevity 26
Luther, Martin and the Ninety-five Theses 13

M

Maimonides, or Moses Ben Maimon, the Rambam
   See Portrait P. 7 5-7
Medical perspectives in Aging See Schema P. 2 1-24
Medical schools, their development in Europe 6
Medicine, European in relation to Arabians 10
Medieval period and Arabian medical influence 6
Menopause, artificial or induced 28
Mental test movement 37-38
Military orders 7
Monasticism, Christian 5-7
Myxedema compared with senility 28

N

National Academy of Science 38
National Committee on Aging 48
National Council on the Aging 48
National Social Welfare Assembly 48
Natural selection and death See Darwin and Wallace 37
Nineteenth century 20-23
Nursing profession 42
   visiting nurse program 45
Nutrition 14, 15, 17

O

Old Age 2, 33
   pensions 43
   public assistance program 43
   human hope and expectancies 34
   impairment of memory 33, 34
   intellectual powers in the old (Cicero) 33
   testing by appreciation of Shakespeare plays 38
   pastoral counseling 47
   portrayal by M. T. Cicero 34
   religion and salvation 35

P

Palestine 4
   scrolls 2
Papyri of Egypt and the Library of Alexandria 2
Pathology of old age in 1867 21
   cellular, in studies of disease 27
Peale, Charles Willson and longevity 20
Peasants' Revolt 4
Perpetuity and Human Personality 33
Pefsonality of the aging individual 33
Petrarch, Father of the Renaissance 12
Philadelphia Almshouse See reproduction of bath card P. 42 41
Physical and life sciences 27
Physiology, human (Erasistratus) 26
   changes in functions and capacities after middle age 37
   experimental 26
   perception of highest audible pitch 37
   visual acuity test 37
Plague in Marseilles 20
Plato 3
Printing in Europe 12
   first medical book 14
Psychology and evaluative procedures 37
Public health concepts 23
   pattern of service in the United States 41
   responsibility to the aging 41

Q

Quacksalvers 23

R

Rabelais in the humanist movement 13
Rambam, the. See Maimonides Portrait P. 7 6
Reformation 8, 16
Regimen Sanitatis Salernitatum See Arnold de Villanova 8
Regimen of health (F. Bacon) 11
Rejuvenation 28
Renaissance 3, 12-13
   men See Leonardo da Vinci 1, 14
Research, scientific 26
Retirement age, "normal" 44
   towns 45
Rome See Schema P. 2 .... 2-3, 25
   physicians 3
Res Romanae 2
Retardation of old age (Zerbi) 14
Rhazes See Arabian physicians 4, 6
Rush, Benjamin 20

S

Saint Augustine 4
Salerno, school and Regimen 8-9
Scholasticism 8
Science, modern from the 16th century 27
Senescence, nature 3
Senectitude 36-37
Senility 11, 37
   endocrine glands 28
   premature 16
   tremors 21
Seventeenth century 16-19
Sensory perceptions by ages 37
Services to the aged, non-institutional 42

Settlement movement 42
Sexual prowess and the beginning of Endocrinology 27
  hormones *See Endocrinology* 28
  ovaries 28
  testicular procedures 27-28
  thyroid gland 27
Shakespeare, William 16, 41
Sheik, definition 24
Sheltered work program 43
Smallpox in 18th century London 20
Sixteenth century 13-16
Social agencies, voluntary 42
  early American development 41
  hygiene of aging 23
  legislation in the United States 41
  provisions for the elderly, transitions 40
  "secular" service as contrasted with church service 42
  social security program and insurance coverage 44
  welfare of the aged 40, 43
Social welfare aspects of aging 40-49
Statistical studies of Galton 28
  mental and physical evaluations 37
  population samples 37
  strength-type tests 37
Sumerian historians and royal longevity 25
Syphilis, early notations 14

T

Taoism, ethical concepts 36
  views on aging 1-2
Testicular extracts *See Sexual prowess* 27-28
  grafting 28
  transplantation operations, animal and human 28
Thirteenth century 9-11
Twelfth century 4

Theocracy 11
Theory of aging (Roger Bacon) 11
Thermometry *See J.-M. Charcot* 21
Thyroid gland *See Endocrinology* 27
Tyndale's martyrdom 35
  Program 35

U

Unemployment insurance 44
Universities, their rise 12
  Montpellier 6
  Padua 12

V

Vatican Library 14
Villanova, Arnold de *See Portrait P. 9 See title-page
  of book P. 10* 9-10
Visual acuity test *See Physiology, human* 37
Vital capacity studies of the aging (1846) 23
Vivisection *See J.-M. Charcot* 26

W

Wallace, Darwin and natural selection 20
White House Conference on Aging of 1950 and 1961 ...... 30, 48
Woods Hole Conference on Aging 29
Work life in relation to biological life 44
Workman's compensation coverage 43

Y

Yin and Yang 2

Z

Zerbi, Gabriele *See Portrait P. 13 and its enlargement P. 28* 13-14
  regimen of health 14
Zoologists 38

Author Index

A
Adams, F. 26, 31.
Addison, J. 34, 39.
Annual Reports of N. Y. State Jt. Legis. Com. 49.
Anon. 30, 31.
Avicenna. 5, 6, 24.

B
Bacon, F. 16, 17, 18, 24.
Bacon, R. 11, 24.
Barker, L. B. 28, 31.
Beard, G. M. 37, 38.
Bible. 34, 39.
Bichat, X. 20, 24.
Birren, J. E. 27, 51.
Boas, E. 30, 32.
Boring, E. G. 26, 31.
Bowen, C. D. 16, 24.
Breasted, J. H. 2, 24, 26, 27, 31, 33, 39.
Browne, L. 36, 39.
Bryan, C. P. 2, 24.
Burstein, S. 9, 11, 24.
Butler, W. F. 39.

C
Campbell, D. 24.
Cannon, W. B. 38, 39.
Castiglioni, A. 27, 31.
Cato. 33, 39.
Cattell, J. McK. 37, 39.
Charcot, J. M. 20, 21, 22, 24.
Chaucer, G. 11.
Cornaro, L. 16, 24.
Cuffe, H. 11, 24.
Cowdry, E. V. 29, 31.

D
Dobson, J. F. 26, 31.
DuNouy, L. 31.

E
Epstein, A. 43, 49.
Edmonds, C. R. 33, 39.
Erasmus, D. 34, 39.

F
Ficinus, M. 11, 24.
Floyer, J. 19, 24.
Franklin, B. 35, 36, 39.
Freeman, J. T. 23, 24, 29, 31.

G
Galen, C. 3, 24.
Galton, F. 28, 31, 37.

Gardner, M. 28, 31.
Garrison, F. H. 3, 5, 6, 24, 27, 31.
Glass, H. B. 31.
Gordon, B. L. 5, 7, 24.
Grant, R. L. 2, 3, 24, 27, 28, 29, 31.
Gruchy, C. de. 38, 39.
Guillain, G. 24.
Gunn, J. A. 19, 24.
Guthrie, D. 25, 26, 31.
Guthrie, W. K. C. 26, 31.

H
Hall, G. S. 28, 31, 38, 39.
Hamilton, E. 3, 24.
Harrington, Sir J. 9, 24.
Haynes, M. S. 3, 24, 25, 31.
Heiken, C. A. 29, 31.
Hoffman, J. G. 26, 22.
Henderson, E. F. 35, 36, 39.
Hoskins, E. R. 28, 32.
Hufeland, C. W. 20, 24.
Hunter, R. J. 41, 49.

J
Johnson, J. N. 13, 24.

K
Kaiser, P. 49.
Kennedy, J. F. 38, 39.

L
Lansing, A. I. 27, 29, 30, 32.
Laurens, A. du. 14, 24.
Layman, C. M. 25, 32.
Linacre, T. 3, 8, 13, 24.
Lorand, A. 26, 28, 32.

M
Man and His Years. 49.
Martin, L. J. 38, 39.
Miles, C. C. 38, 39.
Miles, W. R. 38, 39.
Minot, C. S. 37, 39.
Monroe, R. T. 29, 32.
Mueller-Deham, A. 30, 32.

N
Nascher, I. L. 29, 32.
Nation and Its Older People. 49.
Nat. Counc. on the Aging. 49.

O
Office of Aging. 49.

Old Age Security. 49.

P
Pollak, O. 36, 29.
Potai, R. 25, 32.
Power, D. 24.
President's Counc. on the Aging. 49.
Proctor, R. A. 38.
Putnam, S. 8, 13, 24.

R
Rabelais, F. 13, 24.
Rowse, A. L. 41, 49.
Ruger, H. A. 35, 37, 39.

S
Santorio, S. 19, 24.
Sarton, G. 31, 32.
Schneider, D. 49.
Shakespeare, W. 16, 24.
Sherrington, C. 39.
Shock, N. W. 30, 32.
Sidman, M. 31, 32.
Simmons, L. 26, 32.
Slonaker, J. R. 28, 32.
Soubiran, A. 5, 24.
Souferan, 2.
Stapleton, L. 31, 32.
Steiglitz, E. J. 29, 32.
Stoessiger, B. 35, 37, 39.
Strong, E. K. 38, 39.
Sudhoff, K. 9, 10, 24.

T
Taylor, T. L. 3, 24.
Thewlis, M. W. 29, 32.
Thoreau, H. D. 31, 32.

V
Valee, B. L. 27, 32.
Villanova, A. de. 5, 8, 9, 10, 24.

W
Wendt, H. 25, 28, 32.
Weyer, E. M. 26, 32.
Woodruff, F. M. 10, 24.

Y
Yerkes, R. M. 38, 39.

Z
Zeitlin, S. 6, 24.
Zeman, F. D. 14, 24, 29, 32.
Zerbi, G. 13, 14, 24.

CONCEPTS OF AGING

Richard L. Grant

CONCEPTS OF AGING: AN HISTORICAL REVIEW

RICHARD L. GRANT, M.D.*

> Certain, when I was born, so long ago,
> Death drew the tap of life and let it flow;
> And ever since the tap has done its task,
> And now there's little but an empty cask.
>
> CHAUCER

I. *Introduction*

The aged, and the problems of aging, have been of concern to man from his very beginnings. In common with all other macroscopic living things, he has a limited life span. Man alone, however, aware of his destiny, and by virtue of his powers of thinking, is able to speculate on the cause of this limitation.

As he has slowly discarded the limitations of former days, man has been increasingly rewarded with augmented insight into the causes of the manifestations of aging. He is now able to elucidate a vast number of these in terms of their micropathology, biochemistry, biophysics, physiology, and psychology. This is not because he is more intelligent than his predecessors, but merely because he has accumulated greater knowledge and technical ability—accumulated, in fact, as a direct result of his predecessors' efforts.

On one question, however, modern man is no closer to an answer than were the sages of the past. Although presently he can discard as unfounded or foolish many of the previous attempts at solutions to the question of the

---

* This paper is condensed from a longer monograph, unpublished, detailing a study supported by a grant from the United States Public Health Service, National Institute of Mental Health.

I am indebted to Ilza Veith, Associate Professor of the History of Medicine at the University of Chicago, whose helpful guidance and encouragement provided a needed integrative factor in the preparation of this paper.

Many others assisted in assembling materials and technical work, and I am happy to acknowledge their help. They include: Robert Rosenthal, director of the Department of Special Collections, Miss Angela Rubin, Mrs. Josephine Elliott, Miss Eleanor Johnson, Miss Sabina Wagner—all of the University of Chicago Libraries; and Mrs. Dorothy H. Grant, Mrs. Susan J. Grant, and Mrs. Kathryn Hoare.

ultimate or primary cause of aging, out of which grow the derangements that cause the manifestations of aging so thoroughly studied today, he is unable to offer other than a metaphysical answer—that aging is a natural process inherent in the individual, if not in the species. The reasons given to support this are varied and teleological.

It may be that the solution to this problem partakes of the nature of the inexplicable mystery of man's existence and should rightly remain in the realm of metaphysics, at which level it has been discussed in the past. Our predecessors may not have been at as great a disadvantage as we might suppose.

But it is not my intention to imply that the question of the cause of aging is not answerable, or that an answer may not result from the many fruitful and productive endeavors directed to the general problems of gerontology and geriatrics. I mean only that, as yet, there is no clear indication that the answer to why man and other living beings age will be forthcoming from science or any other discipline. The purpose of this review is to place in historical perspective previous endeavors to explain the process of aging.

II. *Preliterate, Egyptian, and Eastern Contributions*

In times past, a man was thought to be aging when he showed the signs usually associated with old age. As man has gained more insight into the processes of germination, growth, and senescence, he has pushed the onset of old age further and further backward toward the beginning of life. In recent times, senescence has been referred to as merely one aspect of the developmental process, which would place senescent inception coeval with the conception of life. This conclusion, first made in the Greco-Roman period as speculation, and later formulated from knowledge made available by scientific advancement, can be stated today as an accepted fact. It is merely a descriptive fact, however, and there is no implicit notion of causation.

The first full, explicit theory of the causation of aging is found in Greco-Roman medicine. Before this time, a theory of aging must be extracted from thought which was mainly concerned with death and its causes. A survey of this pre-Greek material, scanty as it is, will provide the basis on which the theories of later ages can be more easily understood.

The difficulties encountered in attempting a definition of preliterate thought concerning the aging process are, however, almost insurmountable. With no access to records left by its peoples, the only possibility, with all its pitfalls, is to reason by analogy from the thought of contemporary preliterate societies. Certain generalizations, pertinent to the aim of this paper, are made, but their tenuous basis must be kept in mind. These generalizations are valid for contemporary preliterate societies and may be valid for prehistoric preliterate societies. They are taken mainly from the excellent comparative study by Simmons [1].

First, it is important to note that problems associated with aging and the aged were probably much less frequently encountered in primitive societies. The deadly triad of disease, famine, and warfare probably prevented all but a small fortunate fraction of society from reaching old age. The life span was probably not appreciably less than ours, but certainly the average expectancy was very low, and, in addition, the symptoms of old age began early. Disease and death were generally looked upon as the result of magic and sorcery rather than due to natural causes. Even a death which should seemingly have been ascribed to old age was said to have a supernatural cause. Death was by no means universally thought to be inevitable and, in general, was believed to have a demonistic or theurgic foundation. Unfortunately, no information is available on what possible reasons might have been given for the many manifestations of old age, although we may assume that if they were relatively uncommon, they must have been ascribed to preternatural influence.

Abandoning or putting to death the old, which appears to have been practiced at times, in addition to infanticide and abortion, was almost always secondary to dire necessity and the duress of primitive life. As man gained greater command over nature, a certain repugnance, reinforced by superstitions, arose toward abandoning or killing the old. This superstition is demonstrated in the almost universal belief of primitive societies in the existence of ghosts and the future life of the spirit. The reactions and attitudes of these people to death, including death in old age, would quite evidently be affected by this belief. The spirits of the old had to be propitiated to prevent retaliation or persecution. Clearly, primitive man's thoughts about the causes of aging and death were inextricably interwoven in the spiritual and religious fabric of his existence, as were all other facets of his life. No truly separate theories can be discerned or discussed.

Interpreting the causes of aging and death mainly in the light of religious and magical beliefs has by no means been limited to prehistoric societies. Except for Greek and modern scientific endeavors to find a solution, this has been an almost universal approach, as will be shown.

The Papyrus Smith, probably written in the Old Kingdom, 3000–2500 B.C., contains the first known written statement about treatment of the old, indicating that in Egypt the problems of the aged were beginning to receive enough attention to deserve comment. A portion of the papyrus is a "Recipe for Transforming an Old Man into a Youth." After a detailed description of the preparation of a paste which is kept in a container of semi-precious stone, these instructions are given [2]:

Anoint a man therewith. It is a remover of "wrinkles" from the head. When the flesh is smeared therewith, it becomes a beautifier of the skin, a remover of "blemishes," of all "weaknesses" which are in the flesh. Found effective myriads of times.

According to Breasted, the words in quotation marks are uncertain but mean some of the unsightly external indications of advanced age. Breasted points out that no mention is made of the effect of this material on other than the external physical manifestations of old age.

The context in which this prescription arose is better understood by realizing that medicine in Egypt is thought to have been almost exclusively in the hands of the priesthood, and subject to the distortions, prejudices, and misinterpretations inherent in such an atmosphere. This passage from the Papyrus Smith, although sounding rational or empirical, probably refers to a magical reversal of wrinkling.

One of the earliest attempts to explain the manifestations of aging is recorded in the Papyrus Ebers, which dates from about the sixteenth century B.C. [3]:

As to 'debility through senile decay,' it is (due to the fact) that purulency is on his heart.

Or, as translated by Bryan [4]:

When there is weakness as the result of old age, behold it is the uxedu [painful swelling] at his heart.

Although the exact significance of the terminology is in doubt, it may be assumed that the heart was considered important in the aging process. The role this concept played in later thought is unknown, but somehow, the Egyptians—and later the Greeks and others—concluded that an unknown process affected the heart and caused aging.

This is admittedly just a sampling of Egyptian thought, but it is probably representative. The Egyptians may have had a complete concept of the cause of aging, but today it seems unavailable. We will have to consult later times for a complete theory.

Before we proceed to the first separate formulation of a theory for the cause of aging—in the Greco-Roman period—the sometimes neglected thought of the East should be discussed. In *The Yellow Emperor's Classic of Internal Medicine*, pertinent thoughts on the problems of aging are found, which we will assume to be representative of the Chinese thinking of the pre-Christian era on this subject. Indeed, in many parts of Asia today, these thoughts on aging and their general philosophic understructure as expressed in this ancient Chinese work are still extant with only minor modifications. The *Classic* is probably a compilation, and although most of the text is said to have existed between 200 B.C. and A.D. 200, its roots are undoubtedly in the earliest oral traditions of the Chinese.

The basis of the theory of Chinese medicine is the religious and philosophical doctrine of Taoism—the Doctrine of the Way. Intimately connected with this doctrine is a belief which holds that just as the universe is made up of two opposite principles in harmony with each other—Yin and Yang—so also is the body constituted. Ailments are ascribed to a lack of balance between these two principles. Imbalance can be brought about in several ways, including failure to follow "the Way." According to this theory, health and longevity are identical, thereby making the aging process and its manifestations a disease.

It was recognized that man did not have an unlimited life span [6]: "The limit of man's life can be perceived when man can no longer overcome (his disease); then his time of death has arrived." The "natural" course of a man's life, to which all aspired, was terminated at a very old age, the natural faculties remaining unimpaired until death. That the common man fell far short of this ideal was apparent. Only by foreseeing the workings of Yin and Yang and maintaining his harmony with Tao could he hope to extend his life to an old age. Anything which thwarted this process, including the many changes which occur as a direct result of or concomitant with aging, was unnatural and was a disease. Although a cause of aging is not explicit in this work, there is the implied assumption that aging was due primarily to failure to lead a proper life.

India, like China, very early had a well-developed system of medicine and surgery related to its religious and philosophical beliefs. An extensive branch of Indian medical thought is contained in the *Sushruta Samhita* and deals with the science of rejuvenation and the prolongation of life. The theory of the causation of disease and aging, which would be necessary in order to speculate on this subject, is incompletely available but has been outlined in part by Veith [7]. It was held that harmony of the elementary substances of the body constituted health and that disharmony resulted in disease. Four different types of disease were recognized: traumatic—due to extraneous physical insults; bodily—related to aliments and the blood or humors; mental—caused by excessive emotions; and natural—the result of both privation of physical necessities and the process of aging. Here, then, is a relatively advanced, implicit notion that the process of aging can result in "natural" diseases. The ancient Indians recognized that man was possessed of "innate morbific tendencies" [8] and had a naturally limited life span. The process of aging, the effects of which are described as fully in the *Sushruta* as they are in the more ancient descriptions of old age found in the Hippocratic Corpus and in the Bible, was apparently looked upon as a natural process as well. As a result of the changes occurring during aging, susceptibility to disease was increased. The process of aging could, therefore, have been looked upon as a "cause" of disease. That the ancient Indians held the aging process in part reversible is clearly seen in the descriptions found in the *Sushruta Samhita* of the use of Soma and innumerable other compounds capable of rejuvenation.

The Indians, however, regarded rejuvenation as a means, not, like the Chinese, as an end. While the Chinese desired to extend life merely in order to enjoy it longer, the Indians, in keeping with their religious beliefs, wished to prolong life ". . . as much as possible so as to have a longer period of spiritual preparation for the final goal of Nirvana when [the] soul may be freed from transmigration and can rejoin the World Soul" [9].

It is natural that the less mundane, more exalted, motivation of the Indians for longevity would lead to the very elaborate system for rejuvenation which is given in the *Sushruta Samhita*. In fact, the theories held by the Indians about the causes of illness, death, and even aging, almost certainly were formulated within the limitations, and chosen from the possibilities, imposed by their religious doctrine—an indication that we must look further for a truly rational theory of the cause of aging. In some of the later theories of aging, however, we will see vague but unmistakable vestiges of Eastern thought.

III. Western Thought

The Hippocratic theory (about fourth century B.C.) of the cause of disease, with the emphasis on observation, is divorced from theological or magical beliefs, which were interwoven in the concepts of the preliterate, the Egyptian, and the Eastern peoples. Founded on Greek philosophical doctrines, this theory is one of the first attempts at a rational explanation of the causation of disease.

The essential factor in life was held to be heat. Its source was thought to be the left heart, from which it pervaded the whole body, maintaining the healthful eucrasia of the humors. According to the Hippocratic theory [10],

... growing bodies have the most innate heat; they therefore require the most food, for otherwise their bodies are wasted. In old persons the heat is feeble, and therefore they require little fuel, as it were, to the flame, for it would be extinguished by much. On this account, also fevers in old persons are not equally acute, because their bodies are cold.

This is a concept which is repeated, with variations, by many subsequent authors. Recognizing the inevitable course of man's life, the theory was expounded that at the inception of life, each individual was given a finite quantity of material on which life depended—called, among other things, innate heat, vital spirit, or vital force. This material, not necessarily physical, was utilized during the lifetime of the individual. The rate of utilization and the time needed to utilize it fully varied with the individual. This innate heat could be fortified or replenished by various means, but it could never be completely restored to a given previous level; the total reserve of innate body heat continuously diminished. This attenuation of innate heat was equated with aging and was looked upon, not as the result of preternatural influences or capable of being halted, but rather as the natural and, above all, normal course of events. The logical conclusion which should have been drawn from this general notion seems to be that the aging process itself is not a disease. The diseases to which the natural diminution of the innate heat made the body more susceptible were recognized, but they were confused with the aging process itself and were thought to be essential parts of it.

Overlooking this confusing of aging with diseases in the old, we find the Hippocratic doctrines, based on previous Greek philosophy, to be a remarkable step forward in an attempt to explain the aging process. The groundwork was laid for the conclusion that the aging process was an irreversible and natural event which predisposed the body to certain diseases and eventually set the stage for a fatal illness.

Aristotle, about a century later, expounded in infinite detail a theory of aging and death in his book *On Youth and Old Age, On Life and Death and On Respiration* [11]. He voiced the physiological fundamentals that were the basis for the Hippocratic discourse. I submit that, within the limitations imposed by the general level of knowledge of the times, Aristotle's views, though sometimes mistaken, are astute and, indeed, visionary. Far greater progress was made toward a solution—or, at least, a reason—for aging between man's origin and Aristotle than between Aristotle and the present time; in fact, since Aristotle, we may have just been marking time.

According to Aristotle, everything that lives has a soul whose seat is the heart and which cannot subsist without natural heat. The soul is incorporated in the natural heat which is innate in every animal and also has its source in the heart. The soul and the innate heat are combined at birth; life consists of maintenance of this heat and its relationship to the soul. Aristotle likened the innate heat to a fire which had to be maintained and provided with fuel: just as a fire could run out of fuel or be put out, the innate heat could also be exhausted or extinguished.

Aristotle divided death into natural and violent: natural death had an internal cause and was not the result of an adventitious ailment; violent death was due to external causes. A natural death was the natural course of events and occurred only after a lapse of time and the fulfillment of the natural term of life. The principle, or source, of life was lost when the innate heat could no longer be refrigerated and was consumed by its own activity. Thus, natural death had to be preceded by a long old age.

Aristotle recognized that diseases, and even minor ailments, had a greater effect in old age than in youth and could cause speedy death. He likened the diminished innate heat of old age—the result of exhalation after a long period—to a small feeble flame which could be extinguished with the slightest disturbance. If left undisturbed, this flame would eventually go out by itself when the fuel was exhausted.

This extensive theory, summarized above, was free of theological implications. Clearly, old age was a period when the innate heat was diminishing, and it could be ascribed to this diminution. There is even a hint of the idea that the amount of the innate heat gradually declined all during life, although the most marked effects are seen in life's later years—an idea first explicitly stated by Galen.

The acme of original contributions that stemmed from Greek philosophical doctrines was reached with Galen (*ca.* A.D. 130-200). Basing his thought on Aristotelian philosophy and using the Hippocratic method of observation, Galen expressed several new and penetrating conclusions concerning the aging process in the book *De Sanitate Tuenda*. Equipped with the concepts of aging held by his predecessors and with the doctrine of humoral pathology supplemented by a concept of *pneuma* permeating and animating all the parts, this facile, intelligent mind—and colossal ego—expounded a system which was meant to explain completely the aging process and death.

The conclusions of this remarkable ancient author are important from two standpoints. His theory represents the culmination of all previous ideas. His whole medical system, including his approach to aging, remained unchanged and virtually unchallenged until the Renaissance because its philosophical basis was closely correlated to and compatible with Christian dogmatism. Galen's misconceptions and errors are quite clear and understandable in the light of the level of knowledge of his time. To make him responsible for the perversions of his ideas perpetrated by sterile minds in the subsequent millennium and a half, however, does him great injustice. His own admonition that one ought to be more concerned with things than with words went unheeded by subsequent writers, who enshrined Galen's writings in an almost unassailable temple of admiration; the crumbling foundations may still be seen.

Galen separated the nature and sources of disease into those which are inevitable and intrinsic, with their basis the source of generation, and those which are not inevitable, arising from extrinsic influences. Blood, a substance amenable for any use, and semen, which carried out and established the design of the Creator, were the sources of generation.

In order to produce tissues from the moist combination of blood and semen, it was necessary to add an element with the power of drying. Therefore, fire was added and [12]

... by this means, then, the embryo is first formed and takes on a little firmness; and after this, drying more, acquires the outlines and faint patterns of each of its parts. Then, drying even more, it assumes not merely their outlines and patterns, but their exact appearance. And now, having been brought forth, it keeps growing larger and drier and stronger until it reaches full development. Then all growth ceases, the bones elongating no more on account of their dryness, and every vessel increases in width, and thus all the parts become strong and attain their maximum power.

But in ensuing time, as all the organs become even dryer, not only are their functions performed less well but their vitality becomes more feeble and restricted. And drying more, the creature becomes not only thinner but also wrinkled, and the limbs weak and unsteady in their movements. This condition is called old age.... This then, is one innate destiny of destruction for every mortal creature....

These processes, then, it is permitted no mortal body to escape; but others, which ensue, it is possible for the forethoughtful to avoid. Moreover, the source of these is from attempting to correct the aforesaid inevitable processes.

Thus, the very element which was essential to the original formation of life led directly and unequivocally to its extinction. In fact, even during life, before its inevitable end, the intrinsic warmth (exactly like the innate heat of Aristotle) caused loss of bodily substance, which could only be replaced by respiration (*pneuma*), eating, and drinking. Complete restoration was not possible, however.

Galen's theory of the causation of old age is clearly stated [12]:

... this is why we grow old, some at one age, others at another, sooner, or later, because we either are from the beginning by nature excessively dry, or become so either from circumstance, or diet, or disease, or worry, or some such cause. For that which all men commonly call old age is the dry and cold constitution of the body resulting from many years of life.

The so-called modern theory, that the aging process is not just a condition peculiar to the last part of the life span, but is a process beginning with conception, was presaged by Galen and, in fact, directly stated [12]: "... every mortal creature has in him from the beginning sources of death."

Galen dissented from the concept, then current, attributed to Terrence, that old age is itself a disease. He redefined health and its necessary conditions [12]:

The impaired capacity of function determines health. Nor is weakness of function, strictly speaking, a sign of disease, but only what is contrary to nature.... Such a man we should say has some disease, unless he suffers this on account of old age; and some say that this also is a disease.... For all disease is contrary to nature, but such people are not contrary to nature, any more than the aged.

One ought not, therefore, to determine health and disease merely by vigor or weakness of function, but one should apply to the healthy the term "in accordance with nature," and to the sick the term "contrary to nature," and disease a condition producing function contrary to nature....

For the present consideration it will suffice to have this much only, that the range of health is very wide, and that it does not exist with equal absoluteness in us all.

In different, more modern terminology, Nascher (who coined the term "geriatrics" and whose famous pioneer work by that title was published in 1914) wrote the logical modern paraphrase of Galen [13]:

Senility is a physiologic entity like childhood and not a pathologic state of maturity. Diseases are pathologic conditions in a normally degenerating body; not diseases such as occur in maturity complicated by degenerations. The object of treatment of disease in senility is to restore the diseased organ or tissue to a state normal in senility; not to a state normal in maturity.

This comparison demonstrates just one of the examples of the remarkable similarities between modern thinking and the thought which we sometimes look upon as ancient and out-dated.

Unlike Aristotle, then, Galen clearly differentiates death and aging and offers the first full, internally complete and consistent account of a concept of the cause of aging. His works convey the distinct impression that if one removed the scientific terminology from today's concepts, they would appear remarkably like those of Galen.

Literally and completely, Galen disappeared in the second century and so did rational, observation-based medicine, figuratively but only temporarily. Arabic medicine served the invaluable purpose of preserving Greek thought, Galenic or otherwise, until Europe was once again philosophically equipped to speculate and question the why's on which the Greeks had expounded so thoroughly. Avicenna in particular wrote an excellent résumé of the Greek position. An additional refinement first mentioned by Aretaeus is found in Avicenna's *Canon* [14]: "... on old persons and in the decrepit, the *earthy* element is more predominant than in other ages." The superfluity of this "earthy" element plays a great part in some of the theories of the cause of aging until the nineteenth century, especially those of Santorio, Rowbotham, and Hufeland.

IV. *European Thought Before the Enlightenment*

The material that has been considered up to this time has been drawn from many different parts of the globe—India, China, the Hellenic world, the Roman Empire, and the Arabic world. From this point on, however, we will deal almost exclusively with the ideas of the Western world, principally European, because no other culture contributed ideas on aging which were an advance over those already discussed. In India and China, especially, ideas seem to have stagnated. Traditional Chinese and Indian medicine of today is still based on the principles set down in such works as *The Yellow Emperor's Classic of Internal Medicine* and the *Sushruta Samhita*. In Europe, on the other hand, a reawakening interest in the pursuit of knowledge unshared by any other part of the world began in the eleventh and twelfth centuries. This was made possible by a unique combination of social, cultural, economic, geographical, psychological, and religious factors which did not obtain elsewhere. This is not to say, however, that the ideas which developed in Europe were completely new, nor that they progressed without interruption. Not only must the immense debt owed to ancient Greek thought by a reawakened Europe be acknowledged, but the initially retarding effect of the Christian Church on the advancement of science should be recognized.

The rise of Christianity, with its emphasis on the spiritual side of man's life, almost to the exclusion of his physical well-being, created conditions which did not encourage originality in the natural sciences. Still imminently threatened with dissolution by paganism during the first millennium after Christ, the Church's active persecution of deviators from official dogma exerted a marked dampening effect on what is probably a natural propensity of man to speculate, theorize, and experiment.

The questing minds of the times adopted the scholastic method in an effort to avoid the Church's attempts to stifle intellectual pursuits. Although arising originally in the Church as the accepted theological method of discussion, and at first characterized by slavish adherence to ancient authority and little independent thinking, this method was also peculiarly, perhaps uniquely, suited to the tenor and needs of the independent thinkers of the times. It made available the works of the ancients, after translation from their Arabic repository, and allowed these thinkers to discuss and disseminate the knowledge in a manner acceptable to the Church. Later, by disguising their deviations in the logorrhea of scholasticism, with varying degrees of success, they were able once again to feed the flame of curiosity which had been kindled on the Greek peninsula. The fifteenth-sixteenth century revival of learning was the culmination of two related factors: increasing tolerance on the part of the Church, with augmented enfranchisement of intellectual pursuits; and ever-increasing numbers of fruitful, independent, innovating thinkers.

The works of a Franciscan friar of the thirteenth century exhibit an excellent example of the scholastic method being used to explore the knowledge of the ancients, to criticize their authority where necessary, and to express original ideas, ostensibly within the restrictions of the Church. The friar, Roger Bacon, lived from 1214(?) to 1292. According to Castiglioni [15], who calls Bacon the first great experimental philosopher, the true value of Bacon's works still remains in doubt because of the "care with which he felt compelled to write his thoughts in obscure language." Witness to the fact that Bacon was not completely successful in hiding his deviant thoughts are the fourteen years he spent in prison after being condemned by religious authorities. This persecution did not uproot his unorthodox views and methods, but ecclesiastical proscription prevented his works from exerting a greater influence on the thinkers of later ages.

Bacon, termed by Allbutt [16] the only eminent forerunner of the great naturalists of the seventeenth century, wrote widely on many subjects, including theology, physics, and medicine. Castiglioni has said that a general perusal of his works would indicate [15] "... how well he understood the dangers to science from the infiltration of scholasticism and appreciated the superiority of observation over reasoning as a basis of knowledge." Unfortunately, the parts of his writings which are of interest in a survey of theories of aging are not the best examples of his ability and judgment. Sarton [15] regarded Bacon's book *On Retardation of Old Age* as his earliest, poorest, and best-known medical writing. Although it may not sound the depths of Bacon's powers of reasoning and understanding, this book is very important for our purposes.

In this book and in *The Cure of Old Age, and Preservation of Youth*, Bacon's basic principles adhered strictly to the Greek model. Aging was brought about by diminution of the innate heat. To Bacon, this was the "first cause" of man's demise. Three factors tended to bring about attenuation of innate heat [17]:

From these three things, namely, Infection [from the great increase of living creatures which infect the air], Negligence [in ordering our lives], and Ignorance [of the properties which are in things conducing to Health, which might help a disordered way of Living, and might supply the defect of due Government], the Natural Heat, after the time of Manhood is past, begins to diminish, and its Diminution and Intemperature doth more and more hasten on. Whence, the Heat by little and little decreasing, the Accidents of Old Age come on. . . .

These three factors acted on the innate heat in one of two ways, both of which decreased the amount of heat:

Which Weakness and Intemperance of Heat, is caused two ways: by the Decay of Natural Moisture, and by the Increase of Extraneous Moisture. For the Heat exists in the Native Moisture, and is extinguished by External and strange moisture, which flows from weakness of Digestion, as Avicenna . . . affirms.

Another cause of the diminution of the natural moisture, showing a remarkable resemblance to the mechanistic theories of the seventeenth century which held that aging was caused by the wear and tear of living, is found in this passage:

> The second Cause is the toil proceeding from the Motions of the body and Mind, which otherwise are necessary in Life. To these accrue Weakness and Defect of Nature, which easily sinks under so great Evils, . . . not resisting those imperfections that invade it.

Despite his reliance on rational Greek methods, Bacon was not free. The following passage from *Of the Wonderful Power of Art and Nature* answers our questions on Bacon's philosophy concerning man's life span and also expresses a rationale for the writing of a manual of proper rules of hygiene.

> The Possibility of Prolongation of Life is confirmed by this, that Man is naturally immortal, that is, able not to dye: And even after he had sinned [original sin], he could live near a Thousand Years [the antedeluvian span], afterwards by little and little the Length of his Life was abbreviated. Therefore it must needs be, that this Abbreviation is Accidental; therefore it might be either wholly repaired, or at least in part. But if we would but make Enquiry into the accidental Cause of this Corruption, we should find, it neither was from Heaven nor from ought but want of a Regiment of Health. For in as much as the Fathers are corrupt, they beget Children of a corrupt Complexion and Composition, and their Children from the same Cause are corrupt themselves: and so Corruption is derived from Father to Son, till Abbreviation of Life prevails by Succession. Yet for all this it does not follow, that it shall always be cut shorter and shorter; because a Term is set in Humane Kind, that Men should at the most of their years arrive at Fourscore, but more is their Pain and Sorrow. Now the Remedy against every Mans proper Corruption is, if every Man from his Youth would exercise a complete Regiment, which consists in these things, Meat and Drink, Sleep and Watching, Motion and Rest, Evacuation and Retention, Air, the Passions of the Mind. [The six so-called "Non-Naturals," a term coined by Galen to indicate those things outside of the body, the proper use of which was beneficial to the body.] For if a Man would observe this Regiment from his nativity, he might live as long as his Nature assumed from his parents would permit, and might be led to the utmost Term of Nature, lapsed from Original Righteousness; which Term nevertheless he could not pass: Because this Regimen does not avail in the least against the old Corruption o our Parents.

In this clear, succinct recitation of the cause of man's limited life span, we see, not the spirit of freedom of the Greek period, but the effect of religious dogma on man's thinking: Bacon's explanation is in strict agreement with Biblical sources and ecclesiastical interpretation. Thus, even Bacon, who fought strenuously against the domination of the Church, was unable to free himself completely from its influences. He utilized the Greek philosophies but inclosed them in a shell of religious dogmatism.

Thus Bacon's answer to why a man's life span is limited was patterned after the Christian prototype. It is really not too different from previous attempts. And if we strip from it the trappings of the Church, we see that Bacon recognizes man's life span and the process of aging to be, in some manner, naturally determined. He disregards any possibility of exceeding this natural course of events and proposes a method of hygiene which would allow man to achieve in good health his rightful term of years. A more rational approach could not reasonably be expected from the thirteenth century—or the twentieth.

Arnold of Villanova (1235-1311?), whose writings brought him also into conflict with the Church, was a contemporary of Roger Bacon. Arnold's theory for a cause of aging is identical with Bacon's except that Arnold introduced, in an elaborate form, alchemy and astrology to the already complicated mélange of the then current medicine, natural science, and theology. He also espoused the belief in an elixir of life.

In his book *The Defence of Age, and Recovery of Youth*, Arnold has this to say about prolonging life [18]:

The conservation of youth and withstandyng of age, consysteth in the mayntenynge of the powres, the spyrytes, and the naturall heate of the body in theyr state and temperancy: and in the comfortyng and repayryng of theym beynge defectyve. For so longe as the powres, the spyrytes and the naturall heate of mannes body are not debylitate nor wekened, so long (I saye) neyther shall ye skynne wrynkle, for the debylyte of ye natural heate declynynge to coldenes and drynes throughe the which the fode and nourisshement of the body is corrupted and hyndered: is cause of corrugacyon or wrynklyng of ye skynne [Aging].

Arnold's writings, like those of Bacon, contain much that is contradictory for the twentieth-century reader. These contradictions are probably more apparent than actual, however. Astrology, alchemy, medicine, natural science, and theology were all held to be within the province of the learned man and would thus properly be amalgamated into an integrated whole. This may account for the seemingly incompatible parts of Arnold's theory of aging.

Gabriele Zerbi (1445-1505) and his longer-lived contemporary Luigi Cornaro (1467-1566) were two authors representative of the late fifteenth century. Zerbi's book *Gerontocomia* (Rome, 1489) was the first printed monograph devoted expressly and exclusively to geriatrics [19], wherein lies its importance. It was a product of the revival of art and science in Italy in the last half of the fifteenth century and represents an increased interest in and appreciation for the problems of aging. That Zerbi depended on the older theories to make his new approach does not detract from its significance as an early manual of hygiene for the aged.

Luigi Cornaro's *A Treatise of Health and Long Life with the Sure Means of Attaining It* [20] went through many editions as one of the most popular of many tracts on hygiene. Cornaro's own longevity has been called the best example of the salutary effect of strict adherence to proper hygienic rules.

Shining almost as an isolated but nevertheless brilliant light in the gray dawn before the Renaissance is Paracelsus (1493-1541), a contemporary of Rabelais. His writings in relation to aging must be discussed in the same fashion in which he himself lived and wrote—seemingly alone and unrelated to the world around him, innovating, indeed, revolutionary, and yet in some way a product of his time. Either much maligned or profoundly praised, he and his extensive writings have presented an enigma to almost all who would attempt to understand them. Those with the ability and temperament to peruse his voluminous work—usually Germanic, and not this writer—seem to be able to pierce the bombastic, quarrelsome, sometimes mystical, coarse, and always obscure façade and perceive originality, far-reaching perception, and freedom from dogma in the questing spirit of this capable physician and surgeon of the early sixteenth century.

Any attempt to summarize Paracelsus must simplify his ideas, because of his contradictions and prolixity, and hence risk presenting a thought as having a greater degree of validity than Paracelsus himself meant it to have. This is especially true in trying to discuss his concept of aging. One might assume that Paracelsus formulated and recorded a complete theory of aging, but it is not in either his treatise *Liber de renovatione et restauratione* or *Liber de Longa vita* [21], where one would expect to find it. However, it is possible to extract some of his ideas about aging from these treatises and combine them with his general concept of physiology and causation of disease and his thoughts on life itself to come reasonably close to his concept of aging. It should be kept in mind that this résumé of Paracelsus' ideas on aging is a speculative simplification which is presented for two reasons: first, to demonstrate that the period before the Renaissance was not completely void of independent thinkers; second, to show that some of the ideas to be discussed later were presaged by this brilliant intellect [21, 22].

Paracelsus believed that he effectively refuted the Greek concept of pathology, but he substituted a remarkably similar one. One important difference—his emphasis on the concept of the independent nature of different diseases—was not finally put on a firm foundation until the nineteenth century, when Bichat published his writings on pathology.

Paracelsus thought that life was a "spirit" endowed with "power and virtue" and came from the air. Every material thing had a "spirit" whether it be animal, vegetable, or mineral; animate or inanimate; celestial or earthly. Each different part of the body had a "spirit" which carried function and individual specificity. This idea was later elaborated upon by Stahl and formed the basis of the vitalist doctrine.

As one of his many analogies, Paracelsus compared aging to rust on metal, although man, unlike metal, cannot be reconstructed. In man there was an innate tendency to corruption, separation, and deposition of superfluities. These processes led not only to diseases but apparently to the manifestations of aging. The many things that could retard the processes which tended to bring about dissolution of the body were such concrete conditions as nutrition and geographical location and such mystical measures as a *quinta essentia* (or fifth essence), *prima substantia*, medicines like *lignum vitae* and *lignum anima*, and the *arcanum* of gold or mercury.

Paracelsus said that life was like a fire which could be constantly rejuvenated with new wood; yet he said that life should not be extended in this way because it would be un-Christian and against nature. This attitude points up vividly one of the many paradoxes in his writings. On the one hand, rejuvenation, proper or not, was possible and life could be prolonged; and on the other hand, life had a predetermined natural end.

We can only speculate about what specifically caused aging, according to Paracelsus. Observant physician that he was, Paracelsus must certainly have looked upon the manifestations of aging, such as wrinkling of the skin and graying of the hair, as natural accompaniments of life's later years, despite the fact that they were not universally present. Whether he regarded the diseases which are peculiar to or more prevalent in the senescent period as "natural" or "pathological" is not clearly seen. He seems to have looked upon them as he viewed disease in general—the result of inexorable corrupting influences innate in man.

V. Beginning and Development of the Scientific Method

The century dating from the birth of Galileo to the death of Harvey has been called perhaps the most brilliant in the history of modern knowledge.

The scientific method was born and nurtured in this span from 1564 to 1657. Two great bulwarks—the Church, which hitherto prevented the development of physiology, and the theory of the interaction of the microcosm and macrocosm—were either being stormed directly or outflanked. Ideas arising at this time, although based, as ever, on the thought of the past, imparted a new direction to the pursuit of truth. An increasing mood of skepticism moved slowly toward the demand for verification.

Enlightenment from accumulated facts and hypotheses verified by experimentation was not always progressive, however. Even Harvey's discovery of the circulation of the blood, which ultimately became one of the most significant factors in the breakdown of the Greek doctrine of humoral pathology, was at first ridiculed. Strong forces—conservatism, the Church, personal pride—constantly restrained the pursuit of knowledge. In modern times only the Church has any less effect than it did centuries ago.

During the late sixteenth and early seventeenth centuries, four contemporaries of Galileo and Harvey, all born within five years of one another, clearly revealed the intellectual ferment of the times in their writings on old age. Each man represents a somewhat different approach in the search for knowledge, specifically, in the search for the reason for senescence and death in old age.

Henry Cuffe, or Cuff (1563–1601), is known as both an author and politician—which latter career was abbreviated by his being beheaded for involvement in the Earl of Essex' plot to overthrow the Protestant Queen Elizabeth. What qualified Cuffe to write a book on aging was, rather, his early training. As a scholar and later professor of Greek at Oxford, before he entered Essex' service, he was intimately familiar with Greek philosophy and its reconciliation with Church doctrines. Thus he was able to expound at length on the traditional theory of aging and death.

In Cuffe's book *The Differences of the Ages of Man's Life* [23], printed posthumously in 1607, his recitation of Greek thought takes an interesting tack. Originally the soul and the body were in absolute and perfect harmony in spite of the contrary nature of the four humors which made up the body. In this state a separation of the soul from the body—death—was unknown.

But after that man's pride set abroach by the divels suggestion, ventured to taste of the forbidden fruite for desire of knowledge; ... there grew a disagreement and quarrell among the subject inferior parts of the soule, from whence followed the warre of the elements in the bodie, never to bee ended till the field were lost by blood: . . . and who dares say, the dealing is inequall, that hee should incurre the death of the body, who wilfully rejected the life of the soule? or who marveils that the divell by Gods sufferance tormenteth the bodie with diseases, that gave the divell a place of dwelling in his soule?

This explanation, in keeping with the profound theological influence which shaped Cuffe's approach, is simply a mixture of Greek humoral pathology and Christian dogma.

When he attempts to explain how natural death and aging are brought about, the reader becomes lost in prolixity. With difficulty it can be seen that three explanations seem to be offered. The first is the traditional one which held that death and aging were the result of a decline in the amount of innate heat which arose because the innate heat had consumed the native moisture of the body. For most authors until this time, this explanation would have been sufficient. Cuffe was aware, however, that there were other reasons advanced to account for aging and death. Unable to choose, he set down this theory in another place in his book:

For as in the violent motion of things naturall, we see it comes to passe, that the virtue or power of moving, imprinted by the unnaturall mover [God], by little and little decaying, at length by continuance of moving, or rather by the resistance of the bodies about it, is cleane extinguished: So in the naturall proceeding toward the enemie and end of nature, death, the preserving meanes of life (either by the toilesomenesse of their never-ceasing operation, or by the corruption and mixture of impure moisture, infeebled and disabled to the sufficient performance of their functions, more and more every day) at length of force yeelds to the oppressing violence of their resisting adversaries, not able any longer to maintaine their conquering action. . . .

This mechanistic attitude, first seen in Roger Bacon's work, was the basis for a full separate theory in the eighteenth century. In Cuffe's work, it merely exemplifies his confusion.

The third theory involves those elements of the body which he said were set at war with each other as a result of man's original corruption: "The first cause naturall of naturall death, is contrarietie in the compound." This contrariety is found in the body in the mixture of the four elements—fire, air, water, and earth—and their qualities—heat, cold, moisture, and dryness. The mere fact of a mélange of elements is sufficient, for Cuffe, to account for the resulting corruption. His belief that those things in which there is the least disagreement endure longest constitutes proof. And those things, like the "unmaterial substance of creatures spirituall, void of all contrarietie" last forever.

These examples reveal the mighty effort made by Cuffe to combat the skepticism against which he must have been writing. Had he but given attention to the writings of some of his contemporaries, he would have understood that new forces with new weapons and new tactics were gathering.

Cuffe was an anachronism in the generation which included Galileo, Harvey, Kepler, and other brilliant, progressive minds. A more typical example of the outlook of an intelligent individual of the times is seen in the works of André du Laurens, latinized Laurentius (1558-1609), a French court physician and chancellor of the university at Montpellier. His book *A Discourse of the Preservation of the Sight: of Melancholike diseases: of Rheumes, and of Old age*, published in 1599, was the first work on geriatrics to be published in French.

In the short discourse on old age, du Laurens' aim was to explain how senescence can be relieved. His methods were the familiar Greek ones. Citing as proof for his contentions the works of the ancients—especially Hippocrates, but also Galen, Avicenna, Celsus, and others—he attributed the cause of aging and natural death to two factors inherent in each individual: the contrariety of the elements of the body, and the workings of the natural heat. Du Laurens also proposed the traditional cause for aging—accumulation of excrements engendered by the process of nourishing the body.

But we have met all these concepts before. Where, then, does du Laurens differ from his predecessors; where lies the advantage over the past? The difference becomes apparent in the following passage [24]:

The men of Egypt and Alexandria did beleeve that the naturall cause of olde age did come of the diminishing of the heart: they said that the heart did growe till fiftie yeeres the weight of two drams every yeere, and that after fiftie yeeres it waxed lesser and lesser, till in the end it was growne to nothing: but these are nothing but vaine imaginations and meere fooleries. We have caused many old men to be opened, whose hearts have been found as great and heavie as those of the younger sort.

We have caused many old men to be opened. . . . Here is the step forward—a skeptical and questing mind resorting to experimentation to prove or disprove a theory. Although Roger Bacon probably would have been in complete agreement with this approach, for almost all other men whose works we have discussed since Galen, it would have been an unlikely procedure.

One of the enlightened thinkers of this period who attempted a new approach in the search for knowledge was Francis Bacon, Lord Verulam

(1561–1621), philosopher, statesman, and a friend of Cuffe. Nevertheless, Francis Bacon and Henry Cuffe diverged markedly in their philosophies, Cuffe endeavoring to combat the very skepticism which Bacon expressed.

Bacon's intent was "to extend more widely the limits of the power and greatness of man" [25]. To this end he proposed the inductive approach based on observation and experimentation. He saw the need for proved facts rather than theories, and he hoped to demonstrate the relationship between phenomena and their resultant general laws. He was unable, however, to depart completely from the strong currents of the past. Sometimes thought of as the last of the schoolmen and encyclopedists, he seemed not to comprehend fully the implications of the scientific method, but his writings mark the beginning of the new approach which eventually led to today's wealth of scientific knowledge. While expressing the tenets of the newly awakened quest for verification, Bacon still adhered to the traditional idea that with the proper method the "secrets of nature" could be discovered completely. He seemed to fail to realize the relative smallness of man in nature's scheme—a necessary perspective for the proper study of natural sciences.

These comments are, of course, a generalized characterization of Francis Bacon's philosophical approach to the search for scientific knowledge, which, though evident in his book on aging, is often obscured or abridged. The title, *History Natural and Experimental of Life and Death or of the Prolongation of Life*, suggests a new approach and yet implies the ubiquitous search for a means of opposing nature and prolonging life.

Bacon said that the attainment of old age was easy and only the inquiry about it difficult [25]:

... and so much the rather, because it is corrupted with false opinions [opinions], and vaine reports. For both those things, which the vulgar physicians talke, of radical moisture, and natural heat, are but meer fictions; And the immoderate praises of chymical medicines; First puffe up with vaine hopes, and then faile their admirers.

Thus seeming to dispel completely the basis of almost all of the theories of aging discussed above, Bacon formulated a new theory, but he still did not escape Greek influence. He stated that in every tangible body there is a "spirit, or body pneumatical," inclosed within the tangible parts, i.e., a spirit in blood, flesh, fat, sinews, arteries, veins, bones, cartilages, bowels, and so forth. All dissolution and consumption began from these spirits, which were endowed with the capability of bringing about all the workings of the body. This belief concerning spirits embodies the viewpoint of Realism—a legacy from Plato—as opposed to Nominalism, which would hold the existence of a spirit immanent in matter as only a subjective conception devoid of reality outside man's mind. Bacon, like Harvey, needed a motivating force for his system, and both men drew it from the philosophy of their day. Although unable to verify this idea experimentally, Harvey adopted the innate heat as the cause of motion of blood and heart. For him, the power of the spirit in the blood superseded that of the other body elements. Unwilling to relinquish, as modern science has, the quest for an ultimate source of energy, Bacon also resorted to the superaddition of an essence to account for phenomena, in spite of his desire for objective verification. He withdrew primacy for the cause of aging and natural death from those "meer fictions"—the radical moisture and natural heat—and ascribed it to a superadded spirit or *pneuma*, another of the sophistries of the past. Therefore, only the details of Bacon's theory of aging were different from those of the past.

Despite his initial rational aim of arriving at a relationship between observed phenomena and general principles, Bacon seems to have lapsed further and further into the kind of thinking against which he wrote. While he succeeded in overthrowing the old theory, he became lost in his own. Forced to carry his generally irrational explanation of the first cause of aging to its ultimate logical conclusion because of the incipient rationality of his mind, he said in a section of Aphorisms, "youthful spirits inserted into an old body, might soon turn natures course back again" [25] —an idea prevalent in the sixteenth century, which may have been the basis for attempts at blood transfusions. Were it not for such reservations as "might" in this passage, Bacon's theory would not represent as advanced a position over previous theories as has been claimed. Just as in du Laurens' work, one must look closely for the signs of a new method.

The significance of Francis Bacon's relatively new approach to the explanation of aging seems to have had very little impact on subsequent ages. Few acknowledgments are made to him by later writers on the subject. In fact, his theory of aging presented here stands in contrast to his general reputation, for his use of the inductive method did, of course, exert a profound influence on the scientific thinking of the eighteenth century.

In the writings of Santorio Santorio (Sanctorius; 1561-1636), the last of the four men from the century between the birth of Galileo and the death of Harvey, we find the scientific method and a quest for quantitative confirmation fully applied. But a new road is not necessarily the correct road, and, as we shall see, the theory of aging which grew out of Santorio's studies is far from satisfactory. It is, however, a fresh approach grounded on a new method of study. Clearly and unequivocally, the scientific period was about to begin.

Santorio was a professor of theoretical medicine in Padua until 1629, when he retired to devote his efforts to private practice and experimental study. Best known among his writings is the *Ars de Statica Medicina*, first published in 1614, which subsequently was translated into all European languages and passed through many editions. I draw his theory of the cause of aging from it.

The principal basis for Santorio's physiology and pathology, including aging, is found in what was termed the "insensible perspiration"—again, a concept of Greek origin. (An excellent review of this doctrine is found in an article by Renbourn [26].) Much of Santorio's experimental work was directed toward quantitative measurement of this insensible perspiration, and it is for this striving for quantification that Santorio is best known. Nevertheless, like Francis Bacon, he was forced to apply his method in the context of the accepted Greek doctrine of humoral pathology. It was too early for the overthrow of this ancient system so long as the tools by which it was to be proved false—the experimental method and the increasing amount of scientific knowledge resulting therefrom— were still embryonic. Also, Santorio shared with others before him the belief that the body contained spirits which effected its phenomena. Despite these drawbacks, especially the adherence to unprovable assumptions, we can, by looking beyond the actual applications of his theory to the practice of medicine, see the innovating spirit of this leading representative of the Iatrophysical school of medical philosophy.

The spirits pervading and motivating every part were essential for Santorio's theory of aging because it was by a decay of these "spirits," by diversion of material to other evacuations, and by stress laid upon the parts that insensible perspiration was hindered. The body's inability to rid itself of the superfluities resulted in hardening of the parts and their declining function. He did not explicitly state that hardness of the parts was synonymous with old age, but Quincy, the translator, who seems everywhere to agree with Santorio's principles, said that old age is a "universal hardness of the fibres" [27]. It is assumed that this is the view held by Santorio also, for it is the logical extension of his own statement that old people die "because their fibres are grown hard, and such as possibly cannot be renewed: whence proceeds death" [27].

The idea that aging is a progressive consolidation was thus fostered by Santorio. Combined with the Galenic concept of increased accumulation of "earthy" material, the idea became a full-blown theory in the nineteenth century in the hands of S. Rowbotham and was expressed in his interesting pamphlet on natural death [28]: "Old age, then, is only a name given to certain conditions of the body, which conditions may be brought on sooner or later according as the process of ossification, or consolidation, proceeds with greater or less velocity." And: "We have seen, that what is called natural death, or death from old age, arises from a general ossification or choking up of the body, by the gradual deposition of earthy, or bony, matter. . . ."

This concept of aging was soon discarded, but the total impact of Santorio's approach to problems in the natural sciences was great, though it is impossible to know how great. By the time of his death in 1636, the new spirit and freedom of the seventeenth century had pervaded the thinking of almost every author. Harvey's book on the circulation of the blood was published in 1628. Van Leeuwenhoek, a pioneer in the use of the microscope, was born in 1632. Malpighi, using the microscope, discovered the capillaries in 1661—thus completing the knowledge of the circulation of the blood—and began to study microscopic anatomy. The same century saw Franz de la Boë (Sylvius) launching the Iatrochemical school of medical philosophy. At the same time Sydenham in England established a new standard of achievement for the medical profession. These men and many others were heirs to the growing surety that knowledge could be gained and hypotheses could be tested by experimentation. Santorio stands at the beginning of this development, but the thread of his thought soon became lost in the fabric of scientific knowledge that followed.

With the writings of Santorio and others of his time, the Galenic principle, in the full Greek tradition of observation and experimentation, was once again held as the proper guide for study of the sciences. In the seventeenth century major discoveries were made and new methods were established which were to culminate in the rejection of the mistaken doctrines of the past. In botany, physics, and astronomy, as well as in medicine, the inertia of the past was gradually being overcome. Initial progress was slow, however.

As man's understanding of the physiological principles by which the body functioned slowly increased, he became better able to explain the changes which seemed to accompany old age. But before we come to the time when such ideas as the doctrine of humoral pathology were altogether discarded and scientific rationality fully governed consideration of questions concerning the workings of the body, it would be well to sample briefly the thought of the seventeenth and part of the eighteenth centuries on the question of aging to see how the transition to modern times was made. These centuries by no means, however, mark the end of more subtle Greek influence on the thinking of the Western world.

Sir John Floyer (1649–1734) was a typical representative of the century and a half before the beginning of the modern period. This well-known English physician published in 1724 the first monograph on geriatrics to be printed initially in English. Its title, *Medicina Gerocomica, or the Galenic Art of Preserving Old Men's Healths* [29], indicates his adherence to Galenic doctrines, which position was being increasingly attacked. But Floyer's Galenic principles did not in any way resemble those used before A.D. 1600 by some of the authors discussed here. While Floyer based his ideas on the doctrine of humoral pathology, which had been so fully discussed by Galen, among others, his use of the term "Galenic Art" seems to imply more the spirit of Galen's approach than the letter of his text. In fact, Floyer's ideas about aging were remarkably eclectic; he quoted from Santorio, Francis Bacon, Baglivi, Celsus, Eustachius, and many others, as well as from Galen.

Floyer's theory of a cause for aging is similar enough to Francis Bacon's, with detectable Santorio influence, not to be repeated. His writings in other phases of medicine measurably overshadowed his contribution to aging.

One of the first Americans to write about aging and propose a system from which a theory of its cause might be drawn was the controversial divine Cotton Mather (1662?–1728). In keeping with his theological orientation, his theory of disease and the cause of death (expressed in his unpublished work *The Angel of Bethesda* and discussed by Beale and Shryock [30]) is similar to Henry Cuffe's ideas of a century before: illness was punishment for original sin. Also, Mather was influenced by the vitalistic concept, then prevalent, of an inherent life-directing principle in all living beings, an idea not drastically different from the belief in "spirits" held by Bacon and Santorio. Mather called this spirit the "Nishmath-Chajim" [31], which is

> ... the strength of every part in our body, and that gives motion to it. Here perhaps the origin of muscular motion may be a little accounted for. And this is the spirit, and the balsams, and one might almost say, the keeper, of each part, which is occupied and befriended with it.

Mather did not comment directly about the cause of aging, and he did not mention specifically the manifestations of aging. Because his views on diseases in general and his concept of physiology were not unlike those of his immediate predecessors and contemporaries, it may be assumed that his views on aging, aside from a strong religious bias, were probably also similar to the main stream of thought of his time. Speaking about death, he said:

> After all, we see, death unavoidable. ... My *Angel of Bethesda*, that has express'd so much concern to arm his readers against the approaches of death, yett confesses, I cannot by any means redeem thee; nor find out a remedy for thee, that thou shouldest live forever, and not see corruption.

His book, which resembles greatly the health manuals, thus recognizes the inevitability of man's death and recommends principally temperance to achieve the longest term possible by generally rational methods.

Nearly contemporary with Mather was the English physician and student of Pitcairn, George Cheyne (1671–1743). His *An Essay of Health and Long Life* was in the tradition of the hygienic tracts of the past and achieved great popularity. In spite of its doctrine of humoral pathology, amalgamated with the "perspiration" ideas of Santorio, a single remarkable fact, really an omission, signals the progress of Cheyne's ideas over previous ones. Cheyne seems to dismiss the quest for a "first cause" of aging, limiting his discussion to phenomena and their immediate causes. He accepts the fact that man has a limited life span, during which certain events bring about its termination. He speaks of the process and manifestations of aging, which consist of hardening and condensing of the parts, as "mechanical and necessary" [32]. Because the reason for this necessity is not discussed, Cheyne's writings represent a new approach to aging.

James Mackenzie (1680?–1761) was another author of this period. Although his book *The History of Health and the Art of Preserving It* offers no new concepts pertinent to our review, it contains a reference to a means of prolonging life which distinctly contrasts with the comment of Roger Bacon that ". . . their [the ancients] regiment is as it were the beginning: ours as the end" [17]. Mackenzie's attitude on this question represents the modern approach and is tempered by modesty and skepticism [33]: ". . . yet a sure and easy road to longevity, different from the general rules of health already mentioned, seems to be among the desiderata in our art, the discovery of which is reserved, perhaps, for a more meritorious generation."

Still another member of the generation of Floyer, Mather, and Cheyne was Johann Heinrich Cohausen (1665–1750), a German physician and pupil of Boerhaave. His book *Hermippus Redivivus: or the Sage's Triumph over Old Age and the Grave* [34] was widely received and translated into several languages, although some present-day authors consider it merely a mental exercise by an old man and not to be taken seriously. Cohausen's theory of aging, like that of most of the authors of the sixteenth, seventeenth, and eighteenth centuries, was a mixture of many of the ideas of his predecessors. He solved the problem of "natural" death in old age by saying that if death occurred in an elderly person who appeared in good health, then the only cause for death was old age—a question not settled today. Senescence, then, is a disease, but differing from all others; it is the only one to which man is subject by nature. Had he proceeded just one step further, Cohausen could have said that aging was a natural process, not a pathological one, and because it inevitably brought about the decay of the body and terminated in death, therefore could be considered a type of disease.

During the seventeenth and eighteenth centuries many authors of books on clinical medicine, such as Thomas Sydenham (1624–1689), Richard Mead (1673–1754), and Gerhard van Swieten (1700–1772), the most famous pupil of Boerhaave, were devoting more of their writings to the diseases and problems of the aged. Mead, the inheritor of the celebrated gold-headed cane from Radcliffe, also wrote a whole book of interesting commentaries on diseases described in the Bible, including one of the many interpretations written between the sixteenth and eighteenth centuries on the well-known twelfth chapter of Ecclesiastes. The interpretations of the allegory to which I have had access—those by Mead, Smith, and Lowe—actually contribute very little to a theory for the cause of aging, however.

Advances in physiology, anatomy, pathology, and chemistry made in these two centuries enabled such men to speak with increasing authority and erudition on the problems of aging. Important roles in these advances were played by such people as Giovanni Borelli (1608–1679), a pupil of Galileo and the teacher of Morgagni; George Stahl (1660–1734), the founder of the vitalistic interpretations of physiology; Giovanni Battista Morgagni (1682–1771), the renowned student of pathological anatomy, whose work demonstrated the use, not only of profound powers of observation, but also of logical reasoning concerning disease; Alexander Monro primus (1697–1767), the first and most accomplished of the Monro dynasty to hold the chair of anatomy at Edinburgh; John Hunter (1728–1793), the famous Scottish anatomist and surgeon; and a multitude of others.

One eighteenth century author who used the rapidly increasing store of medical knowledge to strike out in new directions was Erasmus Darwin (1731–1802), the celebrated English physician and biologist and grandfather of Charles Darwin. Drawing on a physiological doctrine first suggested by Francis Glisson in 1672 and fully developed by Albrecht von Haller in 1747—that muscular tissue possessed the innate faculty of irritability and nervous tissue the faculty of sensibility—Erasmus Darwin ascribed aging and "natural death" to a loss of irritability and decreased response to sensation. The succinctness of this theory, found in his comprehensive treatise *Zoonomia; or the Laws of Organic Life*, cannot be improved upon; it stands as a new chapter in the mechanistic approach to an explanation of the physiology, natural or pathological, of aging and death [35]:

> This apposition of new parts, as the old ones disappear, selected from the aliment we take, first enlarges and strengthens our bodies for twenty years; for another twenty years it keeps us in health and vigour, and adds strength and solidity to the system, and then gradually ceases to nourish us properly; and for another twenty years we gradually sink into decay, and finally cease to act, and to exist.
> On considering this subject one should have imagined at first view, that it might have been easier for nature to have supported her progeny for ever in health and life, than to have perpetually reproduced them by the wonderful and mysterious process of generation. But it seems our bodies by long habit cease to obey the stimulus of the aliment, which should support us. After we have acquired our height and solidity we make no more new parts, and the system obeys the irritations, sensations, volitions, and associations, with less and less energy, till the whole sinks into inaction.
> Three causes may conspire to render our nerves less excitable, which have already been

mentioned. 1. If a stimulus be greater than natural, it produces too great an exertion of the stimulated organ, and in consequence exhausts the spirit of animation; and the moving organ ceases to act, even though the stimulus be continued. And though rest will recruit this exhaustion, yet some degree of permanent injury remains, as is evident after exposing the eyes long to too strong a light. 2. If excitations weaker than natural be applied, so as not to excite the organ into action, (as when small doses of aloes or rhubarb are exhibited,) they may be gradually increased, without exciting the organ into action; which will thus acquire a habit of disobedience to the stimulus; thus by increasing the dose by degrees, great quantities of opium or wine may be taken without intoxication. . . .

3. Another mode, by which life is gradually undermined is when irritative motions continue to be produced in consequence of stimulus, but are not succeeded by sensation; hence the stimulus of contagious matter is not capable of producing fever a second time, because it is not succeeded by sensation. . . . And hence, owing to the want of the general pleasurable sensation, which ought to attend digestion and glandular secretion, an irksomeness of life ensues; and, where this is in greater excess, the melancholy of old age occurs, with torpor or debility.

From hence I conclude, that it is probable that the fibrillae, or moving filaments at the extremities of the nerves of sense, and the fibres which constitute the muscles (which are perhaps the only parts of the system that are endued with contractile life) are not changed, as we advance in years, like the other parts of the body; but only enlarged or elongated with our growth; and in consequence they become less and less excitable into action. Whence, instead of gradually changing the old animal, the generation of a totally new one becomes necessary with undiminished excitability, which many years will continue to acquire new parts, or new solidity, and then losing its excitability in time, perish like its parent.

From this idea the art of preserving long health and life may be deduced; which must consist in using no greater stimulus, whether of the quantity or kind of our food and drink, or of external circumstances, such as heat, and exercise, and wakefulness, than is sufficient to preserve us in vigour; and gradually, as we grow old to increase the stimulus of our aliment, as the inirritability of our system increases.

Darwin's theorizing seems to be marked by liberal but insufficient or incomplete observation; he made assumptions which experimentation would have proved mistaken. The value of his work was that he broke free from the bonds of tradition and formulated a theory which, although fallacious or incomplete, contained germs of the ideas of his successors. It should hardly need to be pointed out that this was exactly his contribution in another field of biological investigation—the theory of evolution of the species.

The outstanding American physician of this period was Benjamin Rush (1745–1813). Although his writings contributed little to a theory of the cause of aging, his "Account of the State of the Body and Mind in Old Age; with Observations of its Diseases, and their Remedies" contains several statements worthy of mention. This practical work, soundly based on observation, is a physiological study of the aged with principal emphasis on the clinical implications of the changes seen in senescence.

Rush unequivocally accepted man's limited life span. As he enumerated the many factors which seemed to effect longevity, he dispelled some of the misconceptions of the past. His descriptions of the phenomena of the body and mind which occur in old people are the most accurate and astute to be encountered up to his time. Observing that the fear of death seems to be less in old age than in youth or middle life, he wrote [36]: "This indifference to life, and desire for death . . . appear to be a wise law in the animal economy, and worthy of being classed with those laws which accommodate the body and mind of man to all the natural evils, to which, in the common order of things, they are necessarily exposed." After describing the diseases seen in the elderly, Rush made the following statement, which struck perhaps one of the last blows at the idea that old age is itself a disease: "Few persons appear to die of old age. Some of the diseases which have been mentioned generally cuts [sic] the last thread of life."

Almost contemporary with Rush was Christoph Wilhelm Hufeland (1762-1836), whose book *The Art of Prolonging the Life of Man* (1796) achieved great popularity for several reasons. Because he was the friend and physician of such people as Goethe and Schiller, professor at Jena and Berlin, a well-known philanthropist, and a leader against astrology, phrenology, and mesmerism, his book was certain to be well received. The universal popularity of the subject itself was also a factor.

A thoroughgoing vitalist, Hufeland, like Bichat to follow, believed that vital force activated all bodily processes—an idea first introduced by George Stahl. Hufeland refused to identify this vital force as either a particular matter or only a property of matter. Recognizing it as unknowable and yet needing it for his theory, he wrote [37]:

The vital force is without contradiction one of the most general, powerful, and incomprehensible forces in nature. It replenishes and activates everything. It is probably the source of all the other forces of the physical world, or at least of the organic world. It produces, conserves and renovates all. . . .

This mystical vital force was thus the principle and source of life.

Hufeland wrote that there is a continual renewal in the body by virtue of the action of the vital force. In this renewal he found the means of prolonging life—by augmenting the vital force, fortifying the organs, slowing the consumption of the body, or perfecting the regenerative action. But:

Finally, the diminution of the vital force and the deterioration of the organs are such that consumption surpasses regeneration; it is then that the body is degraded little by little, until the inevitable moment of its complete dissolution.

Aging, for Hufeland, consisted of gradual deterioration of the vital force, the most inevitable of all the causes which shorten life. He seemed to endow aging with the active capacity for drying the body, diminishing and souring the humors, narrowing the vessels, consuming the organs, and accumulating earthy materials—instead of concluding that the aging process is passive and only the result of these events. He did say in another place, however, that aging may be the natural consequence of life:

> The life of man ... like all other physical phenomena ought to have its laws, limits, and determined duration, in as much as it depends on the sum of the forces and on the quantity of material devolved to each being, on the manner in which these elements are put to work, and on many other circumstances, as many external as internal.

This principle was the theme of the rising belief in the infallibility of the scientific method. Hufeland was motivated by this idea and yet he was unable to free himself from the intellectually stifling atmosphere of the philosophy of vitalism. The true value of Hufeland's book lay not in the promulgation of any new theories, but simply in the completeness of his discussion of the vital force and its relation to aging. Any historical study of vitalism would be incomplete without consideration of this book.

Several of the many scientific investigators of the late eighteenth and early nineteenth centuries played especially significant roles in breaking the traditional bonds which heretofore retarded the advance of science. Of course, their work and the flowering of science paralleled increasing enlightenment in other fields. The emphasis on rationality which guided investigations in the sciences as well as endeavors in philosophy, religion, economics, history, political science, education, and so forth was in the spirit of the times. Whether rational methods are the best approach in some of these fields is not within the scope of this paper; the point to be made is merely that the beginning of the modern period was marked by the pervasiveness of this spirit.

To discuss fully all concepts of aging in the nineteenth and twentieth centuries would require as much space again as has already been used. Only one of the earliest writers of this period is discussed below to demonstrate the tenor of the approach.

Xavier Bichat (1771–1802), professor of anatomy, physiology, and medicine, and physician of the Hôtel-Dieu in Montpellier, in his short life advanced a theory of disease based on tissues rather than organs and held that disease in tissue is the same regardless of the organ in which it takes place. Virchow (1821-1902) carried the idea to its fullest expression in his *Die Cellularpathologie*. Bichat was prevented from developing his own theory more fully by his premature death and also by the lack of adequate microscopes, which were not produced until the 1820's. His physiological investigations recorded in *Physiological Researches upon Life and Death* [38] encompassed many reptiles and amphibians as well as humans and other warm-blooded animals. No action of the body seemed to escape his questioning mind. Almost every page describes experiments undertaken to prove or disprove a theory.

Bichat regarded each of the tissues of the body (he described twenty-one kinds, such as nervous, vascular, mucous, serous, connective, and so forth) as endowed with a specific vital property. Disease was an alteration of this vital property. This belief led him to define life as "the totality of those functions [forces] which resist death" [38]. He was, thus, like Hufeland and many previous writers, a vitalist, believing that in every part of the body resided a superadded *vita propria* which, dependent on the laws of nature, regulated function.

In general, Bichat's theory of aging belongs to the category which holds that there is something added to the individual at the beginning of life that is used up during the course of that life. This is certainly similar to the Greek theory. He said:

Such is in fact the mode of existence of living bodies, that every thing which surrounds them tends to their destruction. Inorganic bodies act upon them incessantly; they themselves exercise a continual action, the one upon the other; and would necessarily soon be destroyed, did they not possess a permanent principle of reaction. This principle is life; not understood in its nature, it can be known only by its phenomena: the most general of which is that constant alternation of action on the part of external bodies, and of reaction on the part of the living body, the proportions of which alternation vary according to age.

There is a superabundance of life in the infant, because the reaction is greater than the action. In the adult, an equilibrium is established, and thus this vital turgescence disappears. The reaction of the internal principle is diminished in old age, while the action of external bodies remains the same; thus life languishes and advances insensibly towards that natural term, which must happen when all proportion has ceased.

The real difference from previous writers is Bichat's belief that the nature of the principle of life can be known only by its phenomena—the approach that characterizes the age which believes that all problems can be solved by scientific experimentation. The principles which guided him and many others in their investigations reached their most complete and eloquent expression in Claude Bernard's *Introduction to the Study of Experimental Medicine*, published in 1865. But Bichat stands at the beginning of our modern scientific period.

VI. *Conclusions*

In the one hundred and fifty years since Bichat our understanding of pathological, biochemical, and biophysical operations of the living being has increased enormously—the fruit of the application of the scientific method of study to biological processes. The extent of this kind of understanding appears almost boundless. No scientist would say today, as did Roger Bacon, that our knowledge is the "end." Thus, the future can only augment our knowledge of aging and the senescent period. Yet, it should probably be emphasized that the ultimate cause of aging sought by most of the authors of the past, and occasionally today, may not be found by science at all. The answers available today about various phases of the aging process are given at the phenomenal level only. While they have step-by-step removed the veil obscuring our understanding of the actual workings of the body, they do not in any way provide evidence which could be interpreted as revealing the ultimate or first cause of aging. Nevertheless, some writers, like the authors we have discussed, attempt, or have attempted, to extract by the rational methods of science understanding of a process which all evidence to date suggests is beyond understanding. Numerous recent theories on the cause or causes of aging have been put forward by men who are contributing greatly to the understanding of the phenomena of aging; when they describe an action or process as the cause of aging, however, they are referring, although not always explicitly, only to immediate causes of objective manifestations.

A short summary of these modern concepts demonstrates the paradox that science has advanced over earlier thought, but that our modern ideas bear a remarkable resemblance to some of the ancient theories discussed in this paper. Aldred Warthin, in a book called *Old Age, the Major Involution* [39], published in 1929, looked upon aging as normal or biological and said that it is the ". . . termination of the activities of the protoplasmic energy machine due to the loss of its intrinsic energy, independent of the action of extrinsic forces." Senescence, according to Warthin, was a "normal involutionary process" and not the progressive disease that had been suggested by Brown-Sequard, Metchnikoff, Horsley, or Lorand. Warthin pointed out a curious fact: ". . . the human mind has always shown a definite aversion to the acceptance of old age and death as natural physiologic processes." Whether this aversion has been the basis for denial of aging as a natural process is an intriguing speculation. Reflecting the Egyptian and Greek ideas of the heart as the source of life, he said: "Personally I would regard myocardial atrophy and inadequacy as the most probable natural terminal lesion. The purely senile death should be, therefore, a cardiac death."

Among Warthin's reviews of some of the more recent theories of aging advanced to his time, is the idea of Minot, who ". . . extended the view of senescence and death as natural processes inherent within the cell, explaining them as due to the gradual loss of the energy stimulus which is supplied to the developing organism at fertilization, through its expenditure is cell growth and differentiation, until finally none is left, and the organism dies of old age." The Greeks reached this conclusion two millennia ago.

Another interesting idea cited in Warthin's book is Weismann's thought that the intrinsic nature of biological death may have been acquired through natural selection as a process having advantages to the species as a whole. This theory has certain attractive features. Would the progress of knowledge be as rapid or as virile if new ideas were not interjected by succeeding ages?

One of the most recent works on aging is Robert De Ropp's *Man Against Aging* [40], an interesting and entertaining book which approaches all aspects of the aging process from an historical standpoint. The marked similarity between ancient ideas and modern concepts of aging is demonstrated vividly in his summary of modern viewpoints:

> Summarizing, we can say that the aging process, though still unexplained, appears to be the result of three processes: first, the gradual accumulation of harmful substances (ashes of the metabolic fires) and of injuries produced by the business of living, particularly by penetrating radiation such as cosmic rays or gamma rays; second, the gradual loss of certain vital materials which are consumed somewhat more rapidly than they are replaced; third, the slow physical changes of the body proteins, from a plump, water-rich condition typical of youth to a dried-out leathery state typical of age. Why this loss of water occurs we do not know, but it may have something to do with the cessation of growth. In fact it may be generally correct to say that when growth ceases senescence begins and that the more slowly an animal grows the longer it will live.
> These are all rather vague statements but at the moment we lack those facts that would enable us to be other than vague. It is hoped that a greatly accelerated program of research on aging will, during the next few years, enable us to speak with more precision.

Surely the coming years will bring us increased and more precise understanding of various parts of the aging process, but, as the similarity between the views characterized by De Ropp and the theories put forth by the ancients demonstrates, our age is no closer to accounting for the ultimate cause of aging than was any past age. It may be that empirical science is not the appropriate medium for its discussion.

REFERENCES

1. L. W. SIMMONS. The role of the aged in primitive society. New Haven: Yale University Press, 1947.
2. J. H. BREASTED (trans.). The Edwin Smith surgical papyrus, Vol. I, p. 498. Chicago: University of Chicago Press, 1930.
3. B. EBBEL (trans.). The Papyrus Ebers, p. 117. London: Oxford University Press, 1937.
4. C. P. BRYAN (trans.). The Papyrus Ebers, p. 128. New York: D. Appleton and Co., 1931.
5. F. H. GARRISON. An introduction to the history of medicine, p. 56. Philadelphia: W. B. Saunders Co., 1929.
6. I. VEITH (trans.). HUANG TI NEI CHING SU WEN, The Yellow Emperor's classic of internal medicine, p. 183. Baltimore: Williams and Wilkins, 1949.
7. I. VEITH. Surgery, 49:564, 1961.
8. KAVIRAJ KUNJA LAL BHISHAGRATNA (ed.). An English translation of the Sushruta Samhita, II, 530. Calcutta: Wilkins Press, 1907-16.
9. I. VEITH. In: F. N. POYNTER (ed.). The history and philosophy of knowledge of the brain and its functions, p. 35. Springfield: Charles C Thomas, 1958.
10. HIPPOCRATES. F. ADAMS (trans.). The genuine works of Hippocrates, p. 197. New York: Wm. Wood and Co., 1929.
11. ARISTOTLE. W. OGLE (trans.). On youth and old age, on life and death and on respiration. London: Longmans, Green, and Co., 1897.
12. GALEN. M. GREEN (trans.). A translation of Galen's hygiene, pp. 7, 217-18,.15 15-17 passim. Springfield: Charles C Thomas, 1951.
13. SONA ROSA BURSTEIN. Geriatrics, 12:499, 1957.
14. AVICENNA. O. C. GRUNER (trans.). A treatise of the canon of Avicenna, p. 75. London: Luzac and Co., 1930.
15. A. CASTIGLIONI. E. B. KRUMBHAAR (trans.). A history of medicine, pp. 351, 352, 510. New York: Alfred A. Knopf, 1958.
16. T. C. ALLBUTT. Science and medieval thought, p. 14. London: C. J. Clay and Sons, 1901.
17. R. BACON. R. BROWNE (trans.). The cure of old age, and preservation of youth, pp. 2, 3, 63-64, 136. London: Tho. Flesher and Edward Evets, 1683.
18. A. DE NOVAVILLA. The defence of age, and recovery of youth, A, ii. (Microfilm.) London: Robert Wyer, 1540.
19. F. D. ZEMAN. J. Mount Sinai Hosp. N.Y., 10:710, 1944.

20. L. Cornaro and L. Lessius. T. Smith (trans.). A treatise of health and long life with the sure means of attaining it. London: Hitch, Leake, and Flackton, 1743.
21. Paracelsus. K. Sudhoff (ed.). Sämtliche Werke, Vol. III, pp. 221-45, 203-20. Munich and Berlin: R. Oldenbourg, 1930.
22. W. Pagel. Paracelsus. Basel and New York: S. Karger, 1958.
23. H. Cuffe. The differences of the ages of man's life: together with the original causes, progresse, and end thereof, pp. 73, 4-5, 76. London: Arnold Hatfield, 1607.
24. A. du Laurens. R. Surphlet (trans.). A discourse of the preservation of the sight; of melancholike diseases: of rheumes, and of old age, p. 168. London: Felix Kingston, 1599. In: Shakespeare Assoc. Facsimilies, No. 15, p. 171. London: Humphrey Milford, 1938.
25. F. Bacon. W. Rawley (trans.). History natural and experimental of life and death or of the prolongation of life, preface, B, i, recto and verso, p. 61. London: A. W. for William Lee and Humphrey Moseley, 1658.
26. E. T. Renbourn. Med. Hist., 4:135, 1960
27. S. Santorio. J. Quincy (trans.). Medicina statica: being the aphorisms of Sanctorius, pp. 270, 92. London: J. Osborn, T. Longwan, and J. Newton, 1728.
28. S. Rowbotham. An inquiry into the cause of natural death; or death from old age, p. 10. Manchester: A. Heywood, 1842.
29. Sir John Floyer. Medicina gerocomia: or, the Galenic art of preserving old men's healths. London: J. Isted, 1724.
30. O. T. Beale and R. H. Shryock. Cotton Mather, first significant figure in American medicine. Baltimore: Johns Hopkins Press, 1954.
31. C. Mather. The angel of Bethesda, pp. 47-48, 531 (facsimile reproduction of typescript from original manuscript).
32. G. Cheyne. An essay of health and long life, p. 221. London: George Strahan, and J. Leake, 1724.
33. J. Mackenzie. The history of health, and the art of preserving it, p. 431. Edinburgh: William Gordon, 1759.
34. J. H. Cohausen. J. Campbell (trans.). Hermippus redivivus: or the sage's triumph over old age and the grave, p. 110. London: J. Nourse, 1744.
35. E. Darwin. Zoonomia; or the laws of organic life, pp. 364-5. Boston: Thomas and Andrews, 1809.
36. B. Rush. Medical inquiries and observations, Vol. I, pp. 245, 249. Philadelphia: Johnson and Warner, 1815.
37. C. W. Hufeland. A.-J.-L. Jourdan (trans.). L'art de prolonger la vie de l'homme, pp. 29, 45-46, i. Paris: J.-B. Baillière, 1824.
38. X. Bichat. T. Watkins (trans.). Physiological researches upon life and death, pp. 1-2. Philadelphia: Smith and Maxwell, 1809.
39. A. S. Warthin. Old age, the major involution, pp. 12-13, 5, 148, 155-6. New York: Paul B. Hoeber, 1929.
40. R. De Ropp. Man against aging, pp. 99-100. New York: St Martin's Press, 1960.

NASCHER:

Excerpts from His Life, Letters, and Works

Joseph T. Freeman

Nascher: Excerpts from His Life, Letters, and Works[1]

Joseph T. Freeman[2]

PART I

It was a burgeoning era in which the social and medical particularity of the aging was identified by a physician. Perhaps it is not strange that an element of virtuosity characterized almost everything that this physician, Ignatz Leo Nascher, did.

Starting in 1909, he wrote on a number of aspects of senescence.

He coined a word, geriatrics, and published a text under that title. He lectured on medical care of the aging in several medical schools. He edited a special section on the subject in a medical journal under the name which he had devised. He created a specialty society, stimulated some students, and anticipated many of the problems of motivation and rehabilitation in old age. Despite all this, he failed to win general acceptance for his ideas in his time. These events took place before 1920.

Nascher was a solitary observer who moved along undefined lines. As a rule the efforts of unusual men emerge from an established frame of identification. It would be difficult, for example, to visualize Robert Koch as anything but a medical scientist. The same is true of the Hunters, Osler, and others whose contributions came from a background essentially medical in nature. Despite his clinical talents and medical qualifications, Nascher's interest in aging did not seem to be primarily the result of his knowledge of the physiological mechanisms and diagnostic patterns of older age. It was an expression of the sociological objectivity, of a specified form of humanism with which he viewed everything. In this sense, which is not as absolute as it sounds, geriatrics derived from a social rather than a medical scientist. This is not a denial of his definite ability in medicine as much as an emphasis on his sympathetic nature. It may also explain in part why this field of learning has had more than average difficulty in winning acceptance as a definitive category.

Some source material is available for insight into this energetic and full personality. The outlines of his life are quite clear. Its chronology is essential to the interpretation of the man in his times.

Nascher was born in Vienna, October 11, 1863, and was brought to the United States as an infant. As a boy he recalled living in a cold water tenement with a backhouse, which was not unusual because there was a general lack of centralized sewage facilities. (These backhouses, he commented in a letter, were emptied at three-month intervals and the contents sold to farmers for fertilizer.)

Ultimately he matriculated at the College of the City of New York but did not graduate. His studies were continued at the New York College of Pharmacy, later incorporated into Columbia University, and he was graduated in pharmacy in 1882. After this professional attainment, he entered the medical department of New York University, from which he received his medical degree in 1885. Two years later, when he was 24, he opened an office for medical practice in a house which he noted had been built in 1855.

In 1889 he published his first article, A Young Living Fetus, in the *Medical Record of New York*. It was signed *J. L. Nascher*. This same signature appeared on several of his publications. The second paper, which did not appear until 1908, was on prostitution. The following year his initial paper on aging was printed in the *New York Medical Record*. His next article, dealing with the treatment of diseases in senility, published in the same journal in the same year, was signed *I. L. Nascher*, as were all but one of the remainder of his works.

---

[1] Much of the source material for this biographical excerpt was derived from the Thewlis memoriam (1945) and letters to the late Dr. Thewlis, to the author, and a few others. A deep sense of gratitude is due to Mrs. Thewlis and Mr. Harold Thewlis, her son, for permission to review the letters. Thanks to Mr. Alexander H. Joseph for a critical review are expressed gladly.

[2] 1530 Locust St., Philadelphia 2, Pa.

Reprint from the Gerontologist, Vol. 1, No. 1, March 1961—Printed in U. S. A.

This disparity in signature may be because manuscripts of the period for the most part were handwritten. Despite a writing of unusual clarity, even with a degree of fine-penned elegance, some confusion could result from the configuration of a signature signed with initals rather than a full name. Nascher invariably signed his papers with initials. His letters to close friends were signed Leo, and his more formal signature was I. L. Nascher. His capital I was written in a looping decorative manner that varied a bit from letter to letter, and could readily have been read by an editor or typesetter as a J. It is strange he never corrected the error in proof despite repeated occurrences (Fig. 1).

in which he revealed his deep sympathy for underprivileged and unfortunate people. Graduating when he did, and the author of several minor papers, it was not until two decades later that he seemed to project himself with fully developed ideas into the field of aging in his work, *Longevity and Rejuvenescence,* in his emerging year of 1909, when he was 46. This anticipated many later ideas and approaches to the subject of aging, although at the time he arrived at the concepts of medical care of the aging practically in a complete form:

> Geriatrics, from *geras,* old age, and *iatrikos,* relating to the physician, is a term I would suggest as an addition to our vocabulary to cover the same field, in old age, that is covered by the term 'paediatrics' in childhood . . . to emphasize the necessity of considering senility and its diseases apart from maturity, and to assign to it a separate place in medicine.

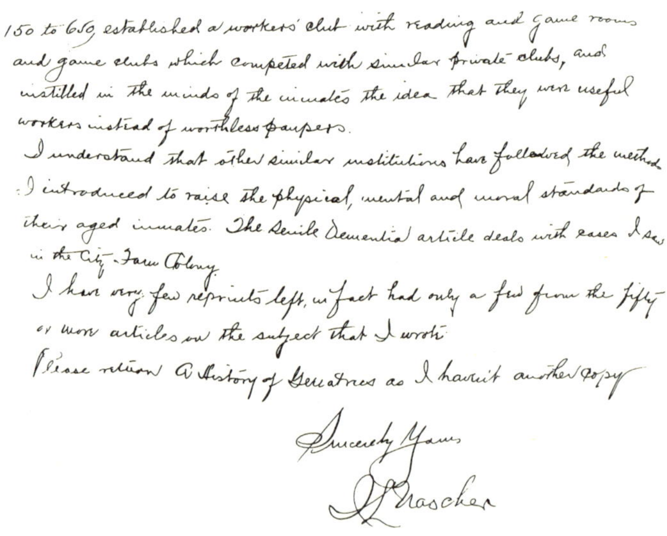
150 to 650 established a workers' club with reading and game rooms and game clubs which competed with similar private clubs, and instilled in the minds of the inmates the idea that they were useful workers instead of worthless paupers.

I understand that other similar institutions have followed the method I introduced to raise the physical, mental and moral standards of their aged inmates. The Senile Dementia article deals with cases I saw in the City Farm Colony.

I have very few reprints left, in fact had only a few from the fifty or more articles on the subject that I wrote.

Please return A History of Geriatrics as I haven't another copy

Sincerely Yours

I L Nascher

Fig. 1. Characteristic letters of Dr. Nascher with his formal-type signature. Informal letters were signed Leo.

It is a little difficult to determine just when Dr. Nascher's interest in the field of aging began. According to one story, he was moved initially by the *laissez faire* treatment which he saw given to old patients while on a trip to the municipal hospital in Vienna. Furthermore, he had observed an arcus senilis, "the bow of age," in his cornea in his early years. It was a matter of amusement to him, if not of challenge, to notice his own lengthening lifespan in view of his personal eye changes, which were supposed to have dire diagnostic implication.

There is an interesting gap in his chronology and bibliography, except for his study of the Bowery, *The Wretches of Povertyville,* published in 1909,

As his ideas expanded, he made three statements decisive for the field as well as revelatory of his insight. His orientation led him to consider senility "a physiological entity, and its diseases not as diseases of maturity with senile complications, but as diseases of senility apart and distinct from maturity." Furthermore, "in senility the flanks, the incidental complications, are more dangerous than the first, the primary disease . . ." He concluded, "So little has been done in the field of geriatrics that until it receives the attention its importance deserves, and we know more about the metabolic changes in the period of decline, we must fall back upon empiricism in the treatment of diseases in senility." No one had said it as well or as clearly except the wide-ranging Charcot over a generation earlier.

Subsequent to publications in 1910 and 1912 pleading for a study of geriatrics, he was invited to deliver a course of lectures on the subject at the College of Physicians and Surgeons of Boston and at the Bennett Medical College in Chicago. He had pointed out that "there is not a lecture given in any medical college on that branch of medicine dealing with senility and its diseases." He spoke with vigor in defense of his view that "the branch of medicine, for which I suggested the term 'geriatrics' is neither a fad, a hobby, nor a recent innovation in medicine."

In 1914, after more than 30 articles on the subject in 5 years, during which time he was active in clinical work he published his text, *Geriatrics*, utilizing the ideas and many of the phrases which he had developed. Acceptance by a publisher did not come readily.

In the introduction, Jacobi, who helped to define pediatrics in the United States, said that it was "the first modern comprehensive book on the normal and morbid changes in old age." He indicated that this was the first American work on senile diseases since the Charcot and Loomis work (1881). Reviews stated that "the author evidences his application to the investigation of a view of physiological pathology which he has made quite his own" (1914).

In a letter to the late Dr. Frank R. Packard of Philadelphia, editor of the *Bulletin of Medical History*, Nascher confirmed the dates:

The name was in a paper published in the N. Y. Medical Journal August 21, 1909. I gave a talk in geriatrics in the N. Y. County Med. Society in 1910 or 1911. Lectured in geriatrics in Bennett Medical College, Chicago (now the Med. Dept. of Loyola University) in 1911 and 1912, and in Fordham Medical College 1913-1914. . . . My book is obsolete, but I may revise it. . . .

This was in 1938 when he was 75 and was written from a hospital where he was under treatment for ischemic complications of the leg secondary to obliterating arteriosclerosis. The second edition of his book had appeared in 1916. There was no later revision, despite the hope and intent expressed even 22 years later.

A review of the titles of some of Nascher's papers indicates just how widely he had thought on the subject of aging.

In 1916 he withdrew from practice and was appointed physician to the New York Department of Public Welfare. Prior to taking this position he had been chief of the Out-Patient Department Clinics of the Mt. Sinai Hospital of that city. At the time he was writing scientific articles for the Sunday magazine of the *New York American*. He mentioned this casually in one of his letters, and such work probably explains not only a clarity of expression, but the fact that he wrote with few errors in grammar, spelling, the need for correction, or any check in the flow of ideas in his letters requiring self editing.

In 1917 he served on a draft board as an examining physician. In the same year the *Medical Review of Reviews* added a section in geriatrics to which he either contributed an article regularly or supervised a contribution. The issue of the journal in which the program was started was dedicated to him (Figs. 2 and 3).

In 1925, 9 years after taking his city position, he was made chief physician in his Department and later chief physician of the Department of Hospitals. He kept this position until he was required to retire in 1929 because of his age (66 years).

Two years after his retirement in 1931 he asked to be put in charge of the 1200 inmates of the New York City Farm Colony, which was a branch of the Home for Dependents. He aimed:

to change the antiquated methods of dealing with aged public dependents (that is, Almshouse inmates) and rehabilitate them as far as possible physically and mentally. In 18 months the number of volunteer workers rose from 150 to 650. . . . I tried to promote incentive to work, stimulated pride in appearance, tried to improve attitudes on life, created reading and game rooms, made workers' clubs, stimulated competition with private clubs, etc. . . .

Subsequently he said that he hoped to see geriatrics become one of the major branches of medicine. Young workers at this institution helped him to collect data for publication. Already visualized were concepts of research, rehabilitation, ideas of motivation, persistence in purposeful activity, and attempts at maintaining ties between older individuals and the life formerly available to them.

He was aware of his accomplishments, despite occasional self-disparagement, since he made a point to return his personal papers to interested institutions during his lifetime. In 1941, a letter stated:

Returned my medical diploma to the New York University, and it hangs in the visitor's room of this medical school; my College of Pharmacy diploma (Columbia) is hung in the dean's office. Today I returned my N. Y. County Med. Soc. certificate, dated 1891, to the office of the Society in the Academy of Medicine Building. . . . I was told that there is considerable interest in geri-

> To
> **I. L. Nascher,**
> The Father of Geriatrics in America,
> who established in this magazine
> the first department
> DEVOTED TO THE DISEASES OF THE AGED,
> this twenty-third volume of
> THE MEDICAL REVIEW OF REVIEWS
> is dedicated by
> The Editor.

Fig. 2. Reproduction of the editor's dedication to Dr. Nascher of volume 23, *The Medical Review of Reviews*, Jan.-Dec., 1917.

GERIATRICS — UNDER THE DIRECTION OF I.L. NASCHER

For the Study of Senile Conditions; The Causes of Ageing, Diseases of Advanced Life, Care of the Aged

I. L. NASCHER, the Father of Geriatrics in America, inaugurates herewith a department devoted to the important specialty which he has done so much to develop. Following his Salutatory he writes on the History of Geriatrics—history which he has helped to make. The diseases of the aged are worthy of the most careful study: an old man may be of more value to the community than a hundred infants. Let us not dismiss his ailments with the facile diagnosis: You are old. Pediatrics must be supplemented by Geriatrics. In this work Dr Nascher is the leader, and the MEDICAL REVIEW OF REVIEWS appreciates the honor of being the first magazine in the world to contain a Department of Geriatrics.

Fig. 3. Heading of Geriatric Section, *The Medical Review of Reviews*, vol. 23, 1917, page 29.

atrics, that many physicians look up articles on senile conditions. Glad to see that my hobby has developed beyond the hobby stage, and hope to see it introduced as a regular subject in the curriculum of medical schools. The dean at my school, Dr. McEwen (now Lt. Col., U. S. A.) said the war put an end, for the present, to the intention to introduce geriatrics as a regular teaching subject, but it may be taken up after the war.

In 1938 he asked for the loan of a copy of Sir John Floyer's book *Medicina Gerocomica*. He wanted to show this first modern book on the subject, printed in 1724, with a copy of his own first article at an exhibition of works by graduates of the New York University in the library of its medical school.

Every aspect of the field attracted and pleased him. When a new edition of a book on geriatrics was dedicated to him, he repeated that this was:

A subject which is becoming daily more important, and may become one of the most important branches of medicine . . . A series of lectures on geriatrics was delivered at the N. Y. Medical School last winter (1940) and will be repeated the coming session (August 12, 1941).

In a letter of advice to a friend, he said: "When I was writing medical articles, I stuck to one subject, geriatrics, until my name was associated with it." It was gratifying when Professor Raymond Pearl of Johns Hopkins University called him "one of the most distinguished of students of senescence and senility now living. . . ." However, in a nostalgic mood, he noted that "I am drifting further and further away from the world of medicine." Nevertheless at this same time (1941) he had received two requests for papers, and his associates were continuing his work at the City Farm Colony and the Goldwater Hospital.

Wherever he went he made inquiries about the field. On a trip to the Congressional Library, he saw "a large number of references to geriatrics and old age. Was agreeably surprised to meet a physician from Cleveland who said he was a geriatrician." In answer to a questionnaire as to his field of medicine, he replied that his specialty was geriatrics. He was rebuffed with the statement that this was not recognized as a specialty, even though there was a New York Geriatric Society, founded by himself, which met in a school on Columbus Avenue, and there was a growing literature on the subject. Apparently, this was part of an effort on his part to promote a specialty in the field, which subsequent students have attempted to avoid.

Dr. Nascher was successful in linking his career to geriatrics, working without interruption for a period of 35 years (Freeman, 1960). One of his most important observations, and a reflection on his objectivity, consisted of notes that he made on a subject most painful to him, the progressive regression of his wife's mental capacity in her older age. Aside from his unhappy concern, endless devotion, and efforts to keep her interested, he drew pertinent conclusions which he summarized in a paper entitled *The Aging Mind,* his last paper, published a month before his death. Reflecting on the situation as he observed it in his own home, he tabulated characteristics of chronic brain syndrome and suggested that it was a primary change of senescence, since an identical situation was seen to occur in mother and daughter at approximately the same age, despite a generation's difference in environment, nutrition, and antecedent medical conditions. This anticipated some of the arguments between primary age changes as a feature of heredity and others which are retarded or accelerated by environmental influences.

There are men of talent and industry, wisdom, and independence of thought, who fail because these qualities are not combined with certain graces. Their merits take longer to get acceptance, if ever, due to a deficit in personal relationships. Nascher apparently suffered because of these beliefs in his own limitations. There are many references in his letters to this concept of himself. However, the introspections may have been more apparent than true. Thewlis (1945), his devoted friend, associate, and student, was impressed with his kindness, his generosity, his gentility, and his affectionate nature.

His letters did not lack humor. Usually a little salty, it consisted of quoted stories containing some rather frank terms. On occasion he made remarks about feminine traits and attractions common to the usual attitude of the public toward the capacities, and regrets, of older men. Moved by situations which he met in his professional and personal life, he was known to have given money to poor patients rather than receive a fee.

Of his personal qualities he had much to say, possibly with the feeling that his letters were being saved. He had observed a lessening of his inhibitions and a weakening of restraints on emotional outlets as he grew older. He was more easily moved to tears by sad things, less tolerant of boring situations, and more susceptible to fatigue, particularly after mental effort. He was aware of his classical picture of angina pectoris, was quite philosophic about it, and predicted his demise from this disease, which occurred almost 20 years after its onset. However, he believed that he could "still adapt myself in thought and action to innovations, keep up with the spirit of the times, discard old notions and manners." When he was admonished to cease bothering about conditions over which he had no control, since they upset him, he replied: "I am mentally and temperamentally unable to let the world roll by without doing something about it." He was 77 at the time that he wrote this and was particularly indignant because, despite his many physical limitations, he had applied for service as an air raid warden and been rejected. This refusal conflicted with his extreme patriotism, his engrossment in politics and the progress of the war, as well as his strong antipathy for chauvinistic and nationalistic immoralities.

His habit was to retire between midnight and 1 a.m. and to nap several times through the day. He walked about a mile daily, gearing his tours to his physical limitations. In diet, although neither a gourmand nor a gourmet, with his weight stable at about 170 pounds, he continued to enjoy coffee, whiskey, and tobacco. At age 81, he regarded himself as an old fogey:

> When a young fellow reaches the four-score mark, he is apt to become senile or childish, an optimist or a crank, looking forward to Nirvana or backward, recalling pleasant things of life or the miserable, sad and unforgivable failures. I am trying to figure out in which of these classifications I belong.

It is doubtful if he realized that he seemed to be asking for an opinion, and his wonder might seem wistful except for the fact that he never failed in his realistic self-judgments.

Despite tendencies to deprecate himself and possibly discouraged at his efforts to get the field of geriatrics fully identified, he was true to his concepts. There was a mixture of pride, persistence, objectivity, and a need for basic understanding which he did not obtain in fullness, not because there were not those who could give it, but because he lacked that special endowment which yields this result. When he referred to a photograph of himself taken with a close friend, he asked: "Who's the old codger alongside of you?" (fig. 4) and then proceeded to paint a most unflattering description of himself. He was sufficiently scientific to ask the professional photographer why a photograph could be good or bad and learned the results in terms of camera angle and light.

From 1938 through the last 6 years of his life he was under quite a bit of stress. His finances were just adequate, he was in poor health, particularly during a bitter 6 months in 1938 with a very painful vascular condition in one foot, as well as the progressive illness of his wife. However, he kept a side of himself free from these limitations. Even when he gave up his home and moved into a boarding house, a change which for a man of 80 must have been extremely difficult, he faced up to it with his usual optimism and high degree of acceptance so typical of his moves, physical or intellectual. He had lived in many parts of his native city. As unhappy as the situation must have been, he said: "I can accommodate myself to almost any environment and condition of life, but miss companionship, especially of persons whom I can talk to on current subjects."

Part II

It is ironic that a man who used travel in every form as a normal part of his life should suffer physical afflictions which are the antithesis of the ability to get around freely. Concerning his cardiac condition, to which he paid a minimum of attention, he observed that when at sea he never had any precordial discomfort. Ten years after its onset he developed intermittent claudication. The circulation of his extremities was so poor that he was able to walk very little without distress. He continued as best he could, even taking long journeys.

In order to avoid tension in his foreign travels, he would pretend that he did not understand the language, or state that European political affairs were too difficult for an American to understand. This was a fabrication that averted trouble by one who wished to keep traveling and who was perceptive enough to note three years before the outbreak of the Second World War that "it's a dismal outlook for Europe . . ."

In an effort to relieve the discomfort in his foot, he tried injections of a tissue extract. Becoming sensitized he suffered an almost fatal anaphylactic reaction. He had a lengthy hospitalization during which time, despite intense suffering, he rejected advice for amputation. He eventually recovered sufficiently to resume many activities.

Apparently he ignored physical restraints. When circumstances became pressing, he took a trip to relax. Every year from 1910 he and his wife took the boat up the Hudson River to Poughkeepsie.

Fig. 4. Photograph of Dr. Nascher taken on his 80th birthday.

He continued these outings even in his wife's older age, when she was unable to remember details, because they gave her momentary pleasure, and probably because he just had to keep going.

Subsequent to World War I, he visited Europe more than a dozen times. It was during these trips that he would follow the play of nationalistic trends and the interplay of political alignments involved with economic adjustments. As a result, he noted quite early the grossness of the Hitlerian regime and the actions of the Soviet under Stalin starting with the latter's behavior in Poland, the pact with Germany, and the delaying diplomatic tactics by which France, England, and Italy were thrown out of gear in arriving at satisfactory diplomatic decisions.

On a 78-day trip through the Mediterranean countries, he exhibited his talent of high sophistication in travel despite offhand avowals that he was not interested in ancient history. He showed a great deal of interest in his traveling associates, although in his status usually as the oldest person on the tour, he was sensitive to the fact that he might not be wanted. He had a splendid grasp of geography, cultural traditions, the flux of politics, and through his insight into nationalities, he was conscious of political trends of the lands through which he traveled. Apparently he traveled without ostentation or thought of money. "Once he became stranded in Holland, and had not the captain of a certain ship belonged to the same Masonic lodge in New York, Nascher would have had some difficulty. As it stood, he was given passage on the ship." (Thewlis, 1945).

He never lost his interest in getting about— whether it was a nocturnal walk in Times Square, a river excursion boat trip, or a trip around the world. He wrote of his tours with enthusiasm and with the intimacy of a well-informed person having an extra talent derived from his knowledge of sociology and the activity of an inquisitively alert mind.

At the age of 73 he wrote of himself:

I thought I was past getting thrills, but riding in a gondola in Venice on the night of a great festival, standing under the leaning tower of Pisa, going through the great Pitti Palace in Florence,[3] visiting the Greek temple in Taormina, the Trulli in southern Italy, the Arab and segregated sections of Casablanca in Morocco gave me real thrills . . .

Despite these pleasures, he believed that he had difficulty making friends, since, in his own opinion, he was too outspoken.

He took pride in attendance at the inauguration of Democratic presidents. This habit was initiated in 1885 as a member of the Democratic party to which he was devoutly attached. He attended every success of his party until 1936. Physical and financial limitations as well as his wife's condition finally prevented him from continuing this tradition.

In 1937 he sailed on the *Exminster* to Greece and countries bordering the Mediterranean. From previous experiences he knew that most of his shipmates would be elderly females, primarily schoolteachers, whom he avoided because he thought that he would be unpopular with them. His efforts to seek younger and what he thought might be more interesting company simply increased his difficulties.

In March, 1940, he outlined a trip on the *Astrea*, a Royal Netherlands Line freighter bound for the Caribbean. Apparently he did not take this trip, since 6 months later he made it on the Dutch freighter, *Hector,* in October, taking his wife with him despite her poor health. He was not well himself. His heart was troubling him; he had shortness of breath and low blood pressure, but was still on his feet. He reflected that with such conditions he might not "reach a hundred, but I won't run much short of that." The following year he took a bus trip to California, which required 4 and a half days. Even the stress of this lengthy trip, the long hours of sitting in one position, did not change his love of getting about, although for a time it seemed to dampen his enthusiasm for this particular mode of travel.

He visited the World's Fair in New York on 4 occasions at the age of 77. He wrote that on one outing he tramped through the grounds for 11 hours. He was quite happy with a vibrating device for relieving foot fatigue which was popular at the Fair. An insurance company had an exhibit by which to estimate life expectancy. He "was told that my life expectancy was about four years. I don't believe it. If I don't reach one hundred, I'll be disappointed. . . ." The actuarial calculation, however, turned out to be remarkably accurate.

On one of his restless little trips, he went to Washington, where he visited Ford's Theater Lincoln Museum and the Congressional Library. During the same day he spent hours in the Smithsonian Institute. By this time it was the middle of the afternoon and he returned to the station for an all-night bus ride back to New York City. This was at age 80.

Altogether, it is estimated that he took 28 major trips, including Europe, Asia, and South America. The number of local expeditions of variable length —by bus, train, foot, and boat—was innumerable. Even short ones were extremely stimulating, if not completely essential to his store of energy. Thewlis pointed out, for example, that he was truly a Doctor Knickerbocker, an expert on odd and forgotten corners of the City of New York. So well versed was he in the metropolis' geography that he served once as an editor of King's *Guide Book of New York*.[4] In addition he wrote a paper, Esthesiomania, his title describing the habits of the odd people in New York's Bohemian quarters.

One of his hobbies was the collection of stamps. He specialized in governmental errors. Apparently this had been an overlooked item in his time, and he was delighted to find that he had acquired some unusual types. His budget, expenditures for his wife's illness, and some minor indulgences reduced his ability to obtain stamps which he wanted for his collection. In 1940 he exhibited two frames at the British pavilion of the International Stamp Exhibit at the World's Fair in New York. At this time he was proud to join the Collectors Club, a select philatelic organization. His display stimu-

---

[3] It is strange that a traveler as well informed and a student as aware of all aspects of aging as Nascher did not mention the famed portrait of Luigi Cornaro in the Pitti Palace in Florence. It seemed to be a case where the father of geriatrics forgot the apostle of senescence. From one of his papers on the history of geriatrics, he knew of Cornaro, but failed to state that the ancient Venetian's portrait, presumably by Tintoretto (or Titian) was in this famed Florentine museum.

[4] Cited by Thewlis (1945), but otherwise unconfirmed.

lated him to add to his stamp collection, even at the need for scrimping on such beloved little pleasures as tobacco or a favorite drink. His collection consisted of 600 frames. Despite the store he put by it, he recognized that this was an intensely personal thing unlikely to mean much to his heirs. For a while he gave some thought to selling his stamps and either increasing the luxuries of his life or taking a long trip with the proceeds.

As a result of insight and precise observations on his travels, he developed a high degree of skill in analyzing political trends. For example, in 1936, three years before Germany moved into Poland, he stated that "Europe is in a mess . . . Germany wants Austria . . . Italy now favors Germany . . . Germany must cut through the Polish Corridor . . ." He was so discouraged by these anticipations, which came true to an unusual degree, that he tried to turn away from the magnetic forces of world activities to limit himself to the health of his wife, his stamp collection, and his trips. Time and time again in his letters he made avowals to quit following politics, yet on the very same page, one or many paragraphs inevitably were devoted to an estimation of the situation.

As his life became circumscribed, after the death of his wife, and with restriction on his activities, both financial and physical, he devoted hours to listening intently to radio commentators, with whom he agreed on occasion and with whom more often he disagreed, often in disgust, usually on the basis of superior knowledge derived from his travels.

Even in the hospital while suffering extreme discomfort with his ischemic foot, he wrote bitterly about the English activities at Munich. Although a great admirer of the English, he began to turn against them because of their political and diplomatic moves at this time. He said that he had heard a tart joke by which the French referred to Chamberlain as J'aime Berlin.

After one of his trips through the Mediterranean he pointed out the strategic position of the fortified Italian island of Pantellaria and indicated that the diplomatic interplay between England and Italy probably was altered by this strategic situation. Obviously, his astute observation of the world's state was based on a traditional European procedure, namely, a close knowledge of ethnic groups contained within political boundaries. In 1938, commenting on the fact that Germany undoubtedly would take Austria and that Russia would violate treaties with Poland, he said: "Treaties are all right when there are reciprocal interests, and then they are unnecessary." The Austrian diplomat, Metternich, more than a hundred years earlier, could not have said it better.

In 1937 he predicted that the United States would enter the war and would help to defeat the dictator nations. A little remorsefully, but in the best American tradition, he said: "I wonder what Grant, Cleveland, or Teddy Roosevelt would have done if Germany tore up a treaty to which the U. S. was a party, without a word of explanation. . . ." In 1941, as his health became worse and he believed that his lifespan was shortening, he regretted that he would not know how Hitler would die. He predicted most accurately, that it would be by suicide.

In the last years of his life, he said that he was "just getting over a bad attack of ergophobia, which I once described as the lazy man's disease." (Apparently he liked to coin words, geriatrics, ergophobia, and esthesiomania.) However, he was energetic enough to travel once more, to Florida, by bus, at the age of 80.

He spoke at a meeting of the American Geriatrics Society in 1944, where he was introduced as "The Father of Geriatrics" who was known to have "broken every rule for a long life." This meeting was dedicated to him and he read his work on mental decline. The occasion and his role as honorary president were very stimulating. He outlined a paper on death, of which his opinion was that "dying is a damned nuisance." Just two months prior to his death, despite a recurrence of constant anginal seizures and recognition of his own physical condition, he planned to act as moderator of a panel and gave thought to a paper, "The Approximation of the Sexes in Old Age," to "show how both sexes in old age approach a neuter type." He always had an interest in pretty women, the relationship between the sexes, and the general nature of feminine attraction, despite self-described senescent limitations.

Learning of the death of a relative at age 75, he commented: "Several of my elderly acquaintances dropped out lately, and I get the foolish idea that I'll drop out some day too. When I think that some day I'll have to die, it takes all the fun out of life." A little later he said, "I guess I'll drop out of circulation soon." In the same letter characteristically he was moved to a vigorous defense of the various minorities in the world and was aroused by social inequities of all kinds. At the same time, he concluded the final draft of his paper, The Senile Mind.

His imagination and vigor remained keen and challenging. He never ceased planning, inquiring, questioning, projecting. It was typical, for example, that he was "curious to know by what process sensory impressions are converted into thoughts."

It is difficult to make a summary about this complex and yet simple man. Attracted to all types of problems dealing with social relationships, he was unable to resolve fully the single issue of himself in relationship to others. Dedicated to certain principles of which the problems of older age attracted him most, he never sought aid in his own older age and continued a line of independent vigor which never asked for succor. Recognizing limitations, he accepted them and resolved them in travel and in many unselfish interests. Marked by courage, guided by integrity, attracted by that which was stimulating and interesting, he thought that he failed to achieve the full acceptance which some men obtain with less effort. As such, his destiny was not too far different than that of many visionaries.

Not only in those externals by which he is identified, but also in letters, Nascher revealed vitality which never seemed to abate. Although he probably did not judge his career generally to have been successful in the common evaluation by his peers, he had a fluidity of nature by which he was able to avoid misanthropy. In economic matters his success was less. Even a minor recognition of his little stamp collection gave him great pleasure. In dealing with matters of travel, he had no mentor. As regards the word and field, geriatrics, he reserved a definite area for his personal stamp. Possibly as a reflection of the total of his successes and failures, there is the ironic affliction of intermittent claudication which, to one who loved to travel as he did, must have been the epitome of rejection. Look as one will in his writings or his personal comments, there is singular absence of terms of resentment or expressions of frustration. His maturity was apparent in practically everything he did, even though he traveled a fairly lonesome road.

In the final identifications of his work and self with the field of aging he seemed to reflect more and more on death. Even here he maintained the little sense of irony which he turned against himself. His devotion to world news, politics, as well as many of the items to which his writings give insight are characteristic of the letter (Nov., 1944) written a month before his death, despite the extreme discomfort of herpes zoster, "I am in my second childhood, and I'm enjoying it. 3:15 a.m., Hurray, just heard Dewey acknowledged defeat." Nascher apparently never did make such an acknowledgement.

He died December 25, 1944.

References

Anonymous. Book review. *Med. Rev. N. Y.*, 1914, **20**, 265.
Charcot, J. M., and Loomis, A. L. *Clinical lectures on the diseases of old age* (Trans. by L. Hunt). New York, W. Wood, 1881.
Freeman, J. T. The first fifty years of geriatrics (1909-1959). *Geriatrics*, 1960, **15**, 216-217.
Thewlis, M. T. In memoriam, Nascher—father of geriatrics. *Med. Times*, 1945, **73**, 140-141.

Nascher Bibliography
Geriatric Subjects
Longevity and rejuvenescence. *N. Y. med. J.*, 1909, **89**, 795.[5]
Geriatrics, *N. Y. med. J.*, 1909, **90**, 359.
The treatment of diseases in senility. *Med. Rec.*, 1909, **76**, 987.
Anatomical changes in senility. *Med Counc. Phila.*, 1909, **15**, 17.
Physiological changes in old age. *Med. Counc. Phila.*, 1910, **15**, 52.[5]
A plea for the study of geriatrics. *Med. Rec.*, 1910, **78**, 536.
Tissue cell evolution; a theory of senescence. *N. Y. med. J.*, 1910, **92**, 918.
Senile debility. *Med. Rec.*, 1911, **79**, 105.
Geriatrics; A neglected branch of medicine. *Therap. Med.*, 1911, **25**, 11.
The danger of routine practice in senile cases. *Amer. J. clin. Med.*, 1911, **18**, 389.
The senile state. *Therap Med.*, 1911, **25**, 47.
Senile mentality. *Internat. Clin. Phila.*, 1911, 21 s., iv, 48.
Sources of error in diagnosis in senile cases. *Arch Diagn.*, 1911, **4**, 270.
Dosage in old age; an important contribution to geriatric therapy. *Amer. J. clin. Med.*, 1911, **18**, 380.
The strenuous life. *Med. Rec.*, 1911, **80**, 722.
The senile climacteric. *N. Y. med. J.*, 1911, **94**, 1125.
Senile rheumatism. *Am. Med.*, 1911, **6** n. s., 670
Geriatrics. *Med. Rec.*, 1912, **81**, 752.
Old age in its medico-legal relations. *N. Y. med. J.*, 1912, **95**, 1089.
Senile arteriosclerosis with alternating cerebral anaemia and cerebral hyperaemia. *Med. Times*, 1912, **10**, 329.
Errors in treatment of senile cases. *N. Y. med. J.*, 1912, **96**, 732.
Diagnostic hints in senile cases. *Amer. Pract.*, 1913, **47**, 61.
Longevity and rejuvenescence. *N. Y. med. J.*, 1913, **98**, 62.
Some remarks on arteriosclerosis. *Amer. Med.*, 1913, 8 n. s., 531.
Rejuvenescence. *Amer. Pract.*, 1913, **47**, 423.
The medical care of the aged. *N. Y. med. J.*, 1913, **98**, 946.
Amorphous phosphorus in senile arteriosclerosis. *N. Y. med. J.*, 1913, **98**, 1042.
Therapetutic problems in senile cases. *Med. Rev.*, 1913, **20**, 88.
The neglect of the aged. *Med. Rec.*, 1914, **86**, 467.
Geriatrics: The diseases of old age and their treatment. Philadelphia, P. Blakiston's Son, 1914.
Lane's auto-intoxication complex and the manifestations of senility. *N. Y. med. J.*, 1914, **100**, 253.
Some geriatric aphorisms. *Amer. Med.*, 1914, 9 n. s., 723.
The importance of geriatrics. *J. Amer. Med. Ass.*, 1914, **63**, 2248.
Evidences of senile mental development. *Amer. J. clin. Med.*, 1915, **22**, 541.
Functional stimulation of senile tissues. *Med. Times*, 1915, **43**, 296.
Diagnostic errors in senile cases. *Arch. Diagn.*, 1916, **9**, 130.
Nephritis in the aged. *N. Y. med. J.*, 1916, **103**, 1214.
Persistent sexual libido in the aged. *Amer. J. Urol.*, 1916, **9**, 407.
Geriatrics: The diseases of old age and their treatment. (2nd ed.) Philadelphia, P. Blakiston's Son, 1916. Revised by A. Klein, Philadelphia.
Diet in old age. *Med Rev. Rev.*, 1917, **23**, 262.
The neglect of geriatrics. *Interstate med. J.*, 1917, **24**, 592.
Diet during old age. *Med. Rev. Rev.*, 1917, **23**, 279.
Institutional care of the aged. *Mod. Hosp.*, 1917, **9**. 4. Also in *Med. Rev. Rev.*, 1917, **23**, 501.
Practical geriatrics, the examination of senile cases. *Med. Counc.*, 1917, **22**, 33.
The treatment of senile constipation. *Amer. J. clin. Med.*, 1917, **24**, 636.
Arteriosclerosis. *N. Y. med. J.*, 1917, **106**, 924.

[5] These papers were signed J. L. Nascher rather than I. L. Nascher.

The institutional care of the aged. *Proc. Nat. Conf. Soc. Work,* 1917, **44,** 350.

A new conception of arteriosclerosis. *Med. Insur. & Health Conserv.,* 1917-1918, **27,** 102.

Bretonneau, Trousseau, and Dieulafoy; three famous French physicians. *N. Y. med. J.,* 1918, **107,** 725 (with M. W. Thewlis as coauthor).

Diagnostic errors in senile cases. *Med. Times,* 1918, **46,** 90.

Physical therapy in senile cases. *Med. Rev. Rev.,* 1918, **24,** 264.

Why old age ends in death. *Med. Rev. Rev.,* 1919, **25,** 284.

Early senescence and rejuvenescence. *Med. Rev. Rev.,* 1919, **25,** 220.

Senile vertigo. *Med. Rev. Rev.,* 1919, **25,** 351.

Senile arthrosclerosis. *Med. Rev. Rev.,* 1919, **25,** 482.

Early signs of ageing. *Med Rev. Rev.,* 1919, **25,** 611.

A noted case of longevity; John Shell; centenarian. *Amer. Med.,* 1920, **15,** n. s., 151.

A little journey to the home of the oldest man in the world; who and what he really is. *Med. Rev. Rev.,* 1920, **26,** 291.

The male climacteric. *Amer. Med.,* 1921, **27,** 242.

A history of geriatrics. *Med. Rev. Rev.,* 1926, **32,** 281.

Hospital problems. *J. med. Soc. N. J.,* 1930, **27,** 507.

The baneful psalm of Moses. *Med. Times and Long Island med. J.,* 1931, **59,** 209.

Senile dementia and senile slump, some differential points. *Med. Times and Long Island med. J.,* 1934 **62,** 314.

Normal duration of life. *Med. Times,* 1942, **70,** 295.

The aging mind. *Med. Rec.,* 1944, **157,** 669.

Subjects Other Than Geriatrics

A young living foetus. *Med. Rec.,* 1889, **35,** 656.[5]

Prostitution. *N. Y. med. J.,* 1908, **88,** 260.[5]

Staining of the conjunctiva, letter to editor. *N. Y. med. J.,* 1909, **90,** 284.[5]

Psychoanalysis of criminality. *Amer. Pract.,* 1914, **48,** 233.

War babies. *Amer. Med.,* 1915, **10,** 623.

Typhoid fever; two unusual cases. *N. Y. med. J.,* 1916, **104,** 394.

Esthesiomania; a study of some of the queer folks in New York's Latin Quarter. *Med. Times,* 1919, **47,** 34.

Racial attractions. *Amer. Med.,* 1925, **20,** n. s., 658.

The wretches of povertyville. Chicago, Joseph J. Lanzit, 1909, 298 pages. Editor, *King's Guide Book of New York.*

---

[5] These papers were signed J. L. Nascher rather than I. L. Nascher.

AGING AND OLD AGE

An Arno Press Collection

(Armstrong, John). **The Art of Preserving Health.** 1744

Canstatt, Carl. **Die Krankheiten des Hoheren Alters Und Ihre Heilung.** 1839

Carlisle, Anthony. **An Essay on the Disorders of Old Age, and on the Means for Prolonging Human Life.** 1818

Cavan, Ruth Shonle, et al. **Personal Adjustment in Old Age.** 1949

Charcot, J(ean) M(artin). **Clinical Lectures on Senile and Chronic Diseases.** 1881

Cheyne, George. **An Essay of Health and Long Life.** 1724

Child, Charles. **Sensecence and Rejuvenescence.** 1915

Cicero, M(arcus) T(ullius). **Cato Major.** 1744

(Cohausen, Johann Heinrich). **Hermippus Redivivus.** 1771

Cornaro, Luigi. **The Art of Living Long.** 1917

Cowdry, E. V., ed. **Problems of Ageing.** 1939

Cumming, Elaine and William E. Henry. **Growing Old.** 1961

Day, George E. **A Practical Treatise on the Domestic Management and Most Important Diseases of Advanced Life.** 1849

Department for the Aging, City of New York. **Older Women in the City.** 1979

Floyer, John. **Medicina Gerocomica.** 1724

Gruman, Gerald J., ed. **The "Fixed Period" Controversy.** 1979

Gruman, Gerald J., ed. **Roots of Modern Gerontology and Geriatrics.** 1979

(Hufeland, Christoph Wilhelm). **Art of Prolonging Life.** 1854

Jameson, Thomas. **Essays on the Changes of the Human Body at Its Different Ages.** 1811

Kirk, Hyland Clare. **When Age Grows Young.** 1888

Kleemeier, Robert W., ed. **Aging and Leisure.** 1961

Lessius, Leonard and Lewis Cornaro. **A Treatise of Health and Long Life With the Future Means of Attaining It.** 1743

MacKenzie, James. **The History of Health, and the Art of Preserving It.** 1760

Martin, Lillien J(ane) and Clare de Gruchy. **Sweeping the Cobwebs.** 1933

Minot, Charles S. **The Problem of Age, Growth, and Death.** 1908

Nascher, I(gnatz) L(eo). **Geriatrics.** 1914

Pearl, Raymond and Ruth DeWitt Pearl. **The Ancestry of the Long-Lived.** 1934

Ramon y Cajal, S(antiago). **El Mundo Visto a Los Ochenta Anos.** 1934

de Ropp, Robert S. **Man Against Aging.** 1960

Stieglitz, Edward J. **The Second Forty Years.** 1946

Sweetser, William. **Human Life.** 1867

Thoms, William J. **Human Longevity.** 1873

Tibbitts, Clark, ed. **Living Through the Older Years.** 1949

Tolstoy, Leo. **Last Diaries.** 1960

Vercors (pseud. Jean Bruller). **The Insurgents.** 1956

Warthin, Aldred Scott. **Old Age.** 1929